EYESHIELD 21

Vol. 28:
Showdown at Tokyo Dome

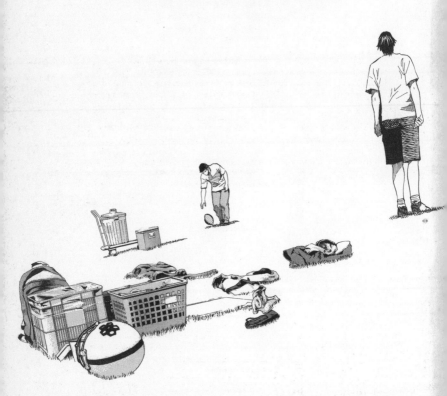

STORY BY **RIICHIRO INAGAKI** ART BY **YUSUKE MURATA**

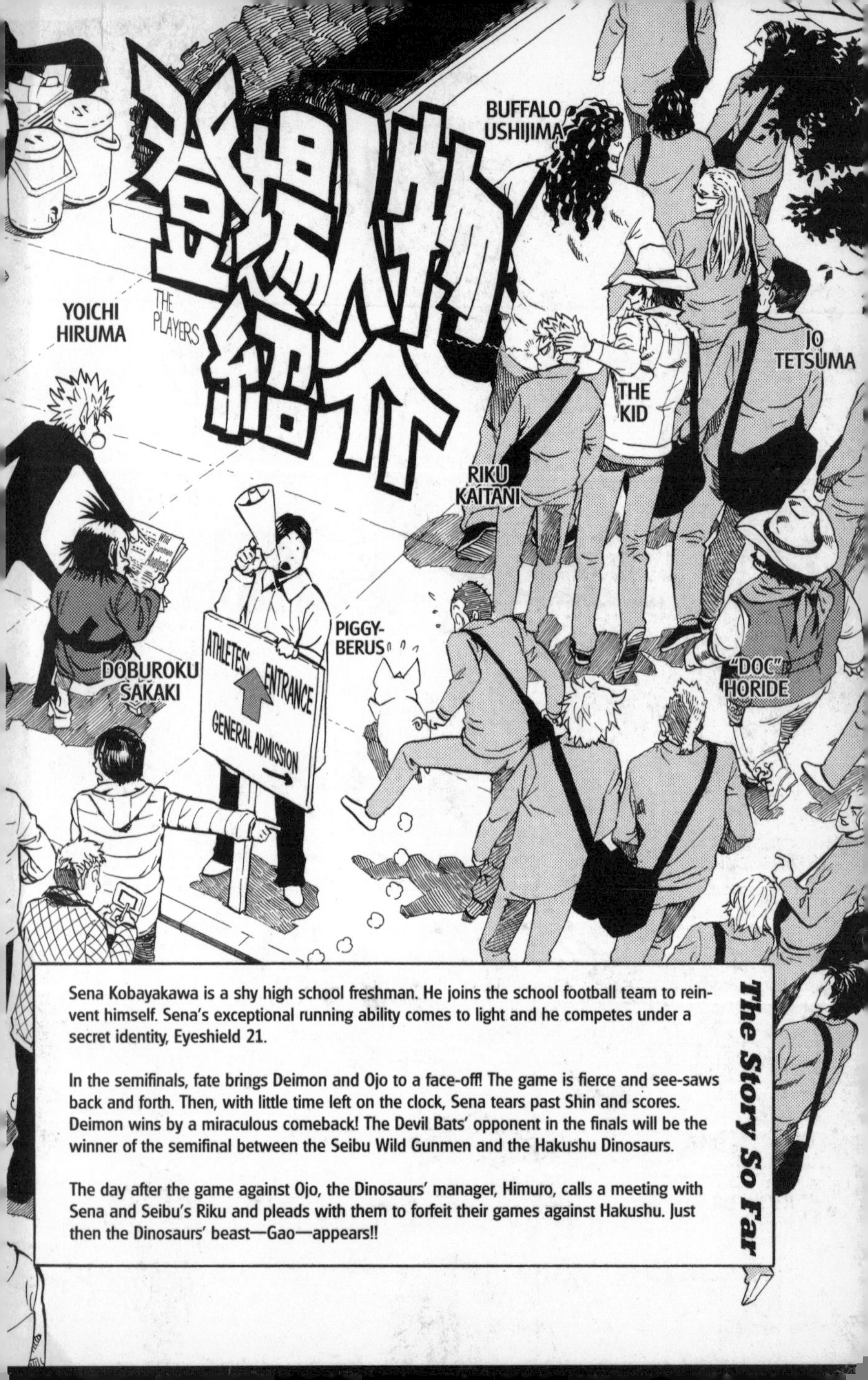
登場人物紹介
THE PLAYERS
YOICHI HIRUMA
BUFFALO USHIJIMA
JO TETSUMA
THE KID
RIKU KAITANI
DOBUROKU SAKAKI
ATHLETES' ENTRANCE
GENERAL ADMISSION
PIGGY-BERUS
"DOC" HORIDE

The Story So Far

Sena Kobayakawa is a shy high school freshman. He joins the school football team to reinvent himself. Sena's exceptional running ability comes to light and he competes under a secret identity, Eyeshield 21.

In the semifinals, fate brings Deimon and Ojo to a face-off! The game is fierce and see-saws back and forth. Then, with little time left on the clock, Sena tears past Shin and scores. Deimon wins by a miraculous comeback! The Devil Bats' opponent in the finals will be the winner of the semifinal between the Seibu Wild Gunmen and the Hakushu Dinosaurs.

The day after the game against Ojo, the Dinosaurs' manager, Himuro, calls a meeting with Sena and Seibu's Riku and pleads with them to forfeit their games against Hakushu. Just then the Dinosaurs' beast—Gao—appears!!

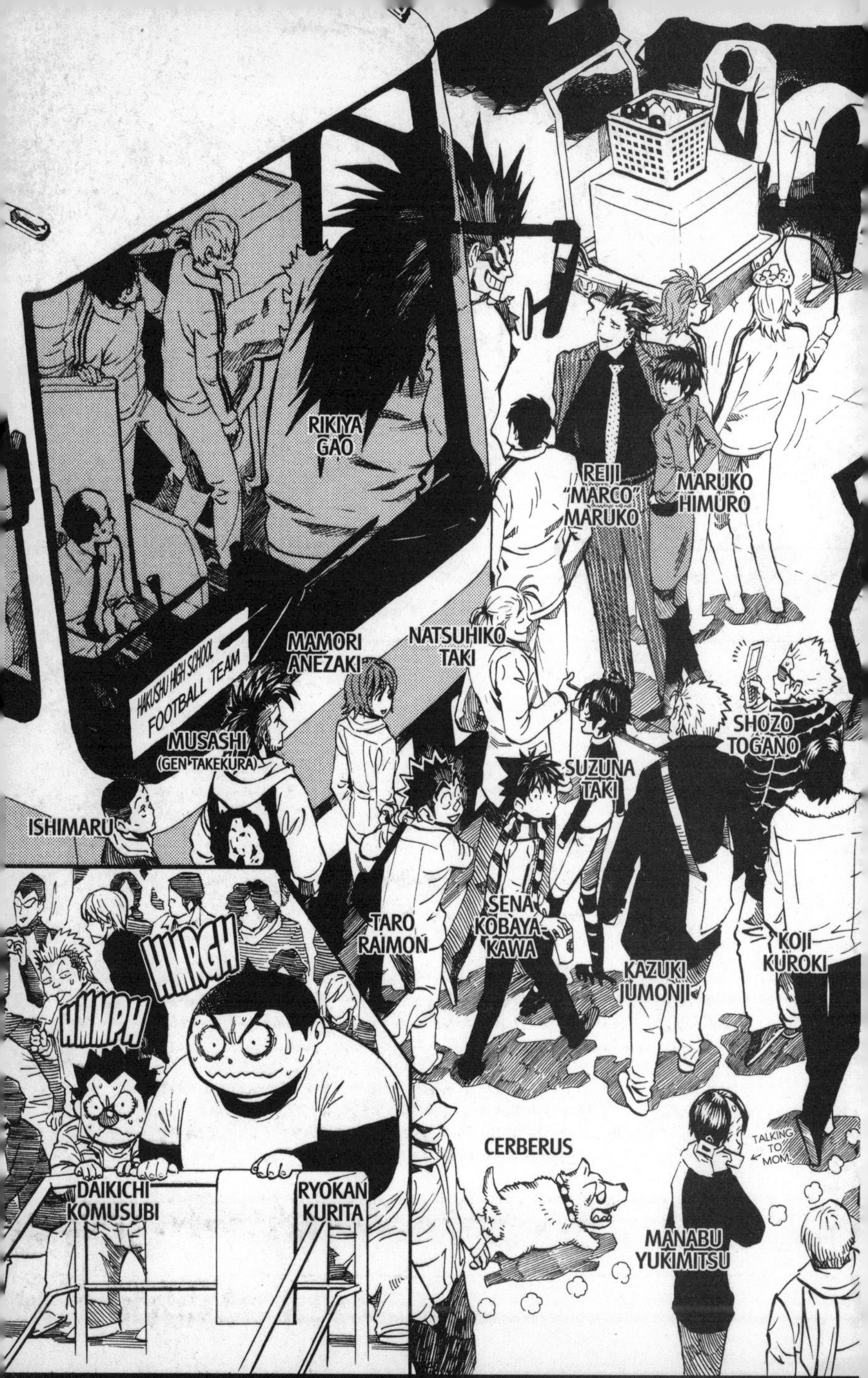

RIKIYA GAO
MARUKO HIMURO
REIJI "MARCO" MARUKO
NATSUHIKO TAKI
MAMORI ANEZAKI
HAKUSHU HIGH SCHOOL FOOTBALL TEAM
SHOZO TOGANO
SUZUNA TAKI
MUSASHI (GEN TAKEKURA)
ISHIMARU
KOJI KUROKI
SENA KOBAYA-KAWA
TARO RAIMON
KAZUKI JUMONJI
TALKING TO MOM.
CERBERUS
MANABU YUKIMITSU
HMRGH
HMMPH
RYOKAN KURITA
DAIKICHI KOMUSUBI

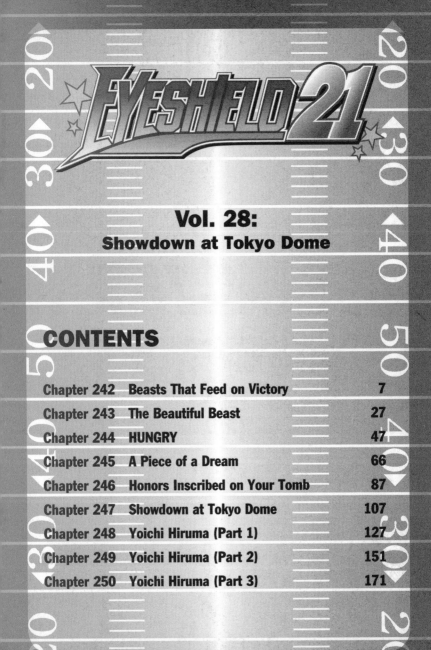

EYESHIELD 21

Vol. 28:
Showdown at Tokyo Dome

CONTENTS

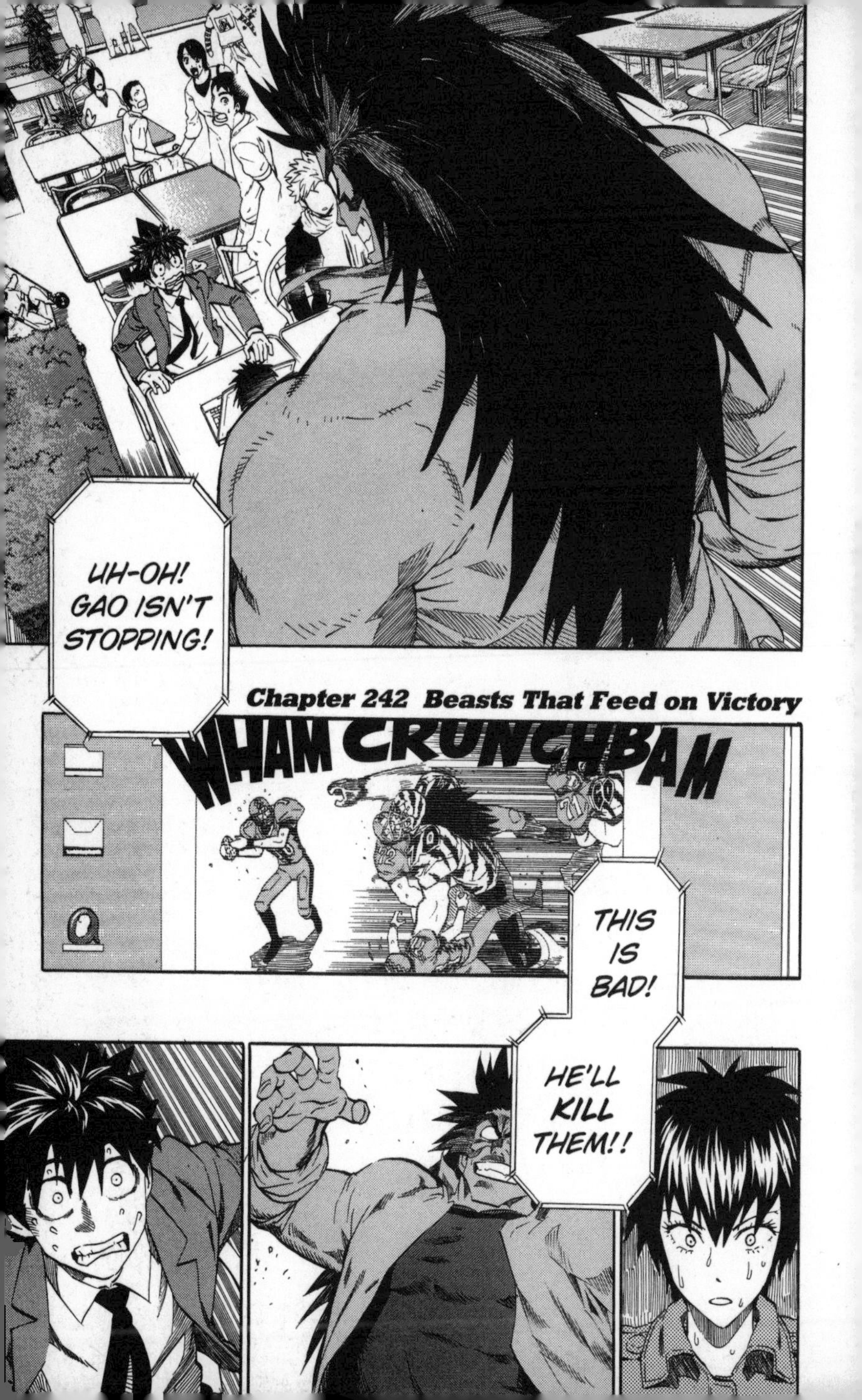
UH-OH! GAO ISN'T STOPPING!
Chapter 242 Beasts That Feed on Victory
WHAM CRUNCH BAM
THIS IS BAD!
HE'LL KILL THEM!!

Chapter 242
Beasts That Feed on Victory

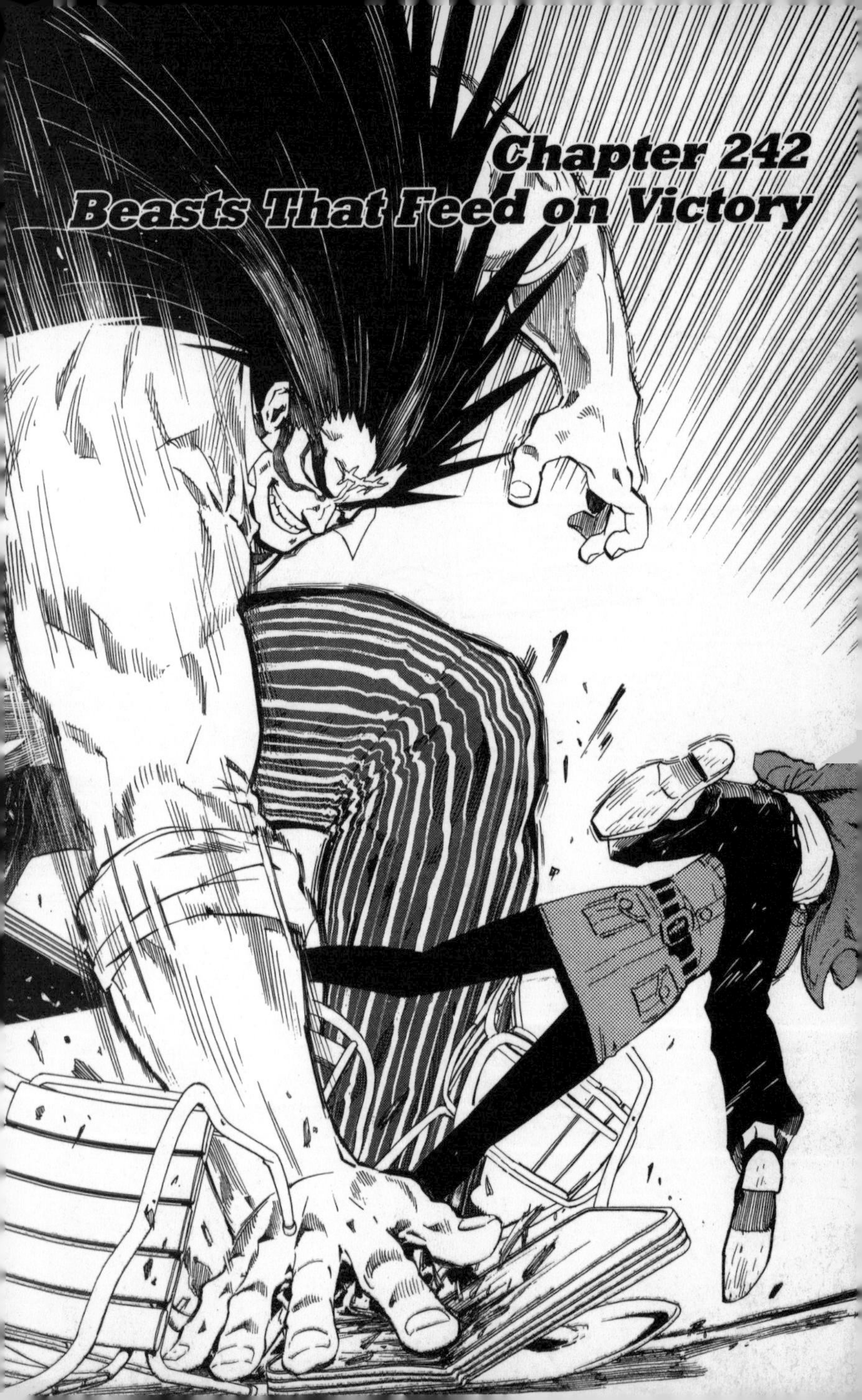

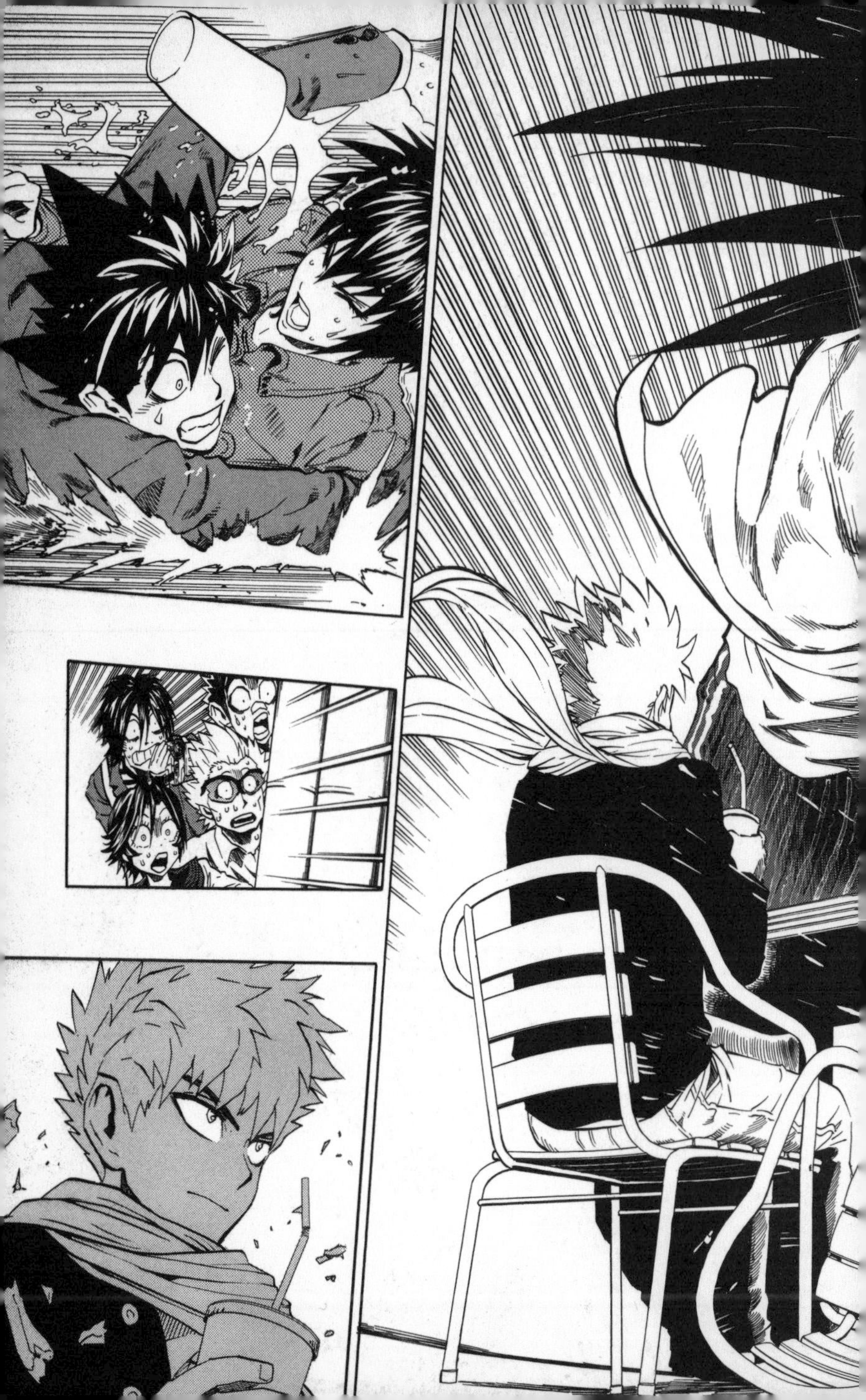

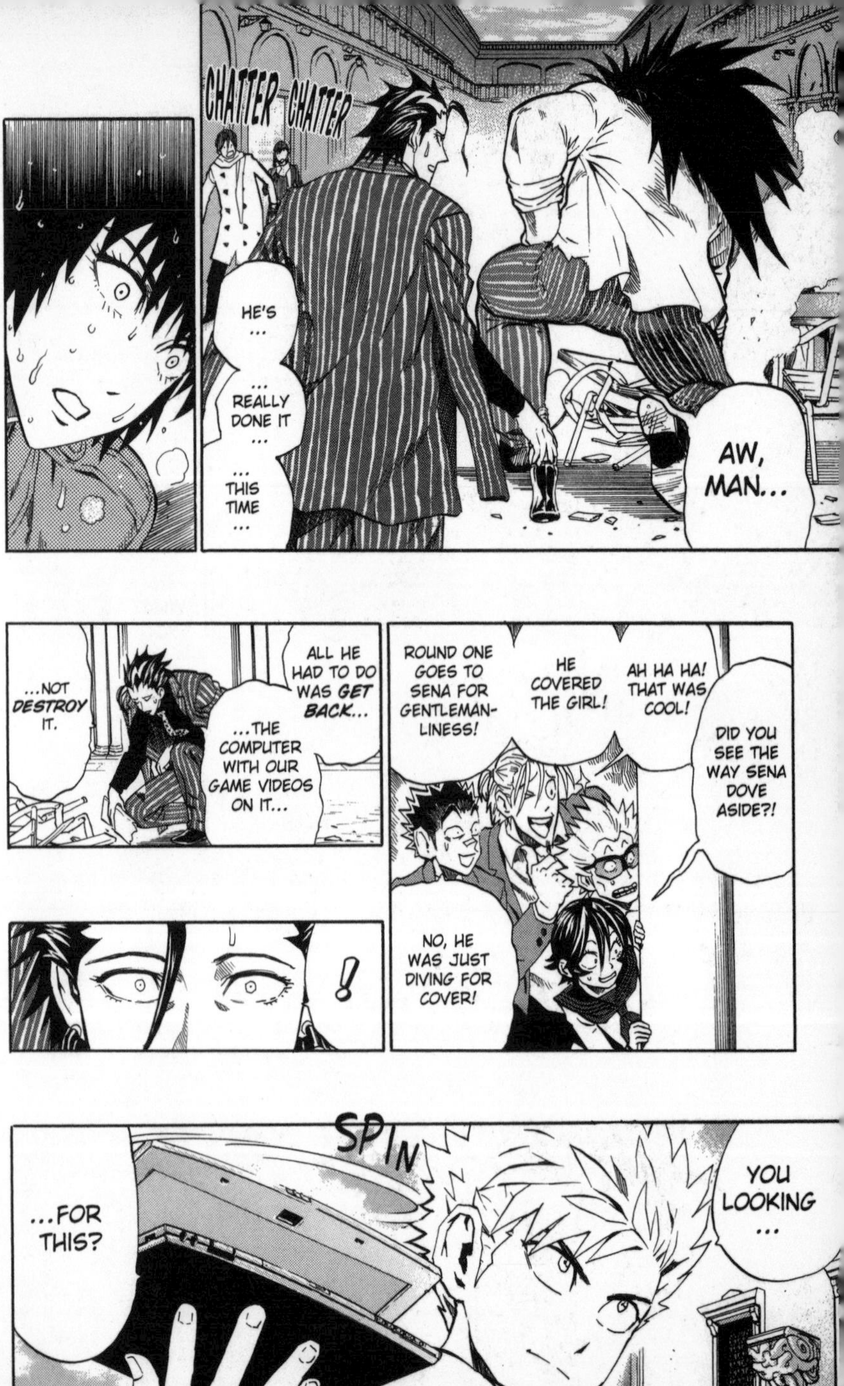
CHATTER CHATTER
AW, MAN...
HE'S ... ... REALLY DONE IT ... ... THIS TIME ...
AH HA HA! THAT WAS COOL!
DID YOU SEE THE WAY SENA DOVE ASIDE?!
HE COVERED THE GIRL!
ROUND ONE GOES TO SENA FOR GENTLEMAN-LINESS!
NO, HE WAS JUST DIVING FOR COVER!
ALL HE HAD TO DO WAS GET BACK...
...THE COMPUTER WITH OUR GAME VIDEOS ON IT...
...NOT DESTROY IT.
!
YOU LOOKING ...
SPIN
...FOR THIS?

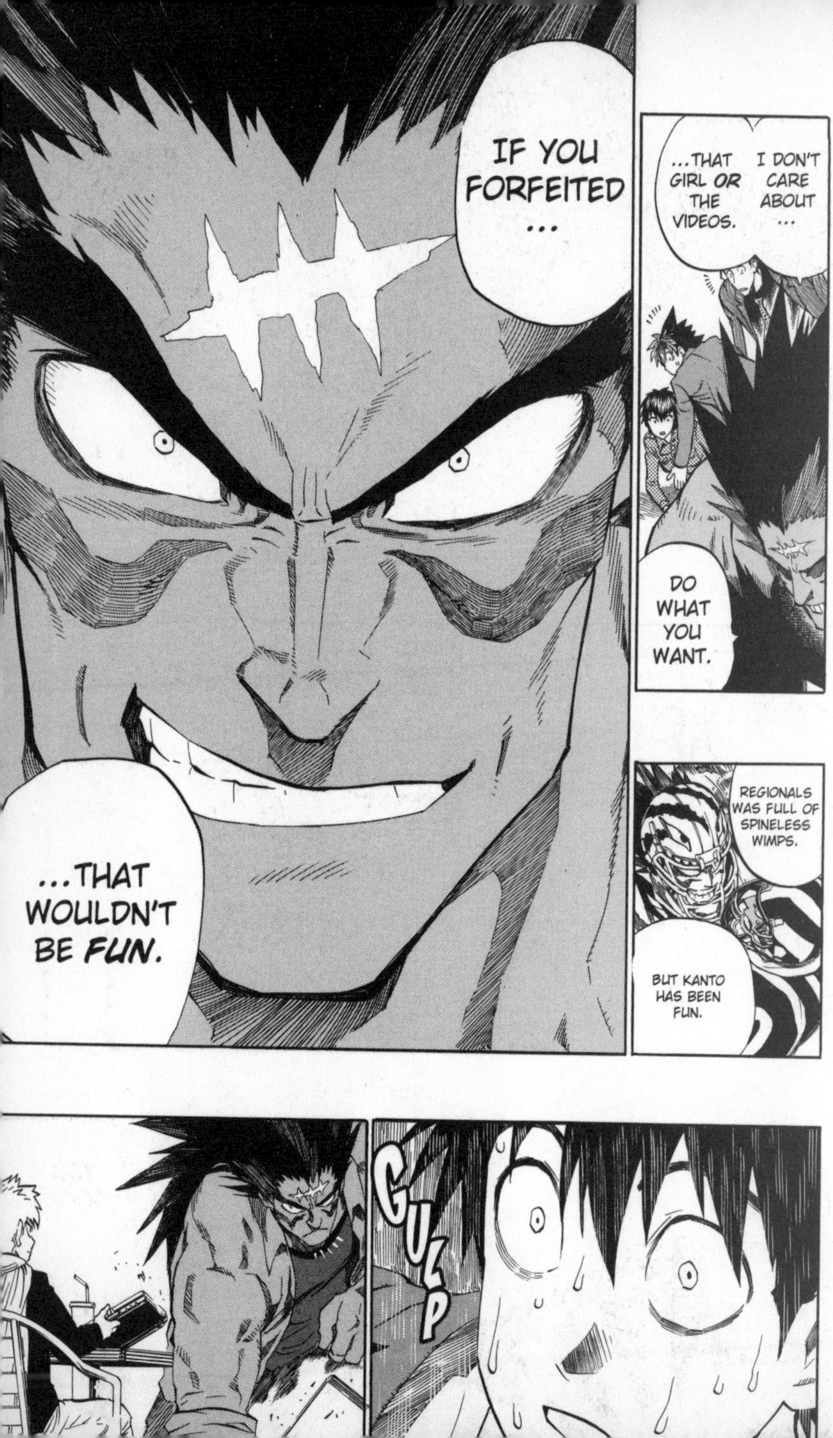
I DON'T CARE ABOUT ...
...THAT GIRL OR THE VIDEOS.
DO WHAT YOU WANT.
REGIONALS WAS FULL OF SPINELESS WIMPS.
BUT KANTO HAS BEEN FUN.
IF YOU FORFEITED ...
...THAT WOULDN'T BE FUN.
GULP

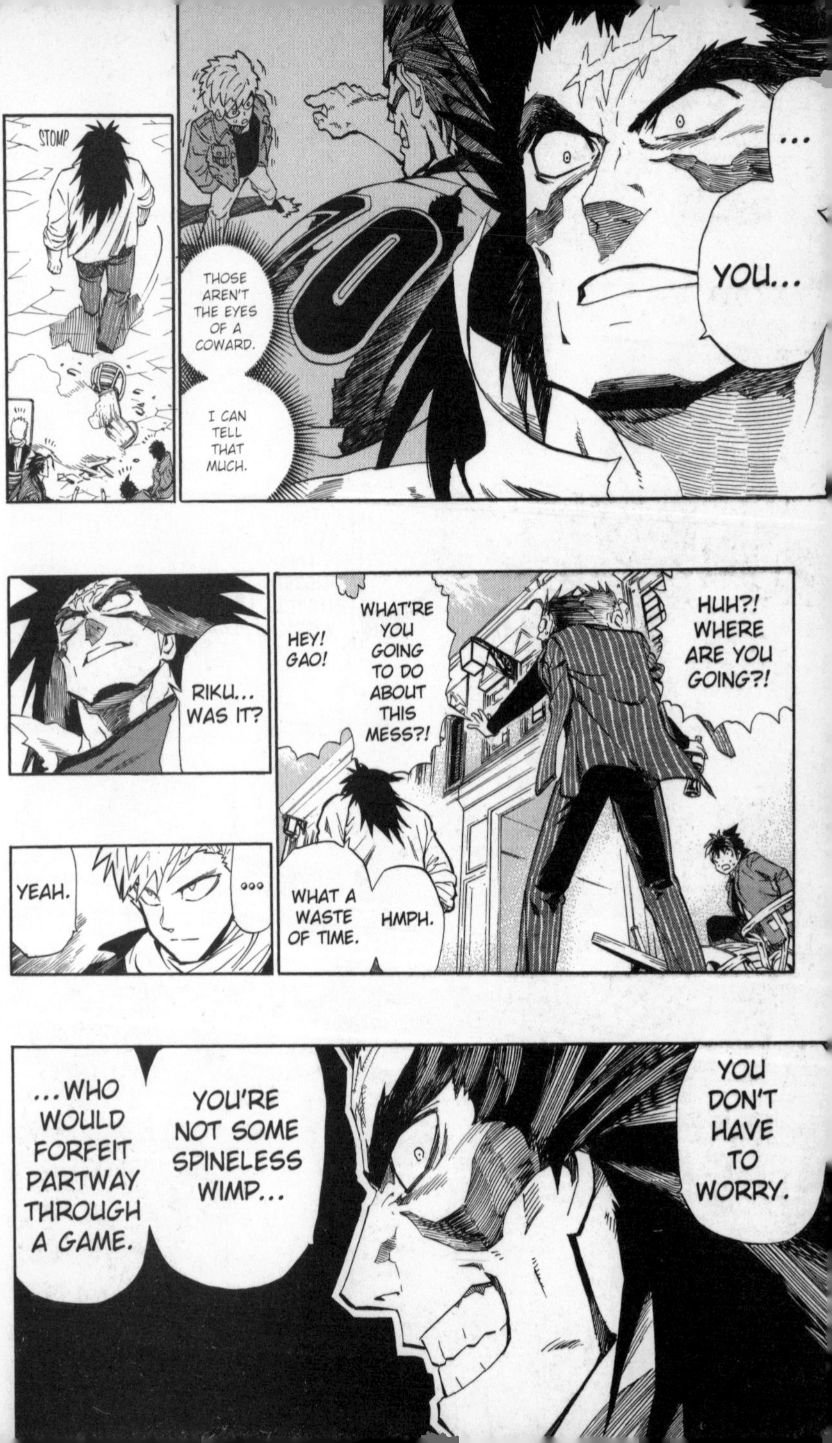
...
YOU...
THOSE AREN'T THE EYES OF A COWARD.
I CAN TELL THAT MUCH.
STOMP
HUH?! WHERE ARE YOU GOING?!
WHAT'RE YOU GOING TO DO ABOUT THIS MESS?!
HEY! GAO!
HMPH.
WHAT A WASTE OF TIME.
RIKU... WAS IT?
...
YEAH.
YOU DON'T HAVE TO WORRY.
YOU'RE NOT SOME SPINELESS WIMP...
...WHO WOULD FORFEIT PARTWAY THROUGH A GAME.

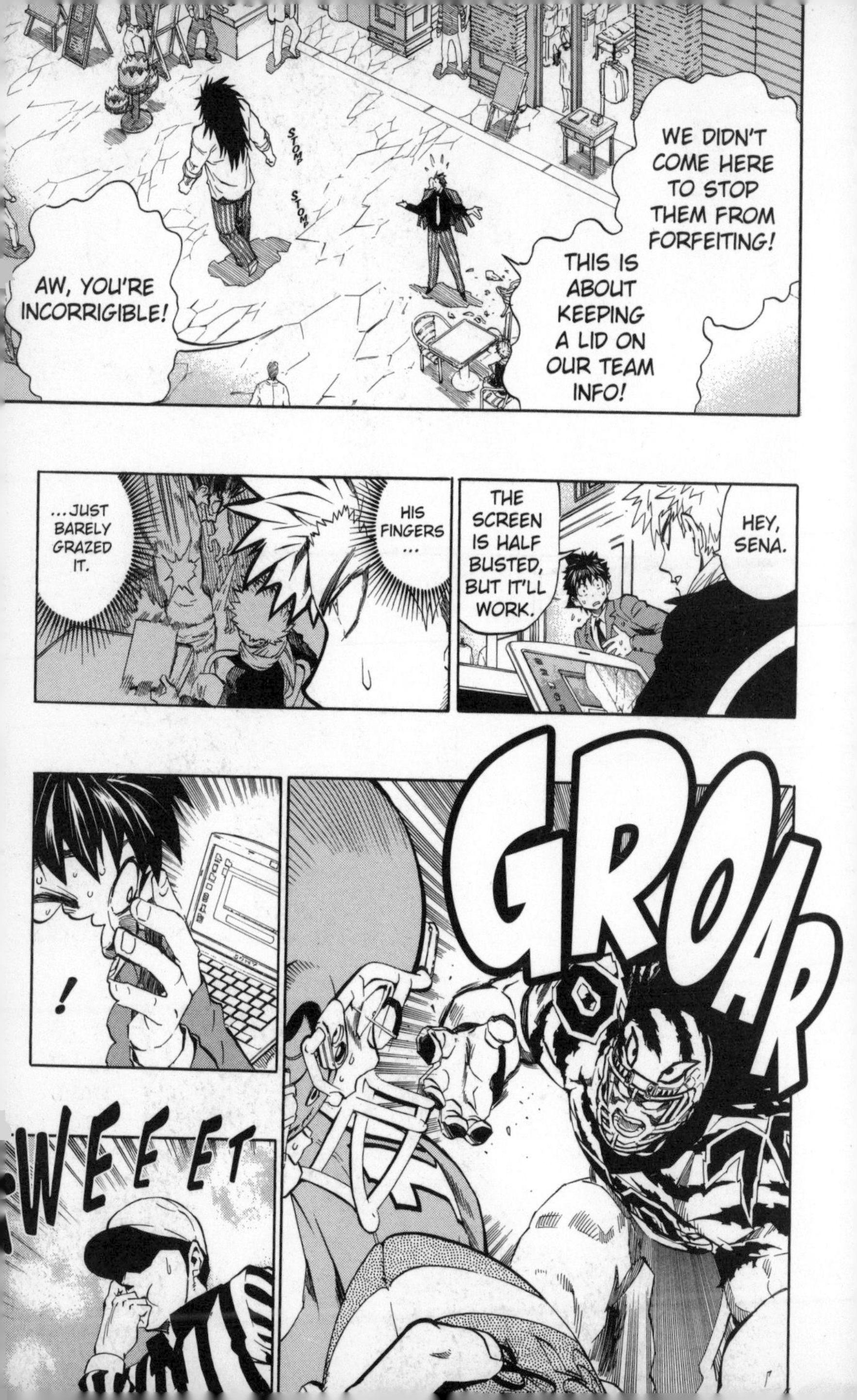
WE DIDN'T COME HERE TO STOP THEM FROM FORFEITING!
THIS IS ABOUT KEEPING A LID ON OUR TEAM INFO!
STOMP
STOMP
AW, YOU'RE INCORRIGIBLE!
HEY, SENA.
THE SCREEN IS HALF BUSTED, BUT IT'LL WORK.
HIS FINGERS...
...JUST BARELY GRAZED IT.
GROAR
!
WEEEET

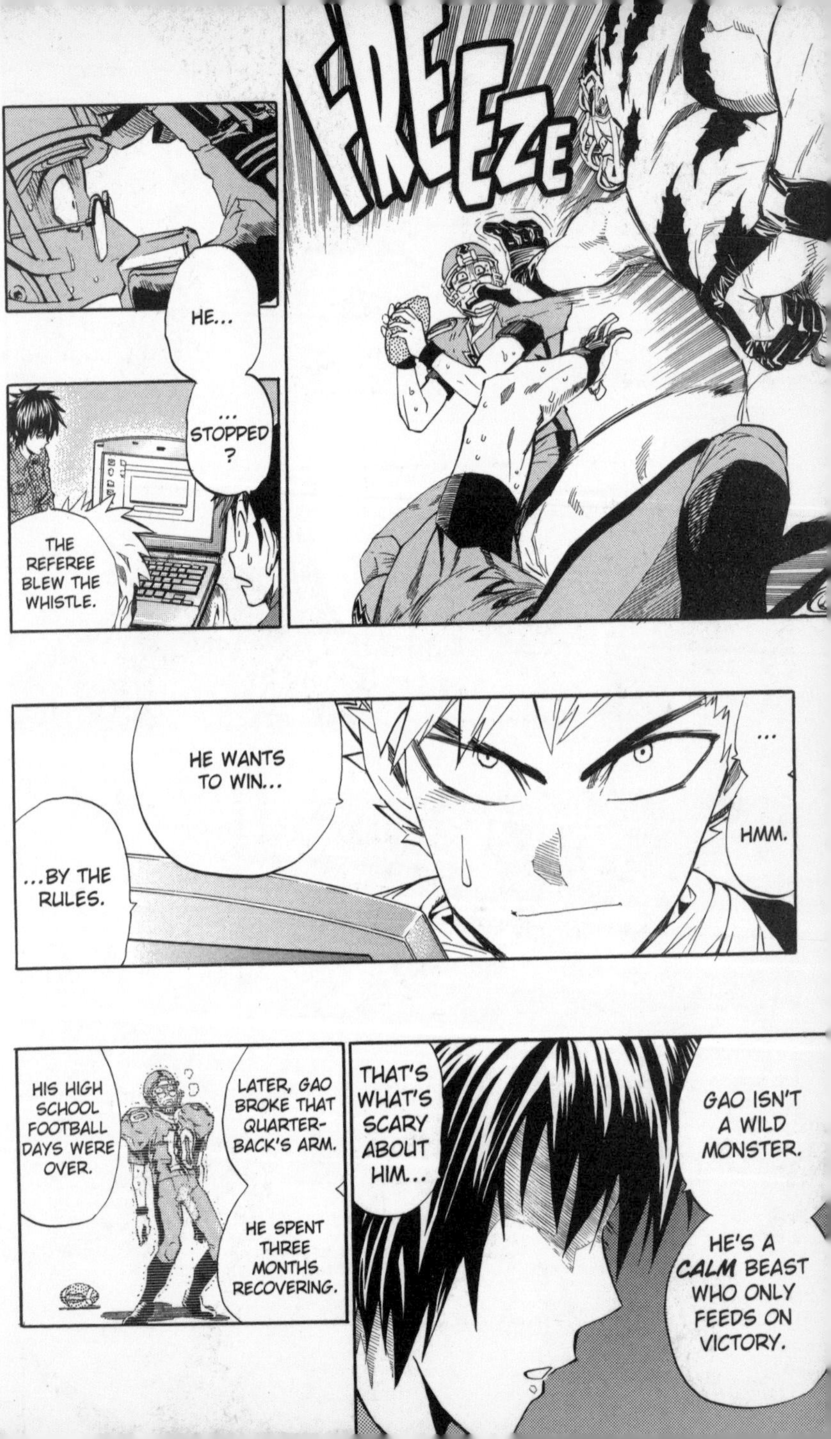
FREEZE
HE...
...STOPPED?
THE REFEREE BLEW THE WHISTLE.
... HMM.
HE WANTS TO WIN...
...BY THE RULES.
GAO ISN'T A WILD MONSTER.
HE'S A CALM BEAST WHO ONLY FEEDS ON VICTORY.
THAT'S WHAT'S SCARY ABOUT HIM...
LATER, GAO BROKE THAT QUARTER-BACK'S ARM.
HE SPENT THREE MONTHS RECOVERING.
HIS HIGH SCHOOL FOOTBALL DAYS WERE OVER.

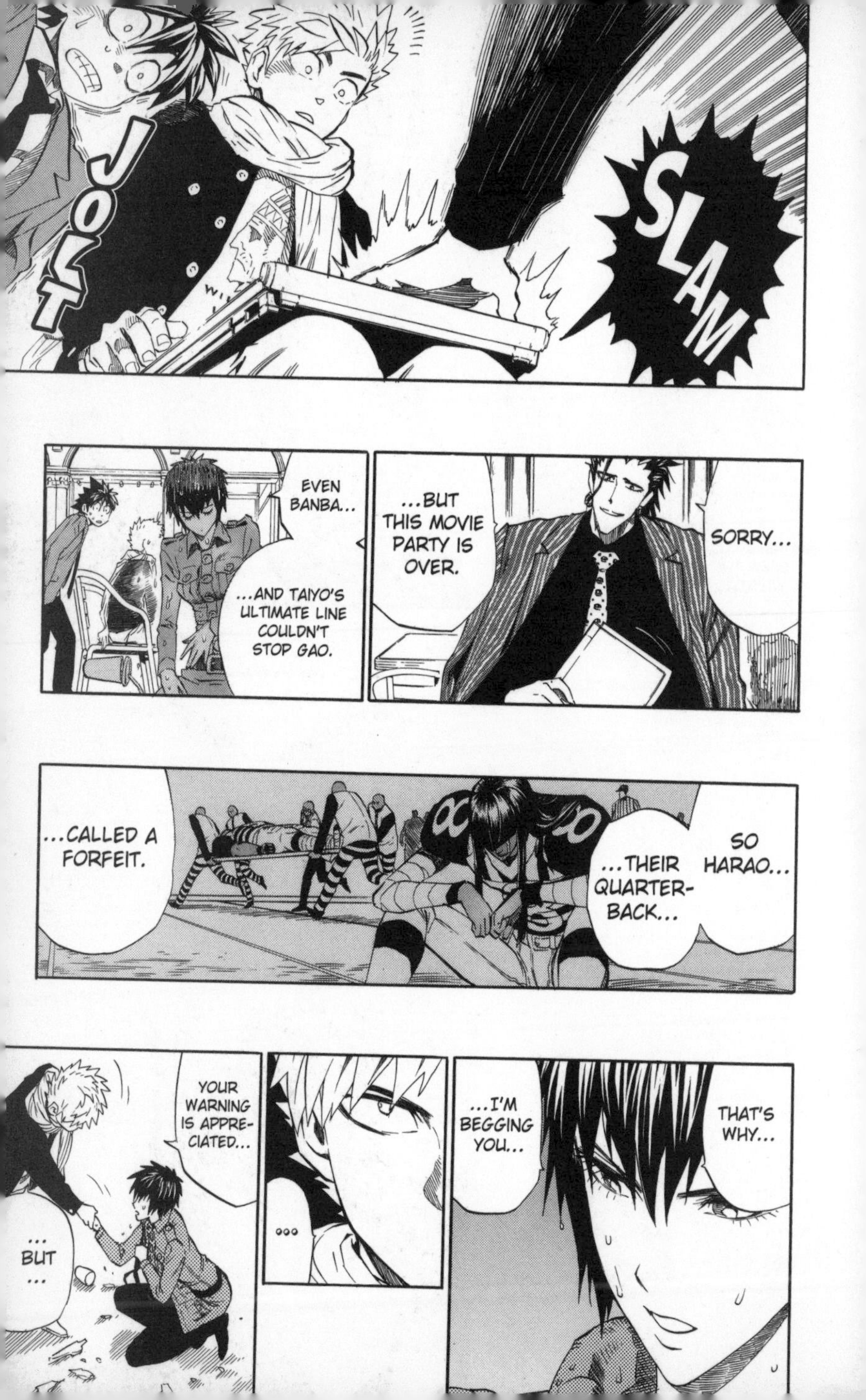
SLAM
JOLT
SORRY...
...BUT THIS MOVIE PARTY IS OVER.
EVEN BANBA...
...AND TAIYO'S ULTIMATE LINE COULDN'T STOP GAO.
SO HARAO...
...THEIR QUARTER-BACK...
...CALLED A FORFEIT.
THAT'S WHY...
...I'M BEGGING YOU...
...
YOUR WARNING IS APPRE-CIATED...
...BUT...

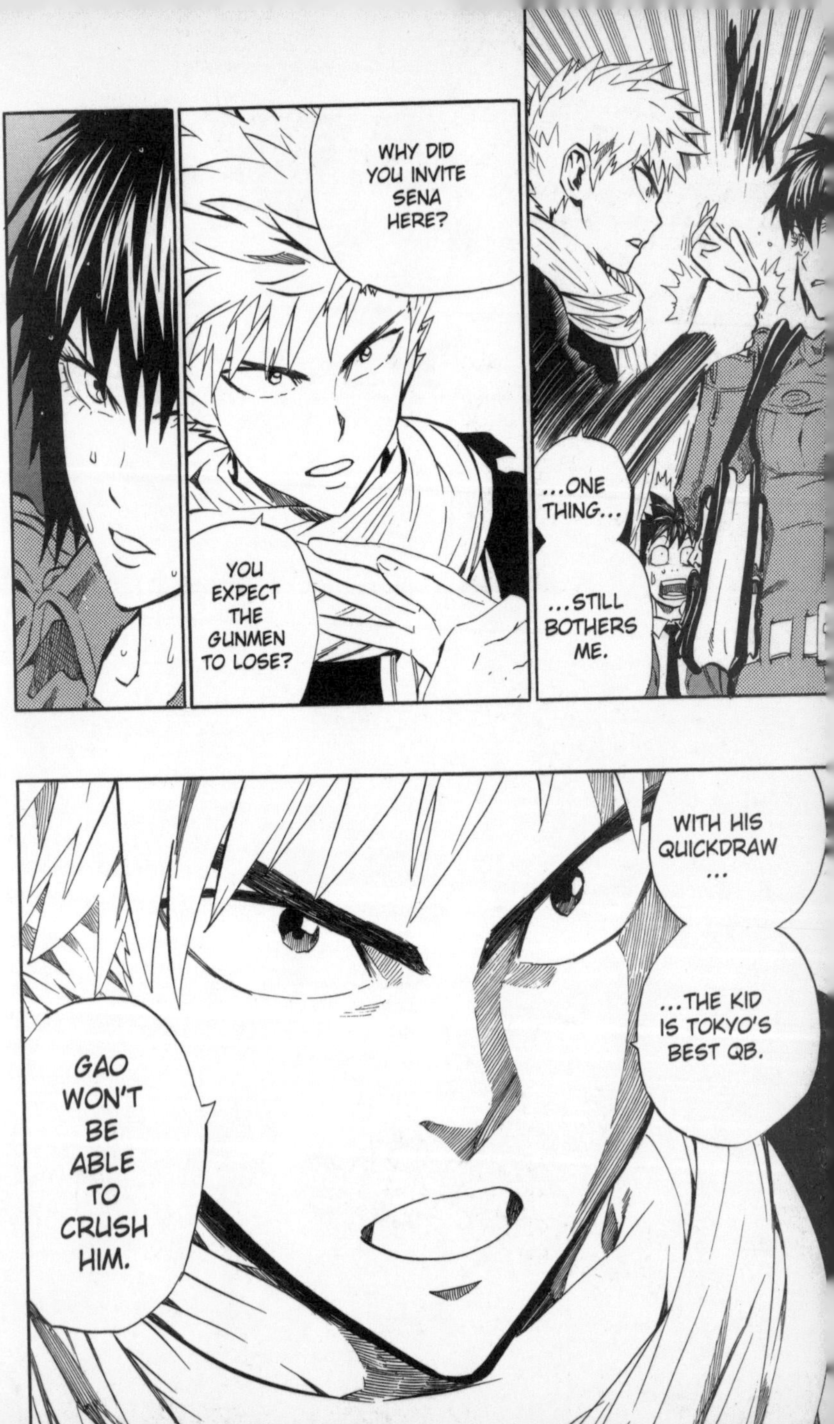
...ONE THING...
...STILL BOTHERS ME.
WHY DID YOU INVITE SENA HERE?
YOU EXPECT THE GUNMEN TO LOSE?
WITH HIS QUICKDRAW ...
...THE KID IS TOKYO'S BEST QB.
GAO WON'T BE ABLE TO CRUSH HIM.

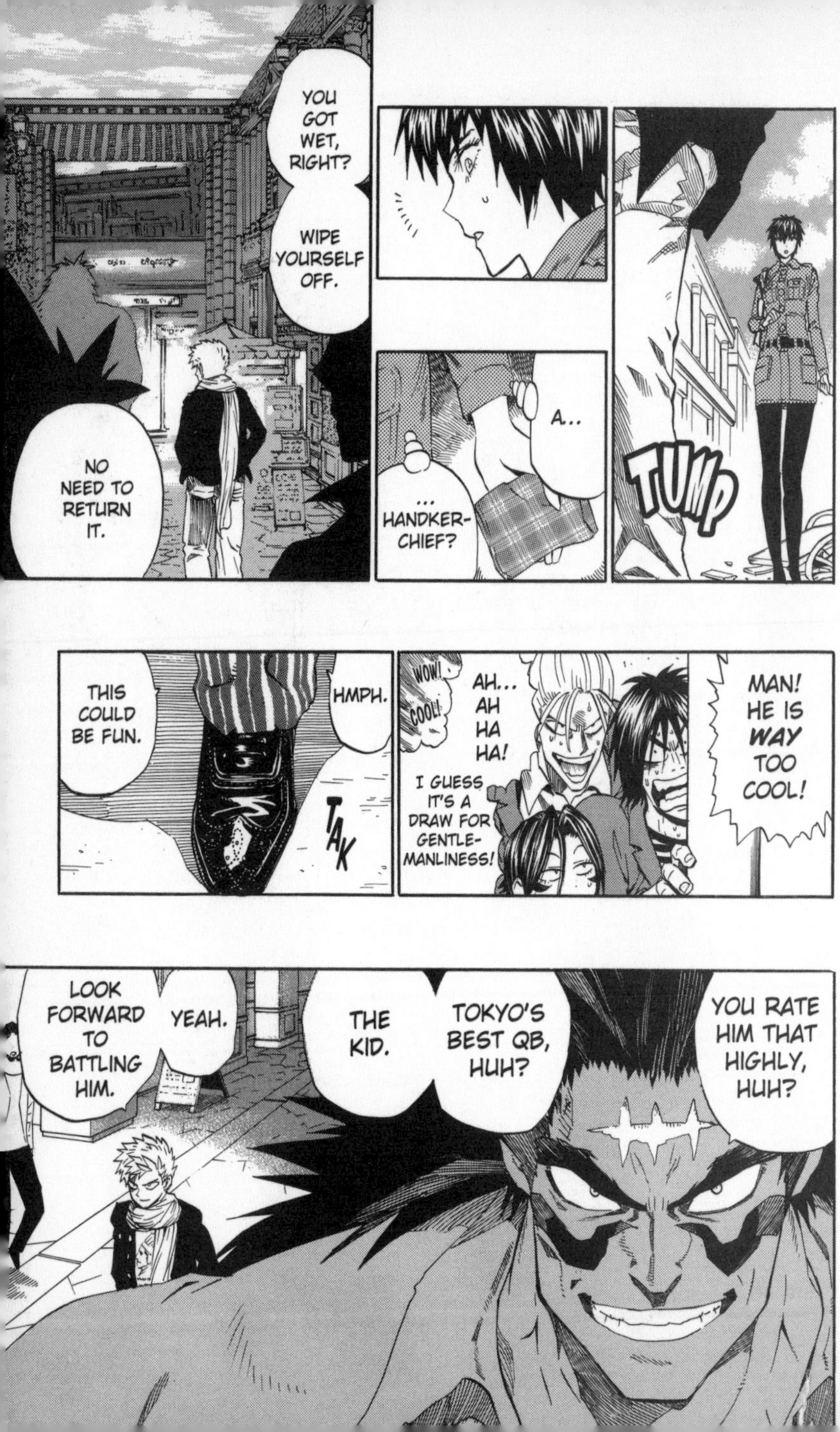
TUMP
A...
...HANDKER-CHIEF?
YOU GOT WET, RIGHT?
WIPE YOURSELF OFF.
NO NEED TO RETURN IT.
MAN! HE IS WAY TOO COOL!
WOW!
COOL!
AH... AH HA HA!
I GUESS IT'S A DRAW FOR GENTLE-MANLINESS!
HMPH.
TAK
THIS COULD BE FUN.
YOU RATE HIM THAT HIGHLY, HUH?
TOKYO'S BEST QB, HUH?
THE KID.
YEAH.
LOOK FORWARD TO BATTLING HIM.

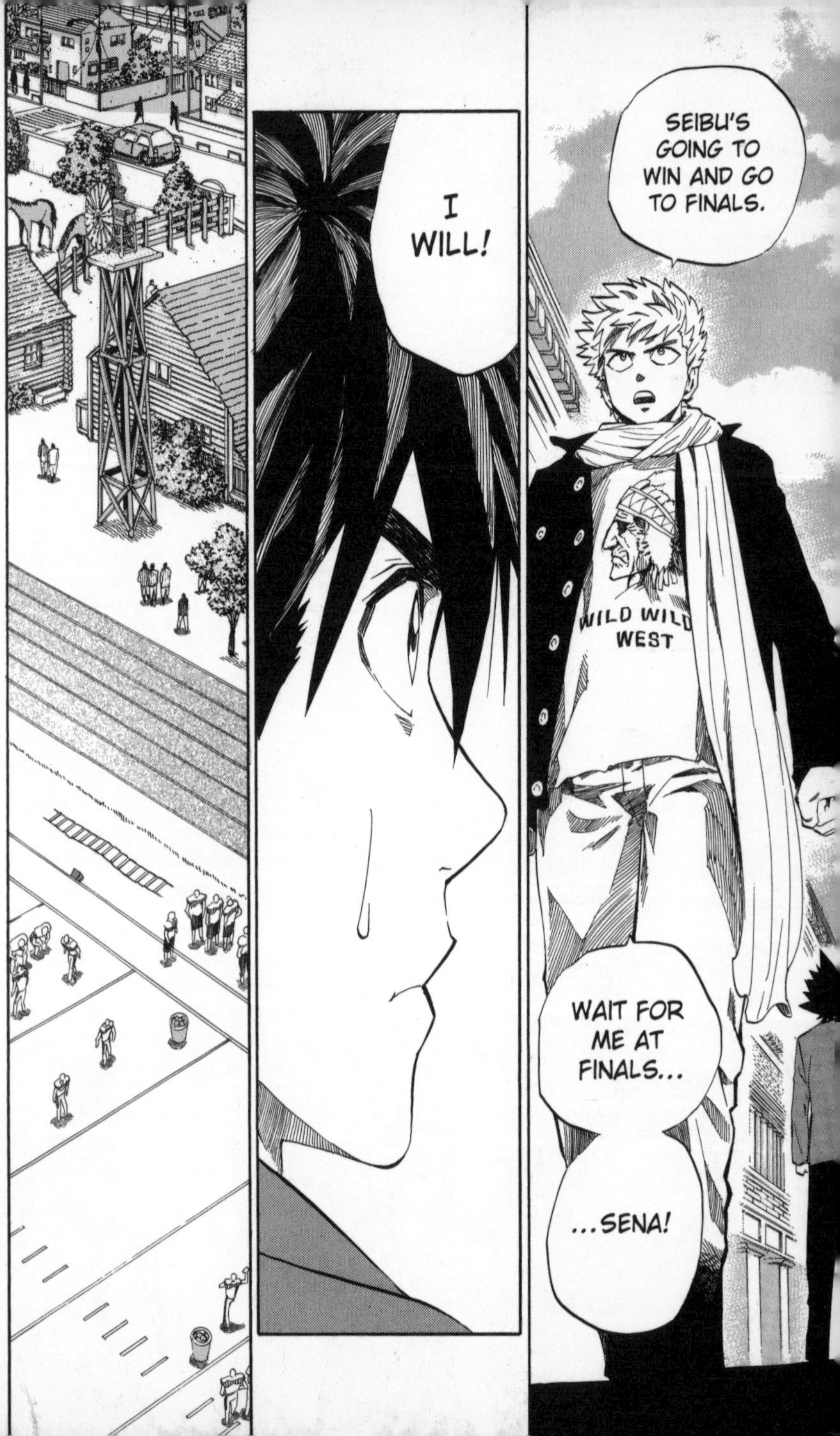
SEIBU'S GOING TO WIN AND GO TO FINALS.
WILD WILD WEST
WAIT FOR ME AT FINALS...
...SENA!
I WILL!

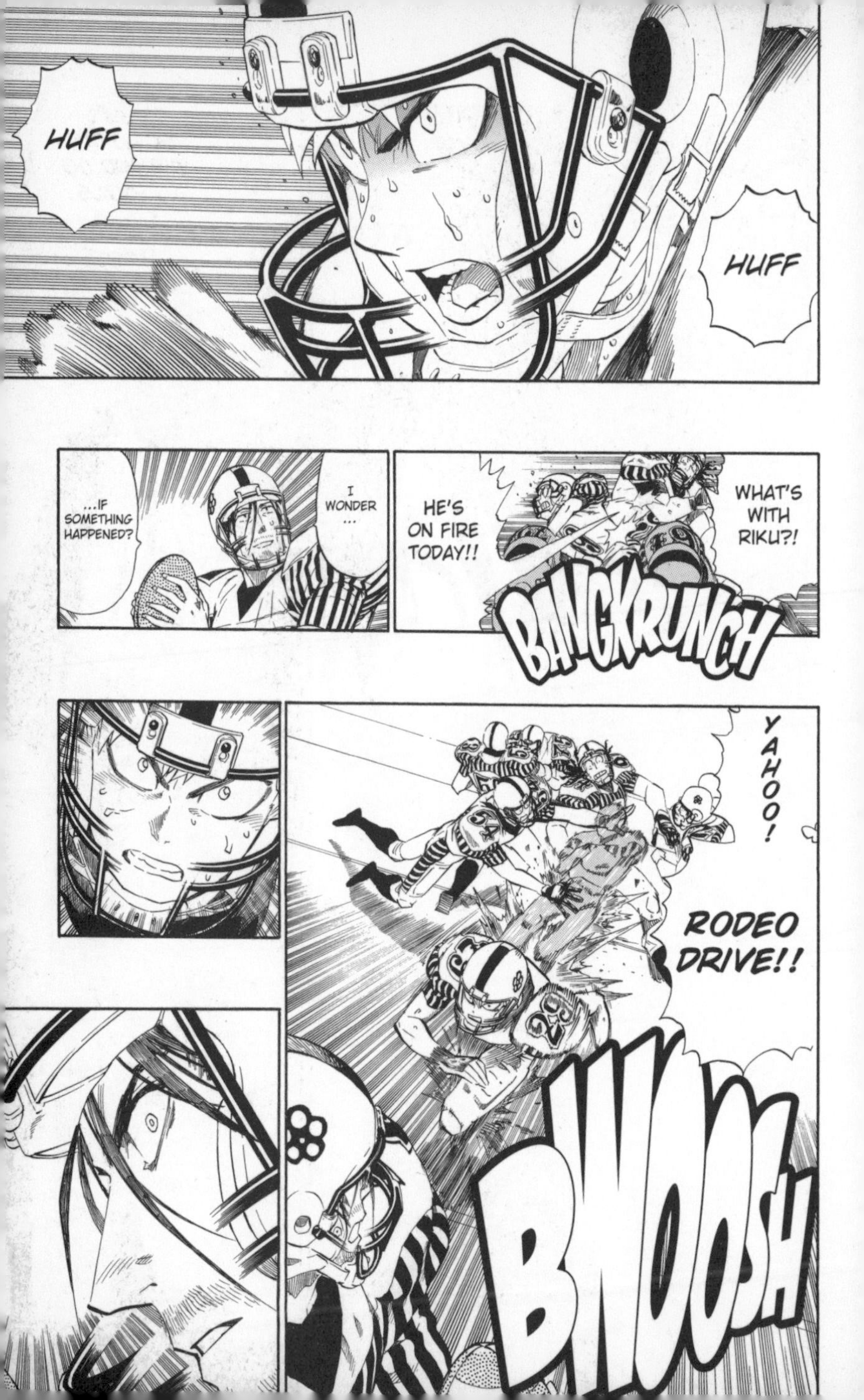
HUFF
HUFF
WHAT'S WITH RIKU?!
HE'S ON FIRE TODAY!!
BANGKRUNCH
I WONDER...
...IF SOMETHING HAPPENED?
YAHOO!
RODEO DRIVE!!
BWOOSH

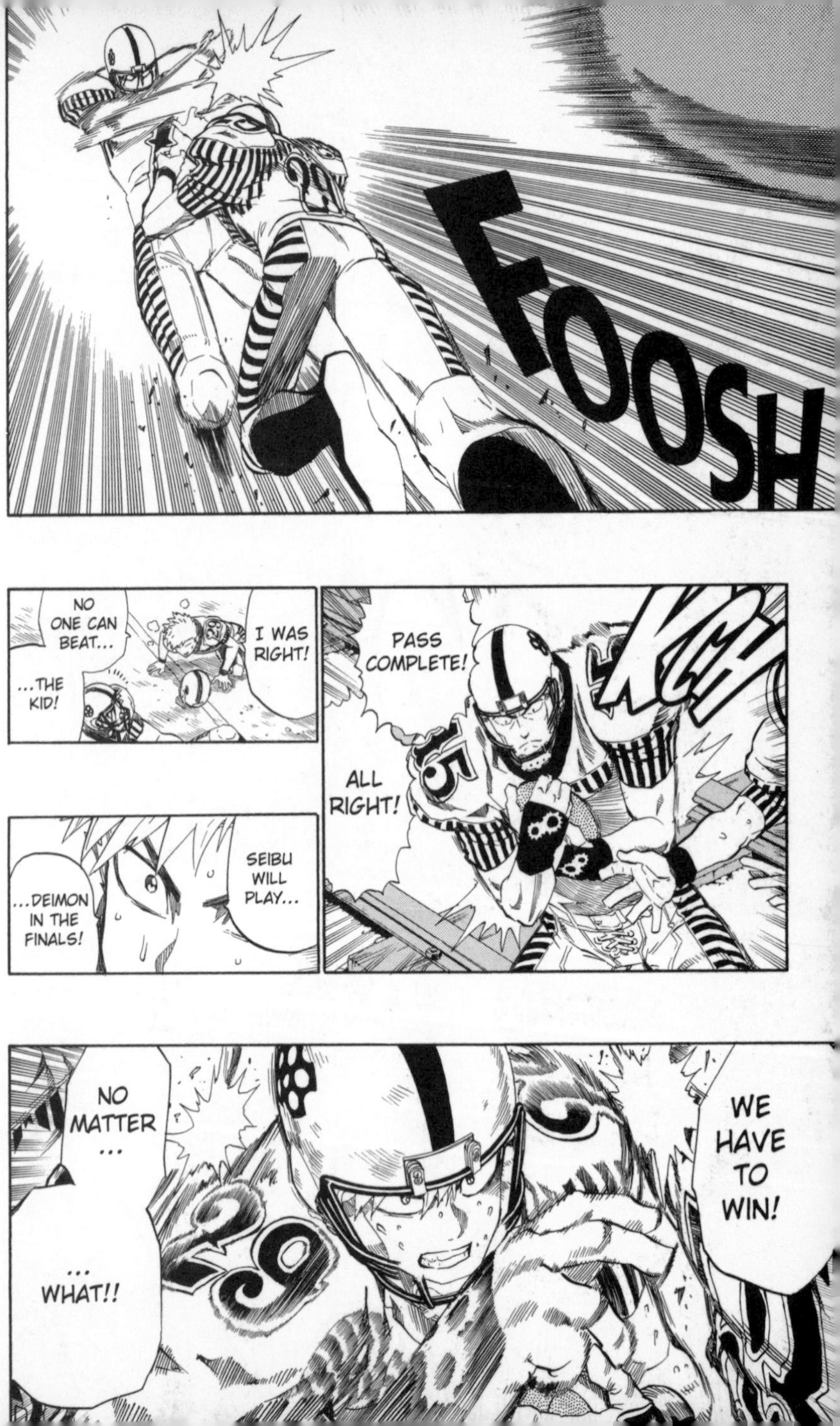
FOOSH
PASS COMPLETE!
ALL RIGHT!
I WAS RIGHT!
NO ONE CAN BEAT...
...THE KID!
SEIBU WILL PLAY...
...DEIMON IN THE FINALS!
WE HAVE TO WIN!
NO MATTER...
...WHAT!!

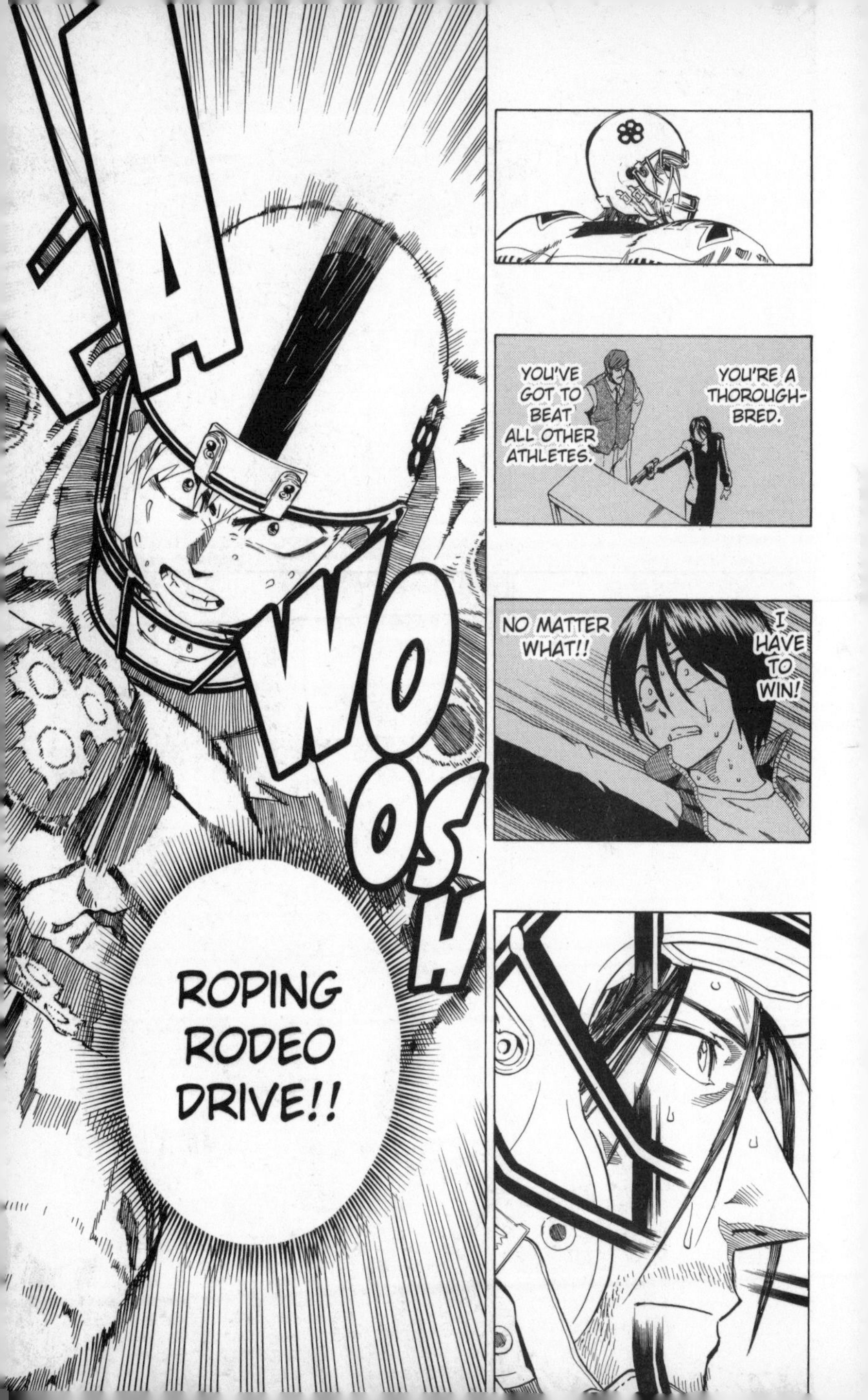
YOU'RE A THOROUGH-BRED.
YOU'VE GOT TO BEAT ALL OTHER ATHLETES.
I HAVE TO WIN!
NO MATTER WHAT!!
WOOSH
ROPING RODEO DRIVE!!

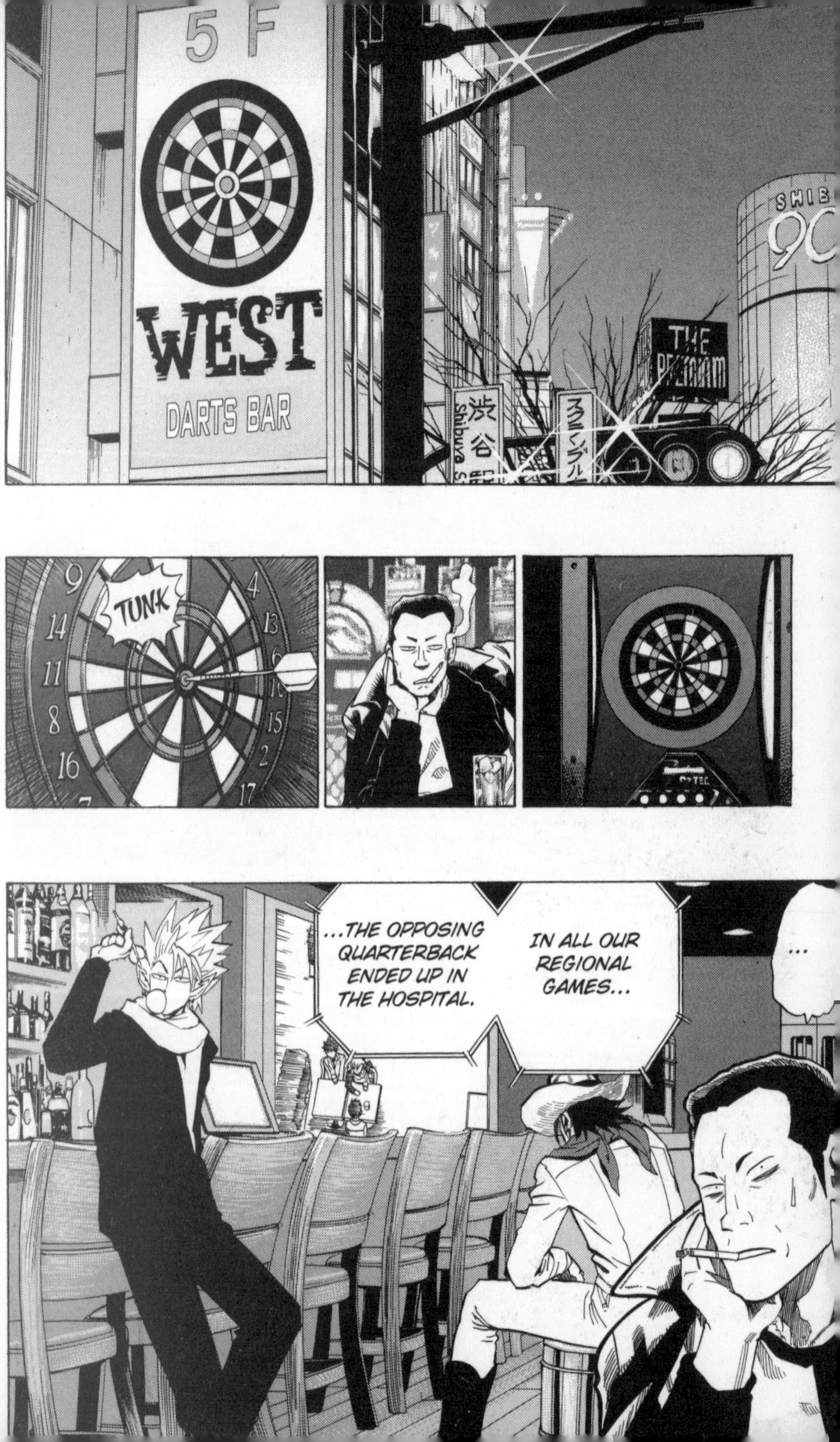
5 F
WEST
DARTS BAR
渋谷
SHIB
90
THE
TUNK
...
IN ALL OUR REGIONAL GAMES...
...THE OPPOSING QUARTERBACK ENDED UP IN THE HOSPITAL.

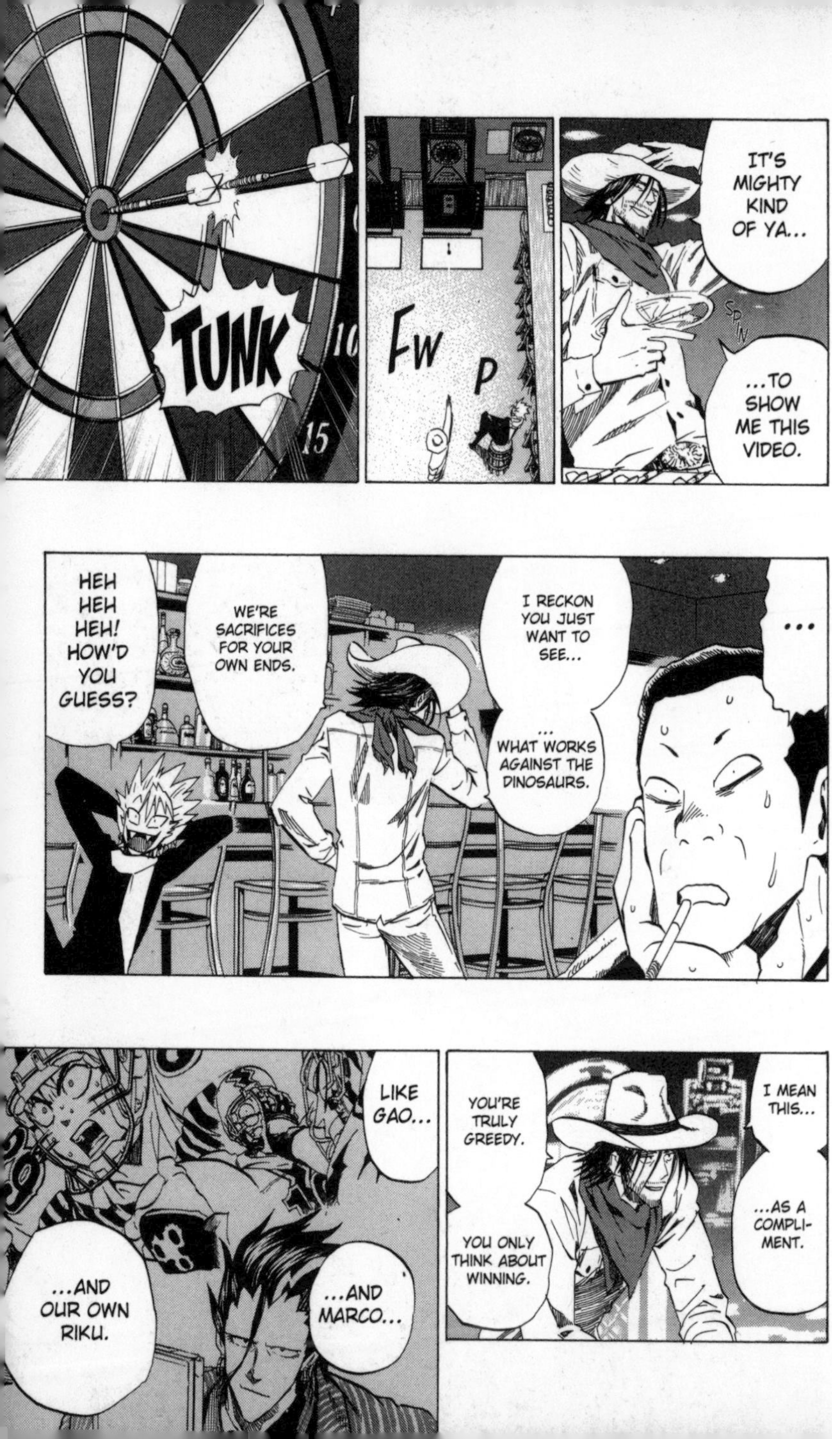
IT'S MIGHTY KIND OF YA...
SPIN
...TO SHOW ME THIS VIDEO.
FWP
TUNK
...
I RECKON YOU JUST WANT TO SEE...
...WHAT WORKS AGAINST THE DINOSAURS.
WE'RE SACRIFICES FOR YOUR OWN ENDS.
HEH HEH HEH! HOW'D YOU GUESS?
I MEAN THIS...
...AS A COMPLIMENT.
YOU'RE TRULY GREEDY.
YOU ONLY THINK ABOUT WINNING.
LIKE GAO...
...AND MARCO...
...AND OUR OWN RIKU.

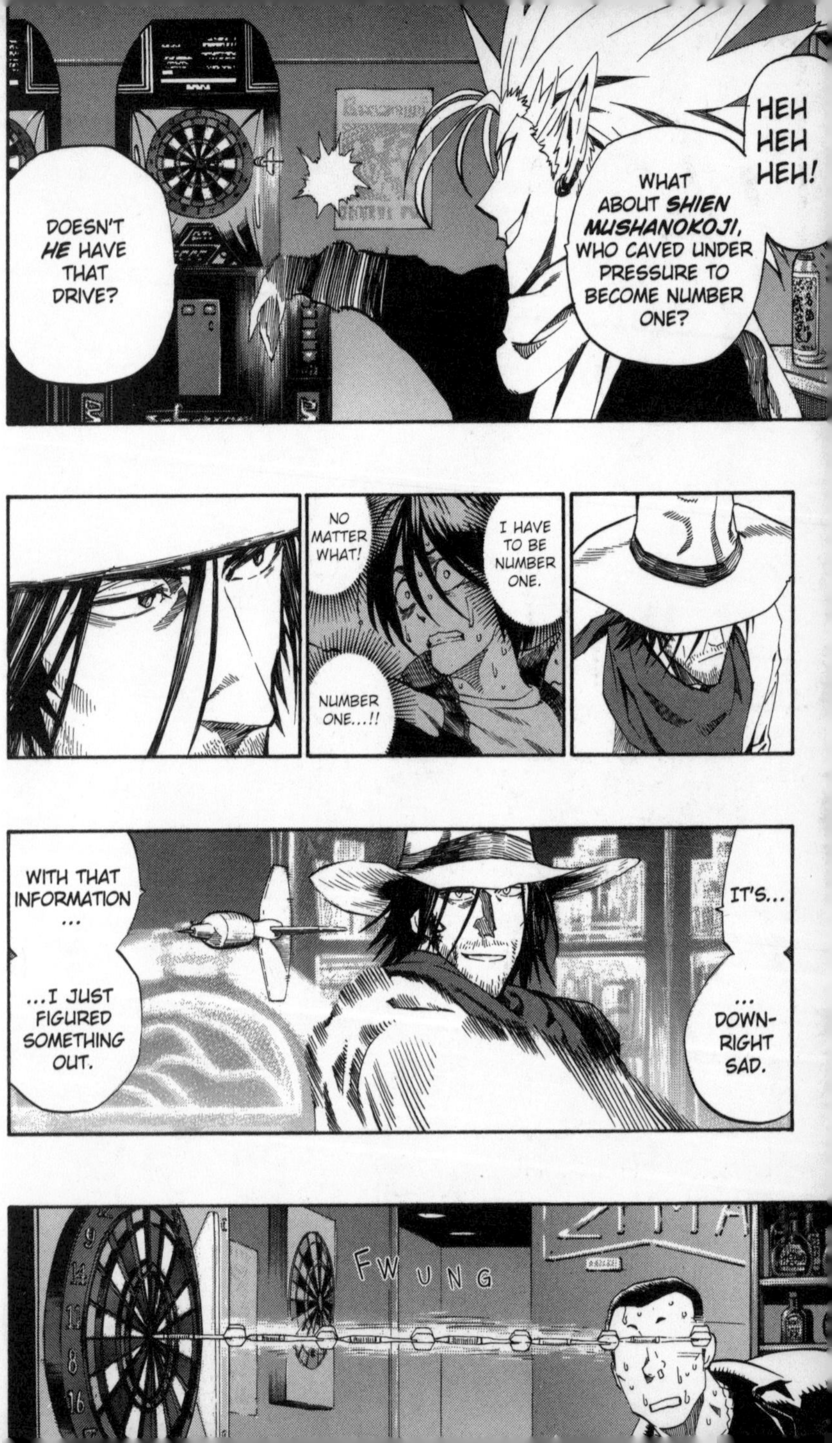
HEH HEH HEH!
WHAT ABOUT SHIEN MUSHANOKOJI, WHO CAVED UNDER PRESSURE TO BECOME NUMBER ONE?
DOESN'T HE HAVE THAT DRIVE?
I HAVE TO BE NUMBER ONE.
NO MATTER WHAT!
NUMBER ONE...!!
IT'S...
...DOWN-RIGHT SAD.
WITH THAT INFORMATION ...
...I JUST FIGURED SOMETHING OUT.
FWUNG

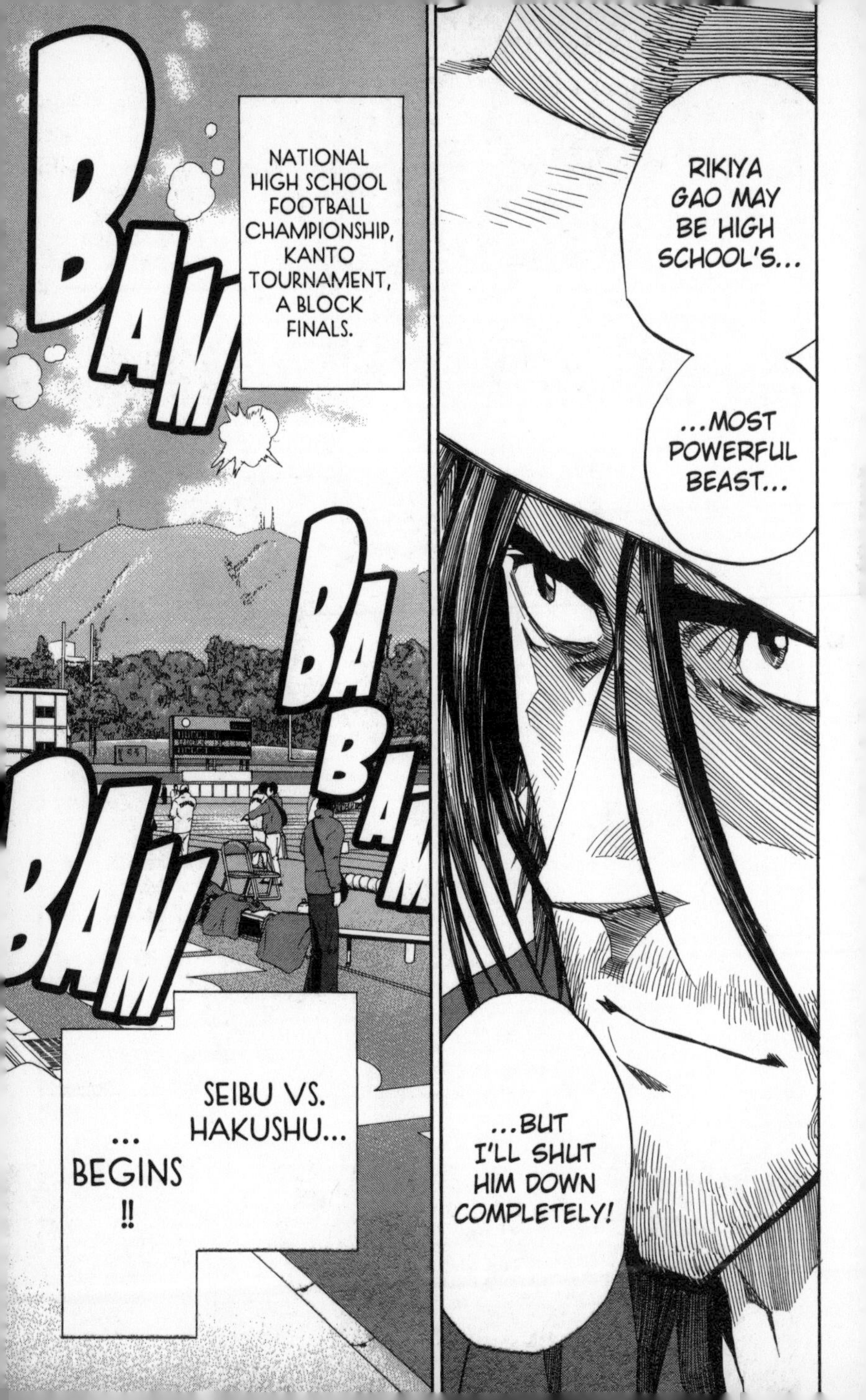
RIKIYA GAO MAY BE HIGH SCHOOL'S...
...MOST POWERFUL BEAST...
...BUT I'LL SHUT HIM DOWN COMPLETELY!
BAM
NATIONAL HIGH SCHOOL FOOTBALL CHAMPIONSHIP, KANTO TOURNAMENT, A BLOCK FINALS.
BA
BA
BAM
BAM
SEIBU VS. HAKUSHU...
... BEGINS !!

Special Supplement!!

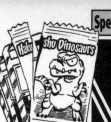

Hakushu Dinosaurs Athlete Card

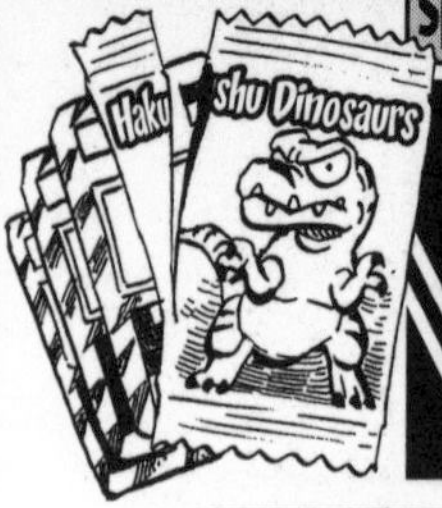

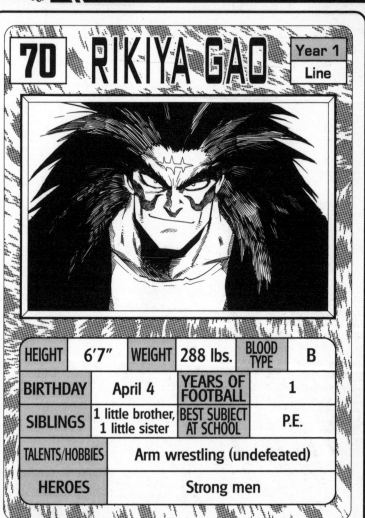

70 RIKIYA GAO

Year 1

Line

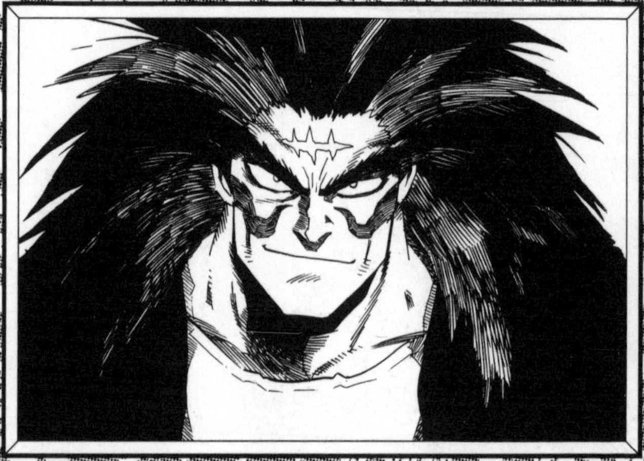

HEIGHT	6'7"	WEIGHT	288 lbs.	BLOOD TYPE	B
BIRTHDAY	April 4	YEARS OF FOOTBALL	1		
SIBLINGS	1 little brother, 1 little sister	BEST SUBJECT AT SCHOOL	P.E.		
TALENTS/HOBBIES	Arm wrestling (undefeated)				
HEROES	Strong men				

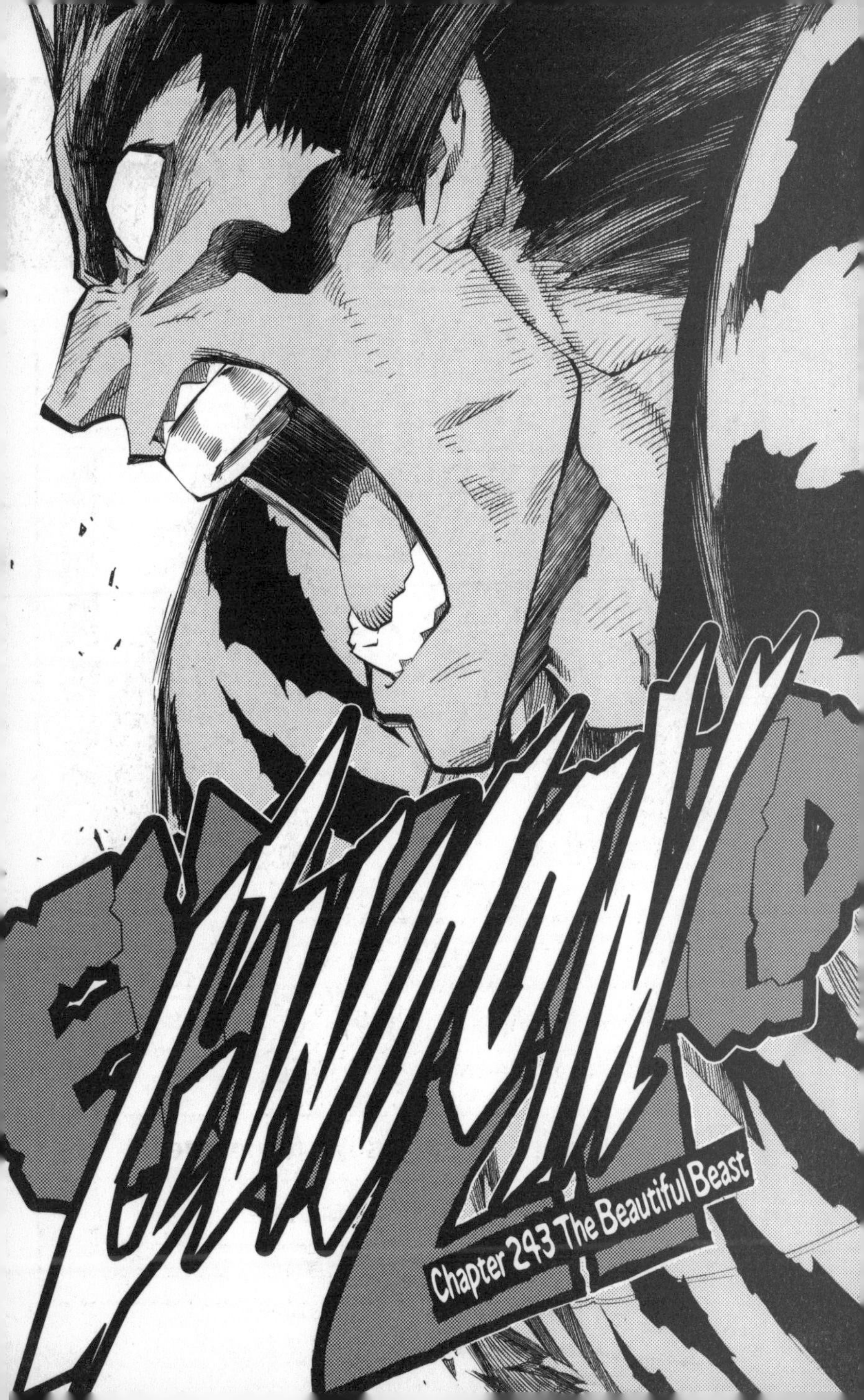
Chapter 243 The Beautiful Beast

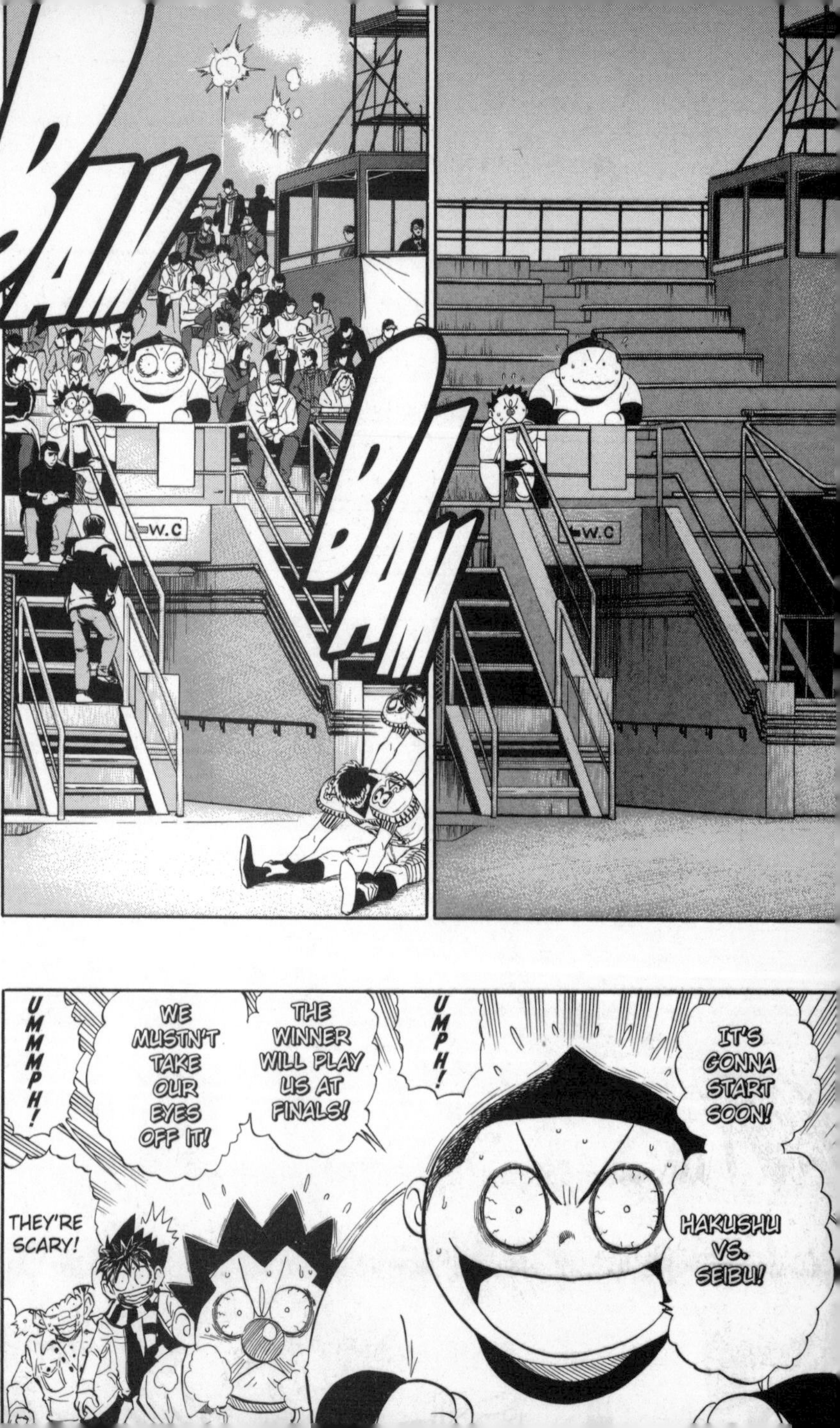
BAM
BAM
IT'S GONNA START SOON!
HAKUSHU VS. SEIBU!
UMPH!
THE WINNER WILL PLAY US AT FINALS!
WE MUSTN'T TAKE OUR EYES OFF IT!
UMMMPH!
THEY'RE SCARY!

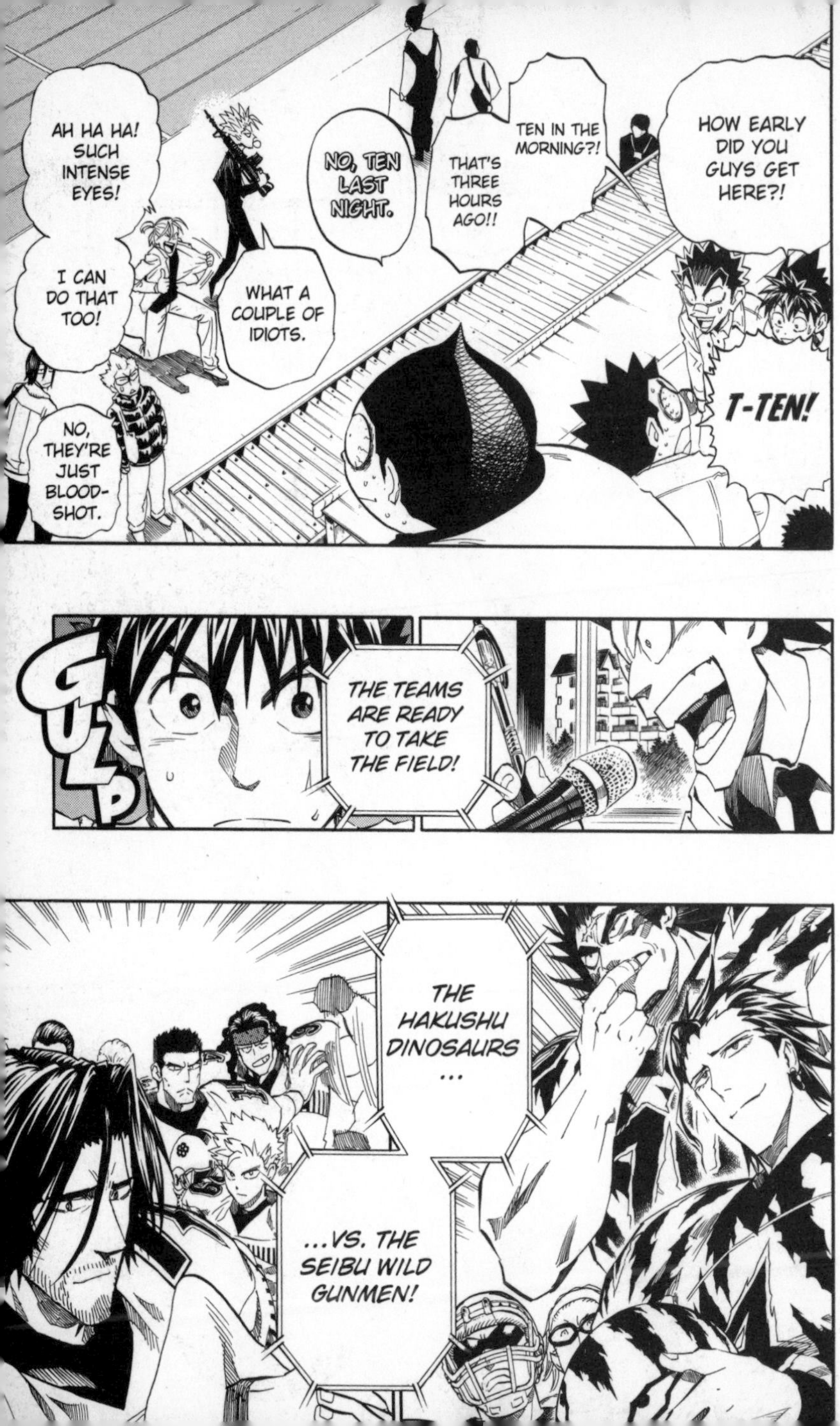
HOW EARLY DID YOU GUYS GET HERE?!
TEN IN THE MORNING?!
THAT'S THREE HOURS AGO!!
T-TEN!
NO, TEN LAST NIGHT.
WHAT A COUPLE OF IDIOTS.
AH HA HA! SUCH INTENSE EYES!
I CAN DO THAT TOO!
NO, THEY'RE JUST BLOOD-SHOT.
THE TEAMS ARE READY TO TAKE THE FIELD!
GULP
THE HAKUSHU DINOSAURS...
...VS. THE SEIBU WILD GUNMEN!

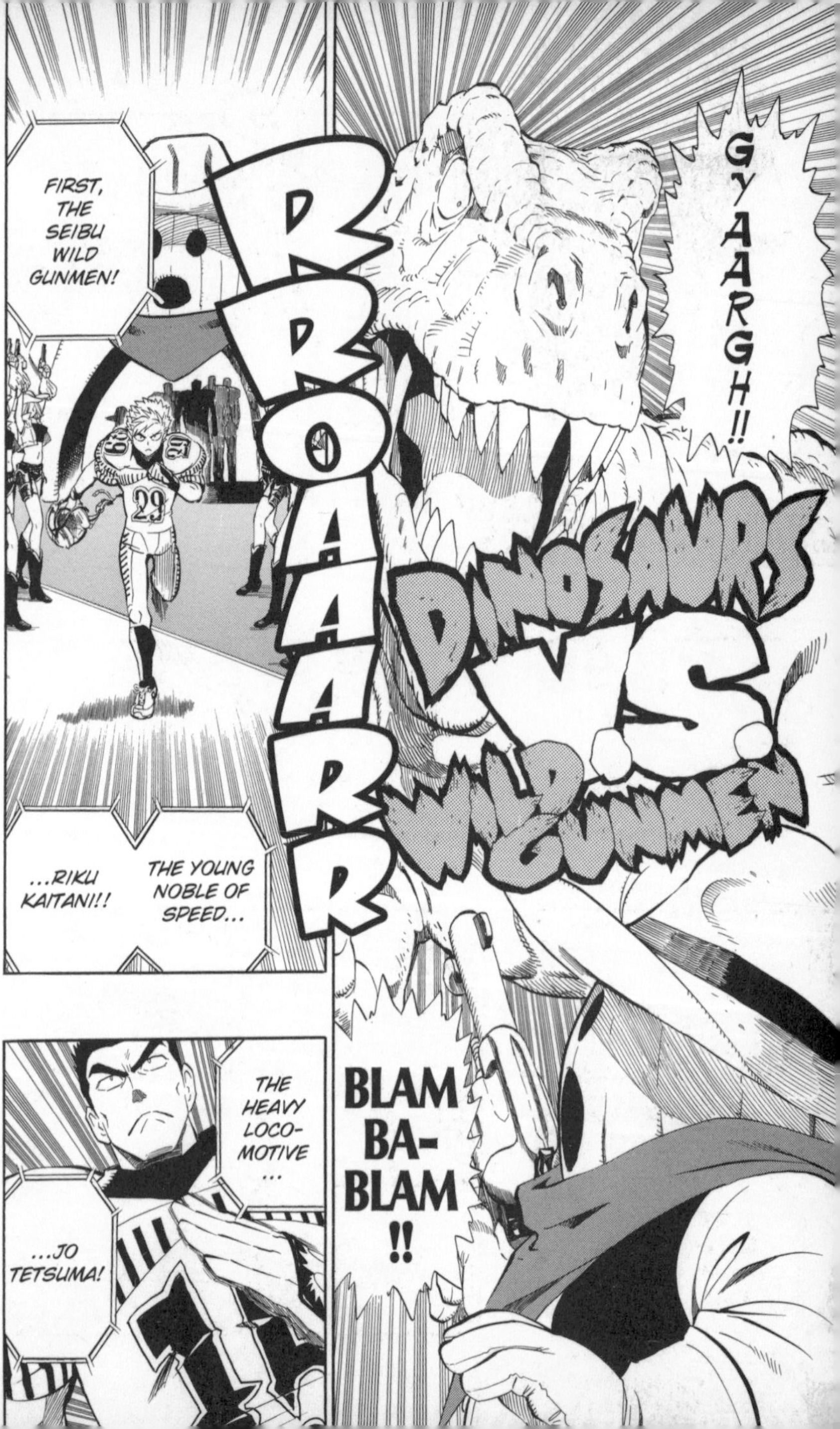
GYAARGH!!
RROAAARR
DINOSAURS V.S. WILD GUNMEN
BLAM BA-BLAM!!
FIRST, THE SEIBU WILD GUNMEN!
THE YOUNG NOBLE OF SPEED...
...RIKU KAITANI!!
THE HEAVY LOCO-MOTIVE ...
...JO TETSUMA!

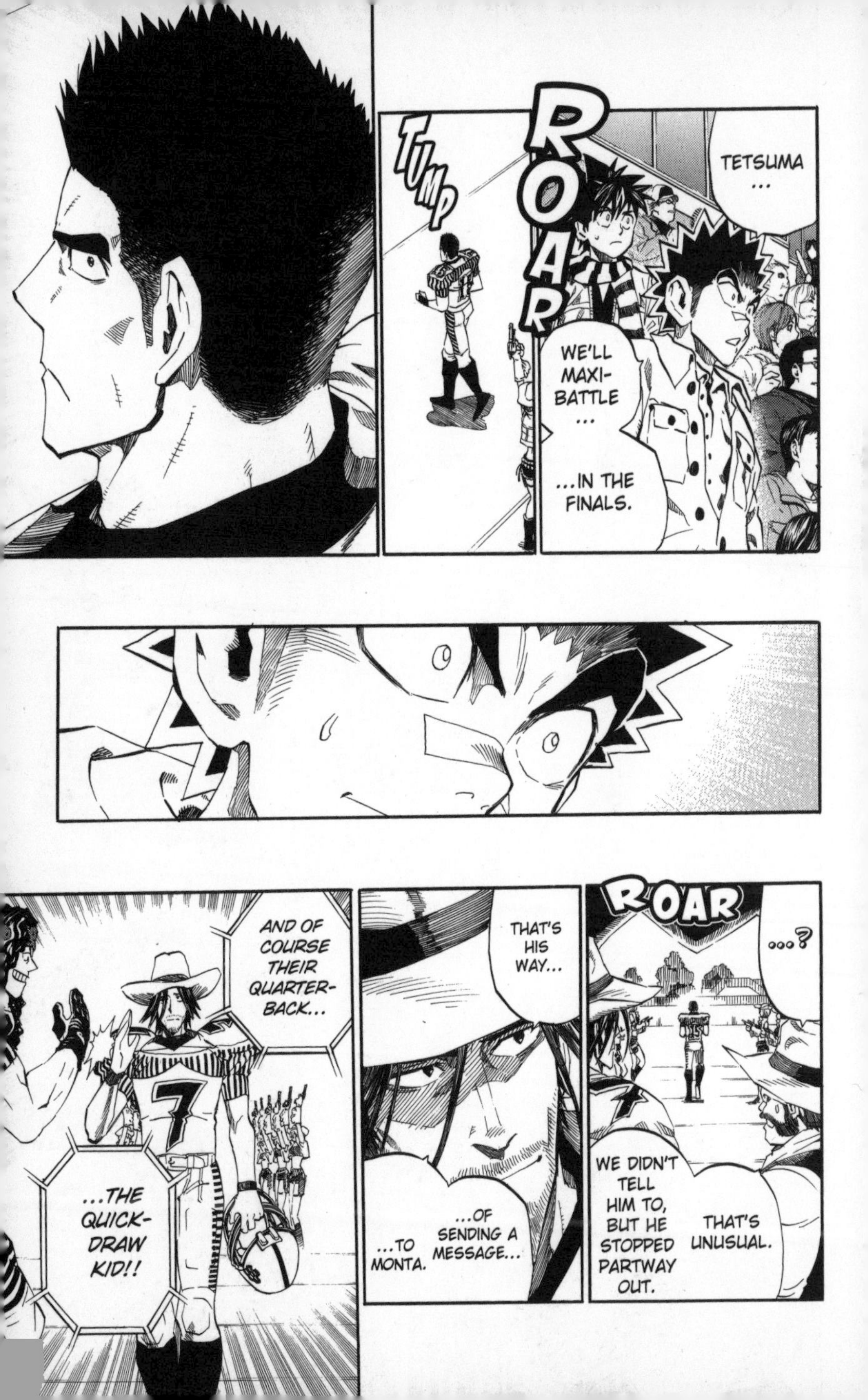
ROAR
TETSUMA ...
WE'LL MAXI-BATTLE ...
...IN THE FINALS.
TUMP
ROAR
...?
WE DIDN'T TELL HIM TO, BUT HE STOPPED PARTWAY OUT.
THAT'S UNUSUAL.
THAT'S HIS WAY...
...OF SENDING A MESSAGE...
...TO MONTA.
AND OF COURSE THEIR QUARTER-BACK...
...THE QUICK-DRAW KID!!

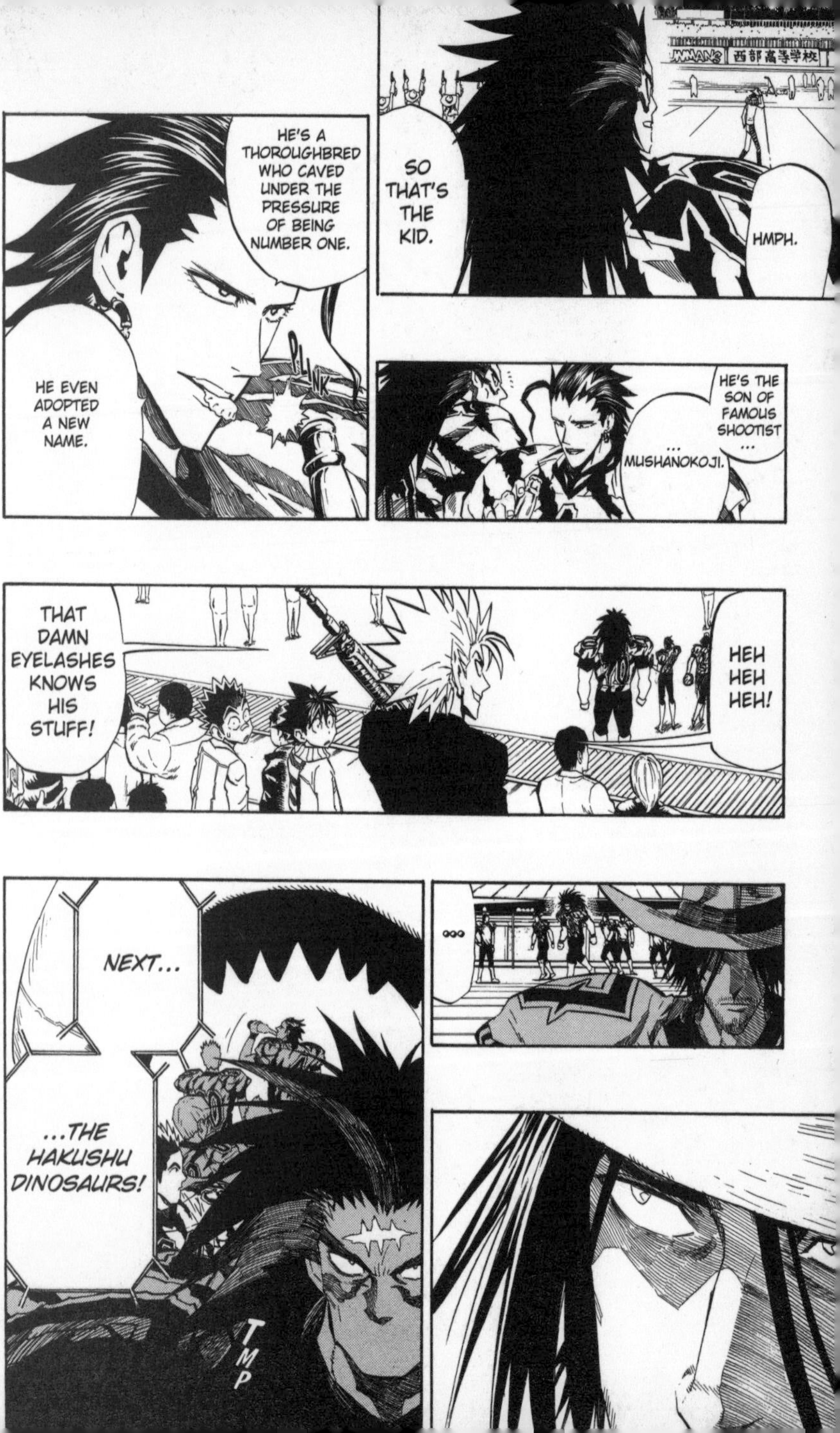
西部高等学校
SO THAT'S THE KID.
HMPH.
HE'S THE SON OF FAMOUS SHOOTIST ...
... MUSHANOKOJI.
HE'S A THOROUGHBRED WHO CAVED UNDER THE PRESSURE OF BEING NUMBER ONE.
PLINK
HE EVEN ADOPTED A NEW NAME.
HEH HEH HEH!
THAT DAMN EYELASHES KNOWS HIS STUFF!
...
NEXT...
...THE HAKUSHU DINOSAURS!
TMP

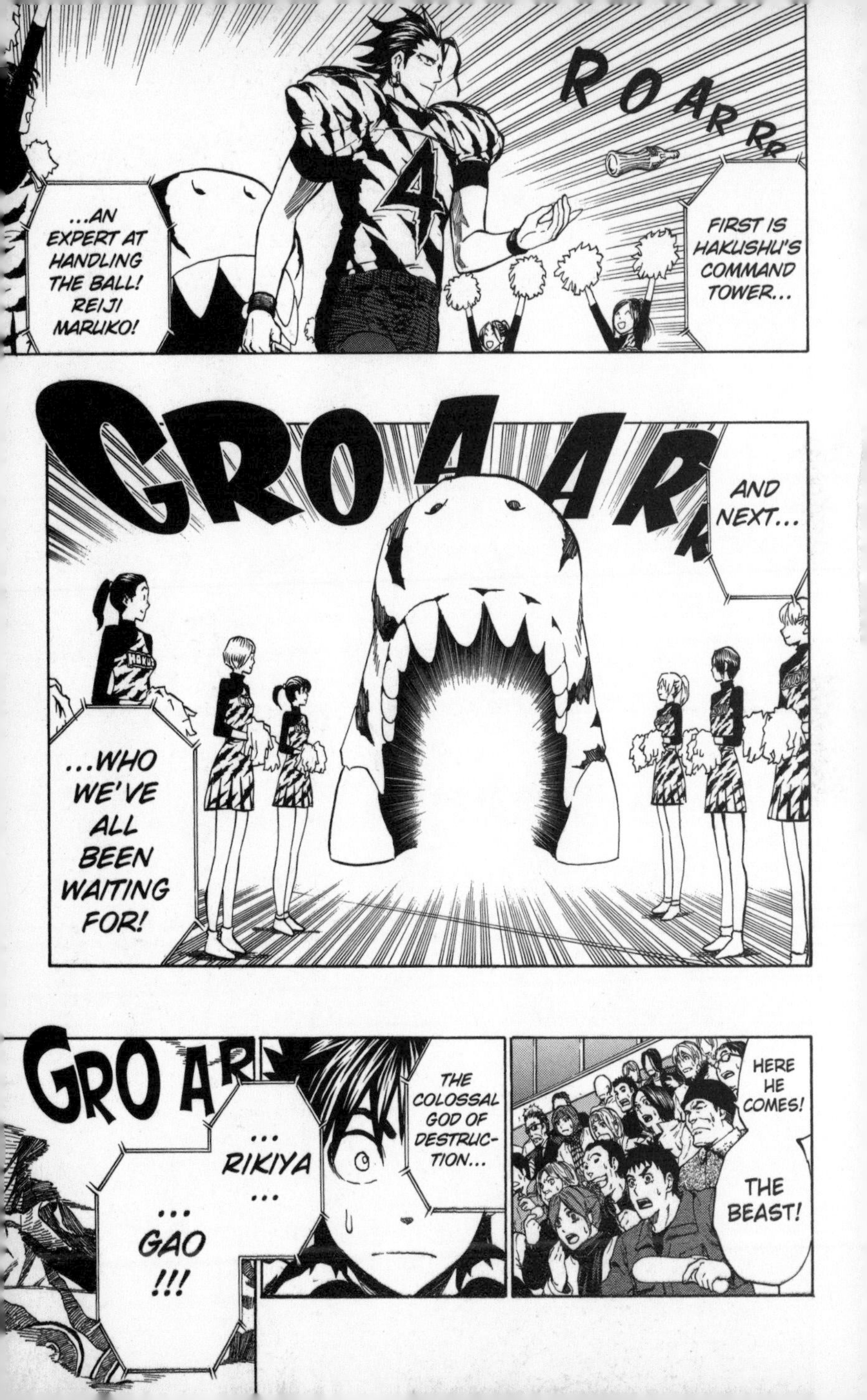
ROARRRR
FIRST IS HAKUSHU'S COMMAND TOWER...
...AN EXPERT AT HANDLING THE BALL! REIJI MARUKO!
GROAARR
AND NEXT...
...WHO WE'VE ALL BEEN WAITING FOR!
HERE HE COMES!
THE BEAST!
THE COLOSSAL GOD OF DESTRUCTION...
... RIKIYA ...
... GAO !!!
GRO AR

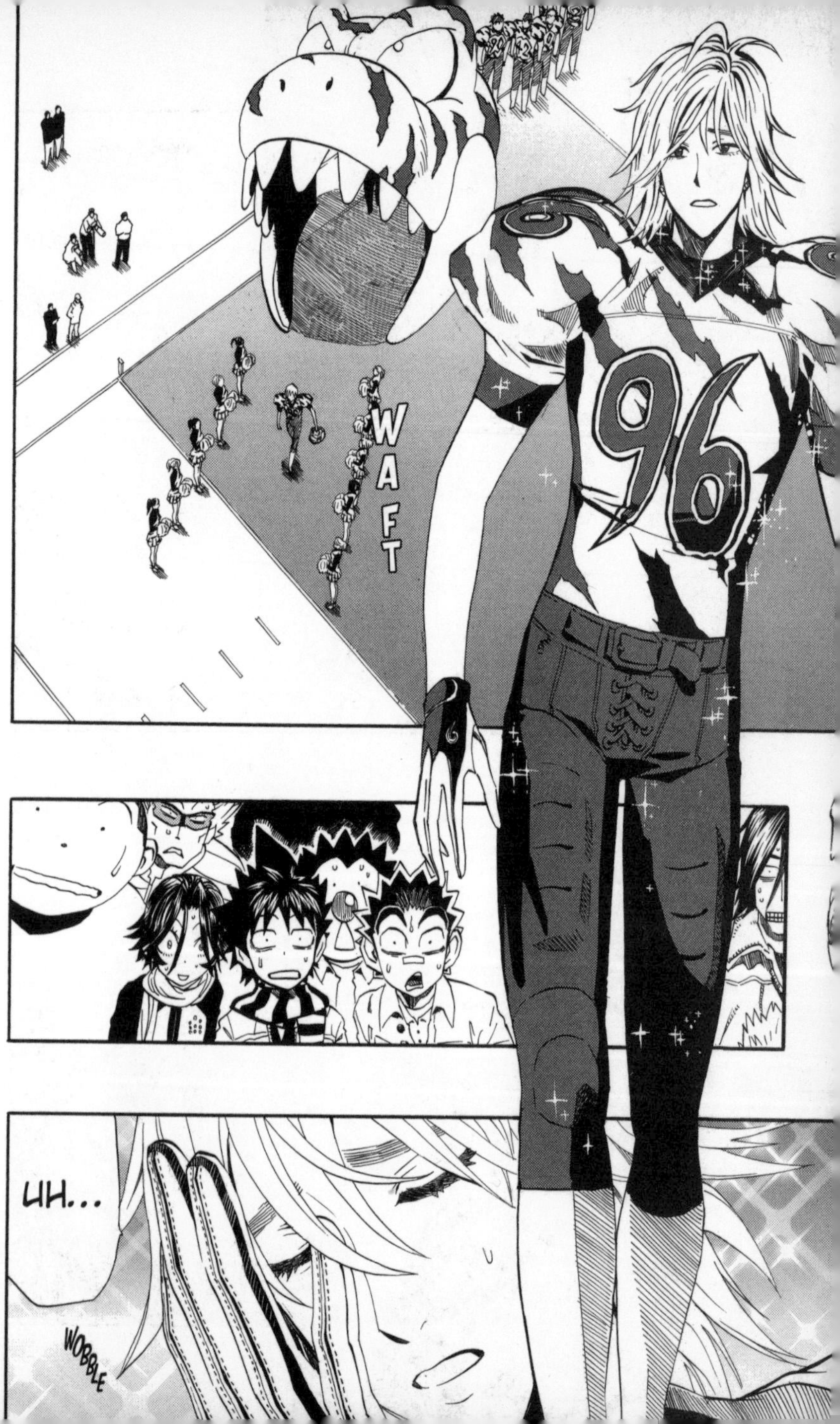
WAFT
UH...
WOBBLE

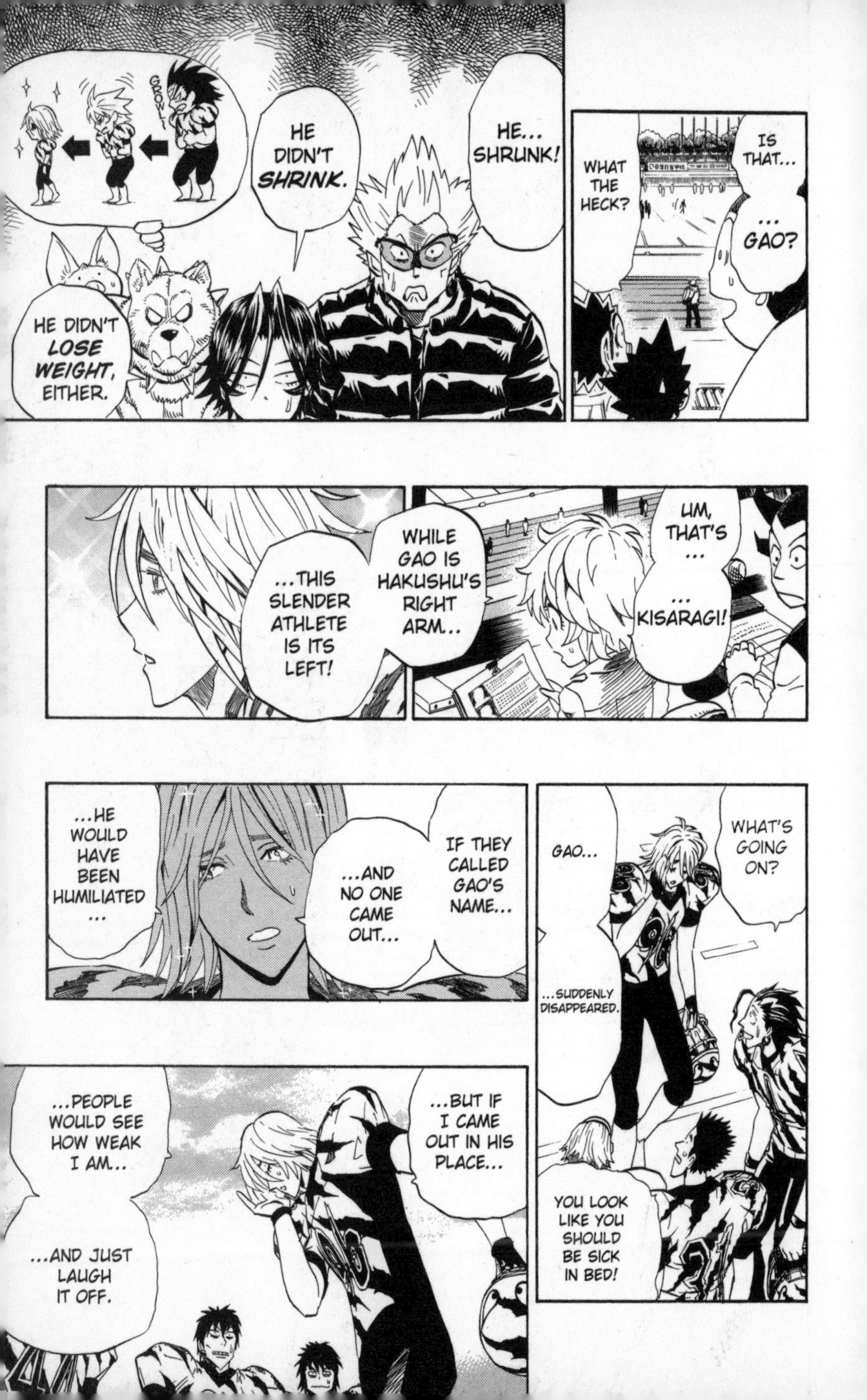
IS THAT... ...GAO?
WHAT THE HECK?
HE... SHRUNK!
HE DIDN'T SHRINK.
GROWL
HE DIDN'T LOSE WEIGHT, EITHER.
UM, THAT'S ...
... KISARAGI!
WHILE GAO IS HAKUSHU'S RIGHT ARM...
...THIS SLENDER ATHLETE IS ITS LEFT!
WHAT'S GOING ON?
GAO...
...SUDDENLY DISAPPEARED.
YOU LOOK LIKE YOU SHOULD BE SICK IN BED!
IF THEY CALLED GAO'S NAME...
...AND NO ONE CAME OUT...
...HE WOULD HAVE BEEN HUMILIATED...
...BUT IF I CAME OUT IN HIS PLACE...
...PEOPLE WOULD SEE HOW WEAK I AM...
...AND JUST LAUGH IT OFF.

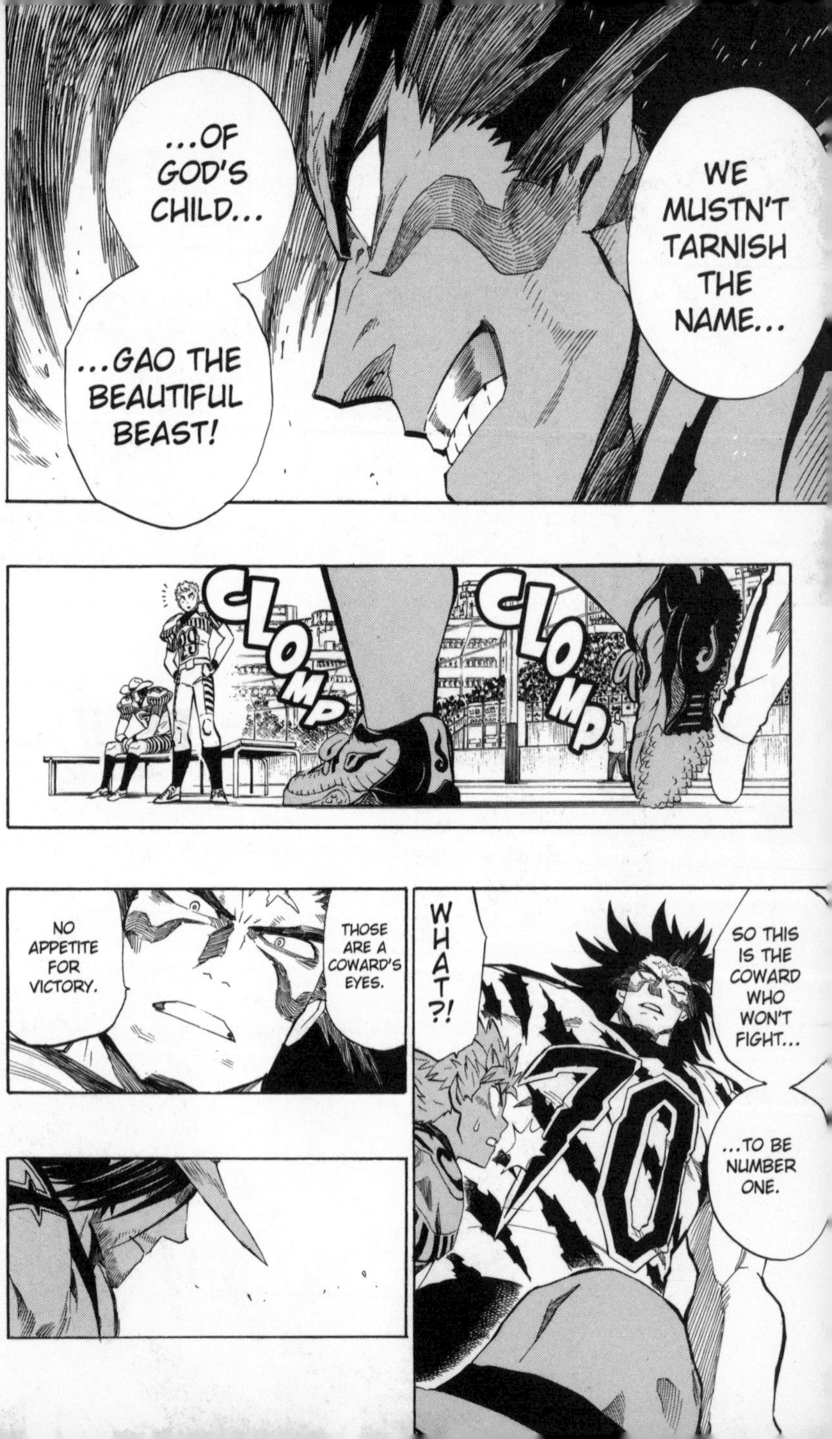
WE MUSTN'T TARNISH THE NAME...
...OF GOD'S CHILD...
...GAO THE BEAUTIFUL BEAST!
CLOMP
CLOMP
SO THIS IS THE COWARD WHO WON'T FIGHT...
...TO BE NUMBER ONE.
WHAT?!
THOSE ARE A COWARD'S EYES.
NO APPETITE FOR VICTORY.

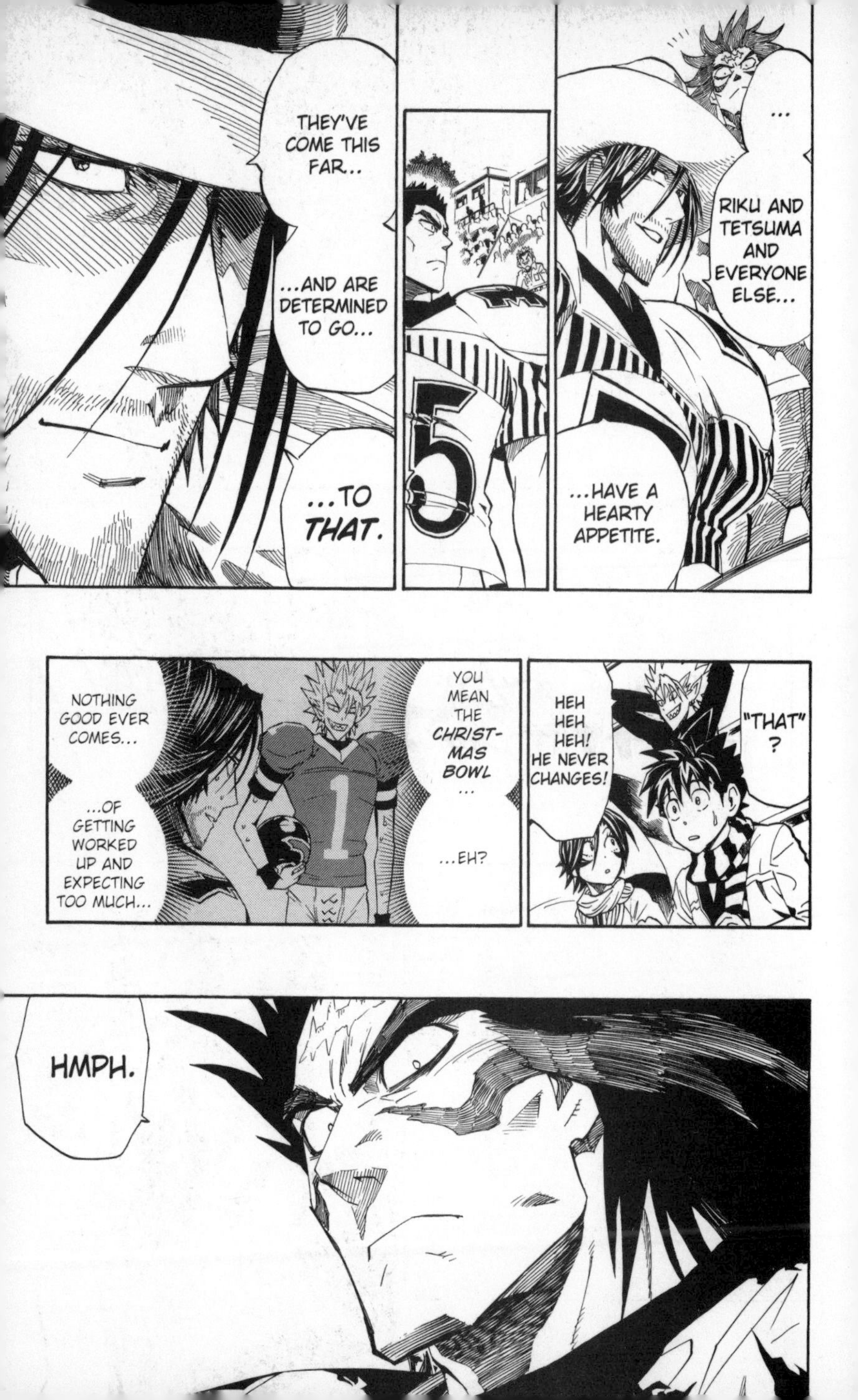
...
RIKU AND TETSUMA AND EVERYONE ELSE...
...HAVE A HEARTY APPETITE.
THEY'VE COME THIS FAR...
...AND ARE DETERMINED TO GO...
...TO *THAT.*
"THAT"?
HEH HEH HEH! HE NEVER CHANGES!
YOU MEAN THE *CHRISTMAS BOWL*...
...EH?
NOTHING GOOD EVER COMES...
...OF GETTING WORKED UP AND EXPECTING TOO MUCH...
HMPH.

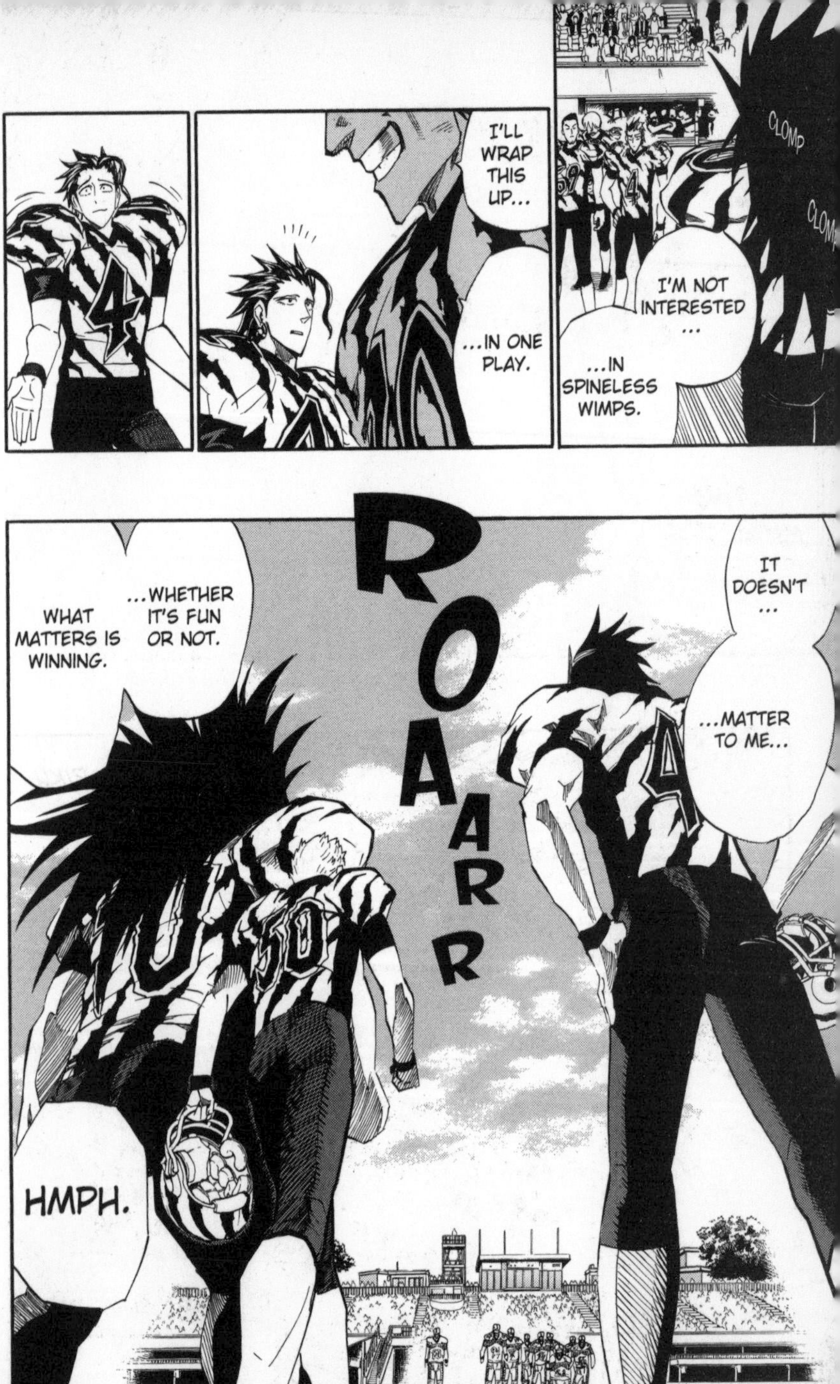
CLOMP
CLOMP
I'M NOT INTERESTED...
...IN SPINELESS WIMPS.
I'LL WRAP THIS UP...
...IN ONE PLAY.
IT DOESN'T...
...MATTER TO ME...
ROAARR
...WHETHER IT'S FUN OR NOT.
WHAT MATTERS IS WINNING.
HMPH.

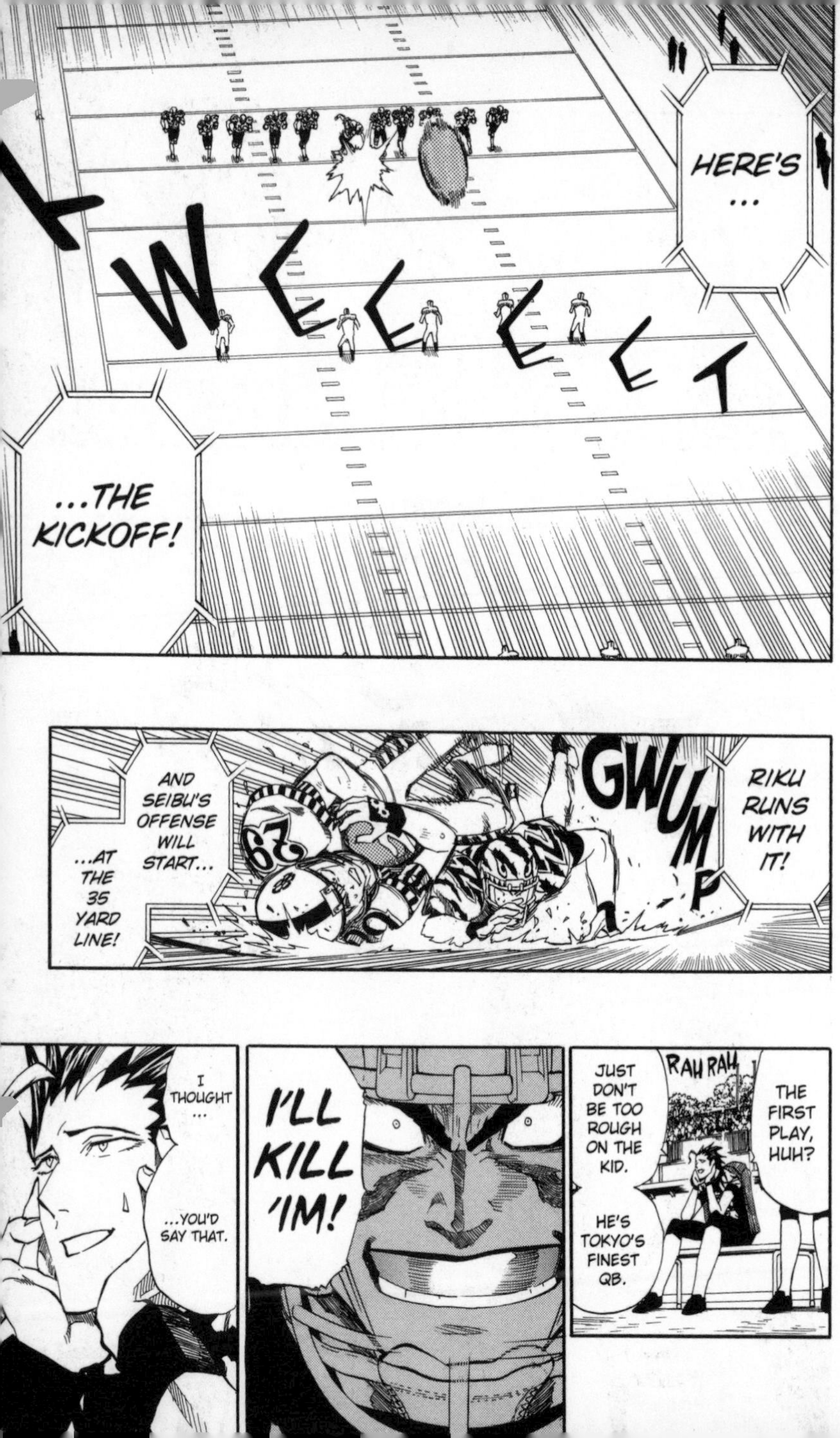
HERE'S...
KWEEEEET
...THE KICKOFF!
RIKU RUNS WITH IT!
GWUMP
AND SEIBU'S OFFENSE WILL START...
...AT THE 35 YARD LINE!
RAH RAH
THE FIRST PLAY, HUH?
JUST DON'T BE TOO ROUGH ON THE KID.
HE'S TOKYO'S FINEST QB.
I'LL KILL 'IM!
I THOUGHT...
...YOU'D SAY THAT.

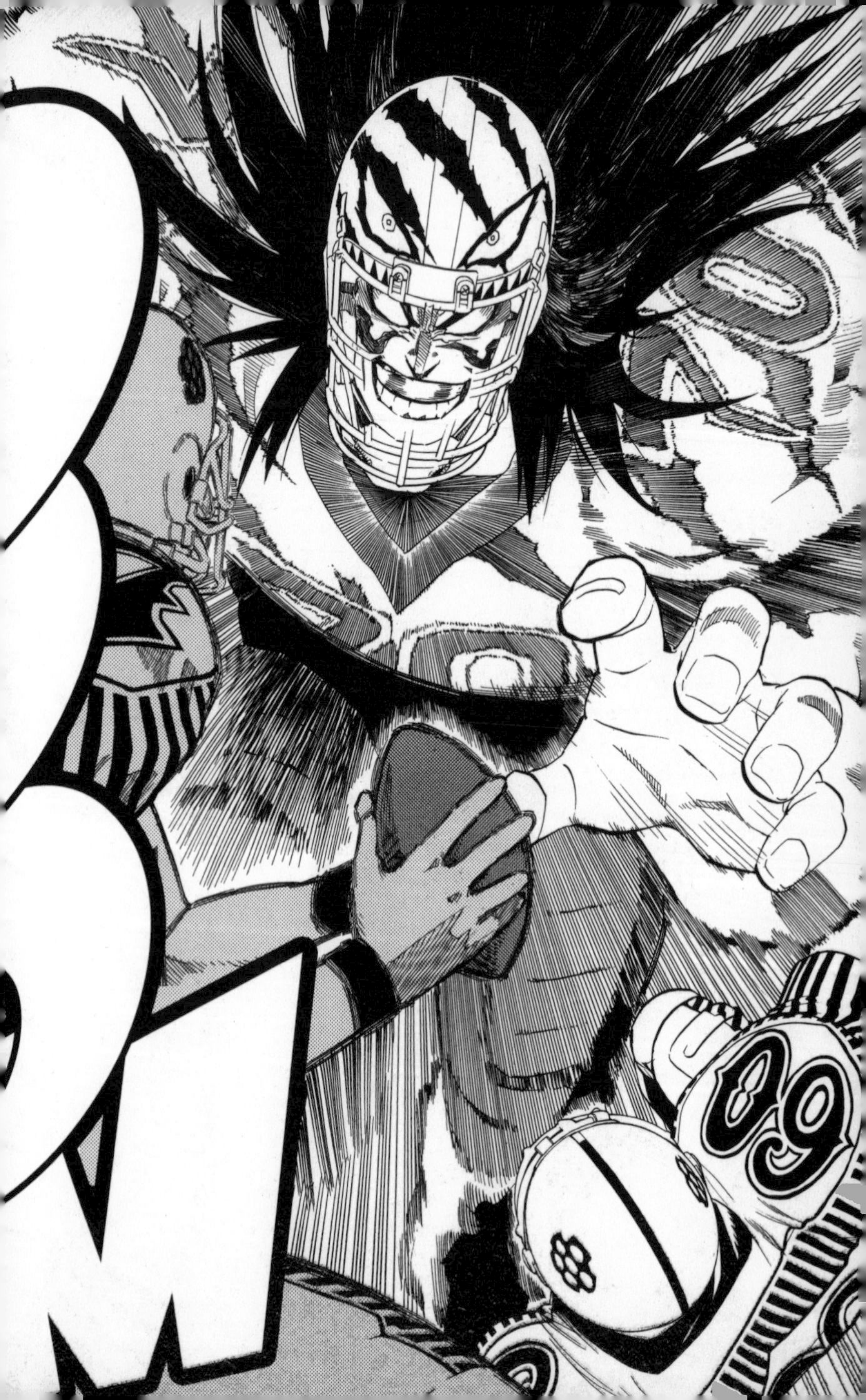

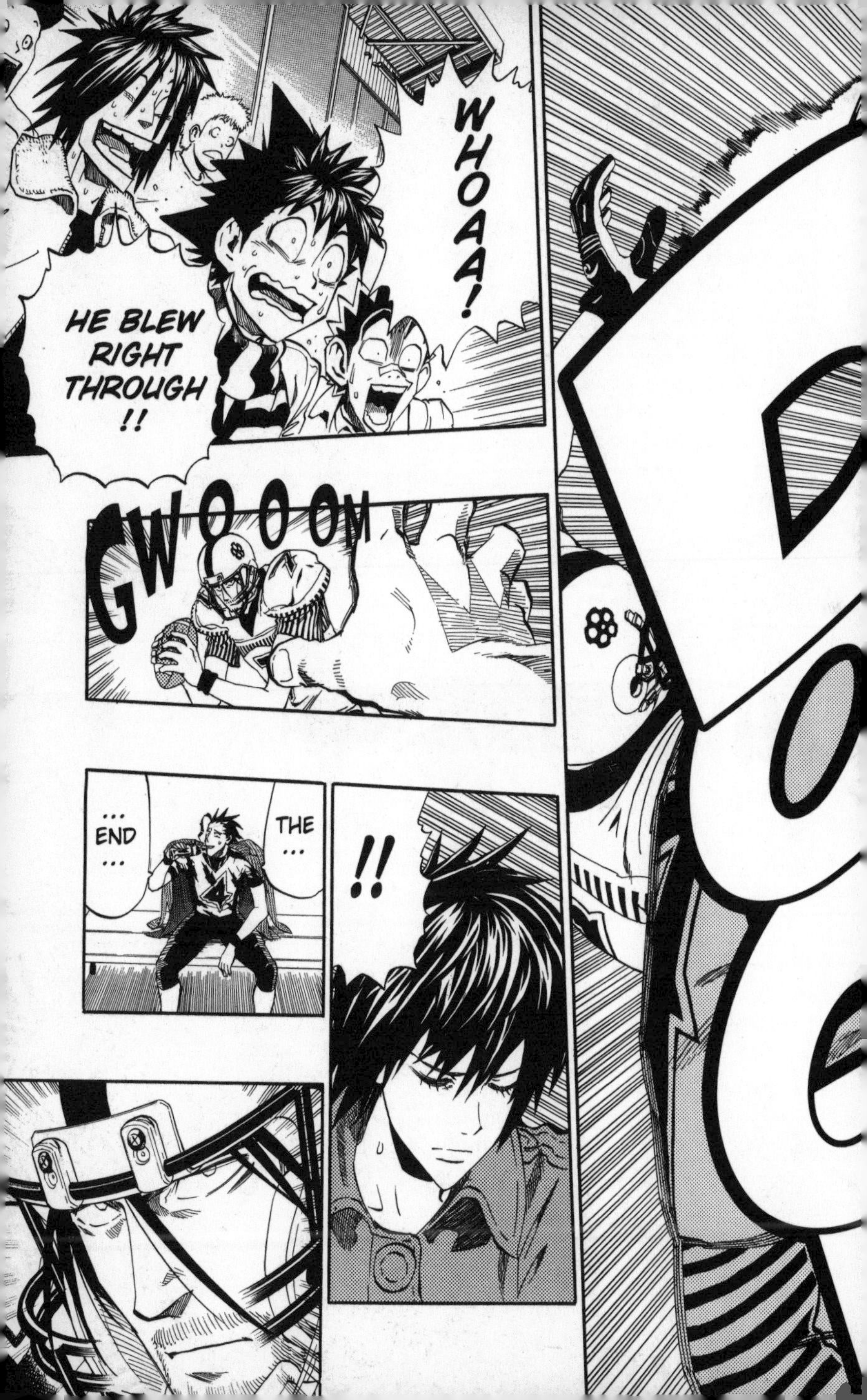
WHOAAA!
HE BLEW RIGHT THROUGH!!
GWOOOOM
!!
THE ...
... END ...

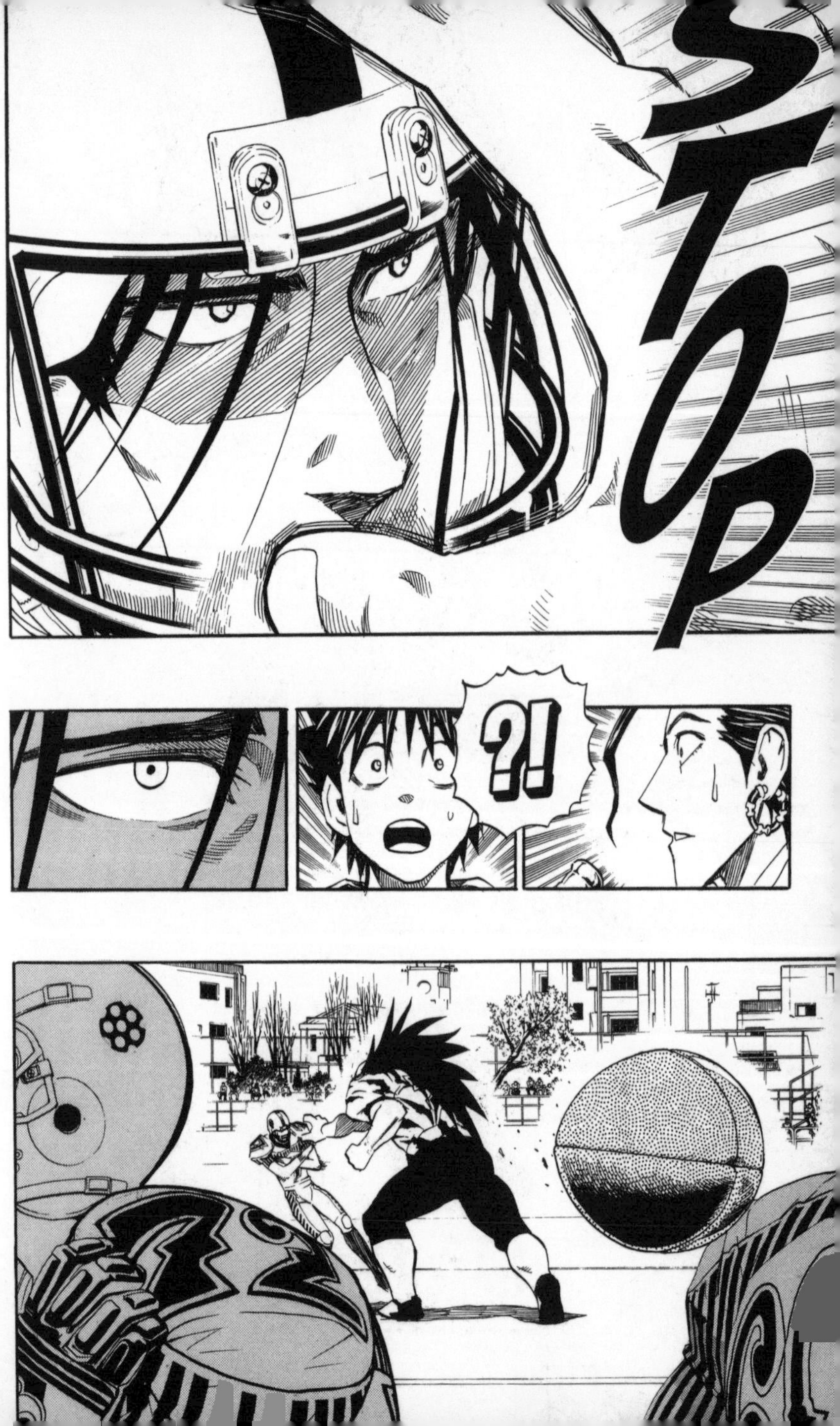
STOP
?!

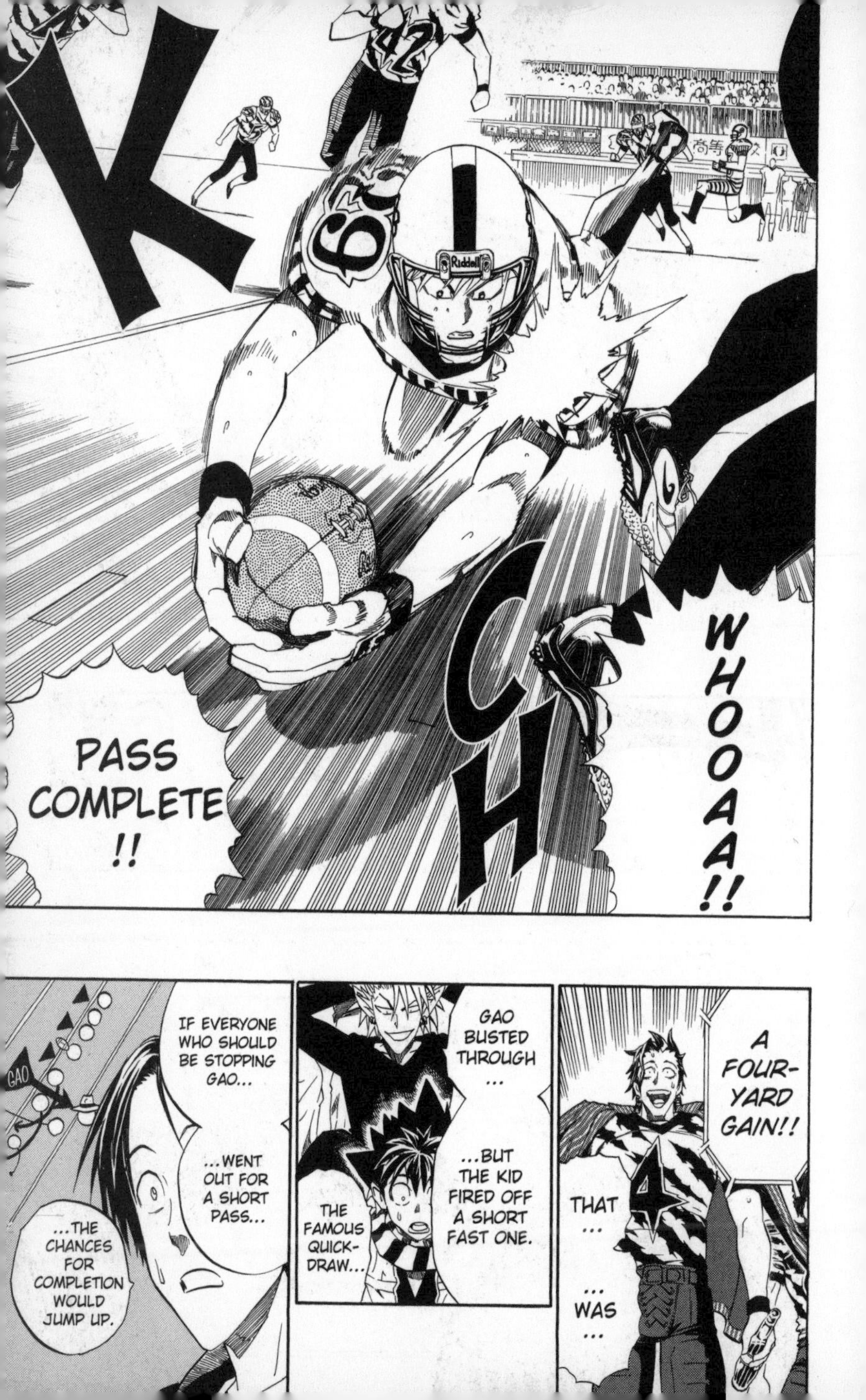
WHOOAAA!!
PASS COMPLETE!!
A FOUR-YARD GAIN!!
THAT...
...WAS...
GAO BUSTED THROUGH...
...BUT THE KID FIRED OFF A SHORT FAST ONE.
THE FAMOUS QUICK-DRAW...
IF EVERYONE WHO SHOULD BE STOPPING GAO...
...WENT OUT FOR A SHORT PASS...
GAO
...THE CHANCES FOR COMPLETION WOULD JUMP UP.

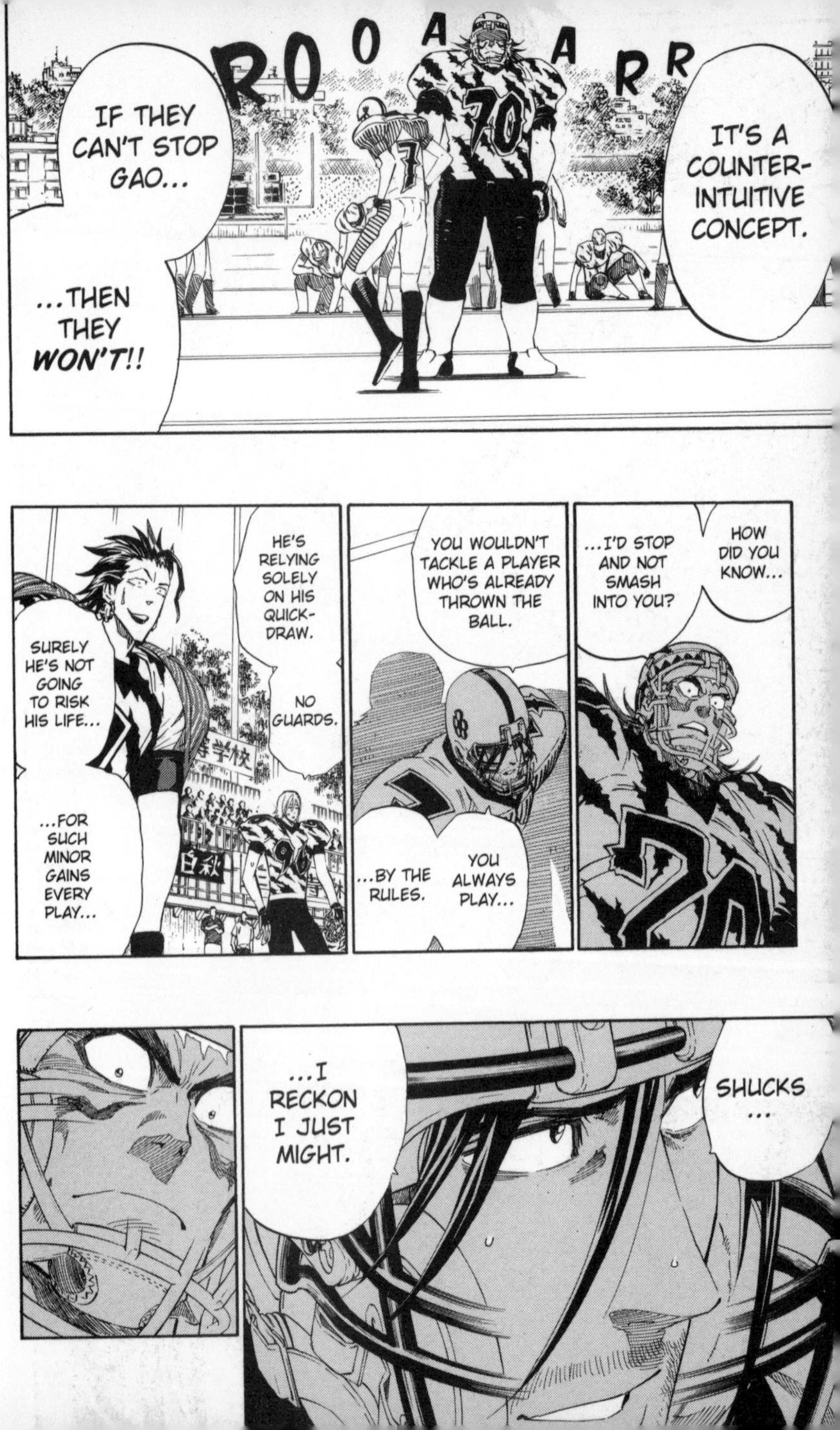
ROOAARR
IT'S A COUNTER-INTUITIVE CONCEPT.
IF THEY CAN'T STOP GAO...
...THEN THEY WON'T!!
HOW DID YOU KNOW...
...I'D STOP AND NOT SMASH INTO YOU?
YOU WOULDN'T TACKLE A PLAYER WHO'S ALREADY THROWN THE BALL.
YOU ALWAYS PLAY...
...BY THE RULES.
HE'S RELYING SOLELY ON HIS QUICK-DRAW.
NO GUARDS.
SURELY HE'S NOT GOING TO RISK HIS LIFE...
...FOR SUCH MINOR GAINS EVERY PLAY...
SHUCKS...
...I RECKON I JUST MIGHT.

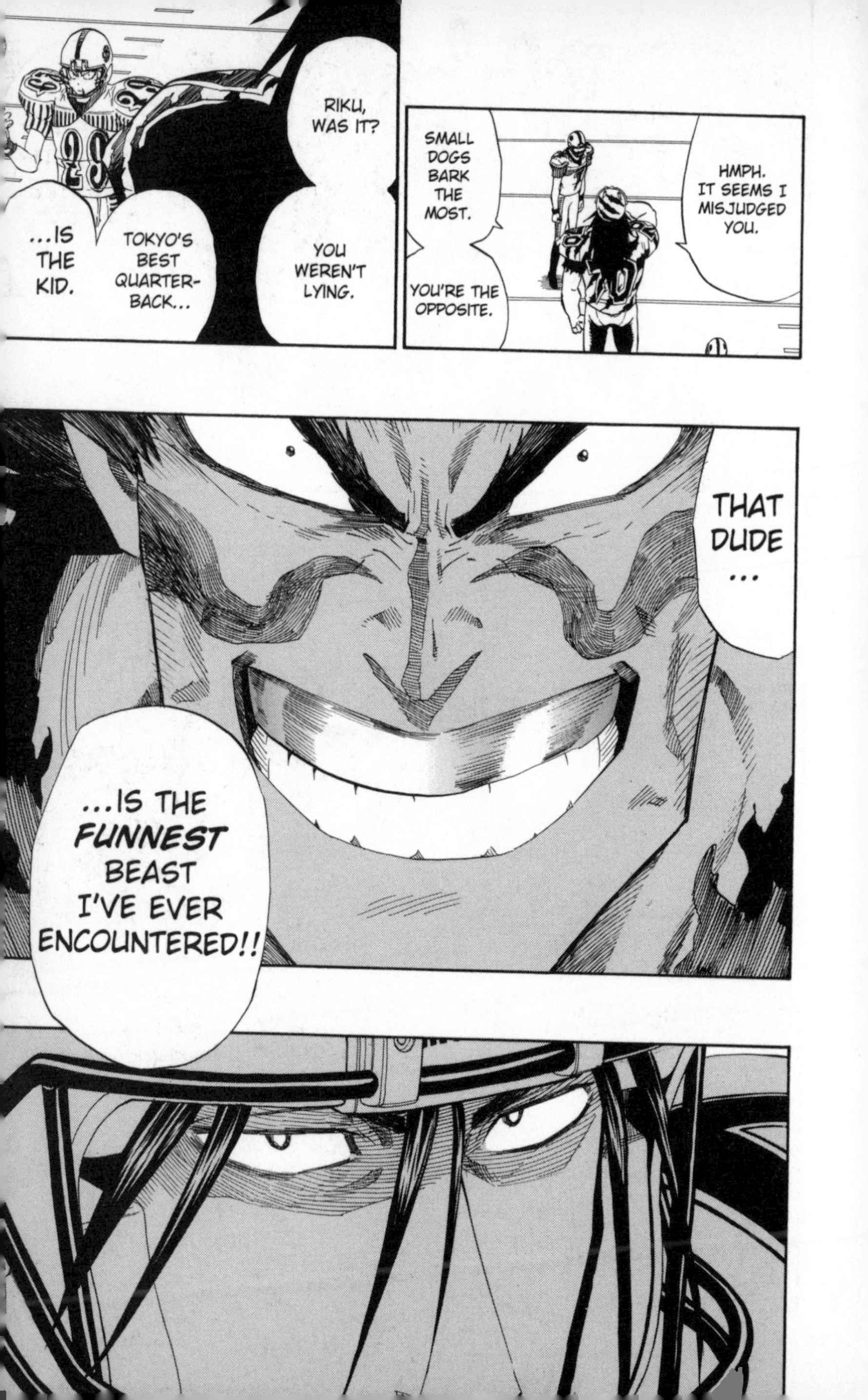
HMPH. IT SEEMS I MISJUDGED YOU.
SMALL DOGS BARK THE MOST.
YOU'RE THE OPPOSITE.
RIKU, WAS IT?
YOU WEREN'T LYING.
TOKYO'S BEST QUARTER-BACK...
...IS THE KID.
THAT DUDE...
...IS THE *FUNNEST* BEAST I'VE EVER ENCOUNTERED!!

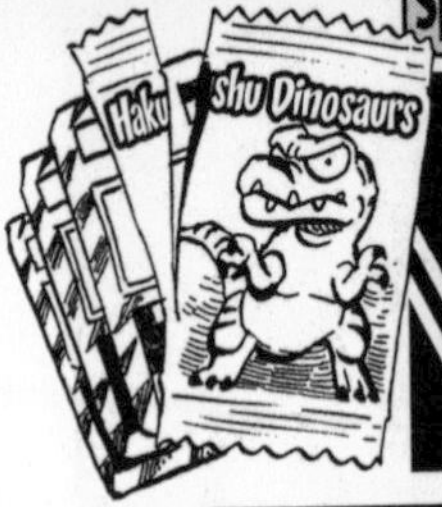

Special Supplement!!

Hakushu Dinosaurs Athlete Card

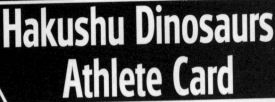

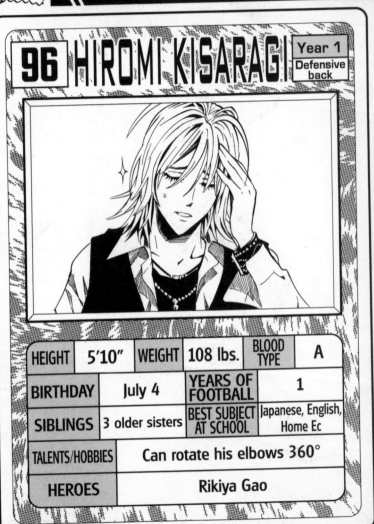

96 HIROMI KISARAGI

Year 1

Defensive back

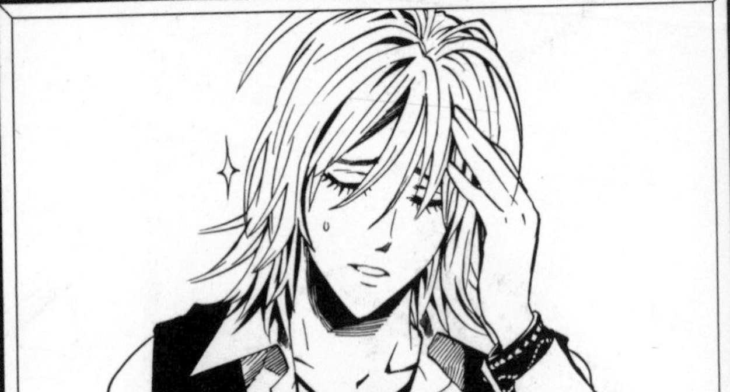

HEIGHT	5′10″	WEIGHT	108 lbs.	BLOOD TYPE	A
BIRTHDAY	July 4	YEARS OF FOOTBALL	1		
SIBLINGS	3 older sisters	BEST SUBJECT AT SCHOOL	Japanese, English, Home Ec		
TALENTS/HOBBIES	Can rotate his elbows 360°				
HEROES	Rikiya Gao				

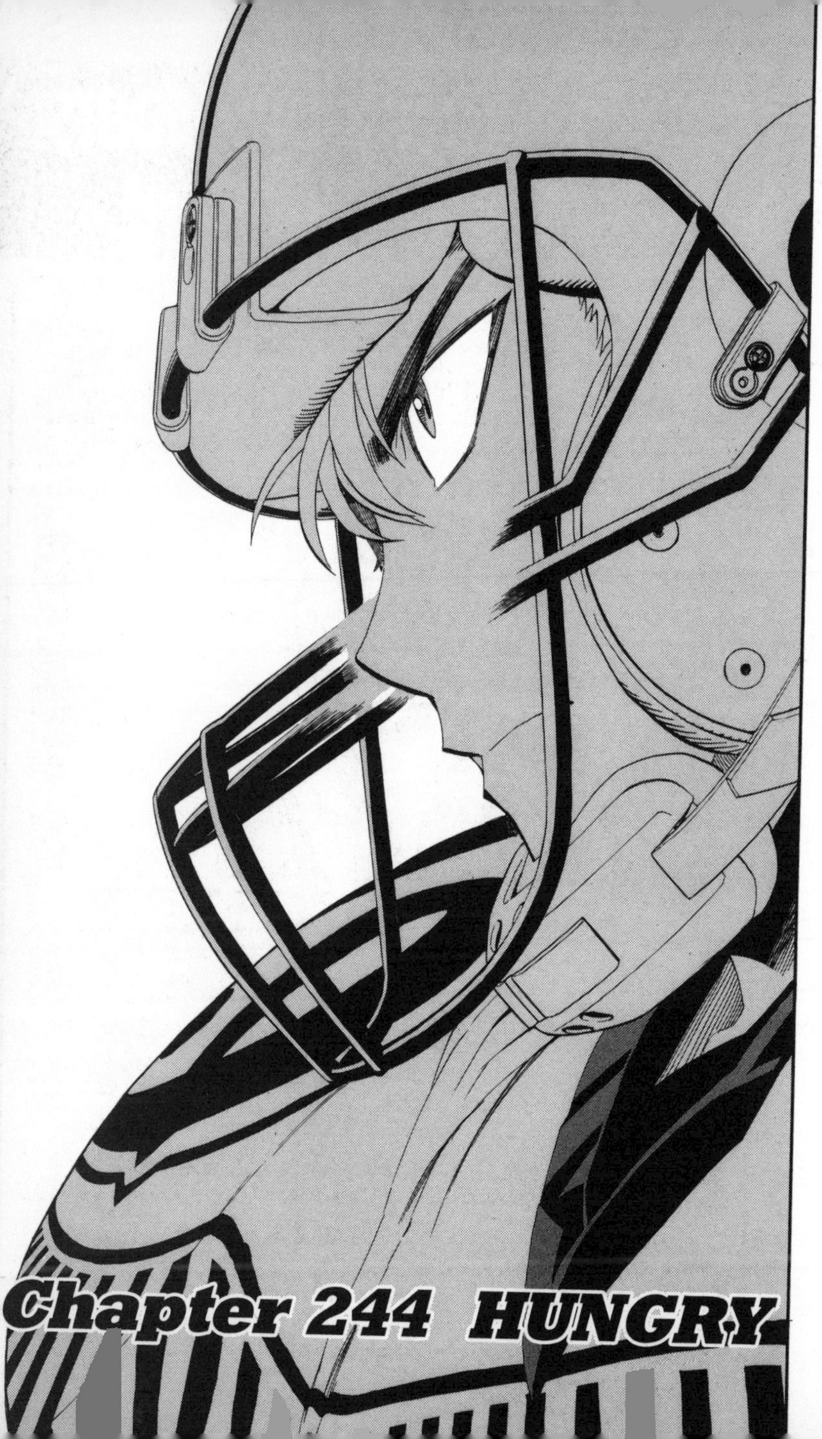
Chapter 244 HUNGRY

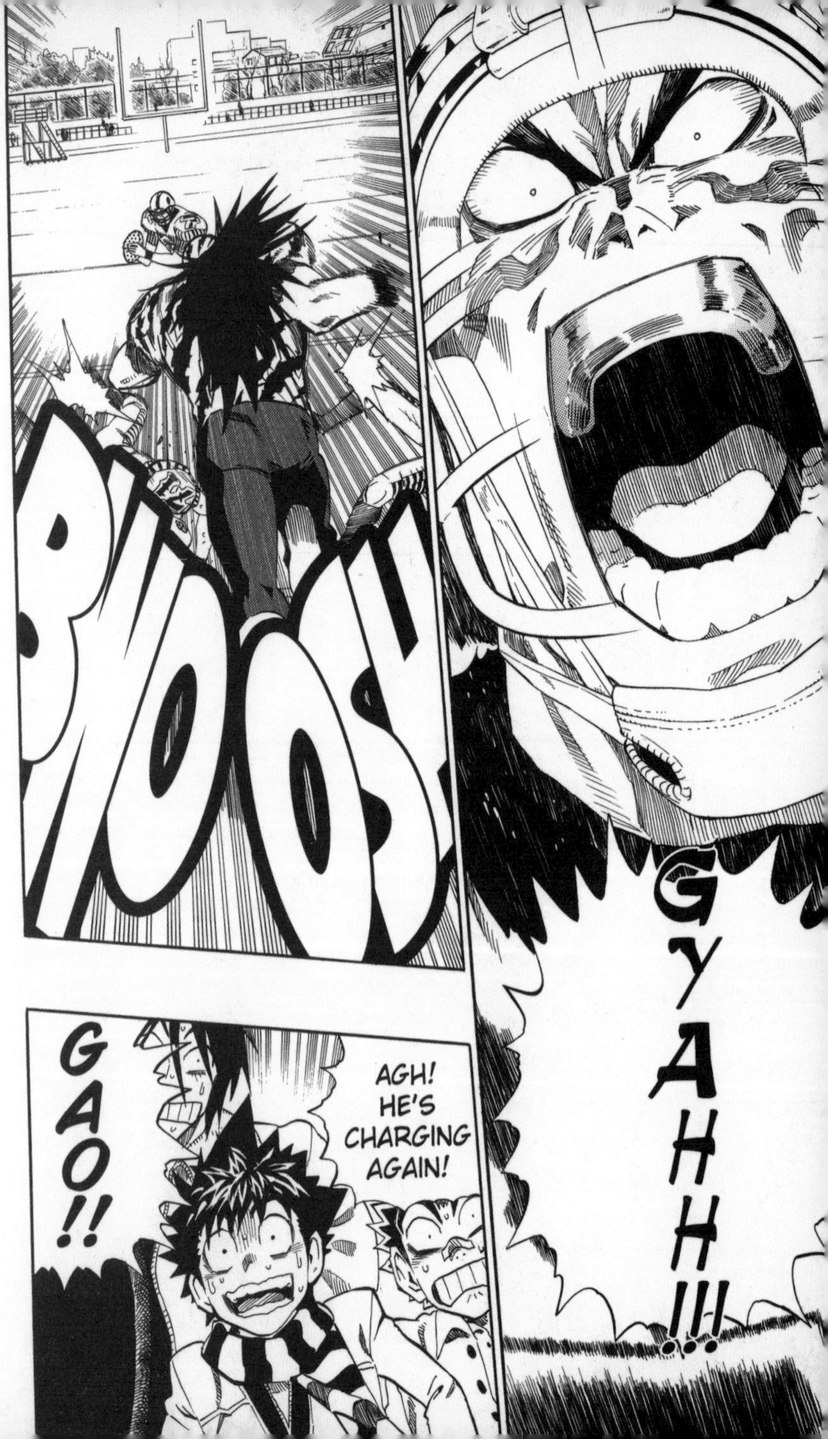
GYAHHH!!!
BWOOSH
AGH! HE'S CHARGING AGAIN!
GAO!!

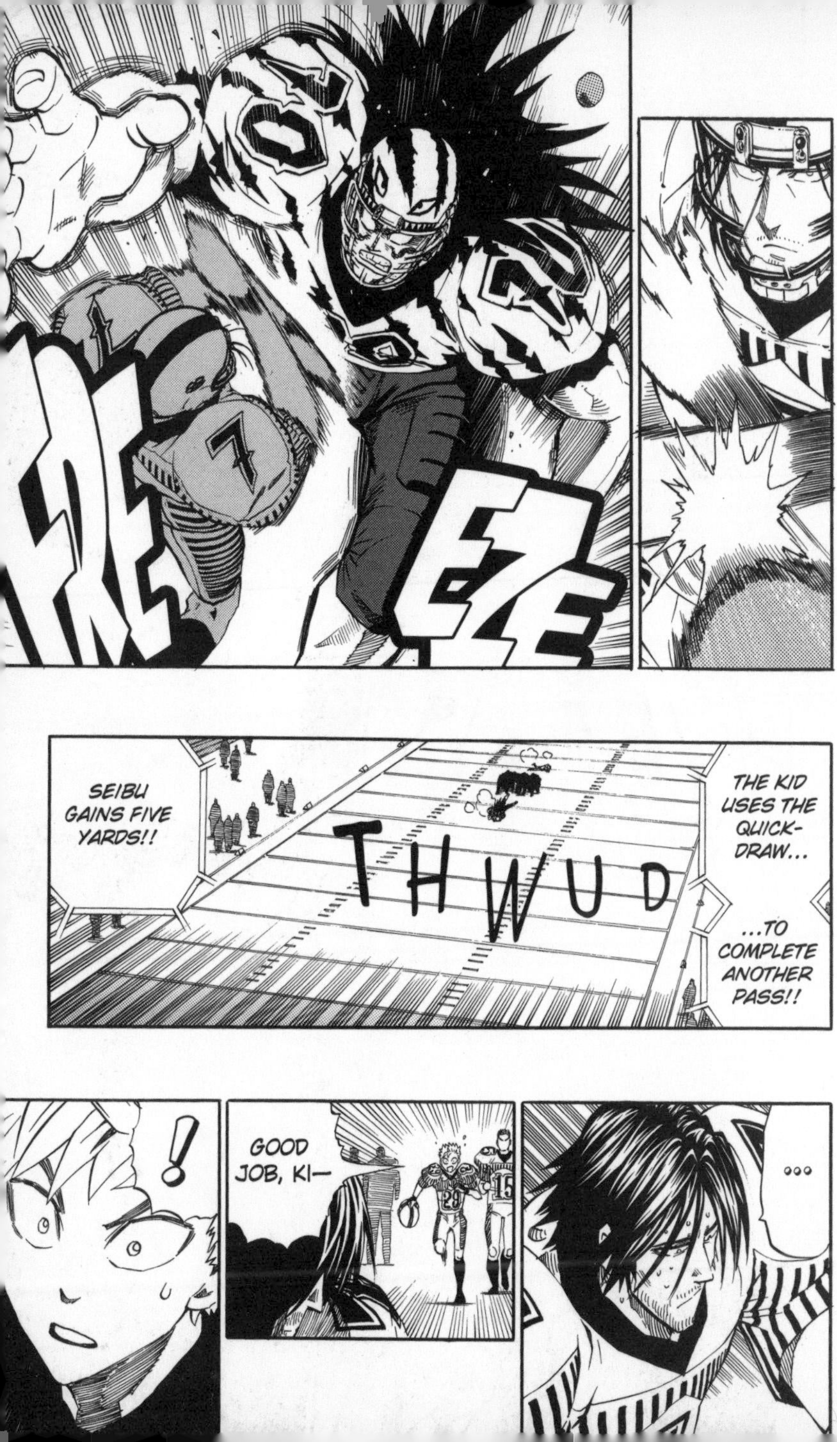
FREEZE
THE KID USES THE QUICK-DRAW...
...TO COMPLETE ANOTHER PASS!!
THWUD
SEIBU GAINS FIVE YARDS!!
...
GOOD JOB, KI—
!

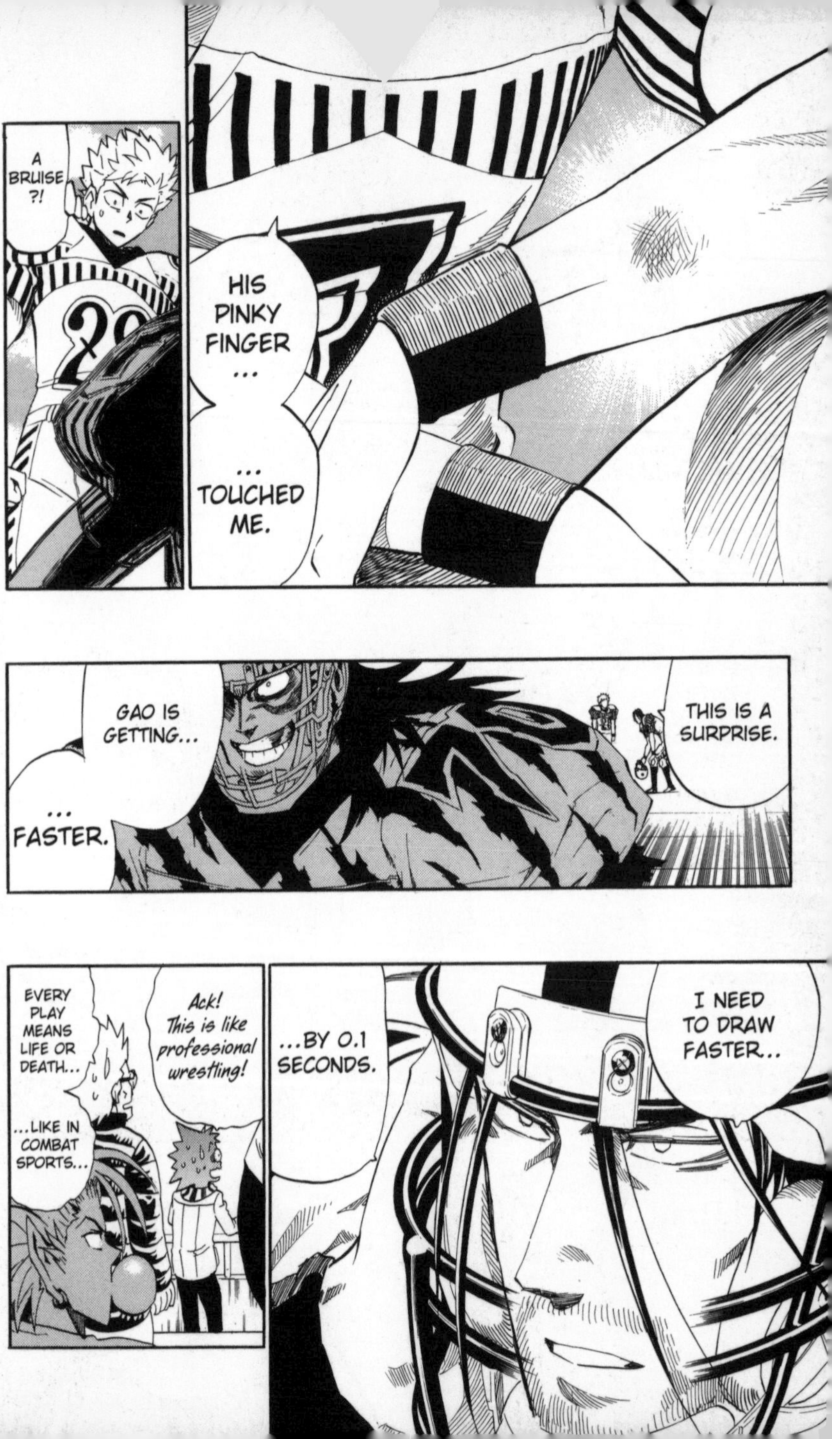
HIS PINKY FINGER ...
... TOUCHED ME.
A BRUISE ?!
THIS IS A SURPRISE.
GAO IS GETTING...
... FASTER.
I NEED TO DRAW FASTER...
...BY 0.1 SECONDS.
Ack! This is like professional wrestling!
EVERY PLAY MEANS LIFE OR DEATH...
...LIKE IN COMBAT SPORTS...

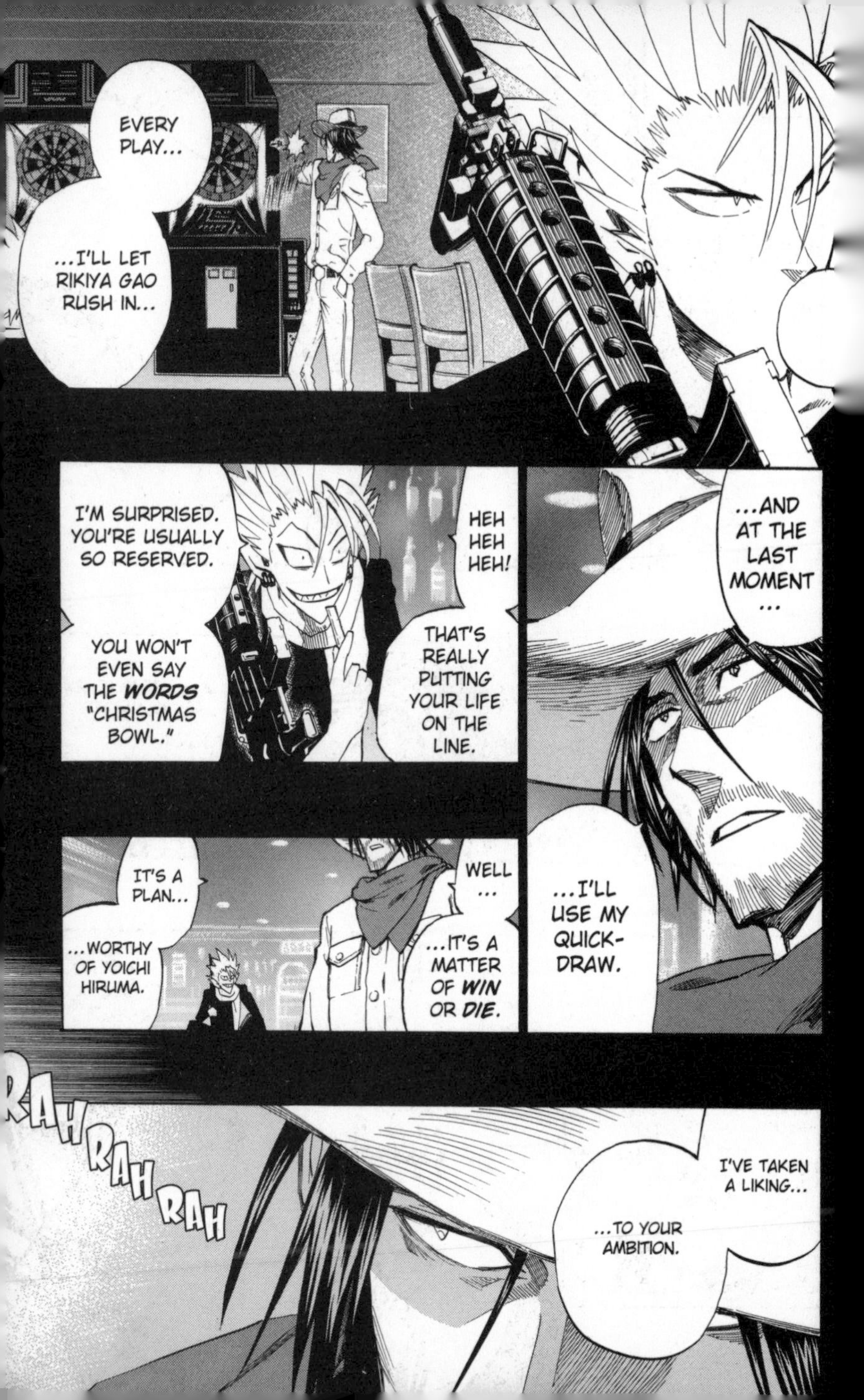
EVERY PLAY...
...I'LL LET RIKIYA GAO RUSH IN...
...AND AT THE LAST MOMENT...
...I'LL USE MY QUICK-DRAW.
HEH HEH HEH!
THAT'S REALLY PUTTING YOUR LIFE ON THE LINE.
I'M SURPRISED. YOU'RE USUALLY SO RESERVED.
YOU WON'T EVEN SAY THE WORDS "CHRISTMAS BOWL."
WELL...
...IT'S A MATTER OF WIN OR DIE.
IT'S A PLAN...
...WORTHY OF YOICHI HIRUMA.
RAH RAH RAH RAH
I'VE TAKEN A LIKING...
...TO YOUR AMBITION.

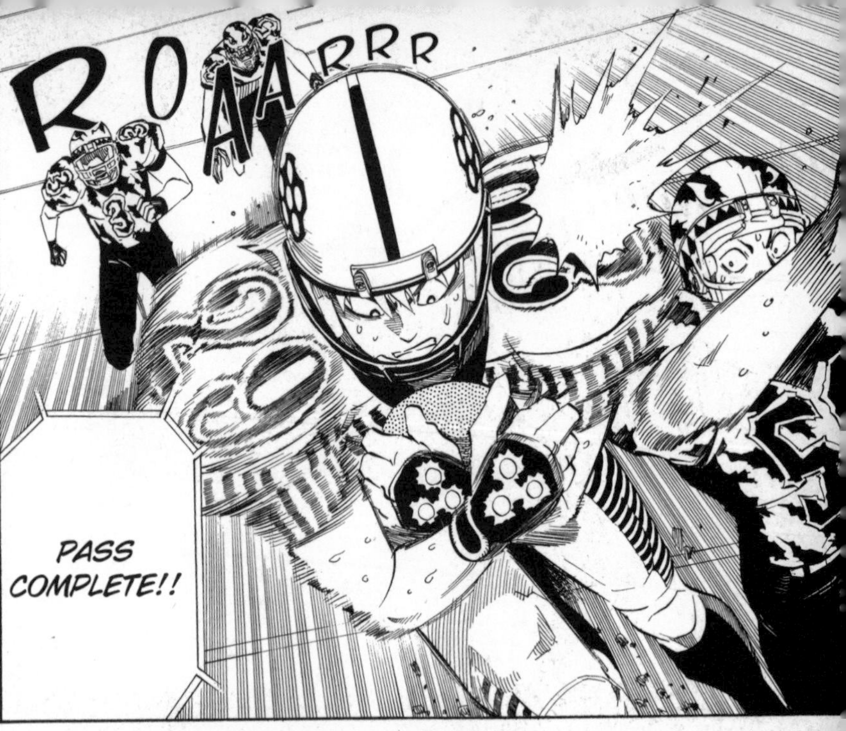
ROAARRR
PASS COMPLETE!!
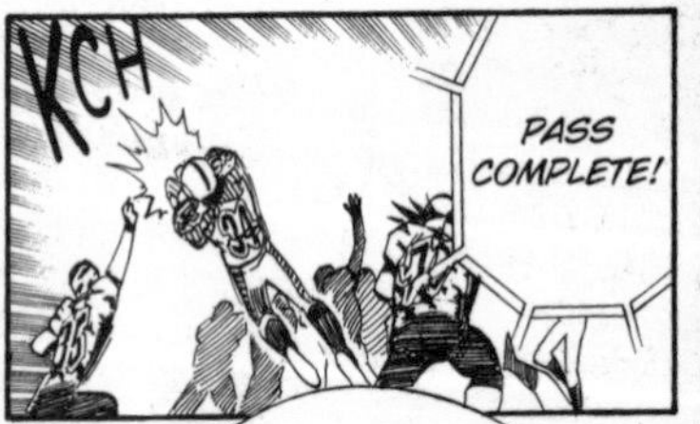
KCH
PASS COMPLETE!
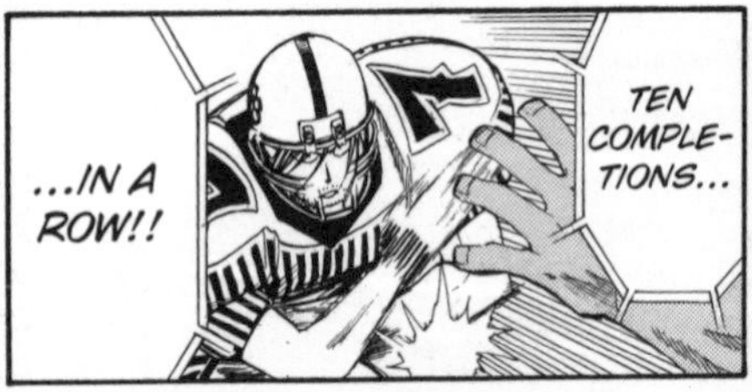
TEN COMPLE-TIONS...
...IN A ROW!!
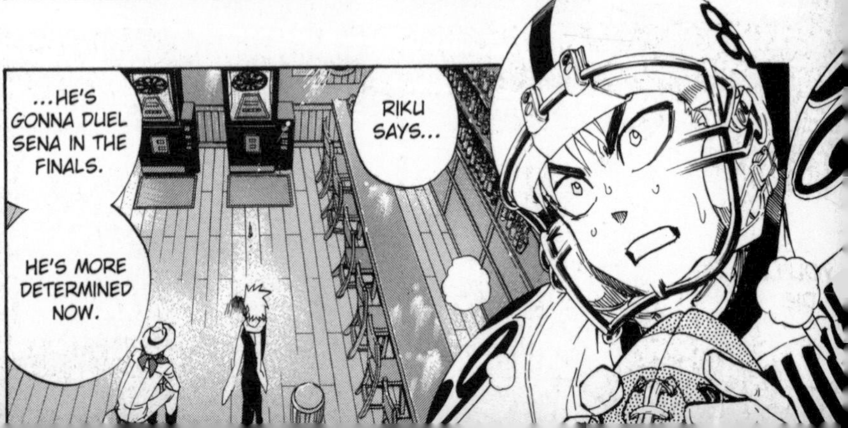
RIKU SAYS...
...HE'S GONNA DUEL SENA IN THE FINALS.
HE'S MORE DETERMINED NOW.

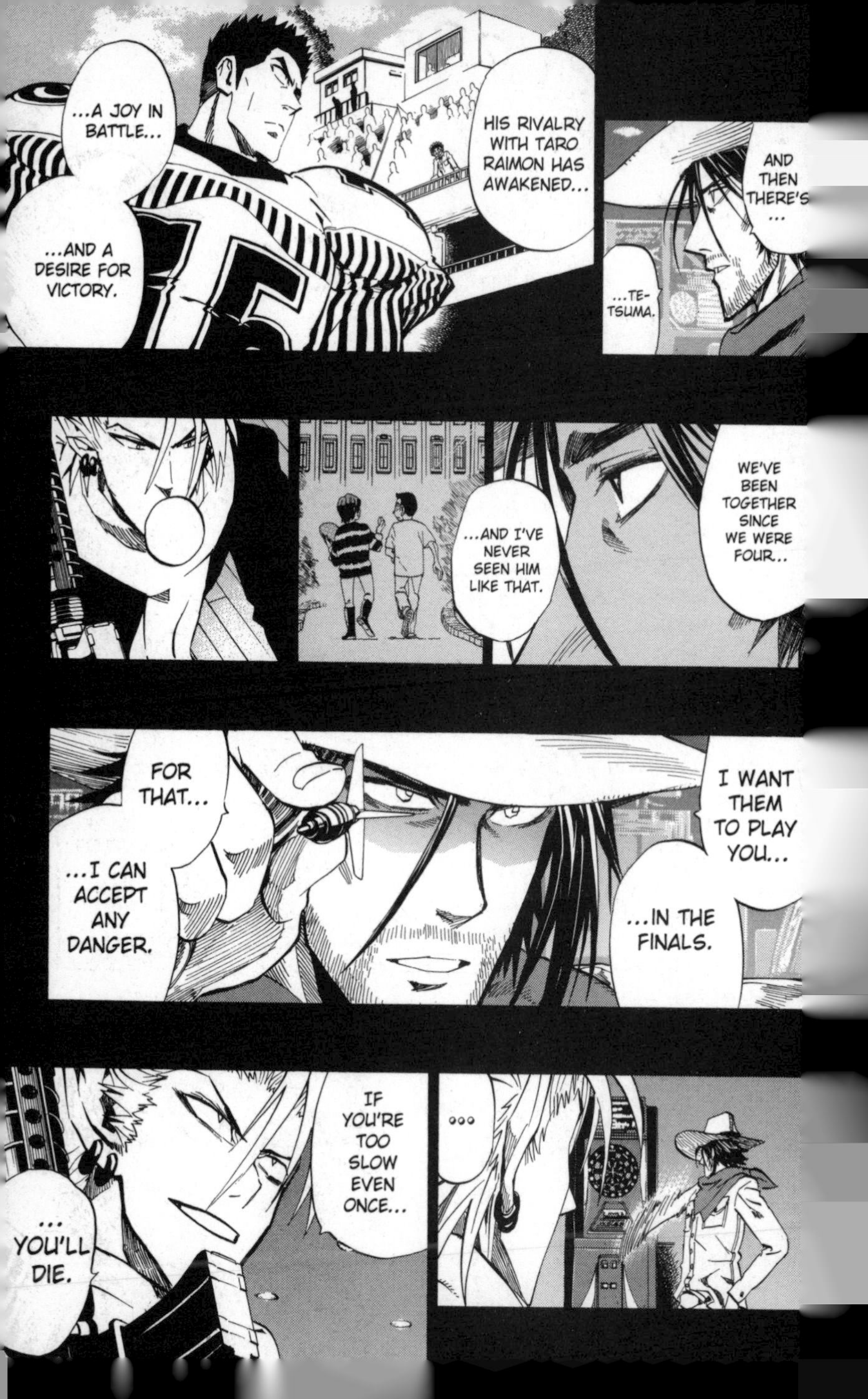
AND THEN THERE'S...
...TE-TSUMA.
HIS RIVALRY WITH TARO RAIMON HAS AWAKENED...
...A JOY IN BATTLE...
...AND A DESIRE FOR VICTORY.
WE'VE BEEN TOGETHER SINCE WE WERE FOUR...
...AND I'VE NEVER SEEN HIM LIKE THAT.
I WANT THEM TO PLAY YOU...
...IN THE FINALS.
FOR THAT...
...I CAN ACCEPT ANY DANGER.
...
IF YOU'RE TOO SLOW EVEN ONCE...
...YOU'LL DIE.

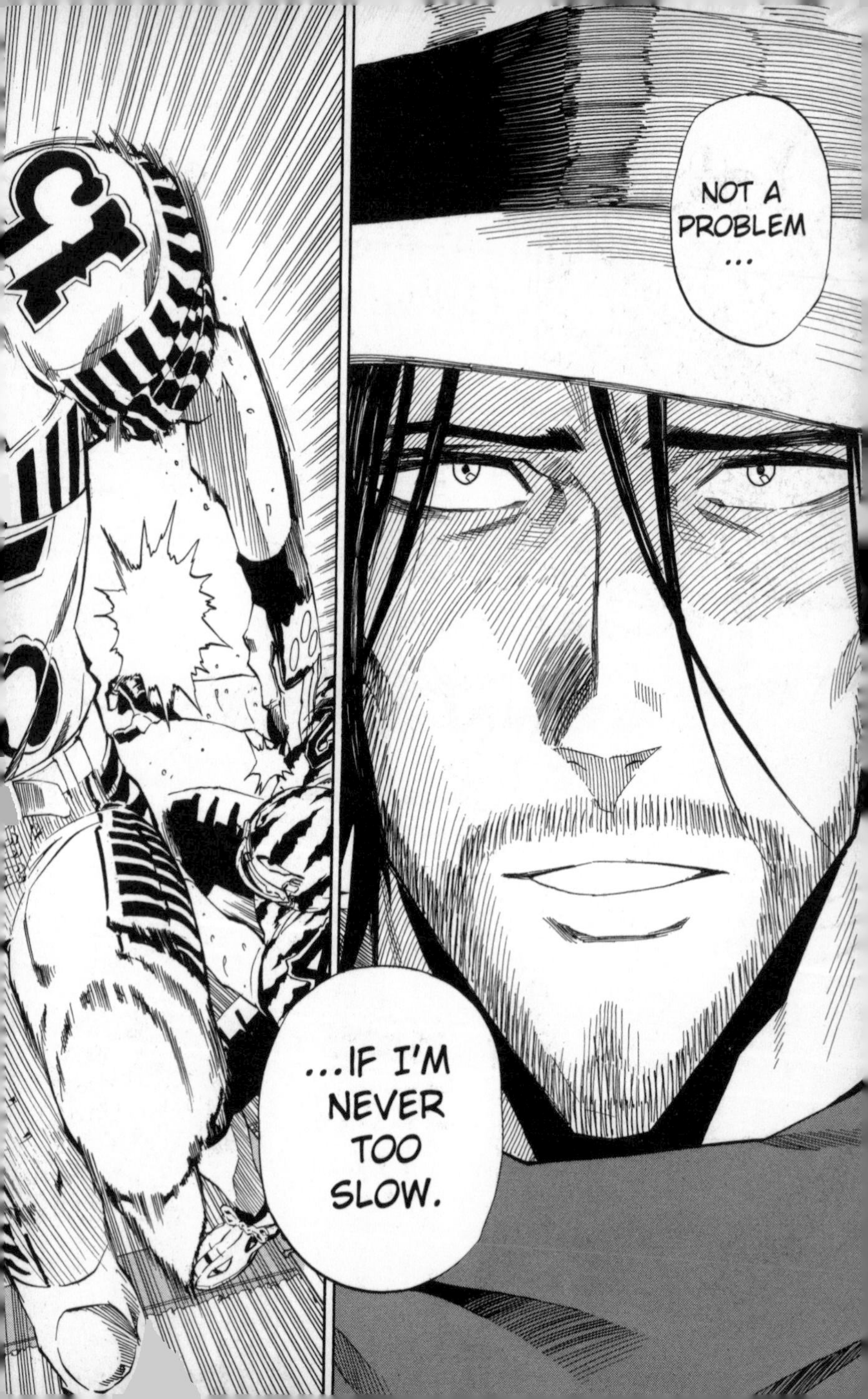
NOT A PROBLEM ...
...IF I'M NEVER TOO SLOW.

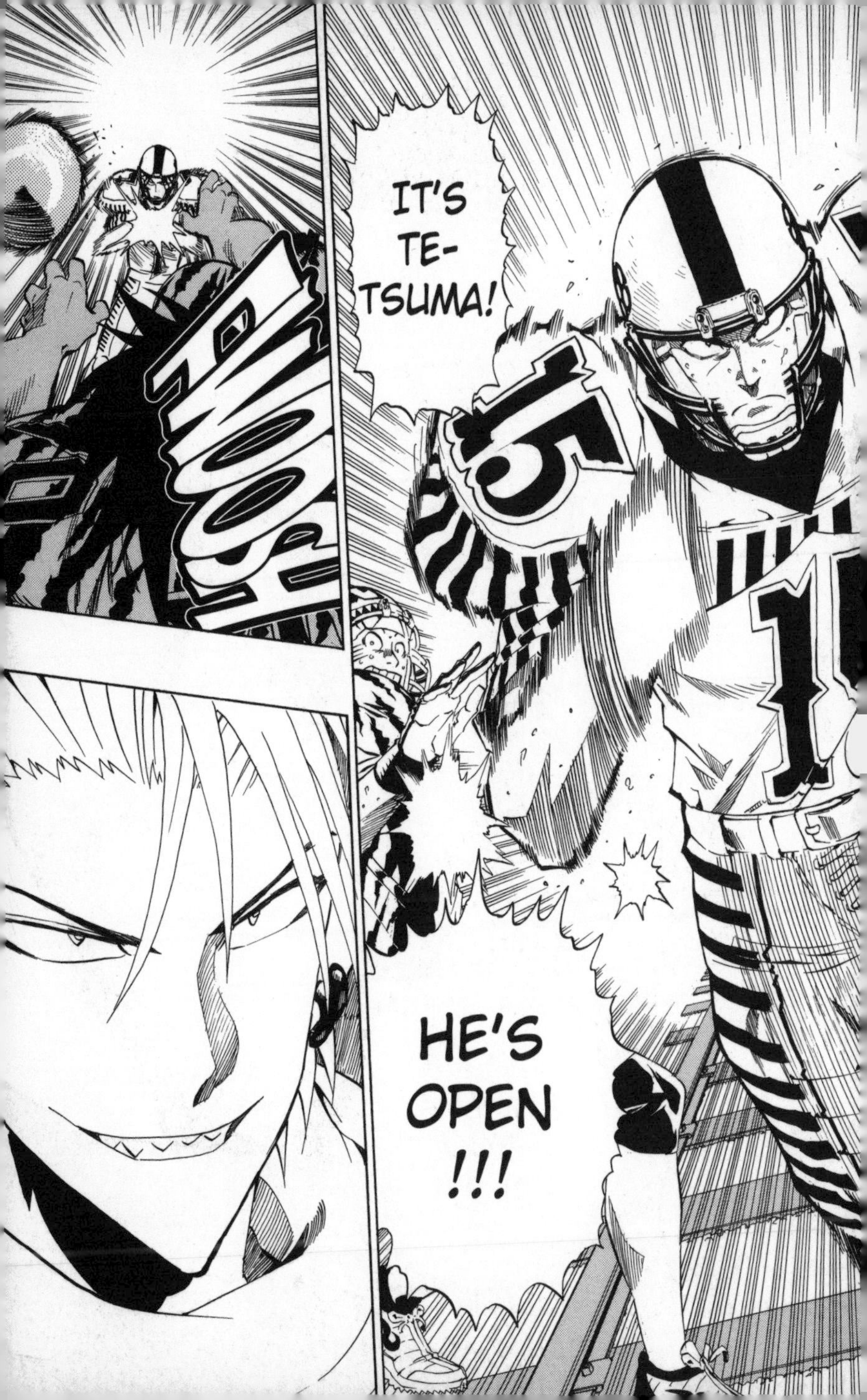
IT'S TE-TSUMA!
HE'S OPEN !!!
WHOOSH

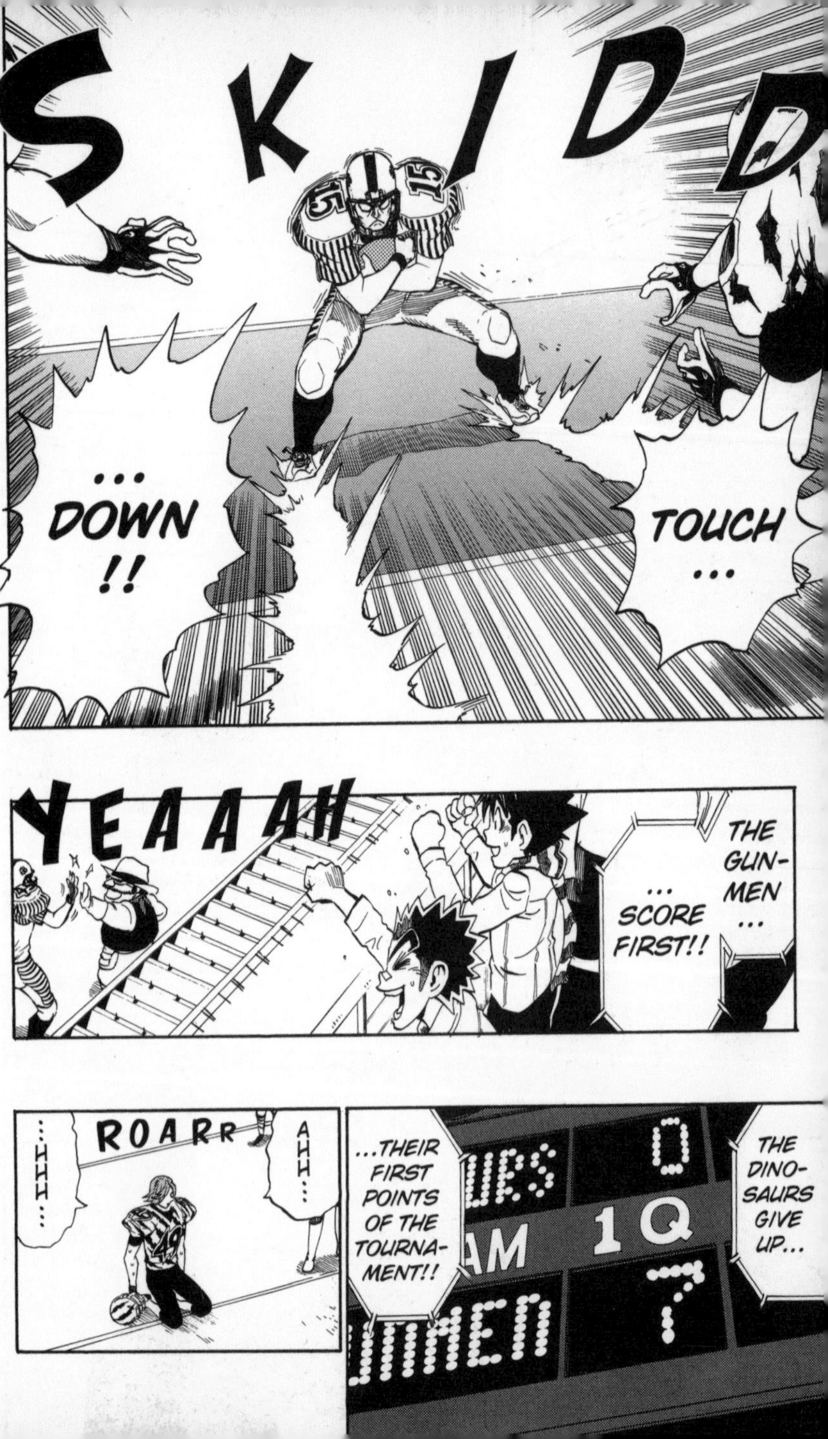
SKIDD
TOUCH...
...DOWN!!
YEAAAAH
THE GUN-MEN...
...SCORE FIRST!!
THE DINO-SAURS GIVE UP...
...THEIR FIRST POINTS OF THE TOURNA-MENT!!
0
1Q
7
AHH...
ROARRR
...HHH...

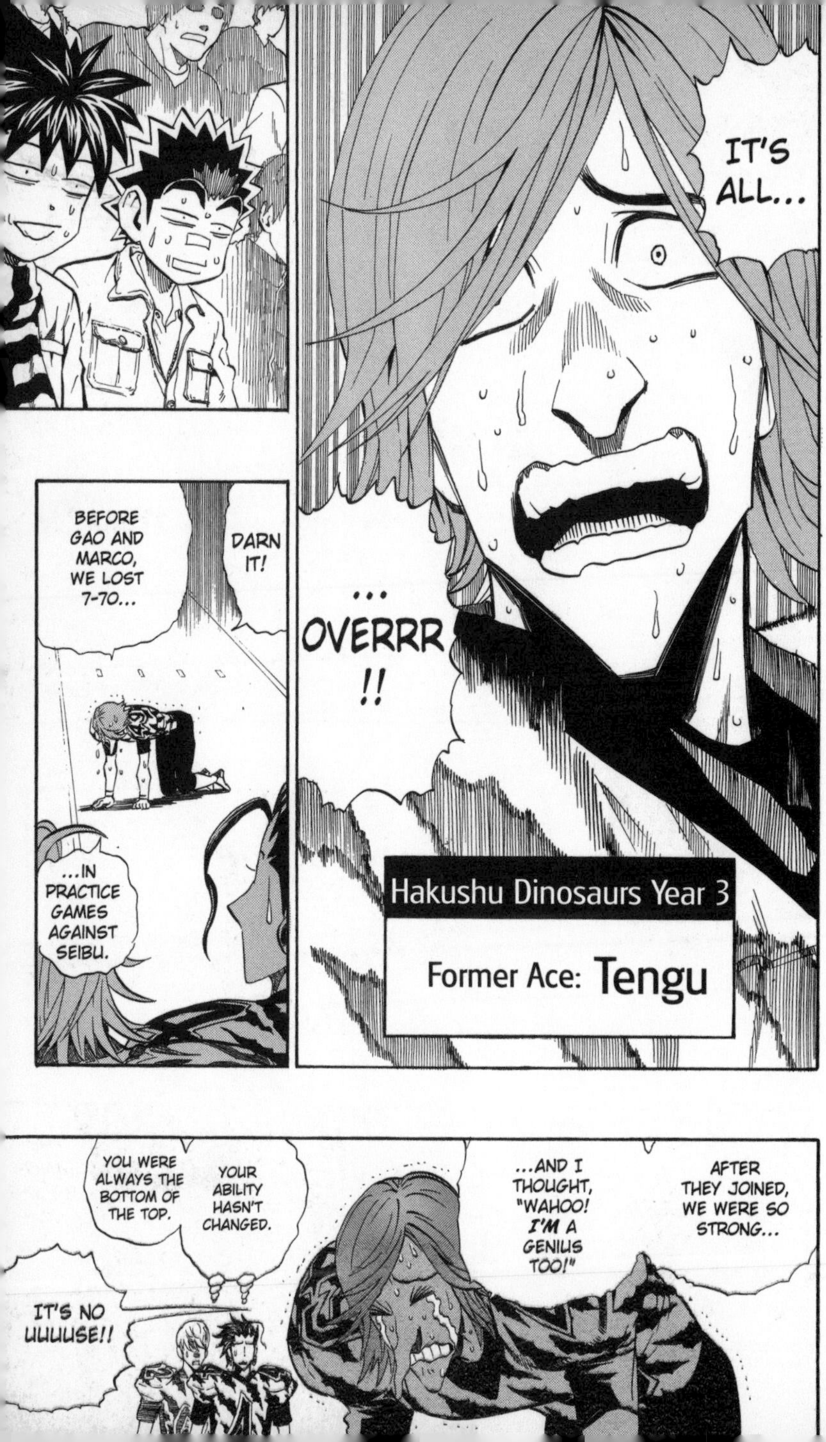
IT'S ALL...
...OVERRR!!
Hakushu Dinosaurs Year 3
Former Ace: Tengu
DARN IT!
BEFORE GAO AND MARCO, WE LOST 7-70...
...IN PRACTICE GAMES AGAINST SEIBU.
AFTER THEY JOINED, WE WERE SO STRONG...
...AND I THOUGHT, "WAHOO! I'M A GENIUS TOO!"
YOUR ABILITY HASN'T CHANGED.
YOU WERE ALWAYS THE BOTTOM OF THE TOP.
IT'S NO UUUUSE!!

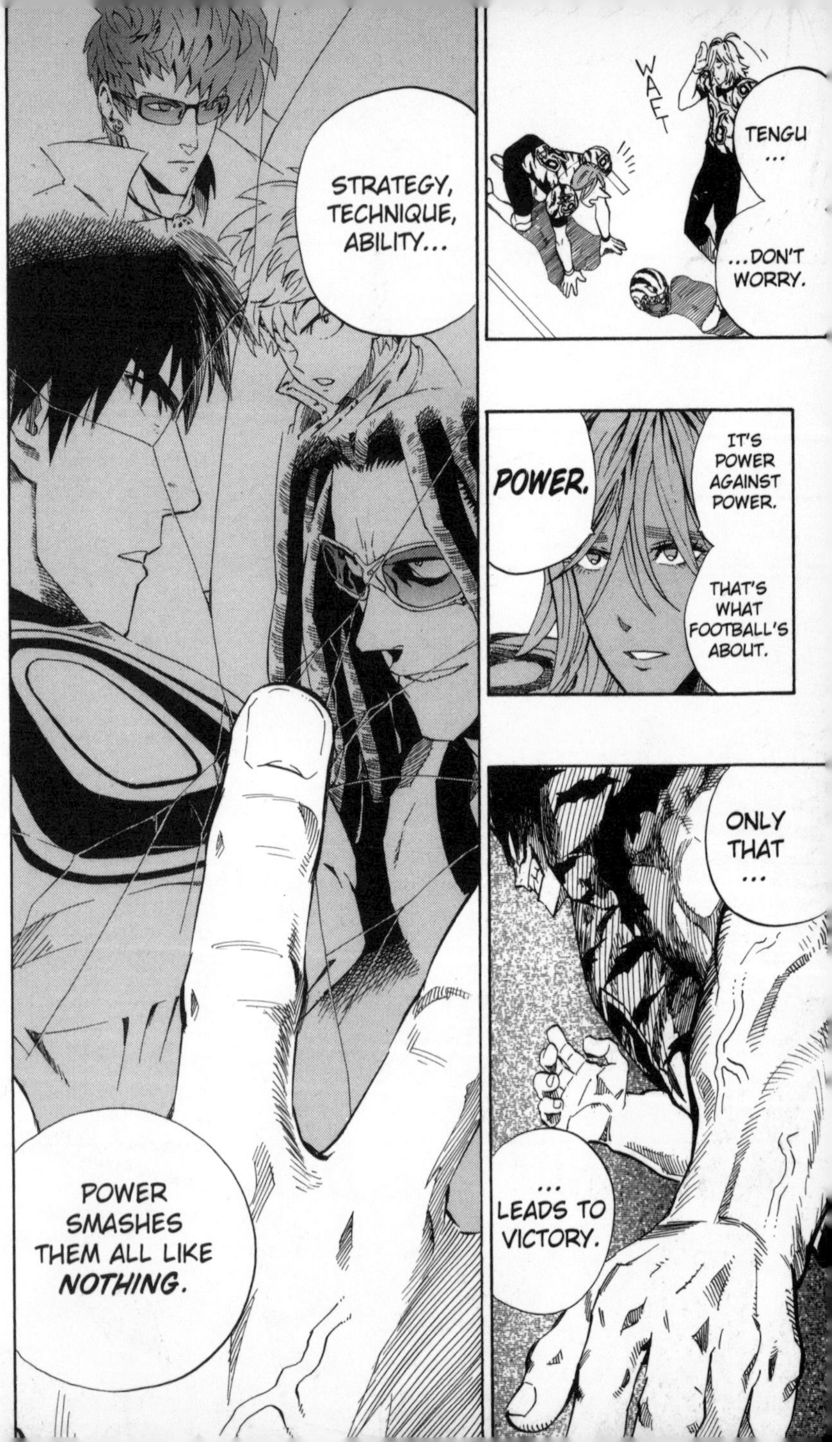
WAFT
TENGU ...
...DON'T WORRY.
IT'S POWER AGAINST POWER.
POWER.
THAT'S WHAT FOOTBALL'S ABOUT.
ONLY THAT ...
... LEADS TO VICTORY.
STRATEGY, TECHNIQUE, ABILITY...
POWER SMASHES THEM ALL LIKE *NOTHING*.

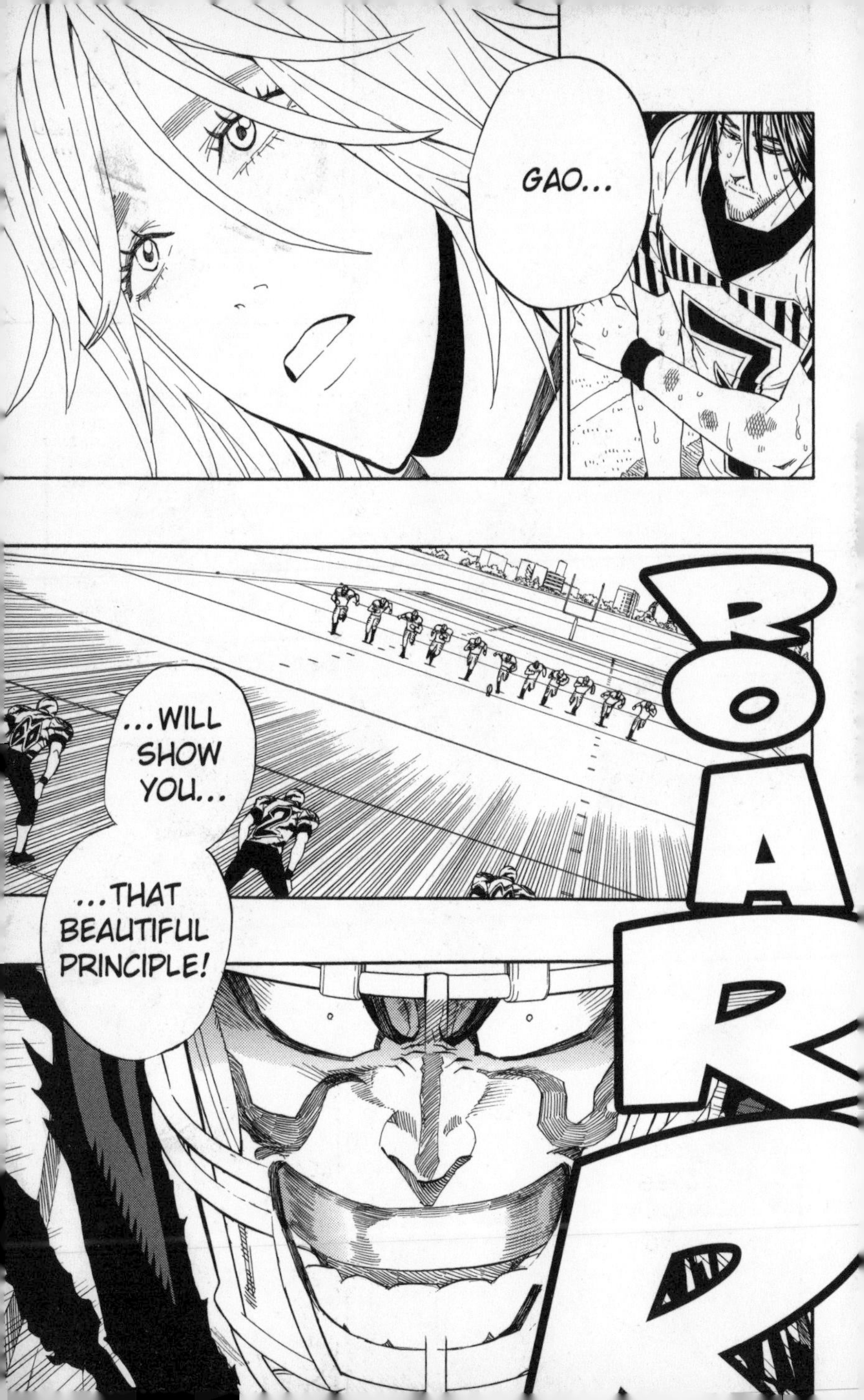
GAO...
...WILL SHOW YOU...
...THAT BEAUTIFUL PRINCIPLE!
ROAR

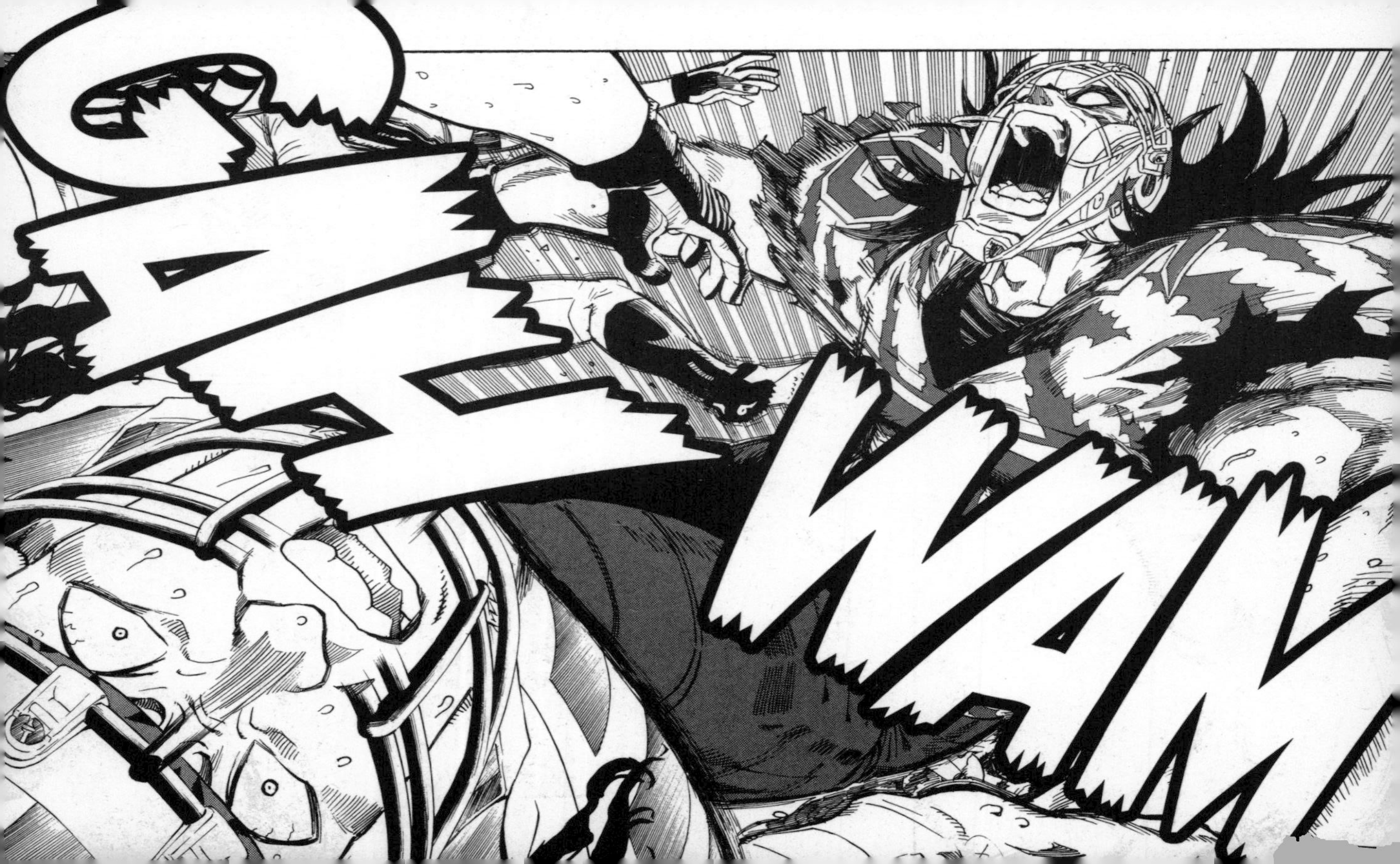
GAWAM

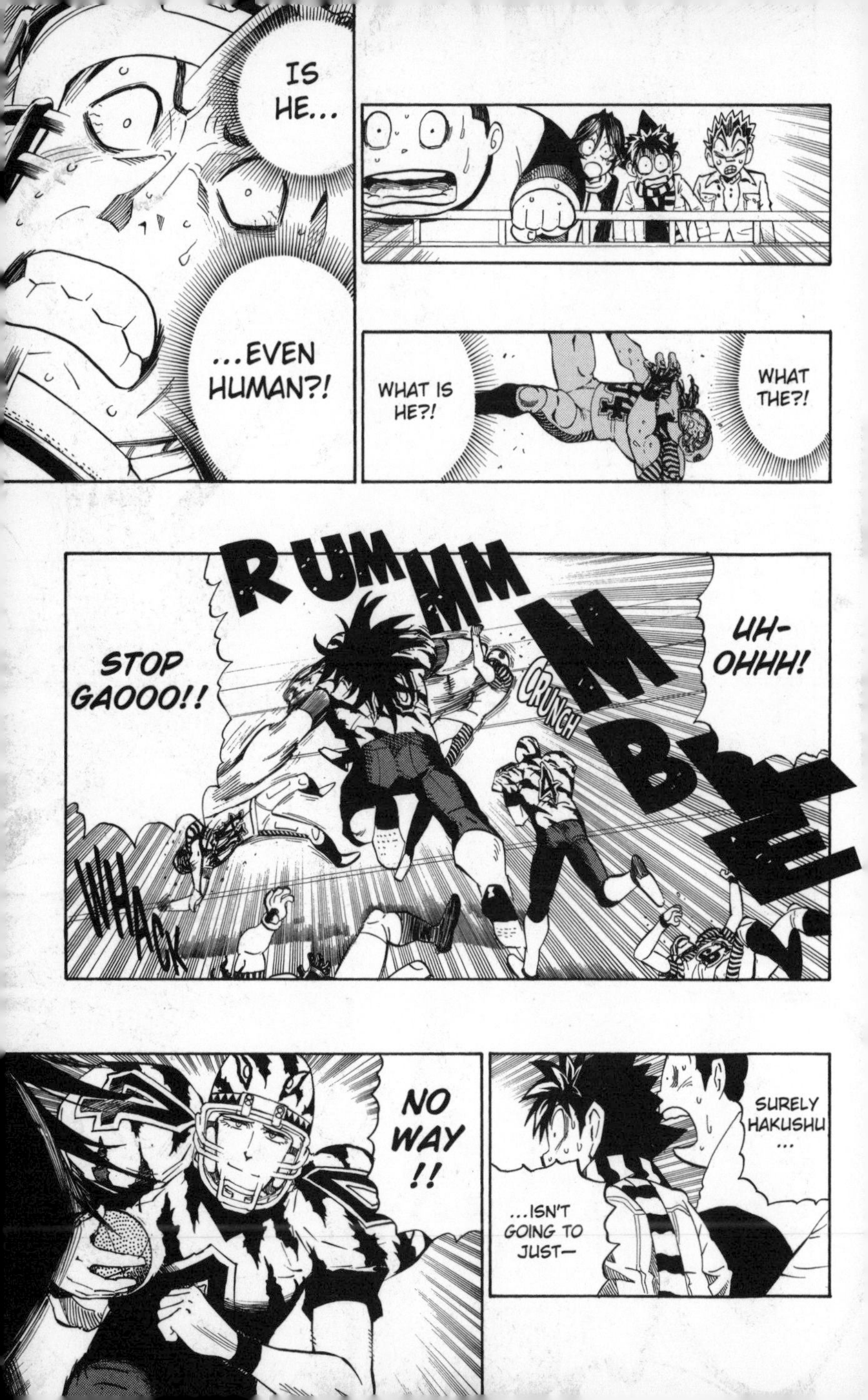
WHAT THE?!
WHAT IS HE?!
IS HE...
...EVEN HUMAN?!
RUMMMMBLE
UH-OHHH!
CRUNCH
STOP GAOOO!!
WHACK
SURELY HAKUSHU...
...ISN'T GOING TO JUST—
NO WAY!!

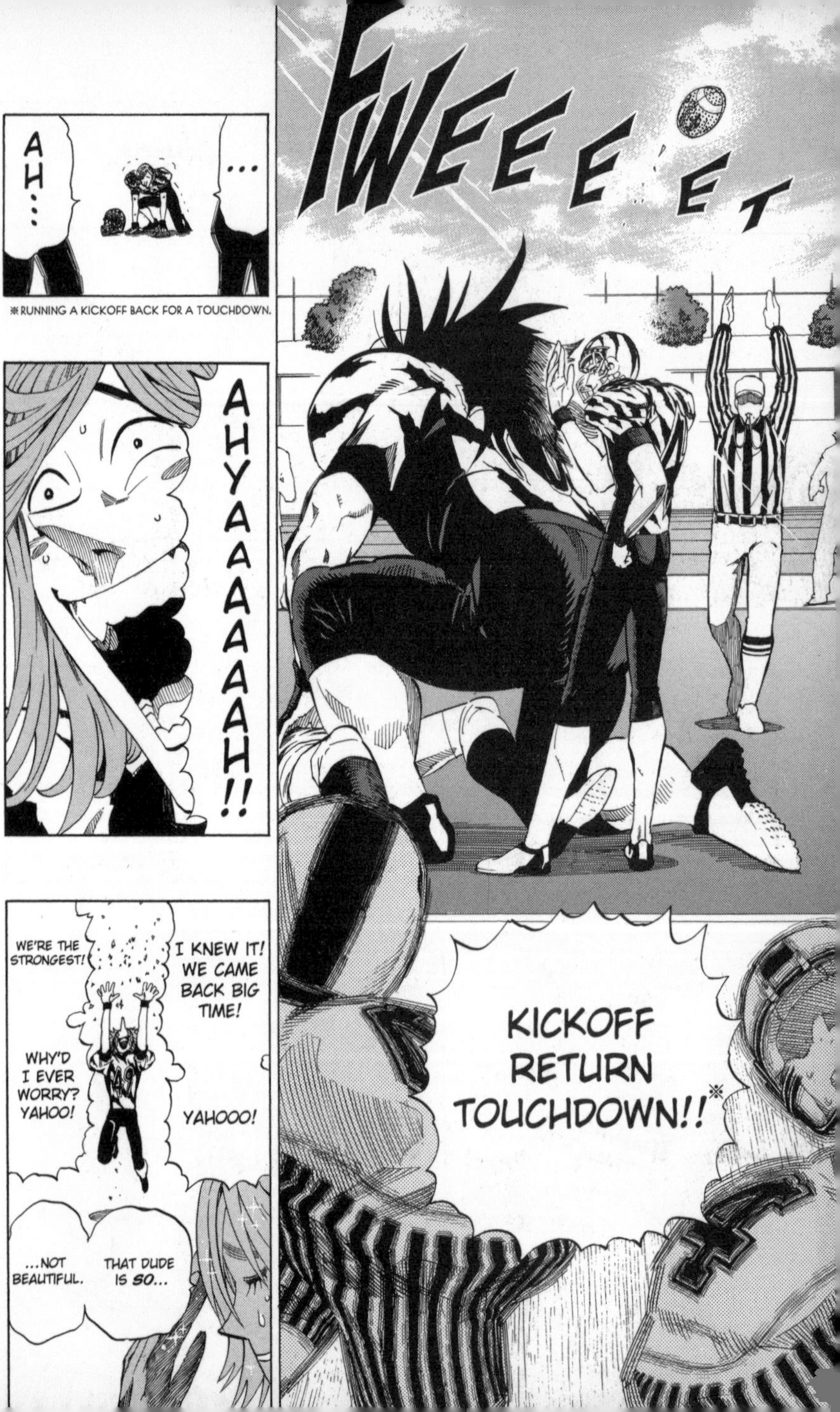
FWEEEEET
KICKOFF RETURN TOUCHDOWN!!※
AH...
...
※RUNNING A KICKOFF BACK FOR A TOUCHDOWN.
AHYAAAAAAAAAH!!
I KNEW IT! WE CAME BACK BIG TIME!
WE'RE THE STRONGEST!
YAHOOO!
WHY'D I EVER WORRY? YAHOO!
THAT DUDE IS SO...
...NOT BEAUTIFUL.

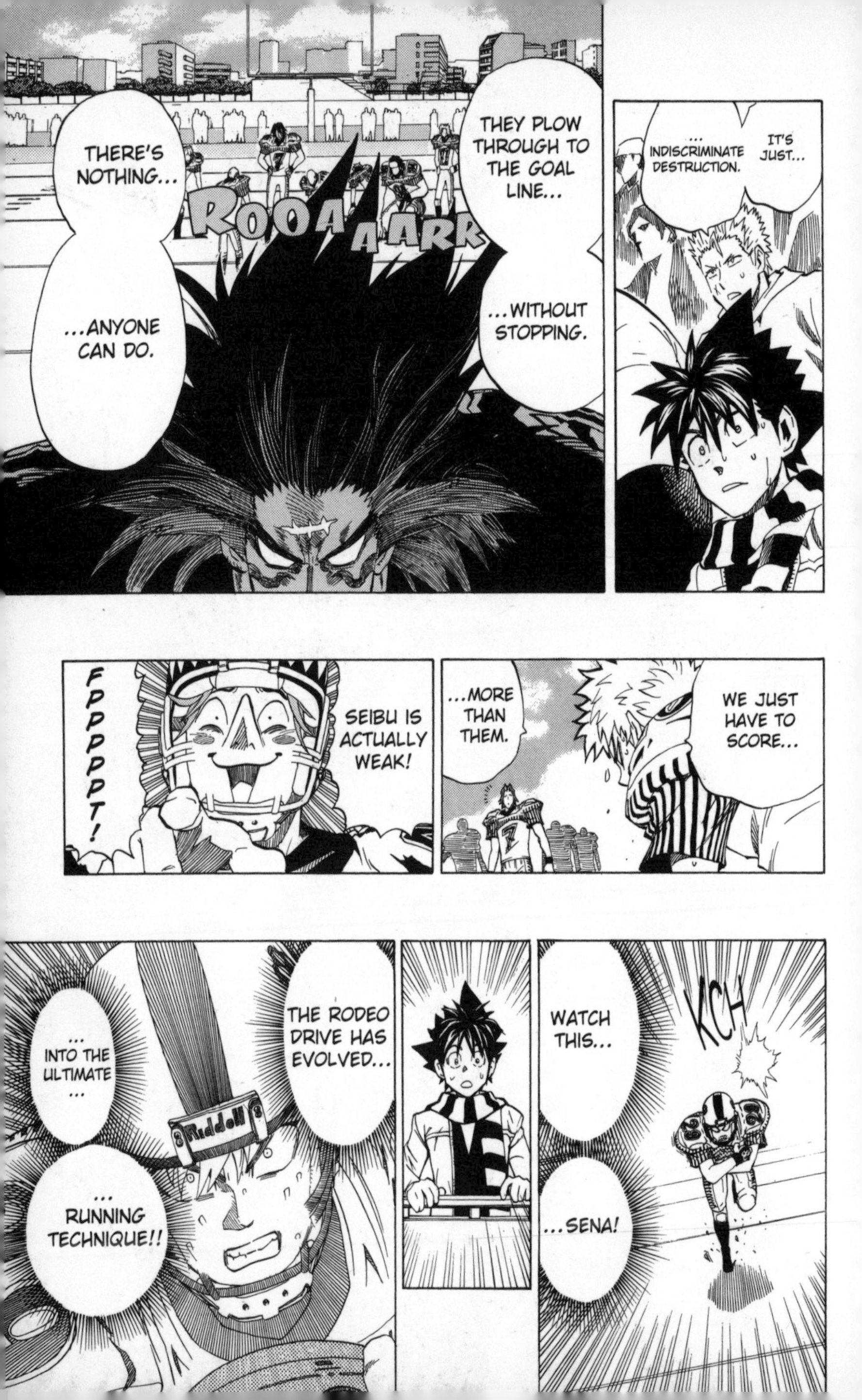
IT'S JUST...
...INDISCRIMINATE DESTRUCTION.
THEY PLOW THROUGH TO THE GOAL LINE...
...WITHOUT STOPPING.
ROOAAARR
THERE'S NOTHING...
...ANYONE CAN DO.
WE JUST HAVE TO SCORE...
...MORE THAN THEM.
FPPPPPT!
SEIBU IS ACTUALLY WEAK!
KCH
WATCH THIS...
...SENA!
THE RODEO DRIVE HAS EVOLVED...
...INTO THE ULTIMATE...
...RUNNING TECHNIQUE!!
Riddell

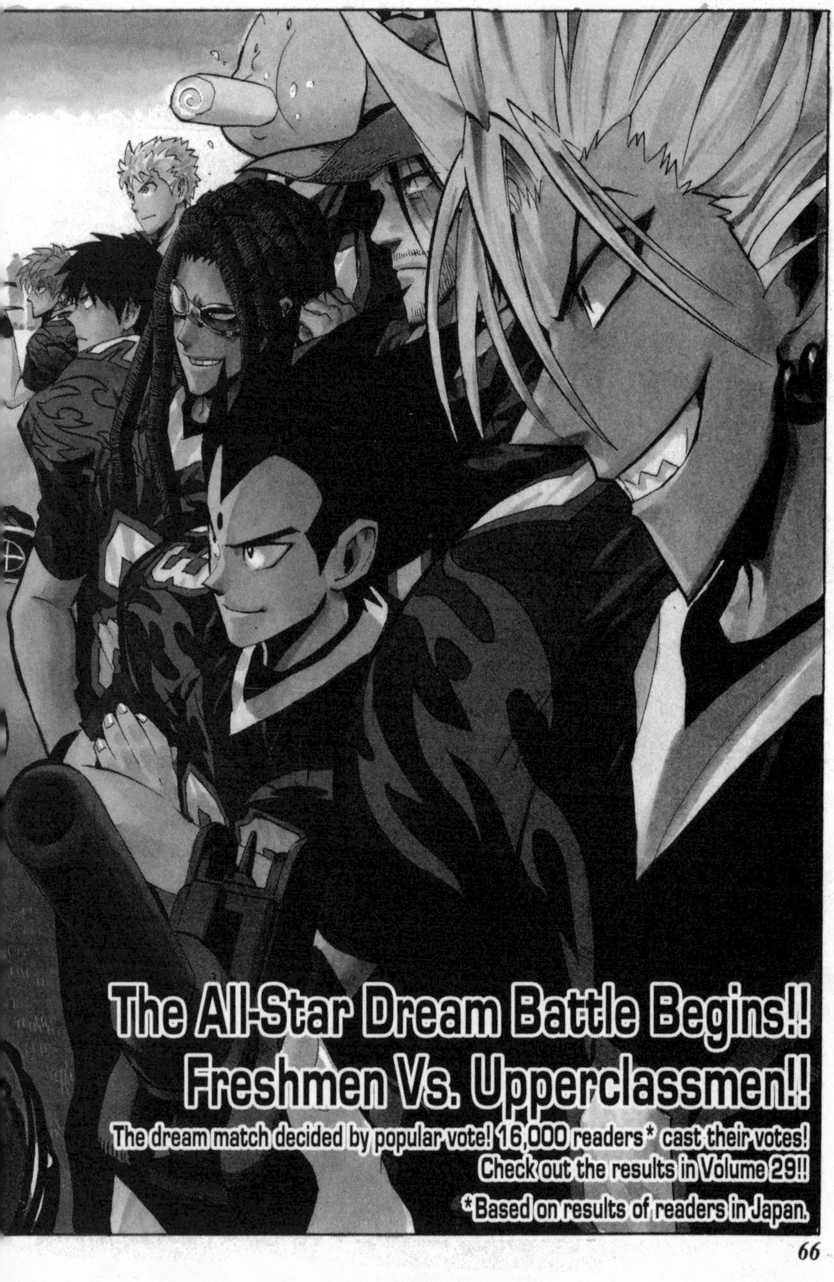
The All-Star Dream Battle Begins!!
Freshmen Vs. Upperclassmen!!
The dream match decided by popular vote! 16,000 readers* cast their votes!
Check out the results in Volume 29!!
*Based on results of readers in Japan.

Chapter 245 A Piece of a Dream

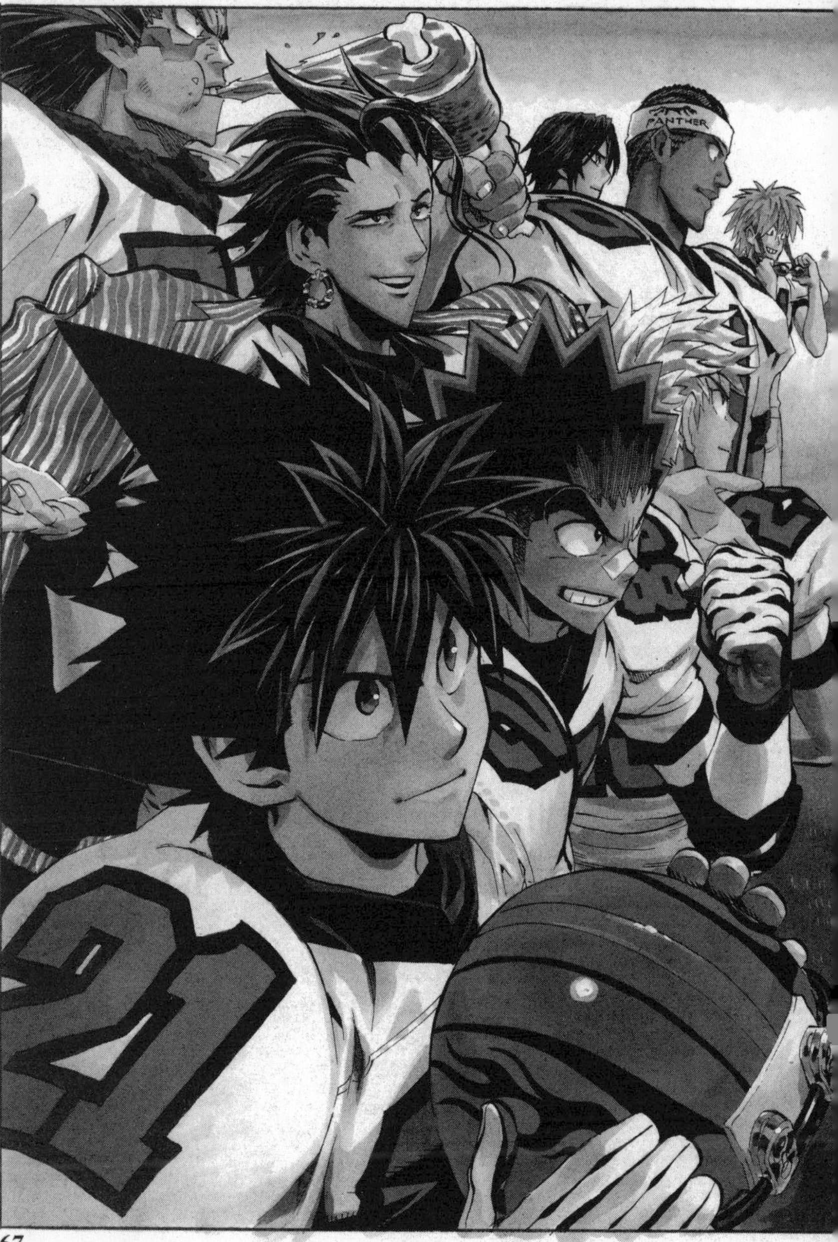
PANTHER

Special Supplement!!

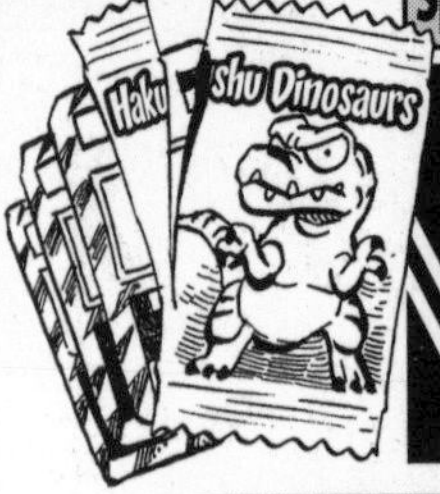

Haku shu Dinosaurs

Hakushu Dinosaurs Athlete Card

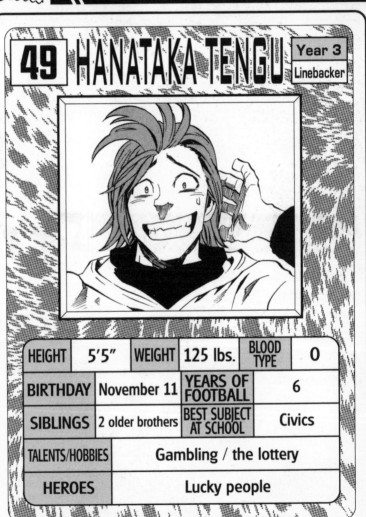

49 HANATAKA TENGU

Year 3

Linebacker

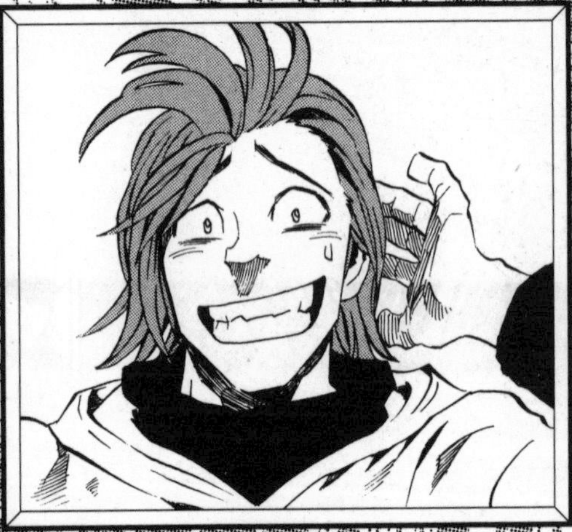

HEIGHT	5'5"	WEIGHT	125 lbs.	BLOOD TYPE	0
BIRTHDAY	November 11	YEARS OF FOOTBALL	6		
SIBLINGS	2 older brothers	BEST SUBJECT AT SCHOOL	Civics		
TALENTS/HOBBIES	Gambling / the lottery				
HEROES	Lucky people				

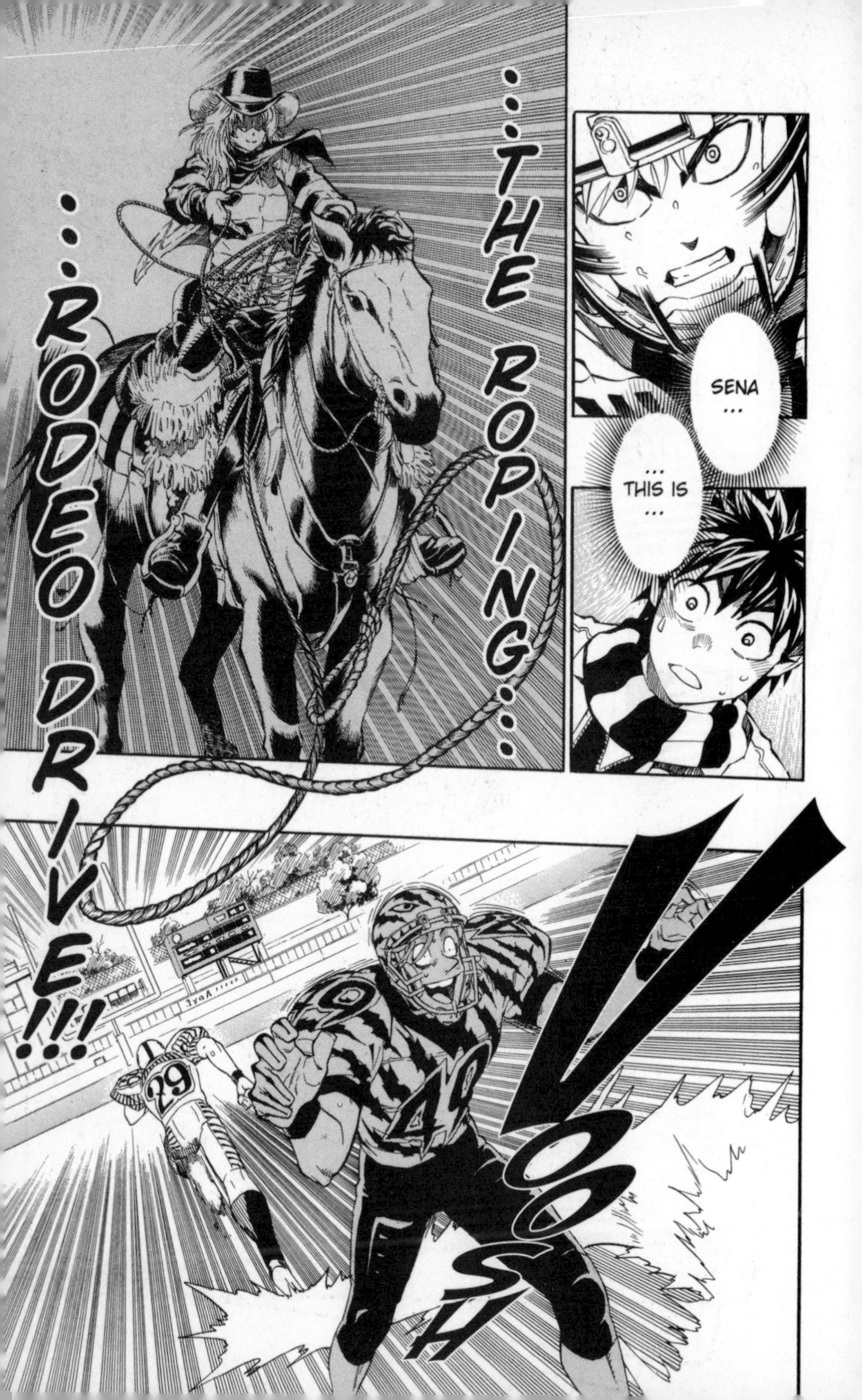
SENA ...
... THIS IS ...
...THE ROPING...
...RODEO DRIVE!!!
VOOSH

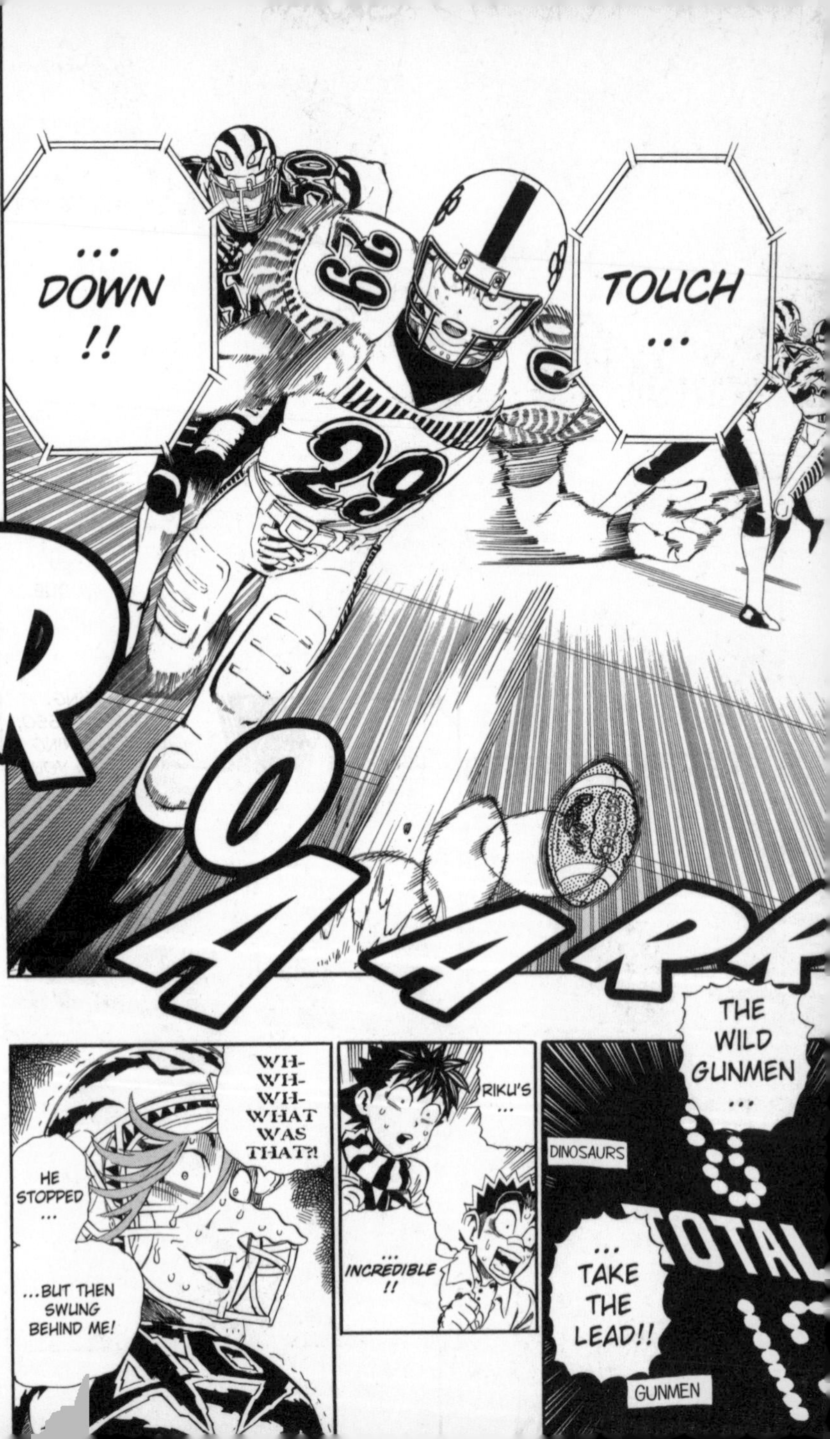
TOUCH ...
... DOWN !!
ROAAR
THE WILD GUNMEN ...
DINOSAURS
TOTAL
... TAKE THE LEAD!!
GUNMEN
RIKU'S ...
... INCREDIBLE !!
WH- WH- WH- WHAT WAS THAT?!
HE STOPPED ...
...BUT THEN SWUNG BEHIND ME!

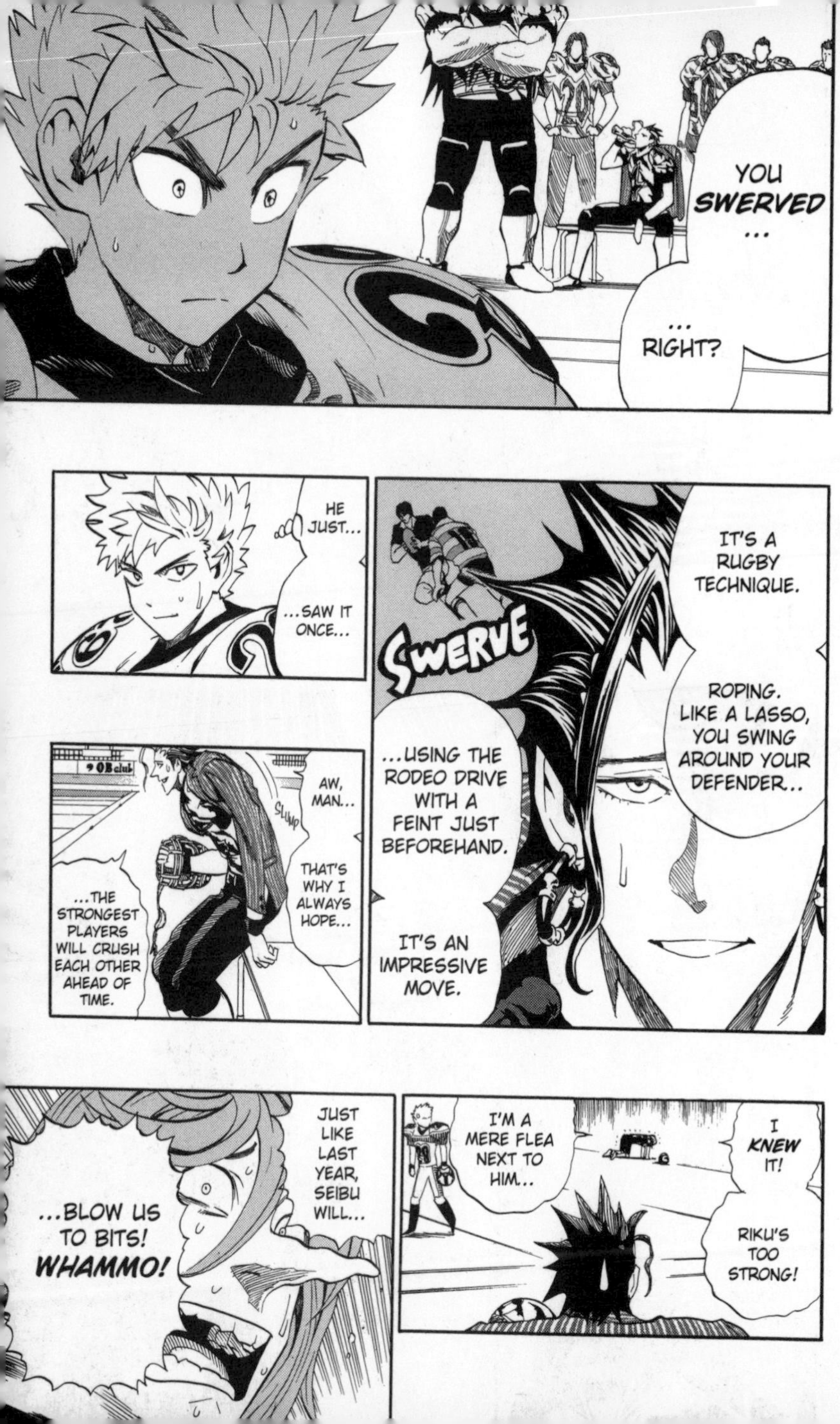

YOU SWERVED ...
... RIGHT?
IT'S A RUGBY TECHNIQUE.
ROPING. LIKE A LASSO, YOU SWING AROUND YOUR DEFENDER...
...USING THE RODEO DRIVE WITH A FEINT JUST BEFOREHAND.
IT'S AN IMPRESSIVE MOVE.
SWERVE
HE JUST...
...SAW IT ONCE...
AW, MAN...
SLUMP
THAT'S WHY I ALWAYS HOPE...
...THE STRONGEST PLAYERS WILL CRUSH EACH OTHER AHEAD OF TIME.
I KNEW IT!
RIKU'S TOO STRONG!
I'M A MERE FLEA NEXT TO HIM...
JUST LIKE LAST YEAR, SEIBU WILL...
...BLOW US TO BITS! WHAMMO!

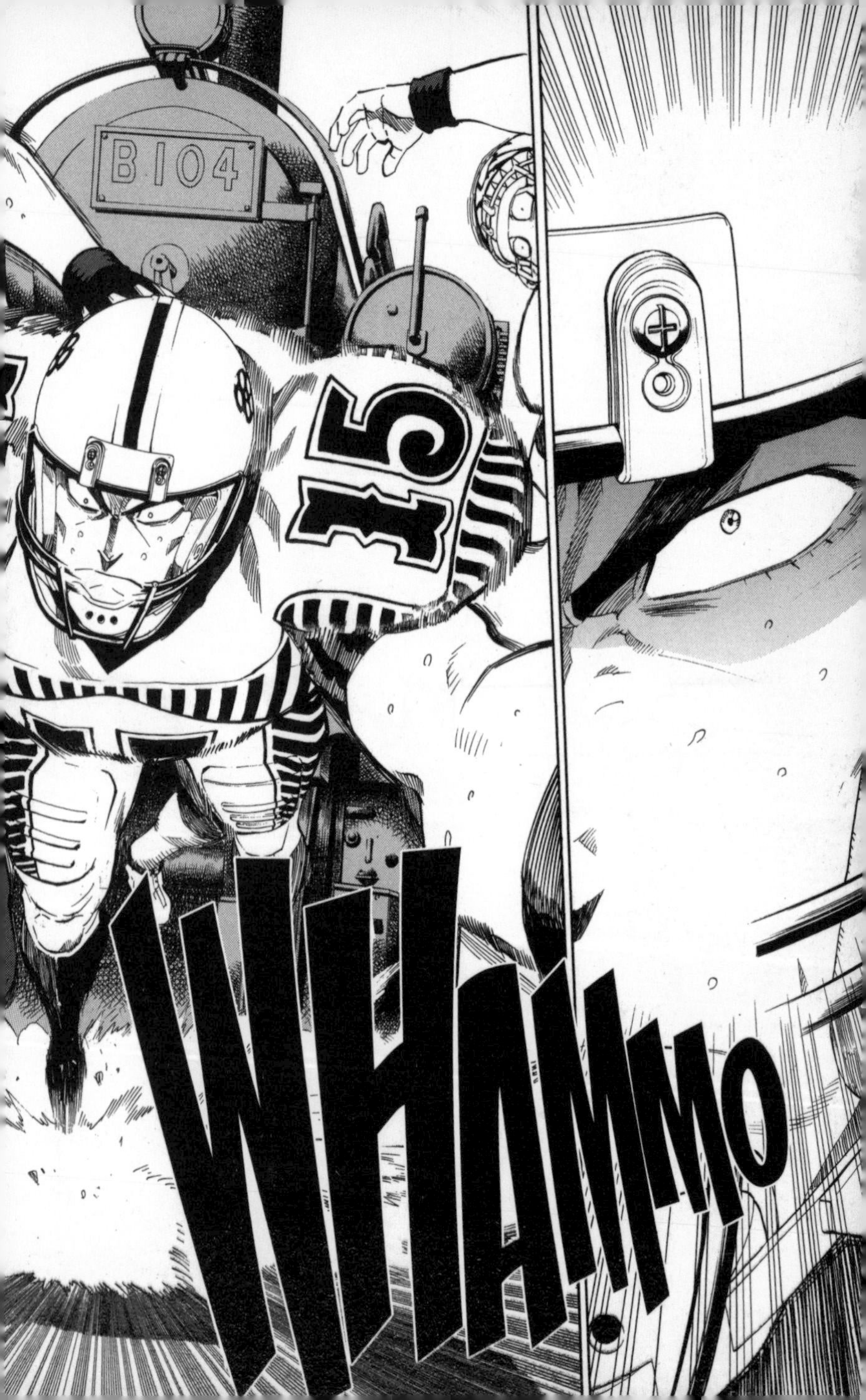
WHAMMO

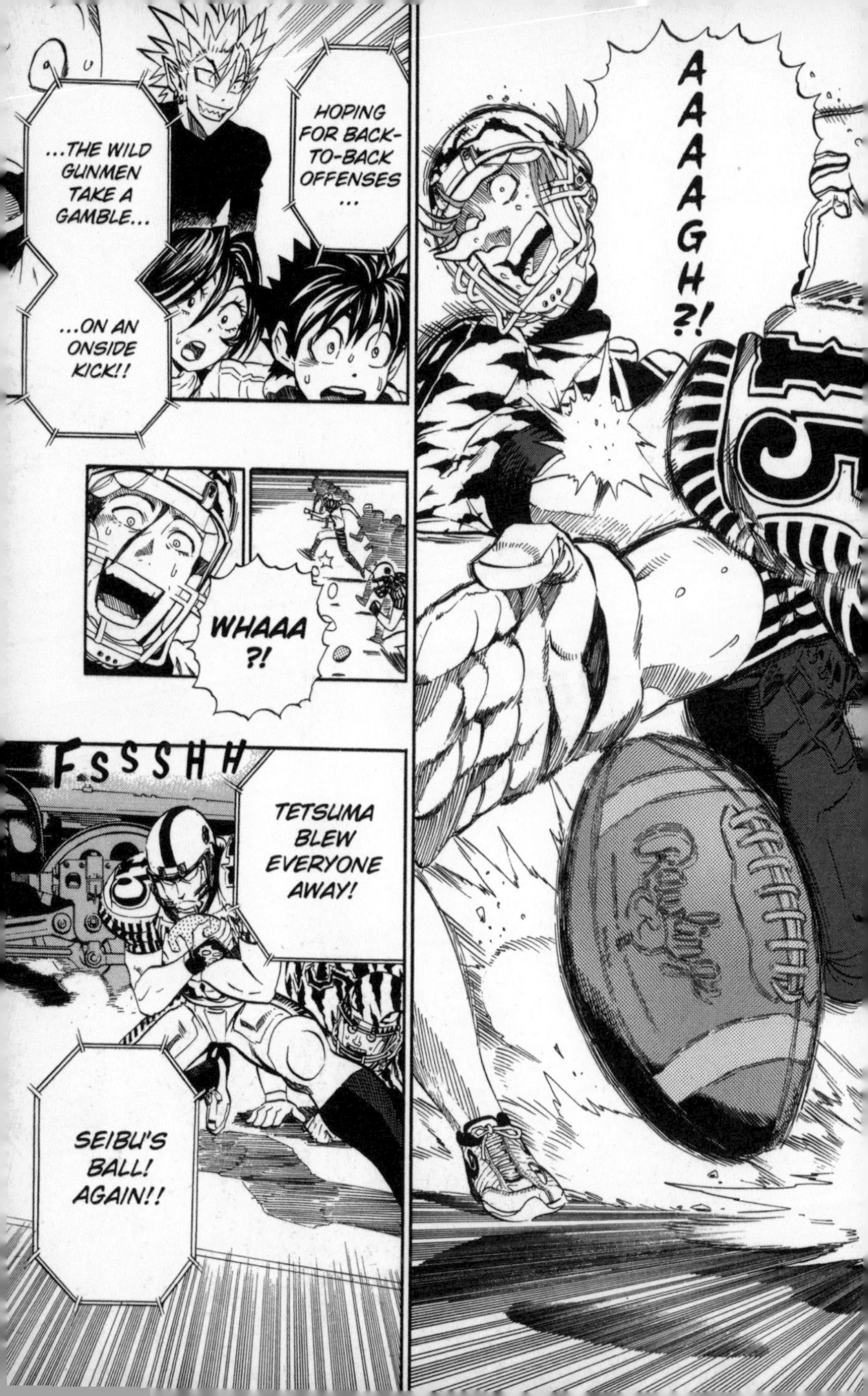
AAAAAGH?!
HOPING FOR BACK-TO-BACK OFFENSES...
...THE WILD GUNMEN TAKE A GAMBLE...
...ON AN ONSIDE KICK!!
WHAAA?!
FSSSHH
TETSUMA BLEW EVERYONE AWAY!
SEIBU'S BALL! AGAIN!!

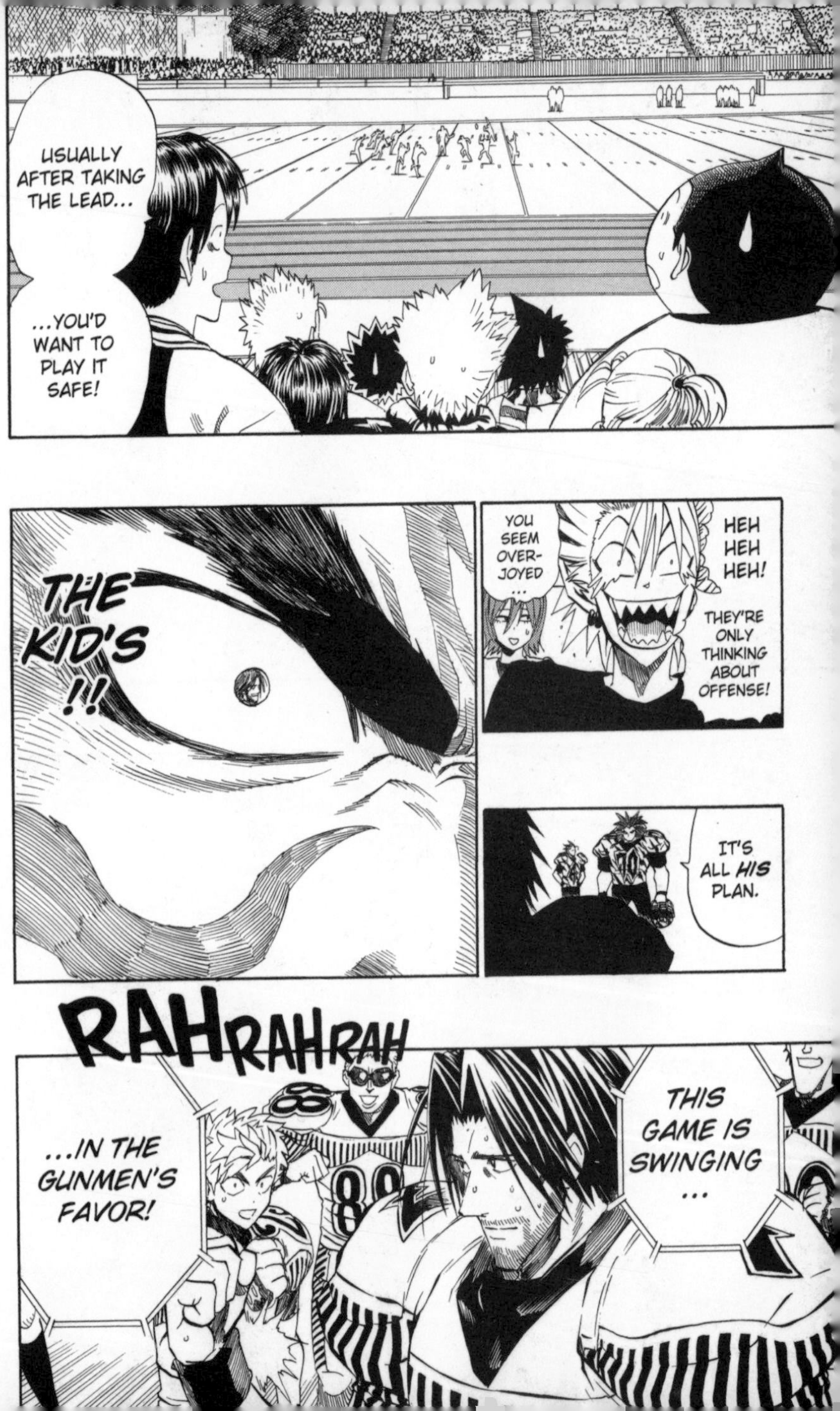
USUALLY AFTER TAKING THE LEAD...
...YOU'D WANT TO PLAY IT SAFE!
HEH HEH HEH!
THEY'RE ONLY THINKING ABOUT OFFENSE!
YOU SEEM OVER-JOYED ...
IT'S ALL HIS PLAN.
THE KID'S !!
RAHRAHRAH
THIS GAME IS SWINGING ...
...IN THE GUNMEN'S FAVOR!

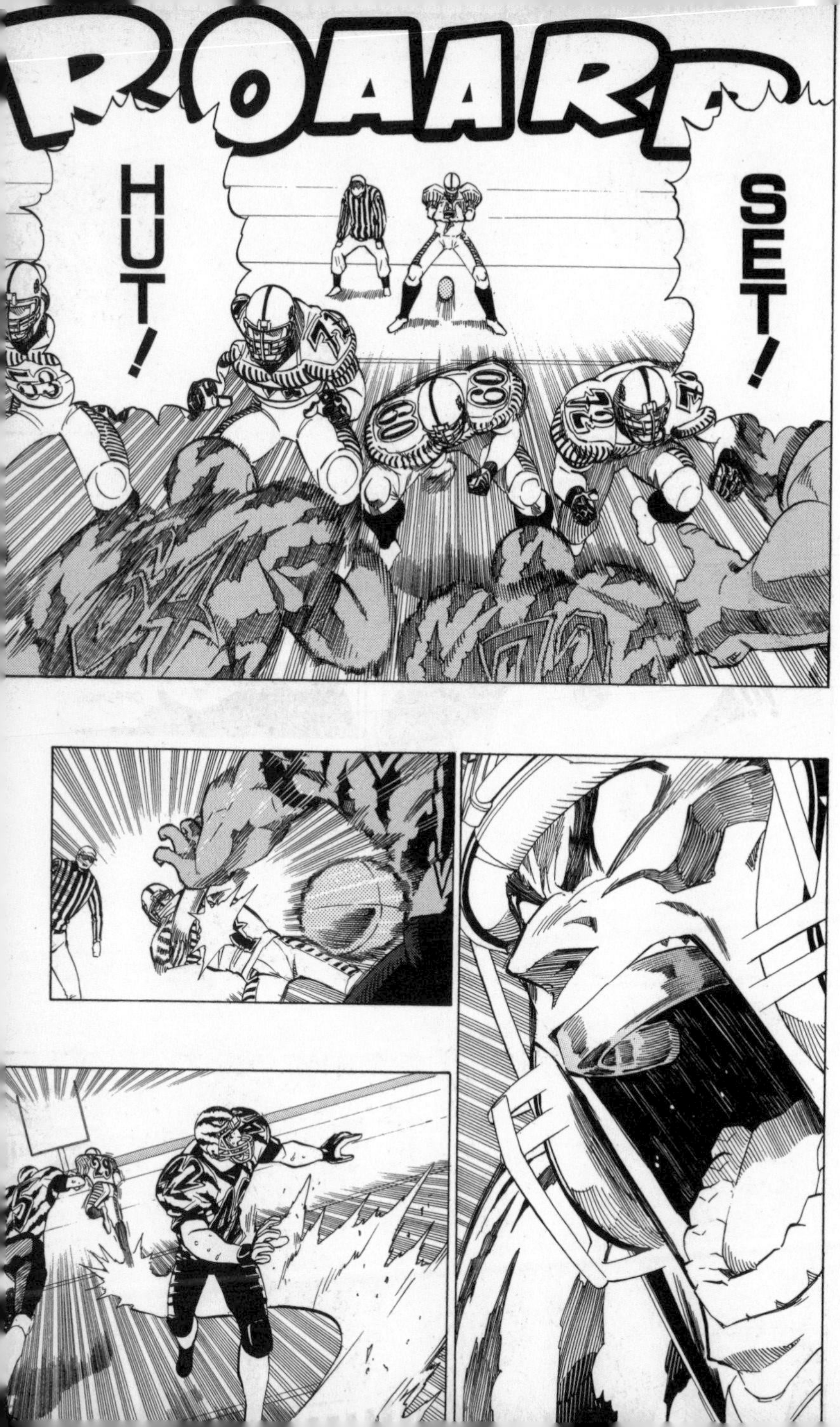
ROAARR
SET!
HUT!

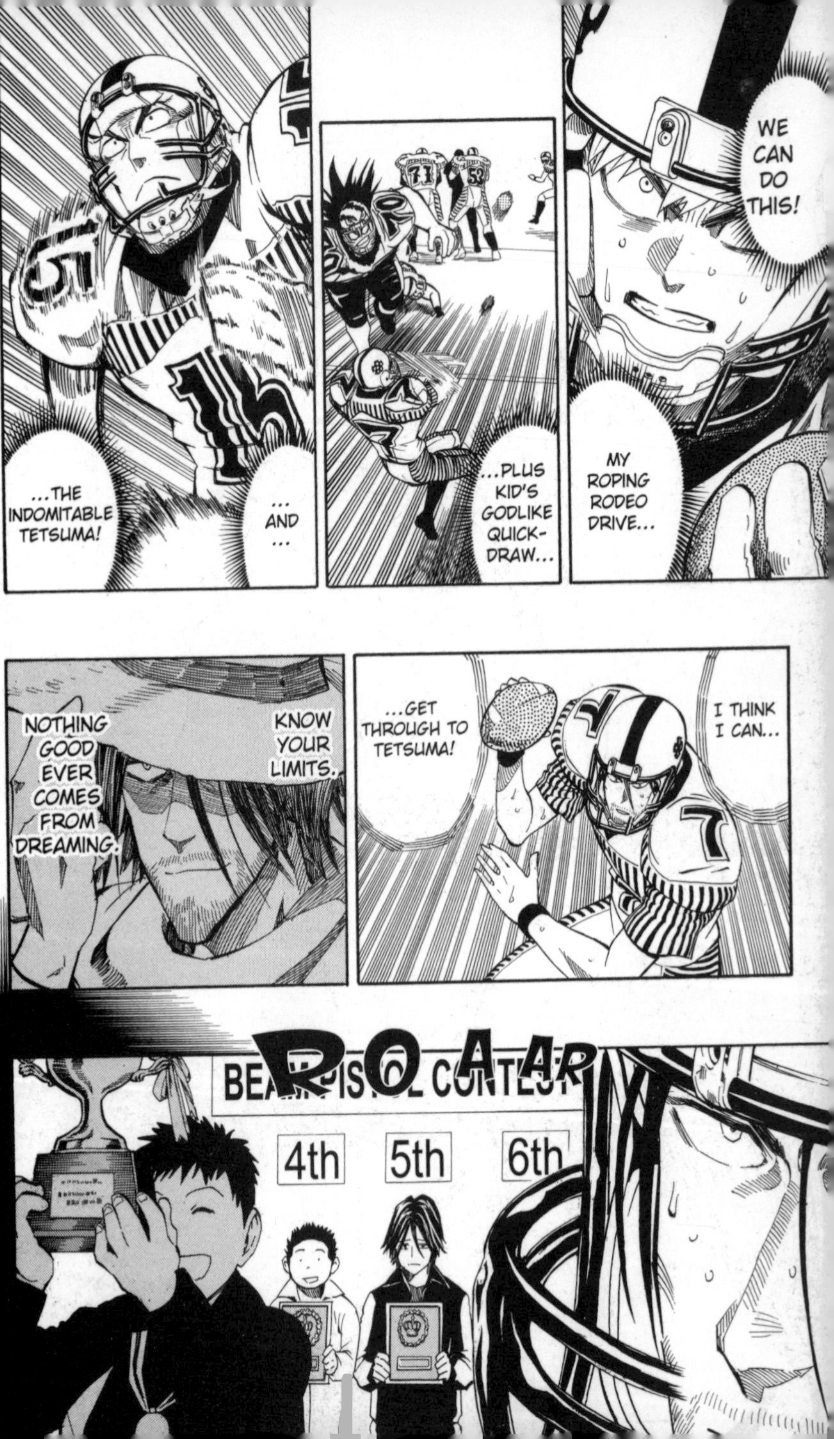
WE CAN DO THIS!
MY ROPING RODEO DRIVE...
...PLUS KID'S GODLIKE QUICK-DRAW...
... AND ...
...THE INDOMITABLE TETSUMA!
I THINK I CAN...
...GET THROUGH TO TETSUMA!
KNOW YOUR LIMITS.
NOTHING GOOD EVER COMES FROM DREAMING.
ROAAR
4th
5th
6th

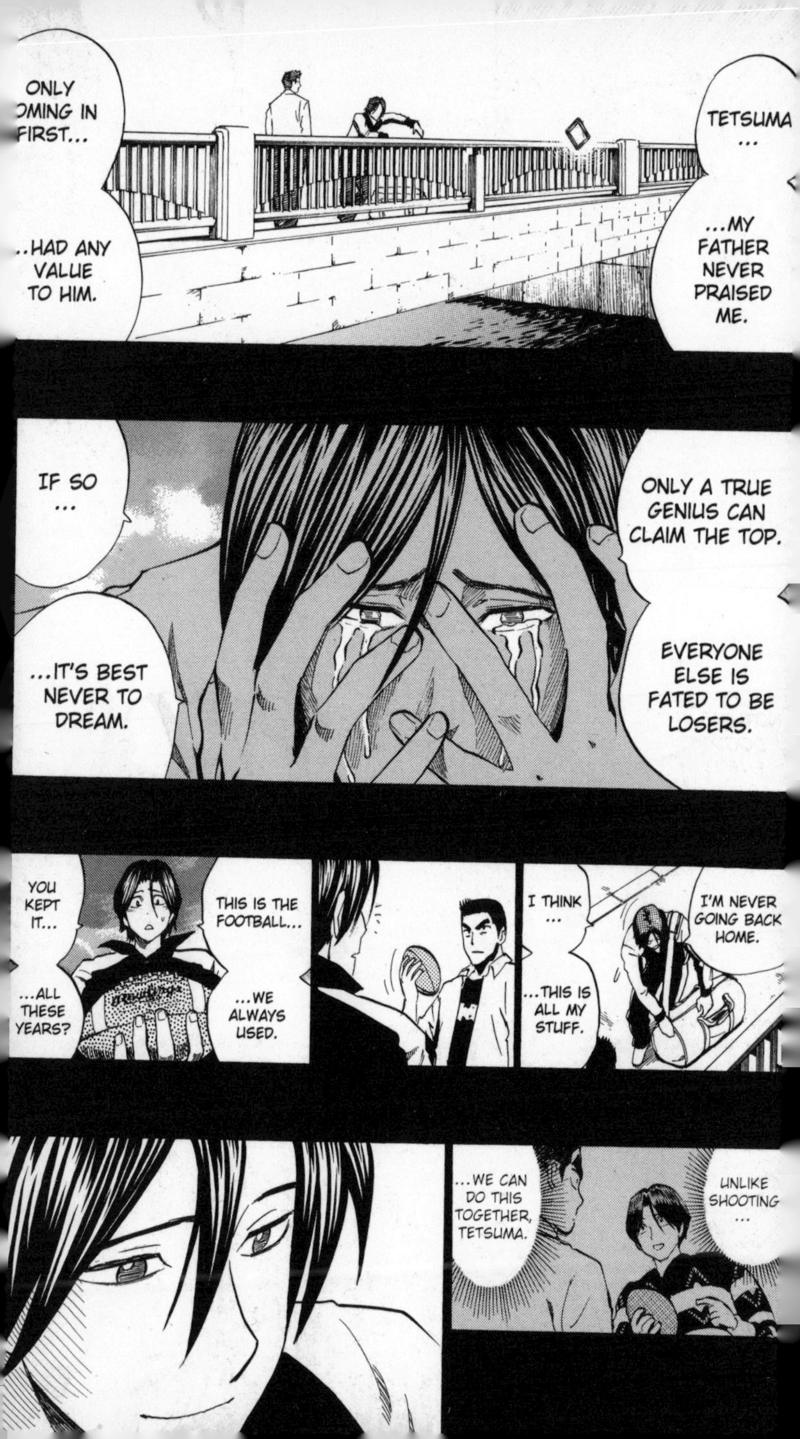
TETSUMA ...
...MY FATHER NEVER PRAISED ME.
ONLY OMING IN FIRST...
..HAD ANY VALUE TO HIM.
ONLY A TRUE GENIUS CAN CLAIM THE TOP.
EVERYONE ELSE IS FATED TO BE LOSERS.
IF SO ...
...IT'S BEST NEVER TO DREAM.
I'M NEVER GOING BACK HOME.
I THINK ...
...THIS IS ALL MY STUFF.
THIS IS THE FOOTBALL...
...WE ALWAYS USED.
YOU KEPT IT...
...ALL THESE YEARS?
UNLIKE SHOOTING ...
...WE CAN DO THIS TOGETHER, TETSUMA.

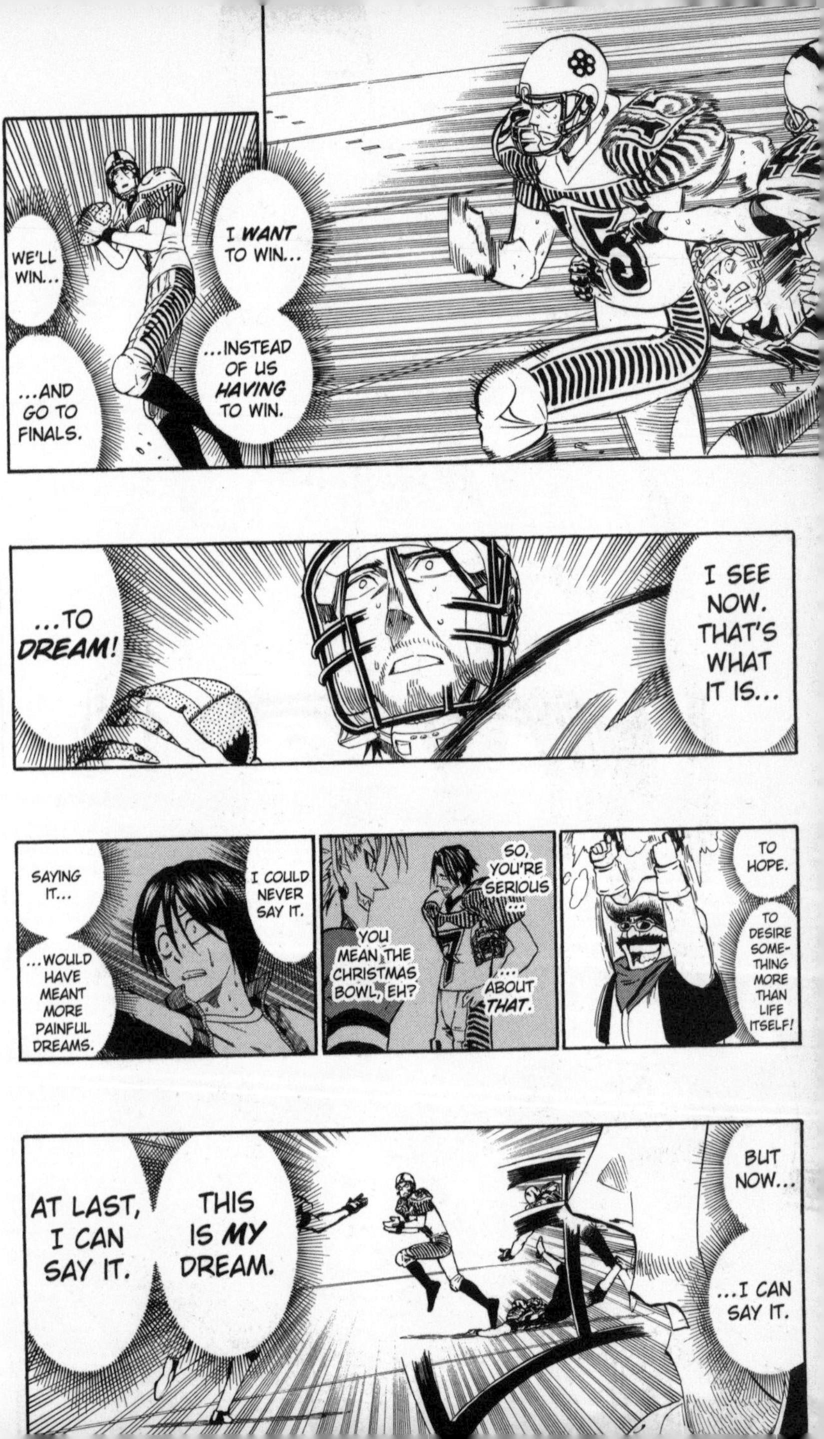
I WANT TO WIN...
...INSTEAD OF US HAVING TO WIN.
WE'LL WIN...
...AND GO TO FINALS.
I SEE NOW. THAT'S WHAT IT IS...
...TO DREAM!
TO HOPE.
TO DESIRE SOME-THING MORE THAN LIFE ITSELF!
SO, YOU'RE SERIOUS...
...ABOUT THAT.
YOU MEAN THE CHRISTMAS BOWL, EH?
I COULD NEVER SAY IT.
SAYING IT...
...WOULD HAVE MEANT MORE PAINFUL DREAMS.
BUT NOW...
...I CAN SAY IT.
THIS IS MY DREAM.
AT LAST, I CAN SAY IT.

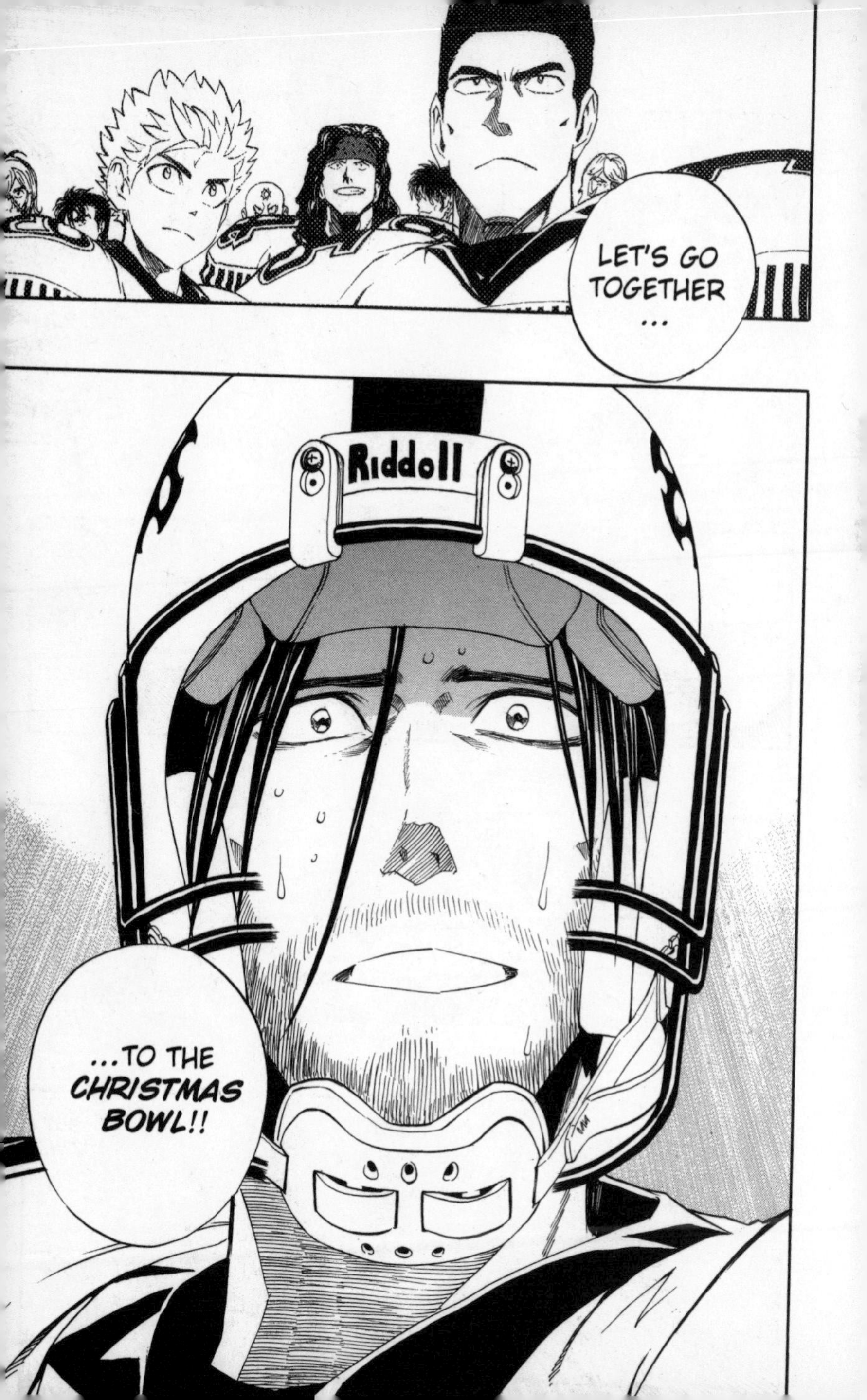
LET'S GO TOGETHER ...
Riddoll
...TO THE CHRISTMAS BOWL!!

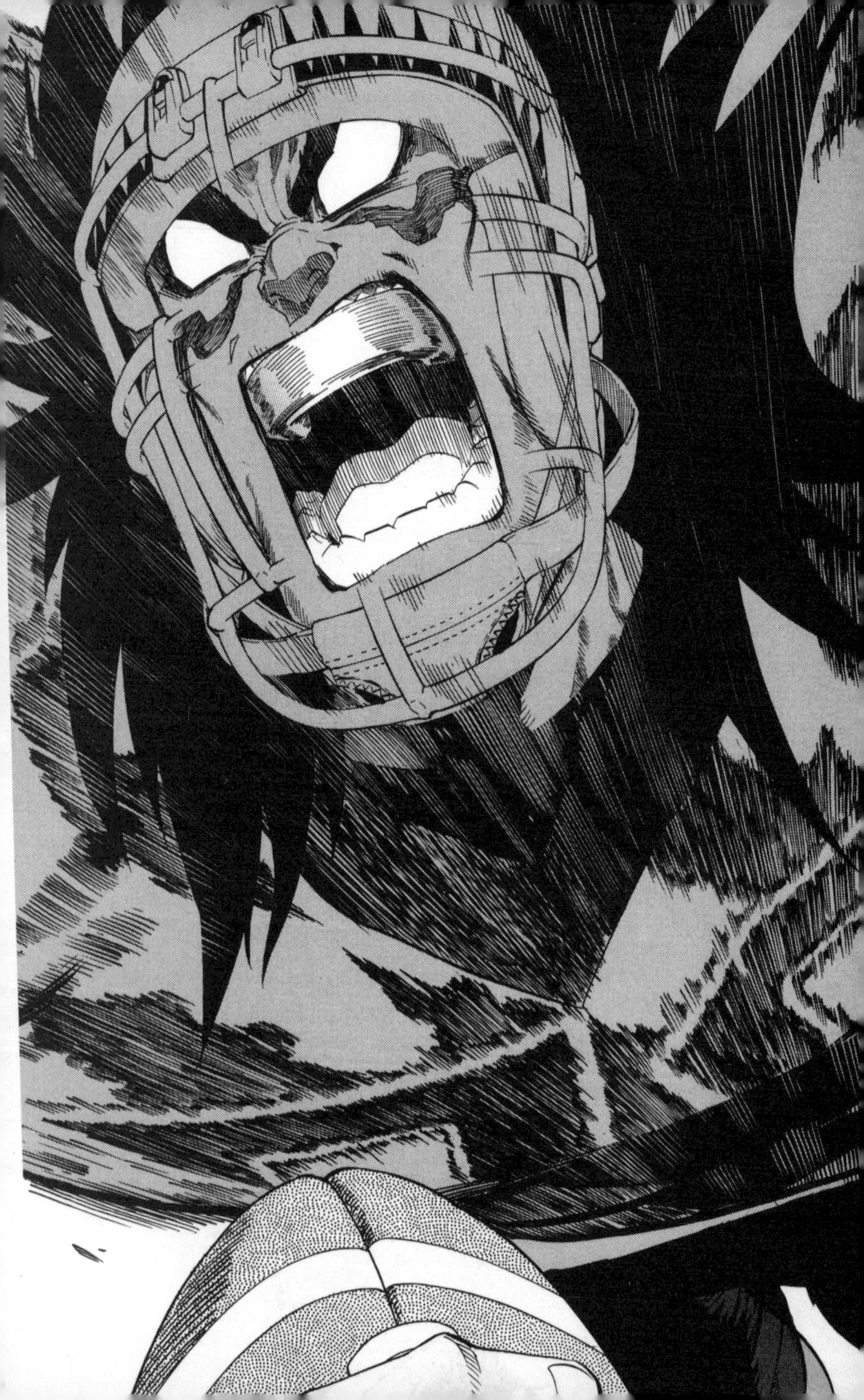

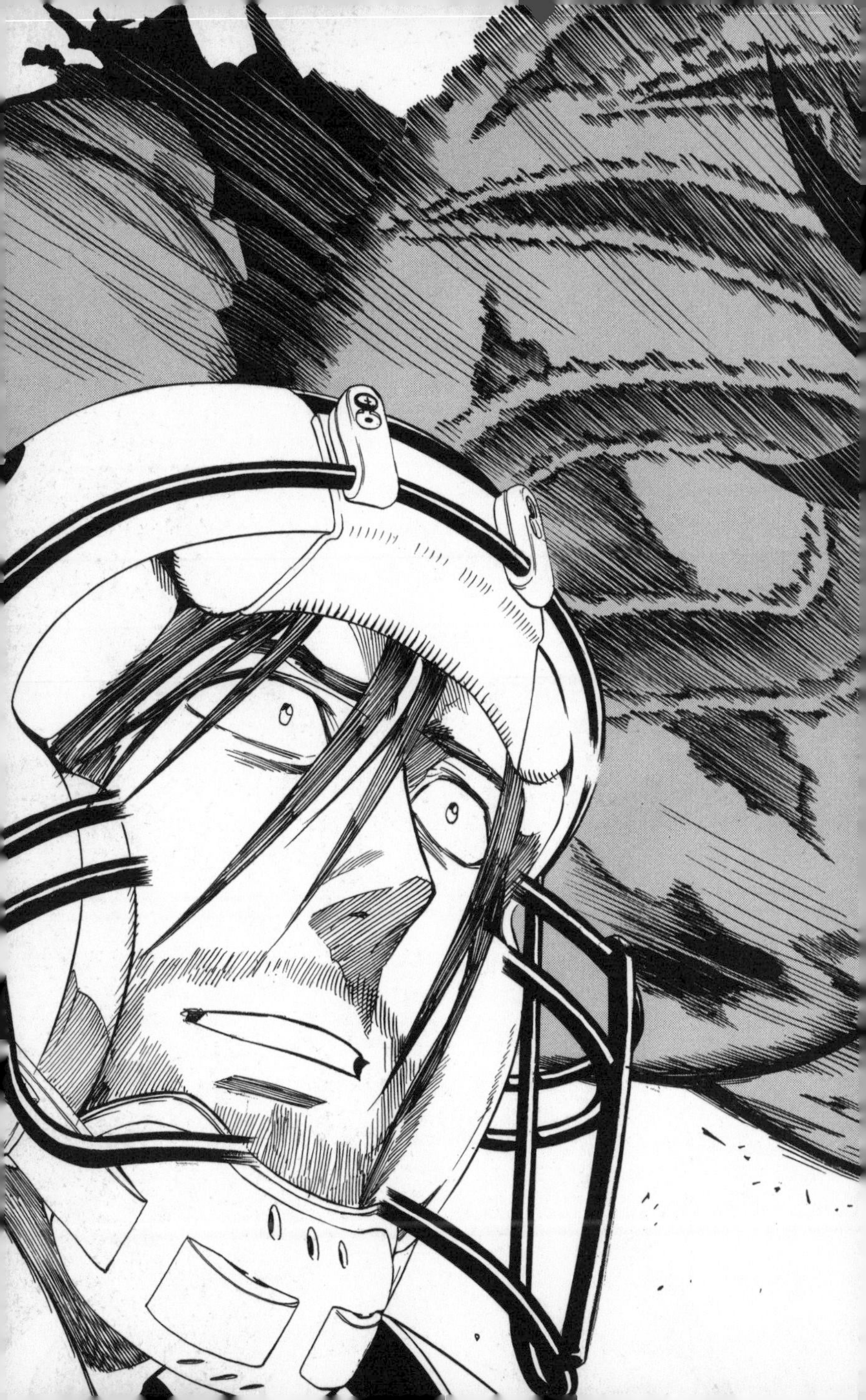

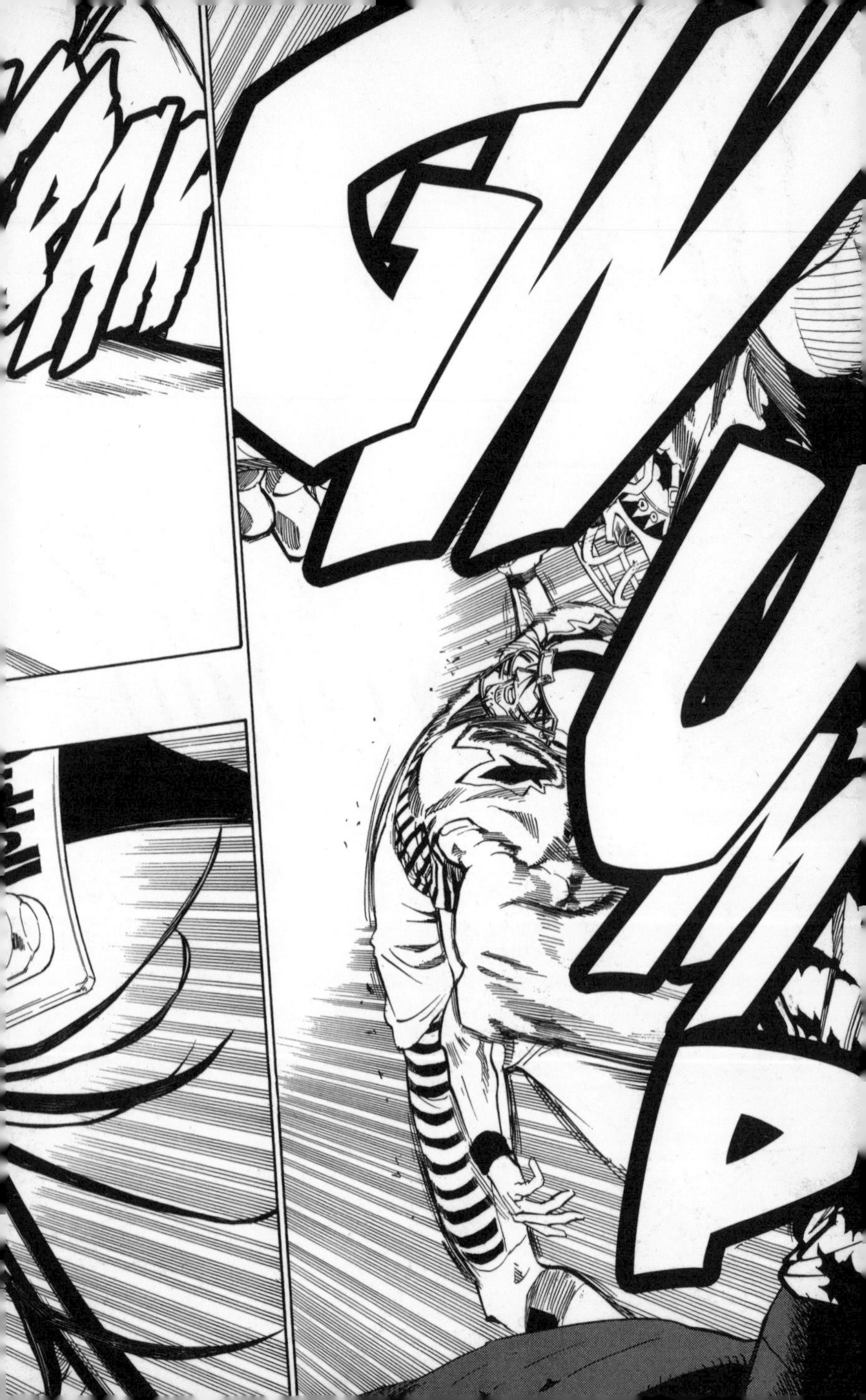

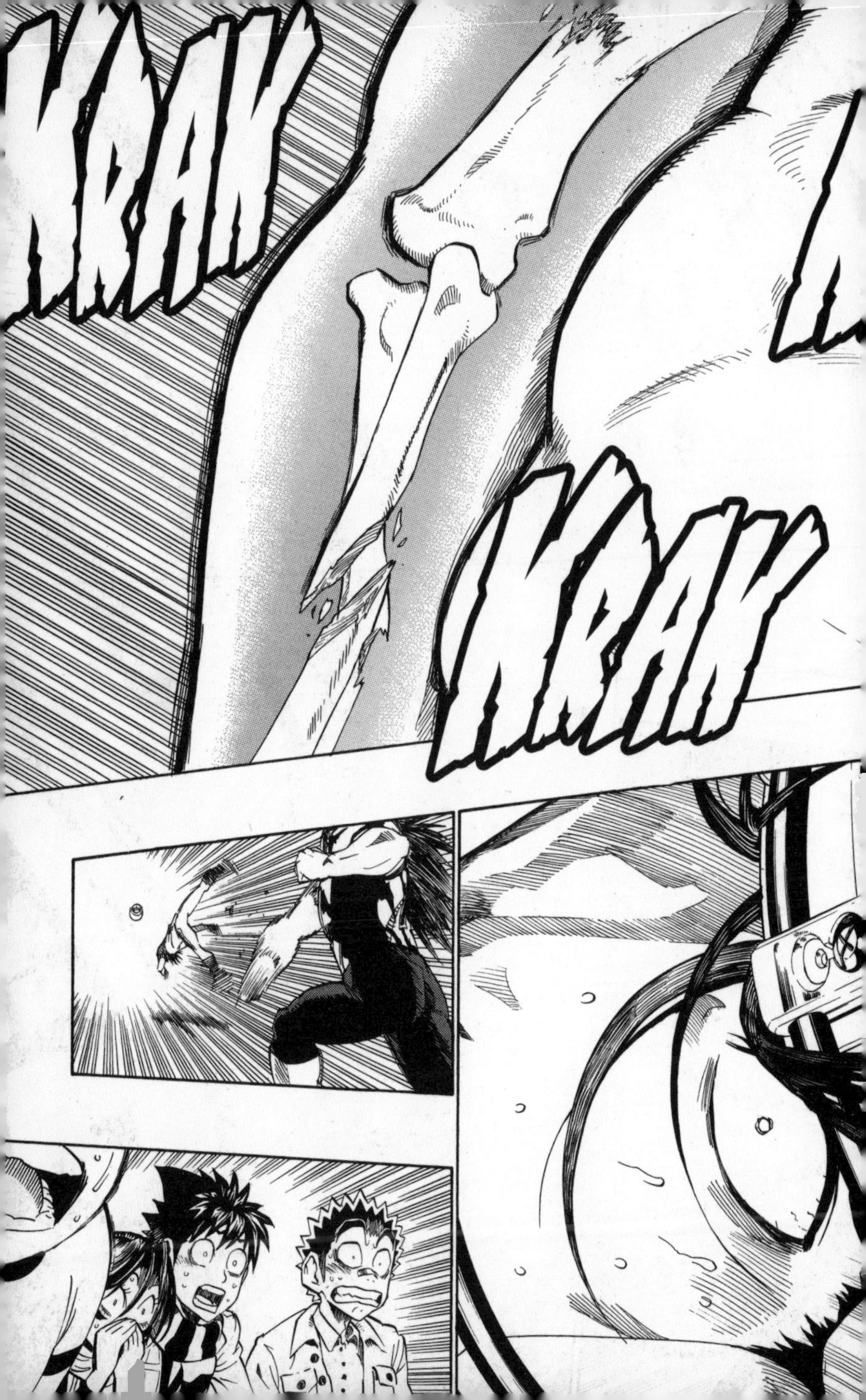
KRAK
KRAK

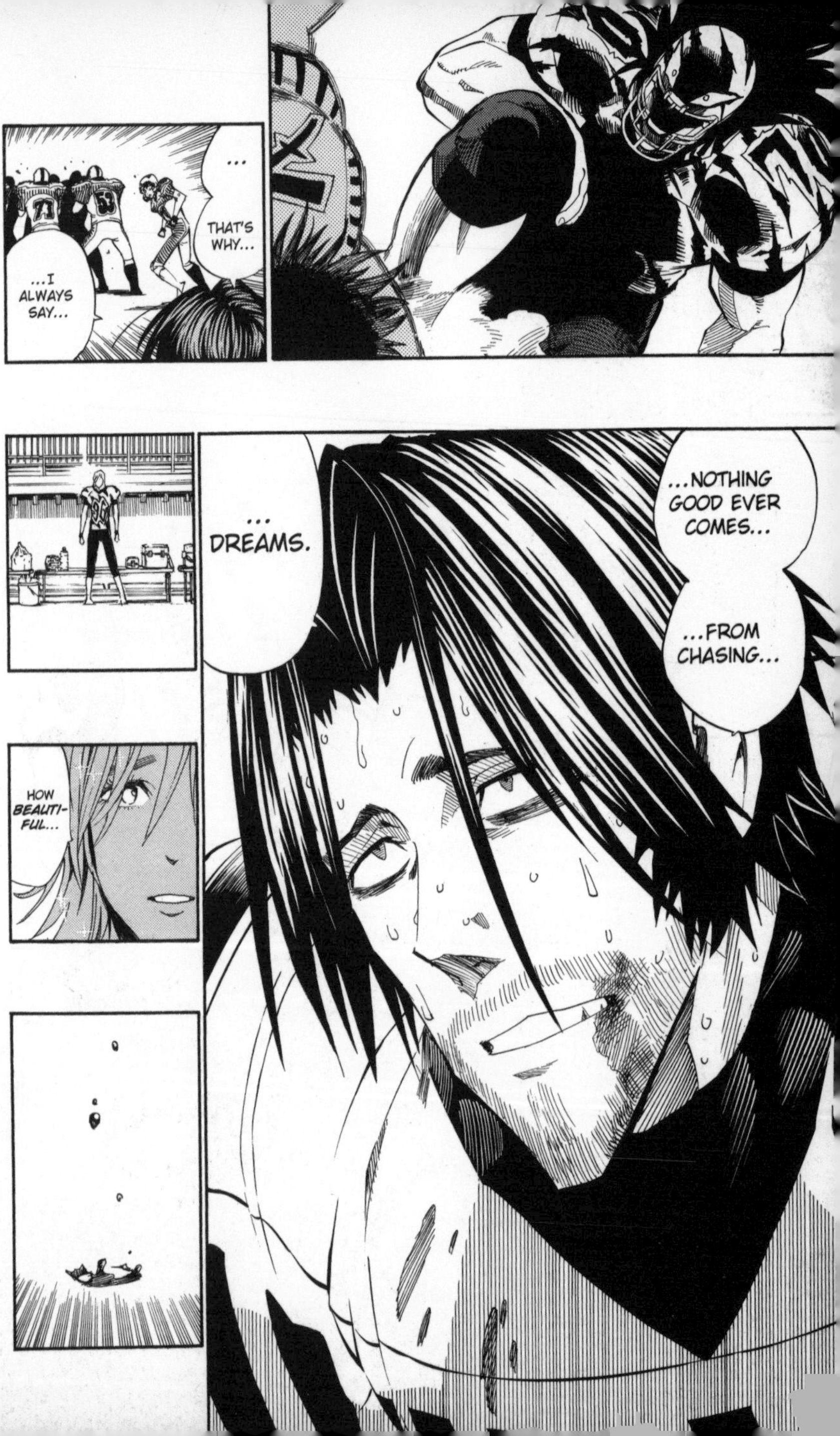
...
THAT'S WHY...
...I ALWAYS SAY...
...NOTHING GOOD EVER COMES...
...FROM CHASING...
...DREAMS.
HOW BEAUTI-FUL...

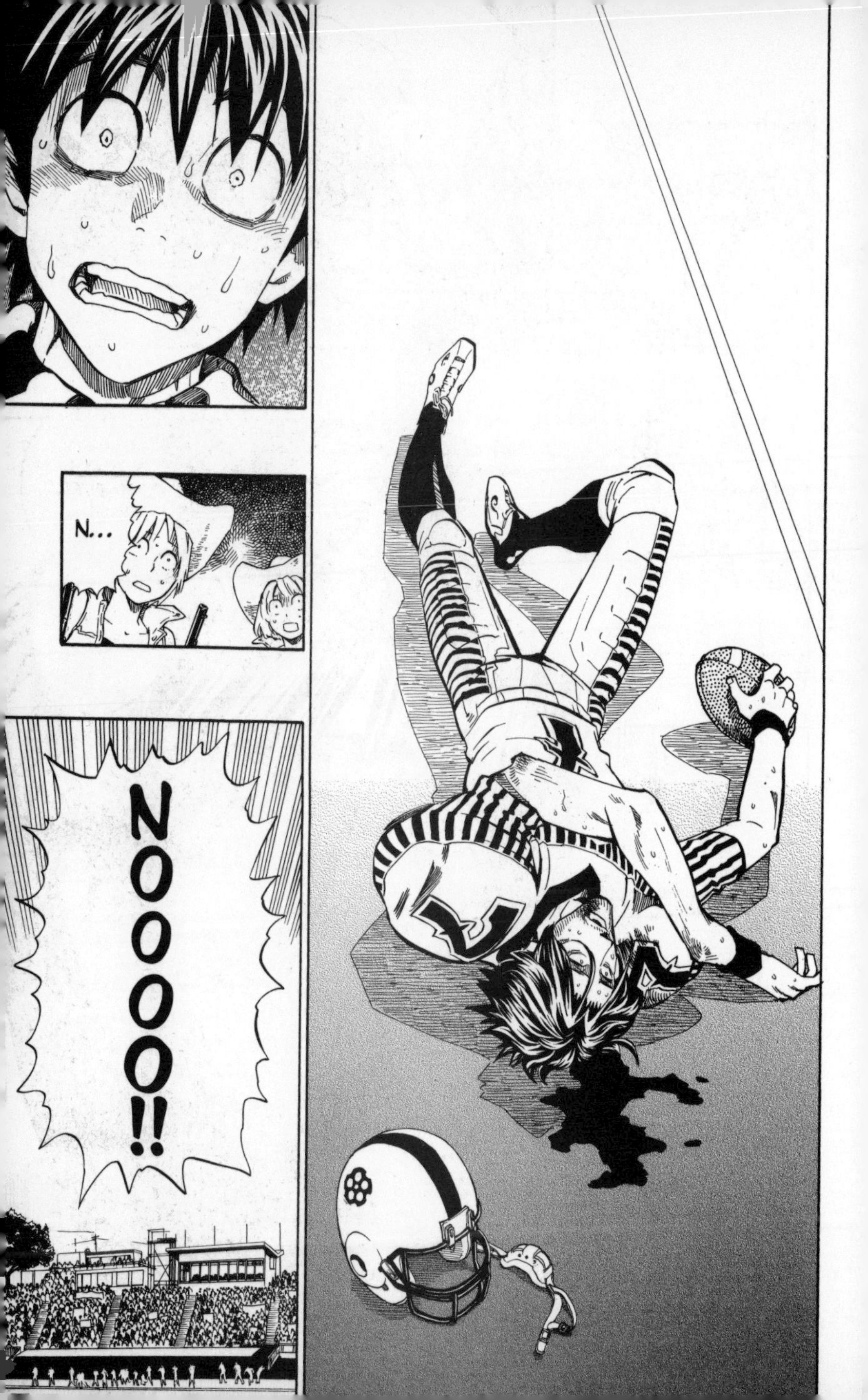
N...
NOOOO!!

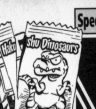

Special Supplement!!

Hakushu Dinosaurs Athlete Card

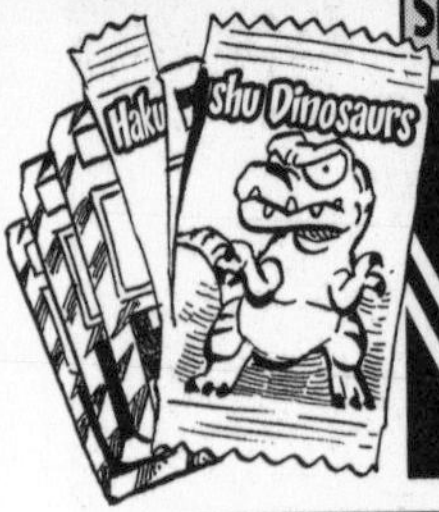
Hakushu Dinosaurs

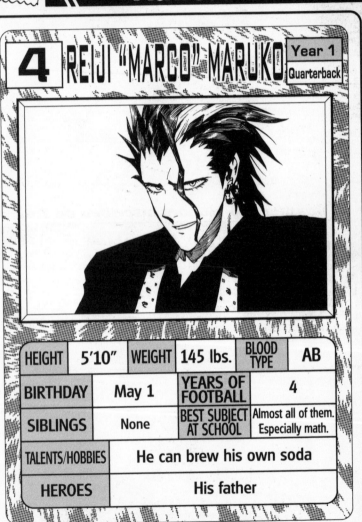

4 REIJI "MARCO" MARUKO

Year 1

Quarterback

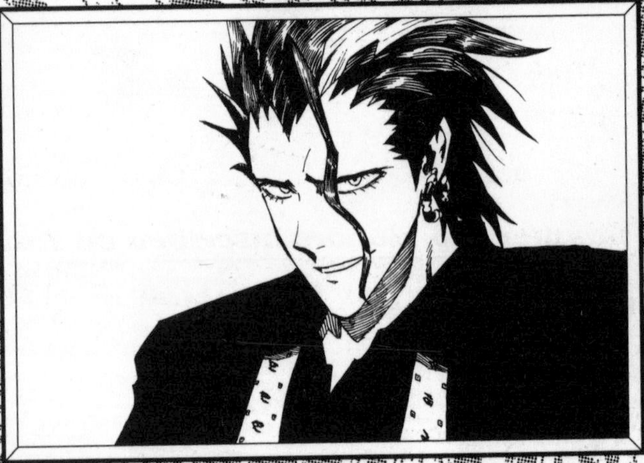

HEIGHT	5'10"	WEIGHT	145 lbs.	BLOOD TYPE	AB
BIRTHDAY	May 1		YEARS OF FOOTBALL	4	
SIBLINGS	None		BEST SUBJECT AT SCHOOL	Almost all of them. Especially math.	
TALENTS/HOBBIES	He can brew his own soda				
HEROES	His father				

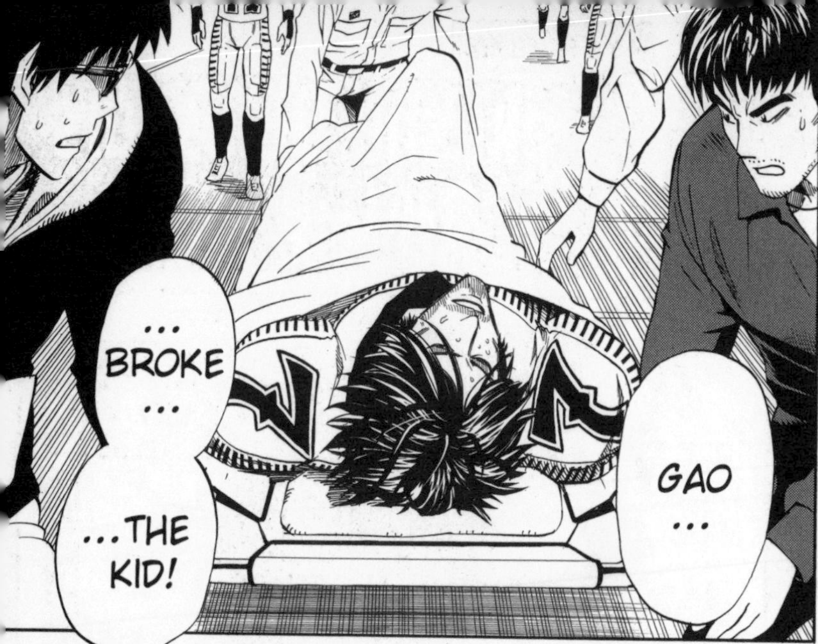
GAO ...
... BROKE ...
...THE KID!

Chapter 246 Honors Inscribed on Your Tomb

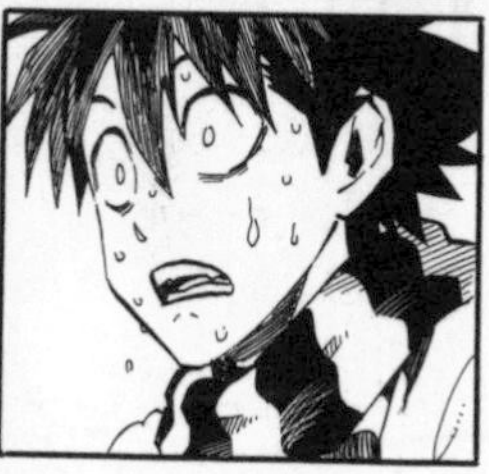
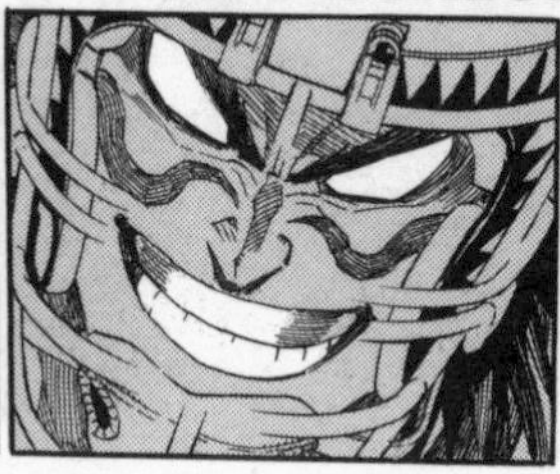
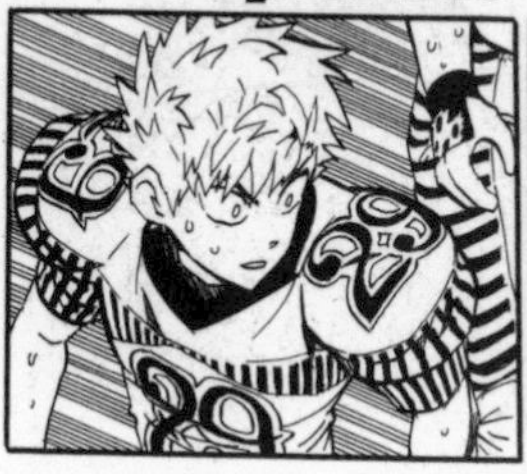
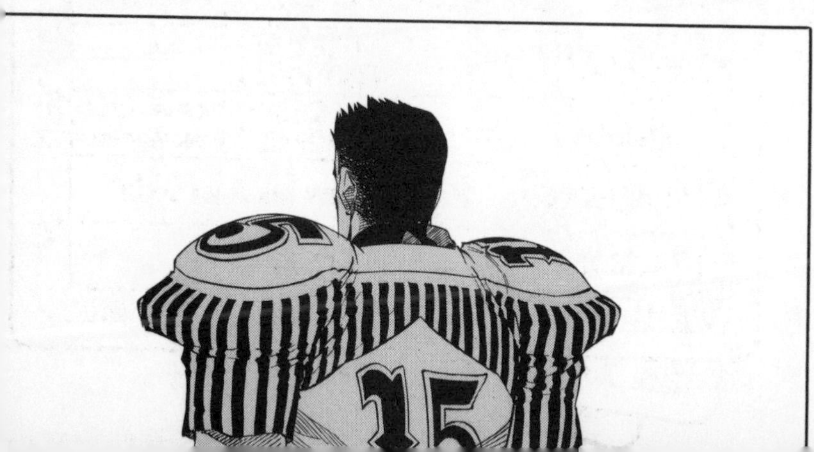

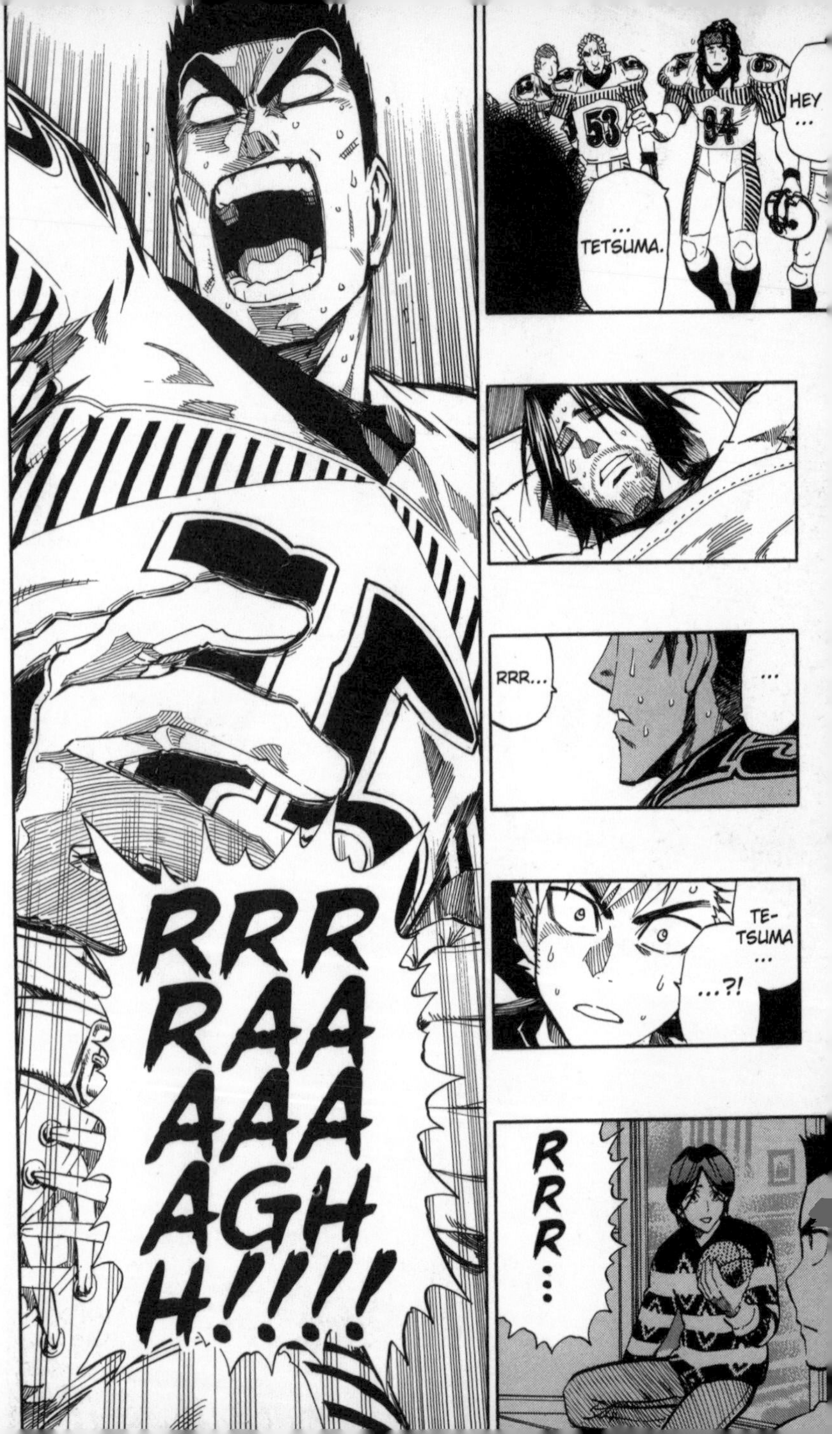
HEY ...
... TETSUMA.
...
RRR...
TE-TSUMA ...
...?!
RRR...
RRRRAAAAAAAGHH!!!!

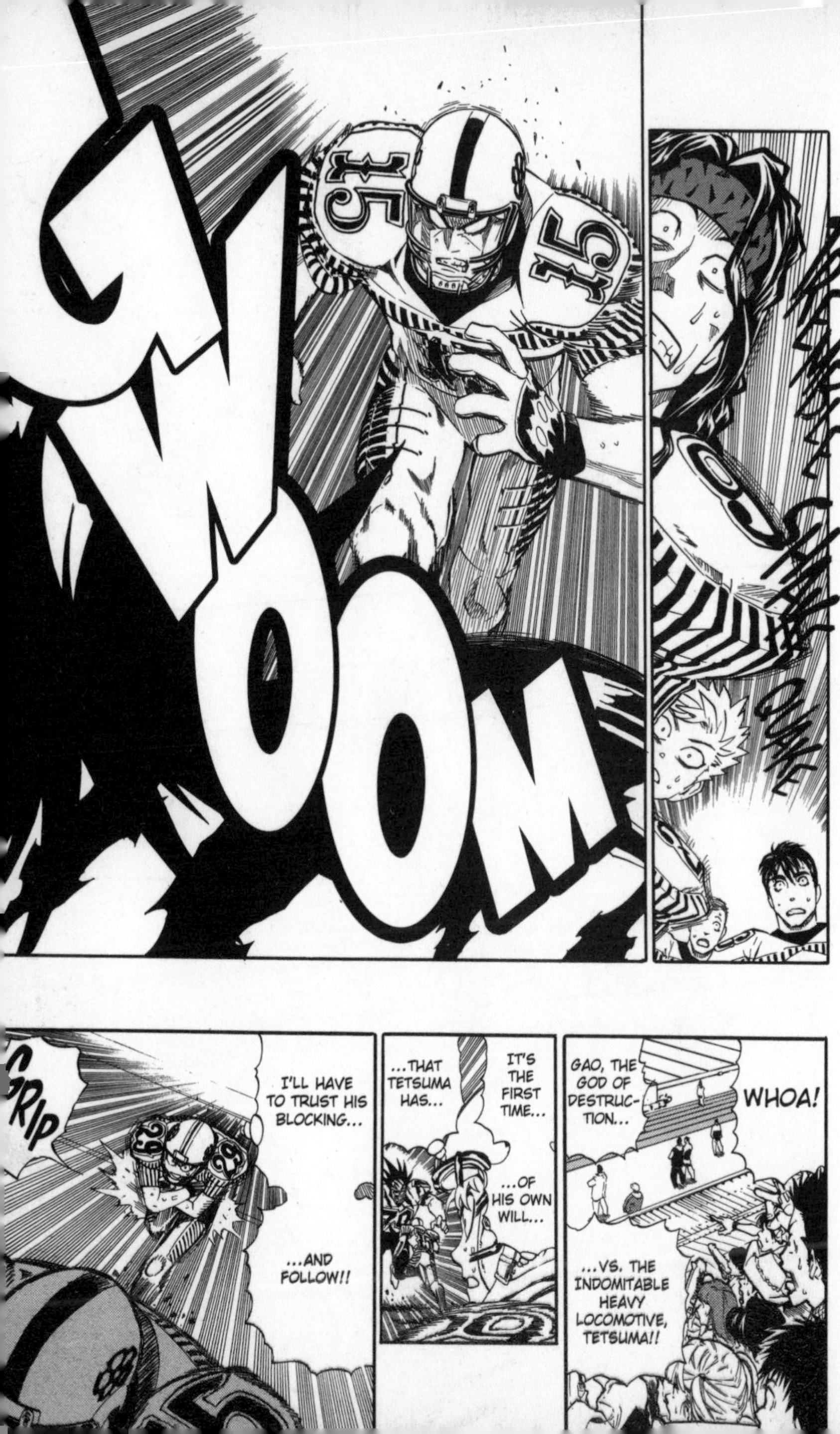
TREMBLE SHAKE QUAKE
WOOM
WHOA!
GAO, THE GOD OF DESTRUC- TION...
...VS. THE INDOMITABLE HEAVY LOCOMOTIVE, TETSUMA!!
IT'S THE FIRST TIME...
...THAT TETSUMA HAS...
...OF HIS OWN WILL...
GRIP
I'LL HAVE TO TRUST HIS BLOCKING...
...AND FOLLOW!!

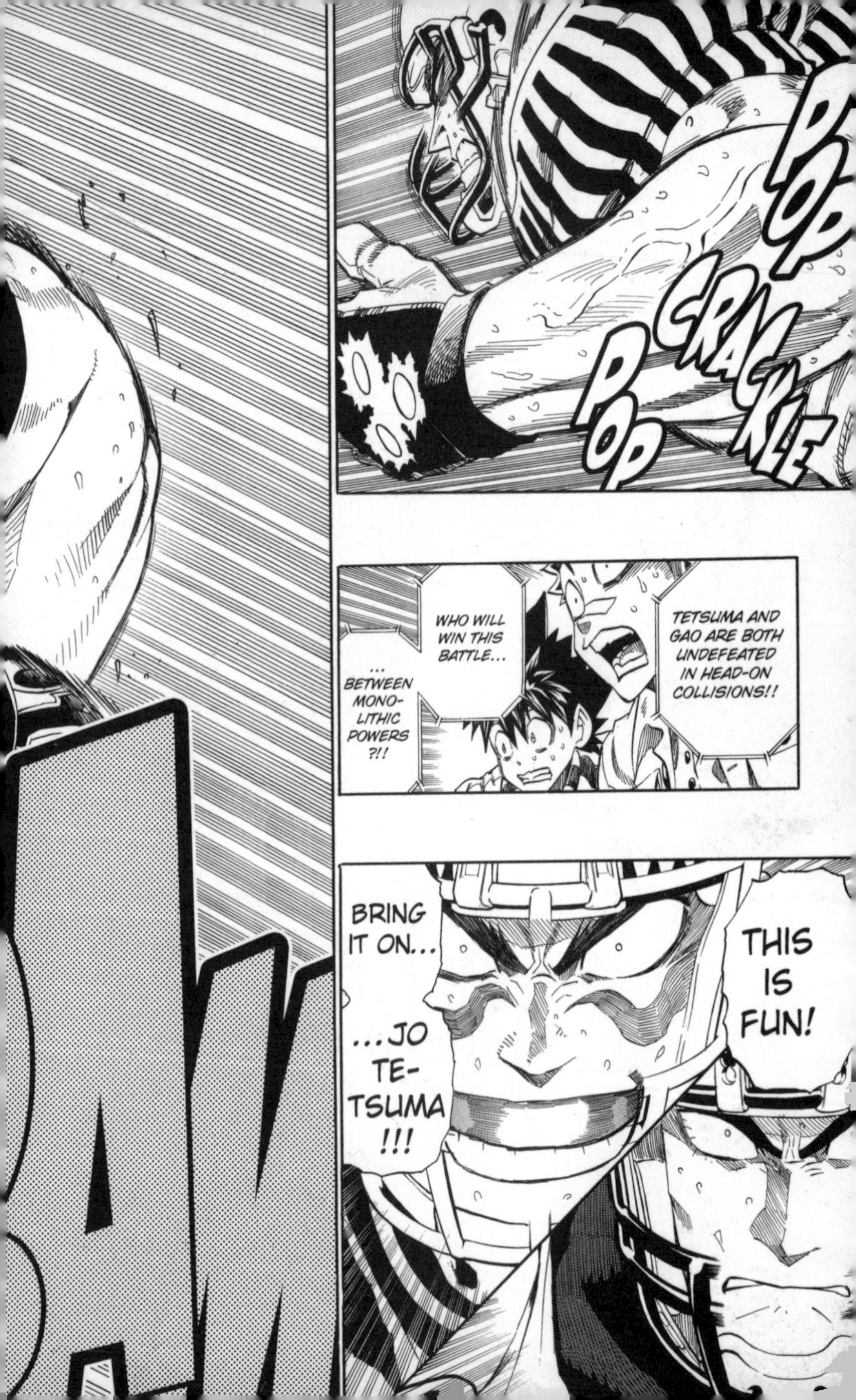
POP
CRACKLE
POP
TETSUMA AND GAO ARE BOTH UNDEFEATED IN HEAD-ON COLLISIONS!!
WHO WILL WIN THIS BATTLE...
...BETWEEN MONO-LITHIC POWERS?!!
THIS IS FUN!
BRING IT ON...
...JO TE-TSUMA!!!

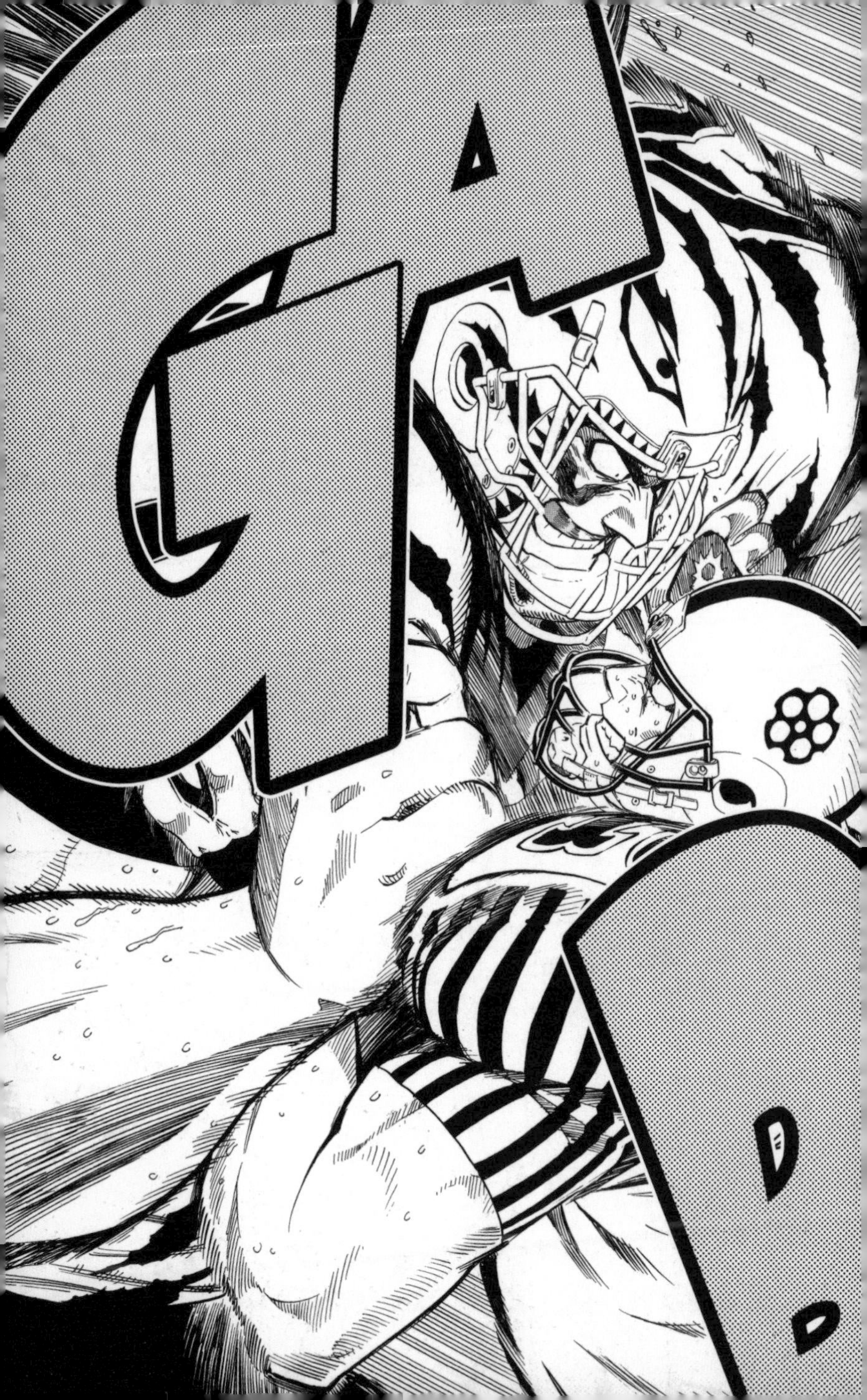

EYE SHIELD 21

Chapter 246
Honors Inscribed on Your Tomb

ROAR

RAH RAH RAH

TMP TMP TMP TMP TMP TMP

DINOSAURS 64

TOTAL

GUNMEN 14

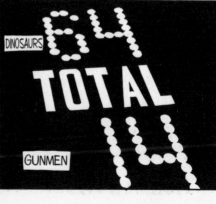

...MA!!

TETSU...

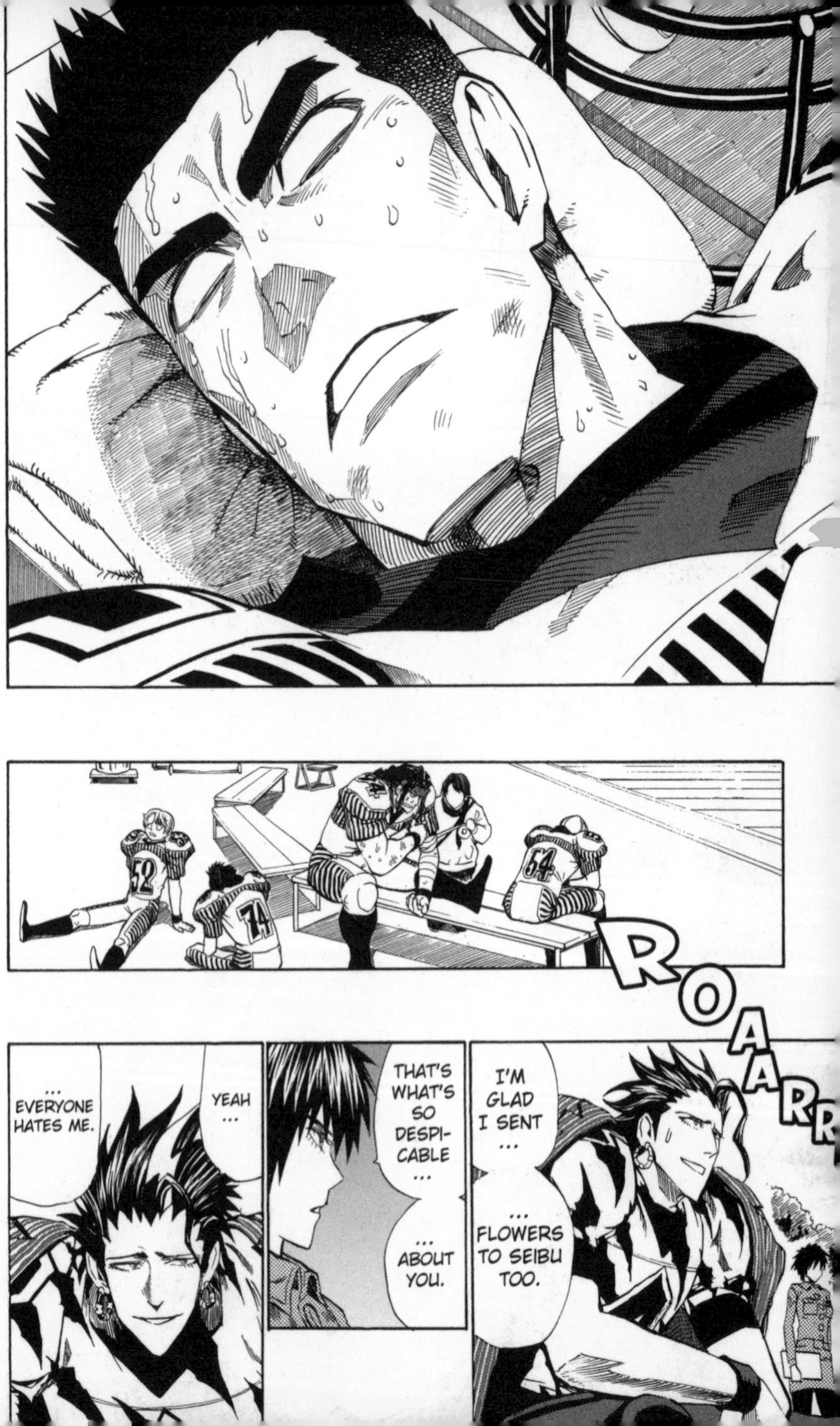
ROAARR
I'M GLAD I SENT ...
... FLOWERS TO SEIBU TOO.
THAT'S WHAT'S SO DESPICABLE ...
... ABOUT YOU.
YEAH ...
... EVERYONE HATES ME.

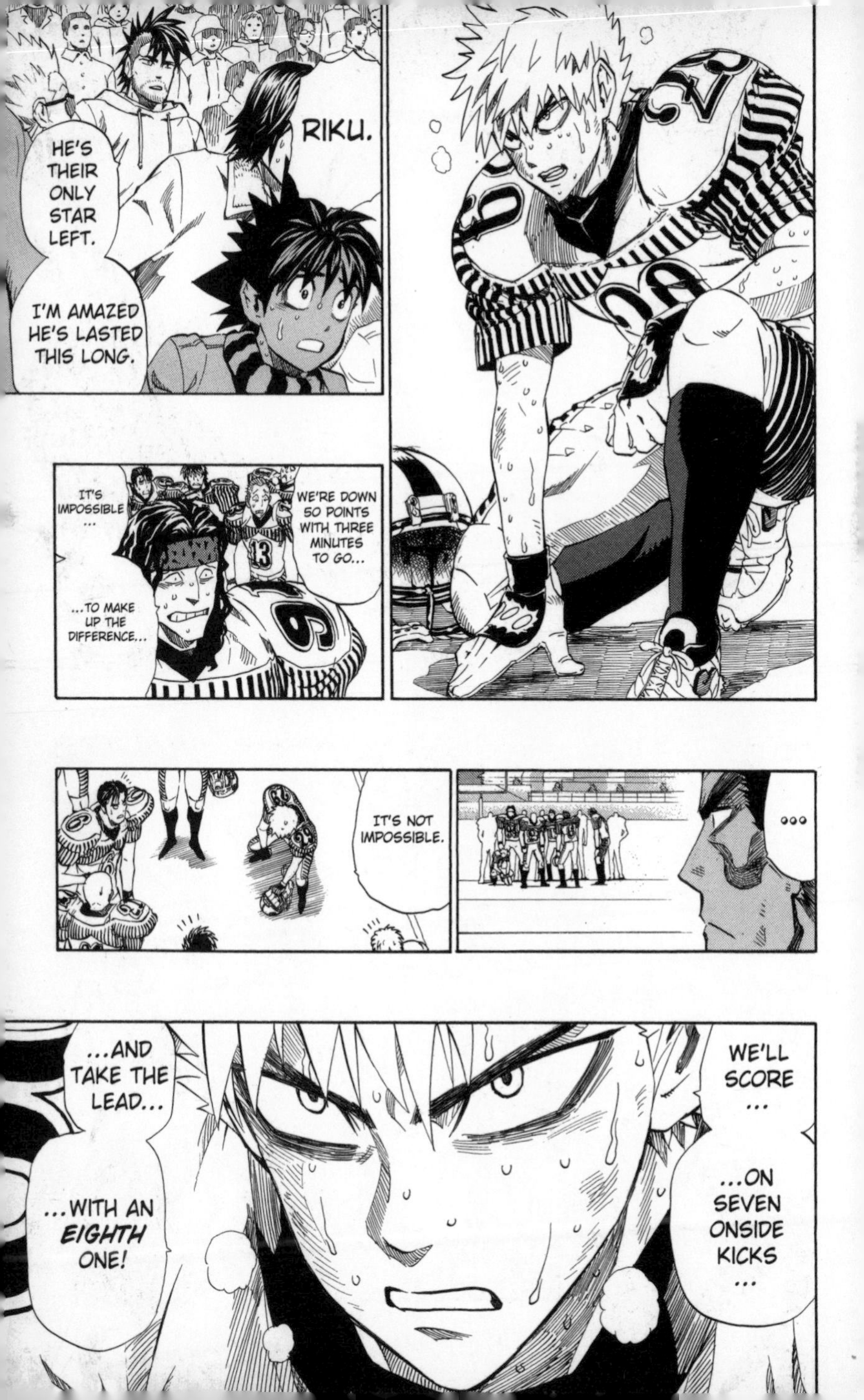
RIKU.
HE'S THEIR ONLY STAR LEFT.
I'M AMAZED HE'S LASTED THIS LONG.
WE'RE DOWN 50 POINTS WITH THREE MINUTES TO GO...
IT'S IMPOSSIBLE...
...TO MAKE UP THE DIFFERENCE...
...
IT'S NOT IMPOSSIBLE.
WE'LL SCORE...
...ON SEVEN ONSIDE KICKS...
...AND TAKE THE LEAD...
...WITH AN *EIGHTH* ONE!

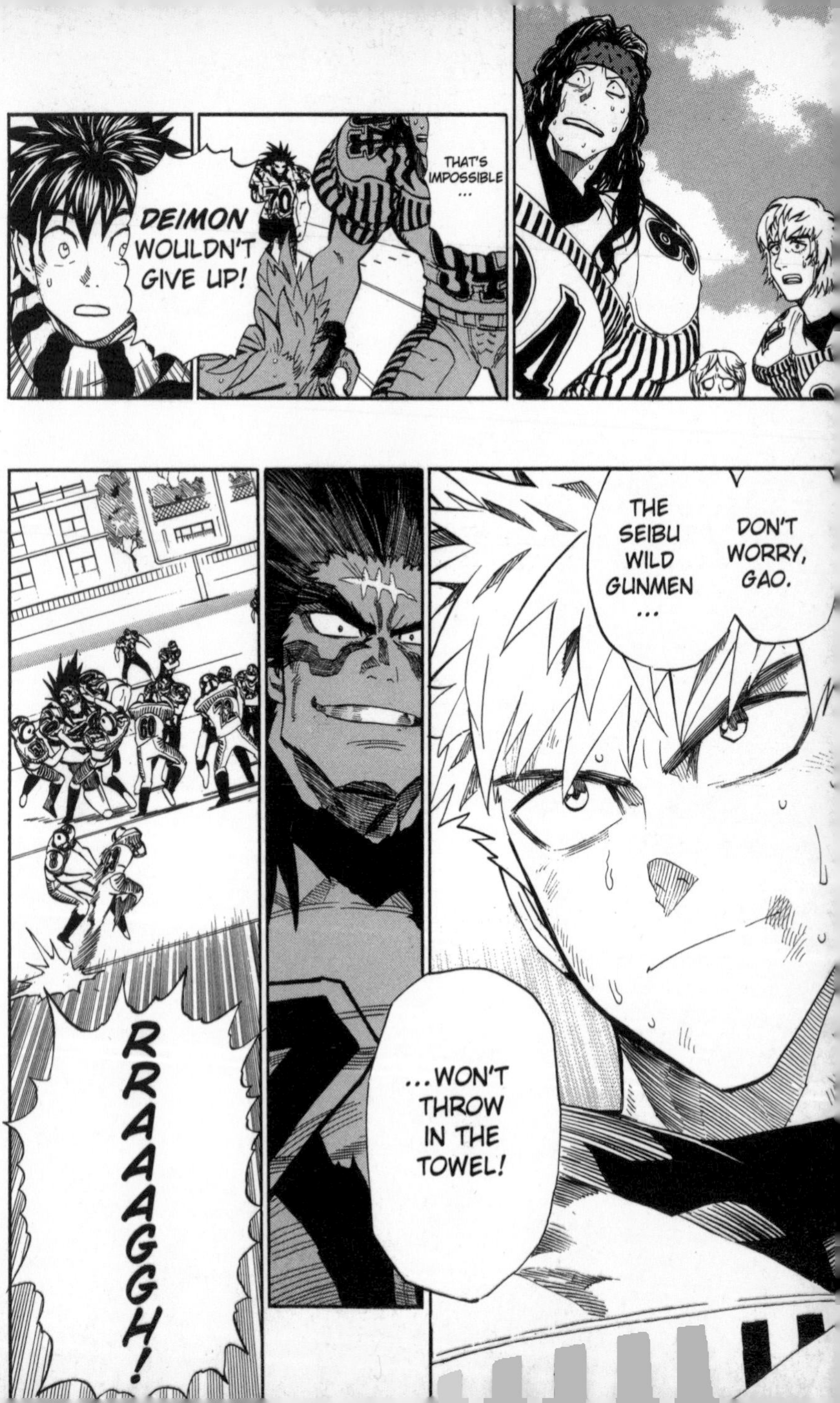
THAT'S IMPOSSIBLE ...
DEIMON WOULDN'T GIVE UP!
DON'T WORRY, GAO.
THE SEIBU WILD GUNMEN ...
...WON'T THROW IN THE TOWEL!
RRAAAGGH!

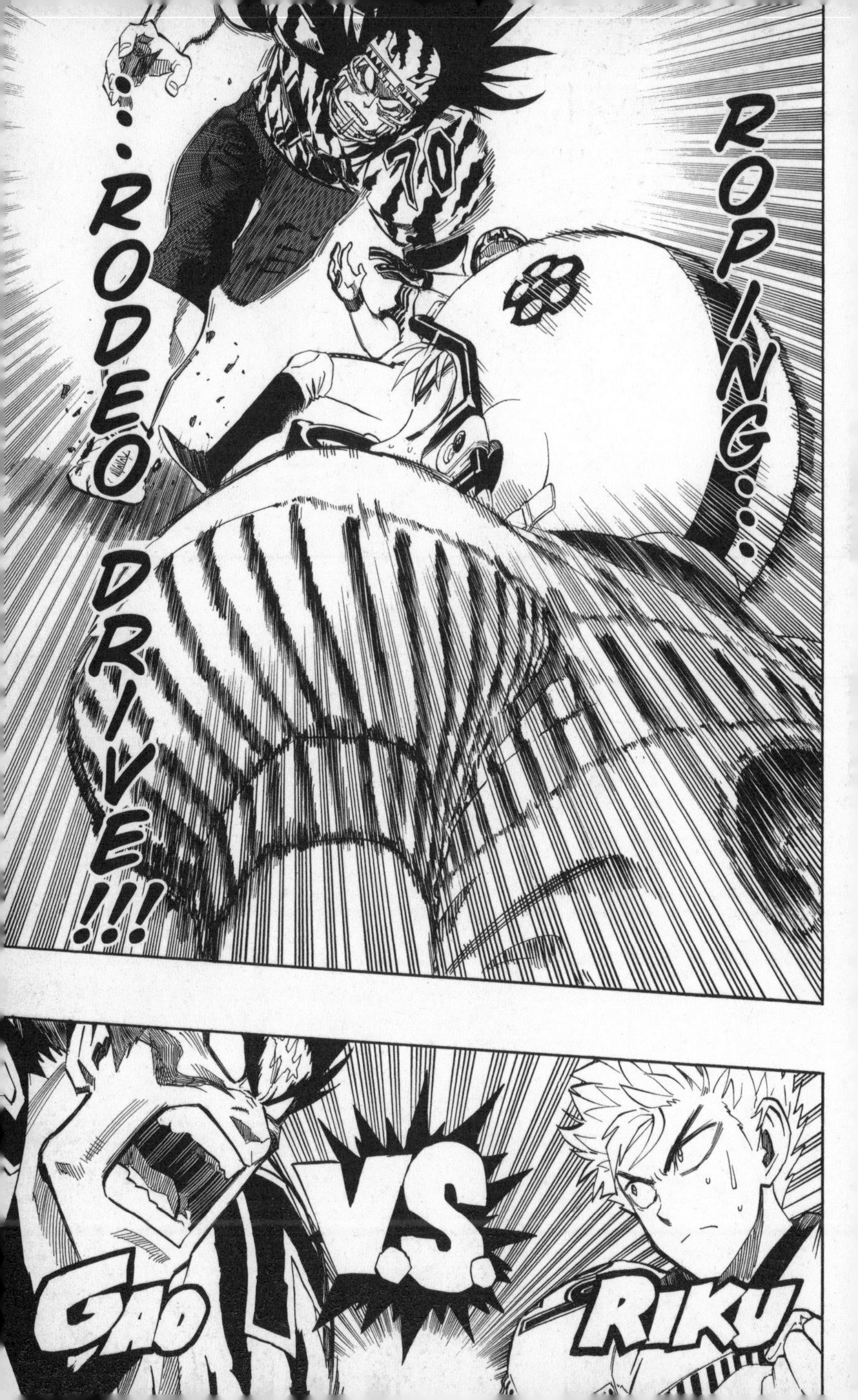
ROPING...
...RODEO DRIVE!!!
GAO
V.S.
RIKU

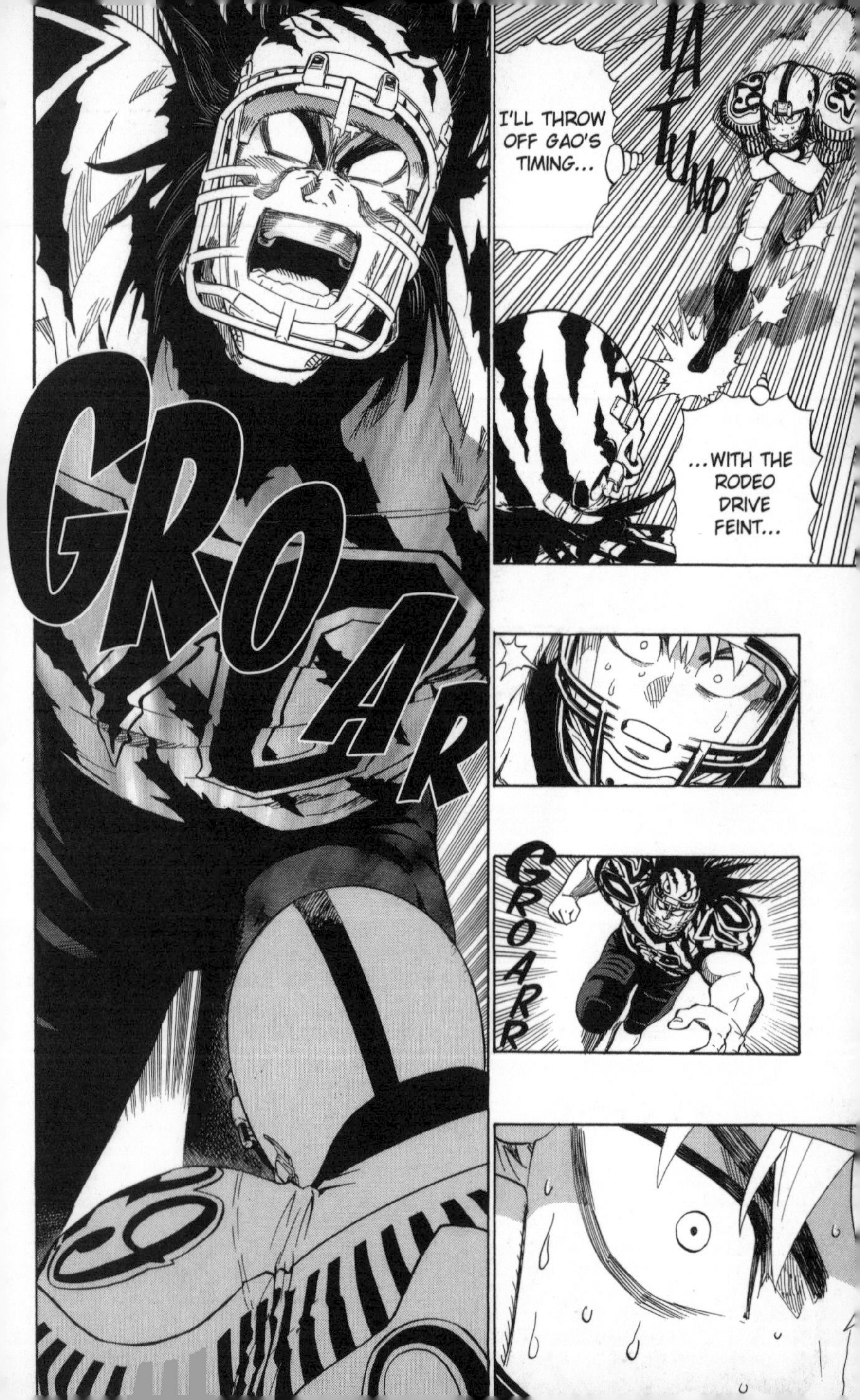
TA TUMP
I'LL THROW OFF GAO'S TIMING...
...WITH THE RODEO DRIVE FEINT...
GROARR
GROAR

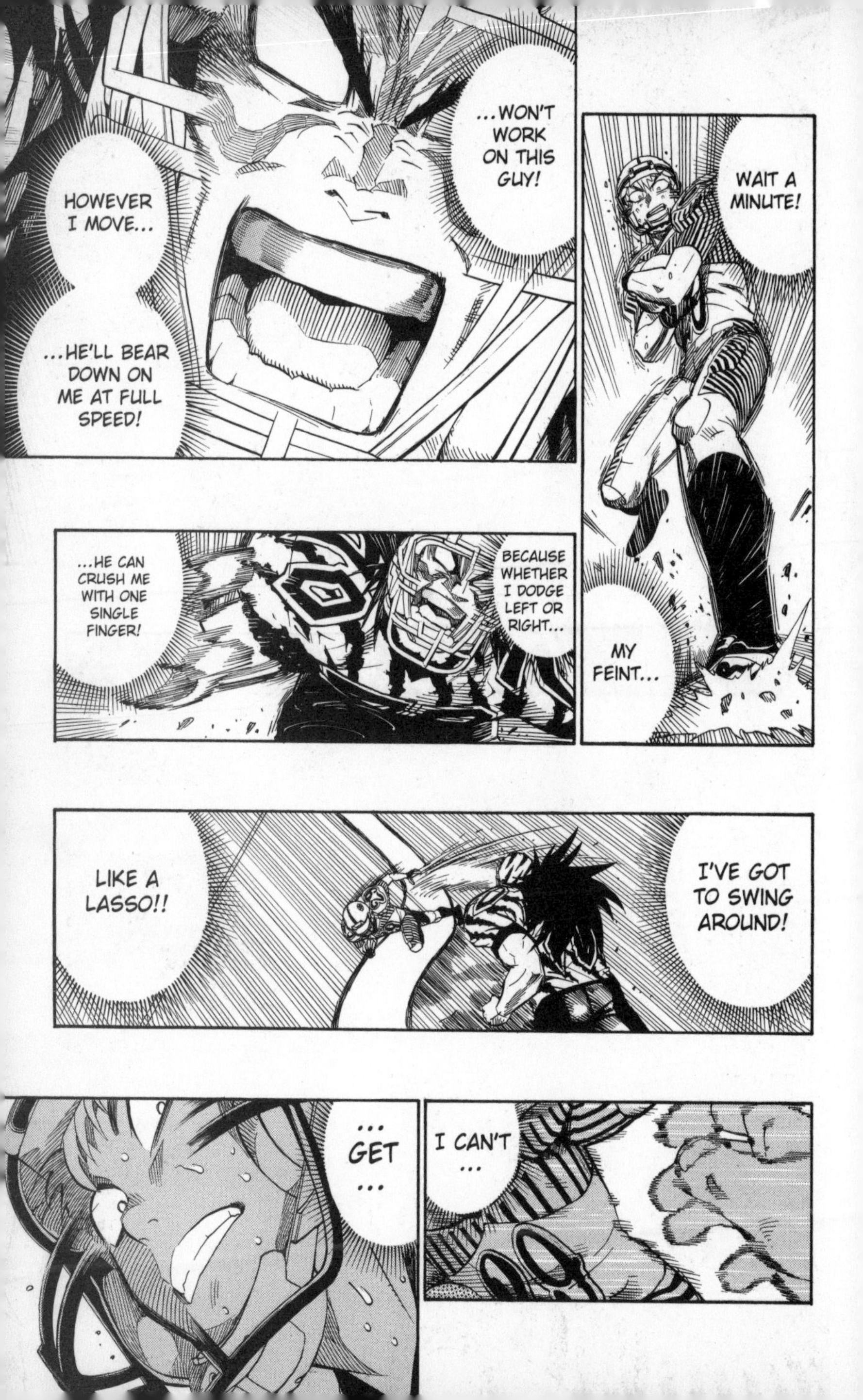
WAIT A MINUTE!
MY FEINT...
...WON'T WORK ON THIS GUY!
HOWEVER I MOVE...
...HE'LL BEAR DOWN ON ME AT FULL SPEED!
BECAUSE WHETHER I DODGE LEFT OR RIGHT...
...HE CAN CRUSH ME WITH ONE SINGLE FINGER!
I'VE GOT TO SWING AROUND!
LIKE A LASSO!!
I CAN'T ...
... GET ...

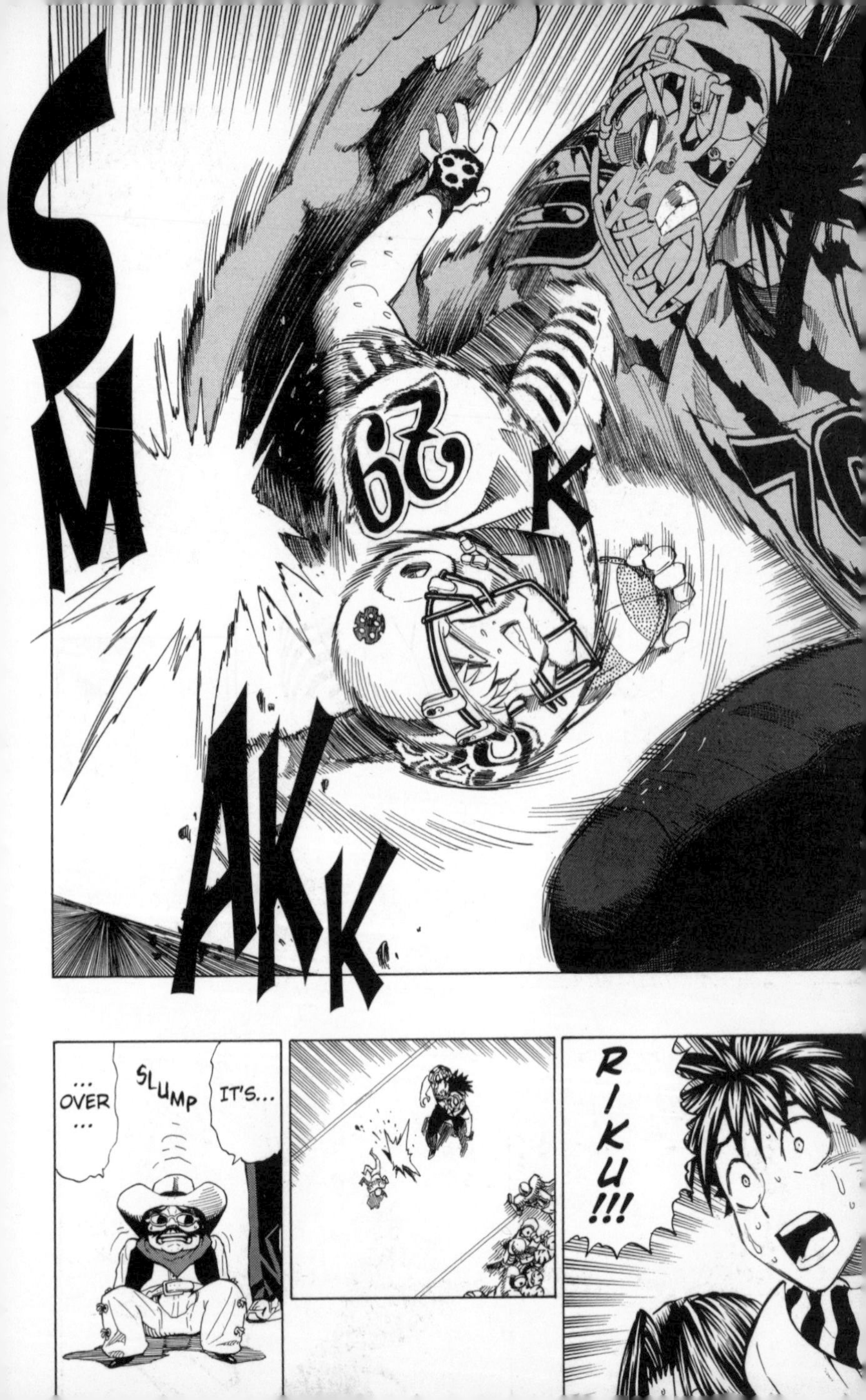
SMAKK
RIKU!!!
IT'S...
SLUMP
...OVER...

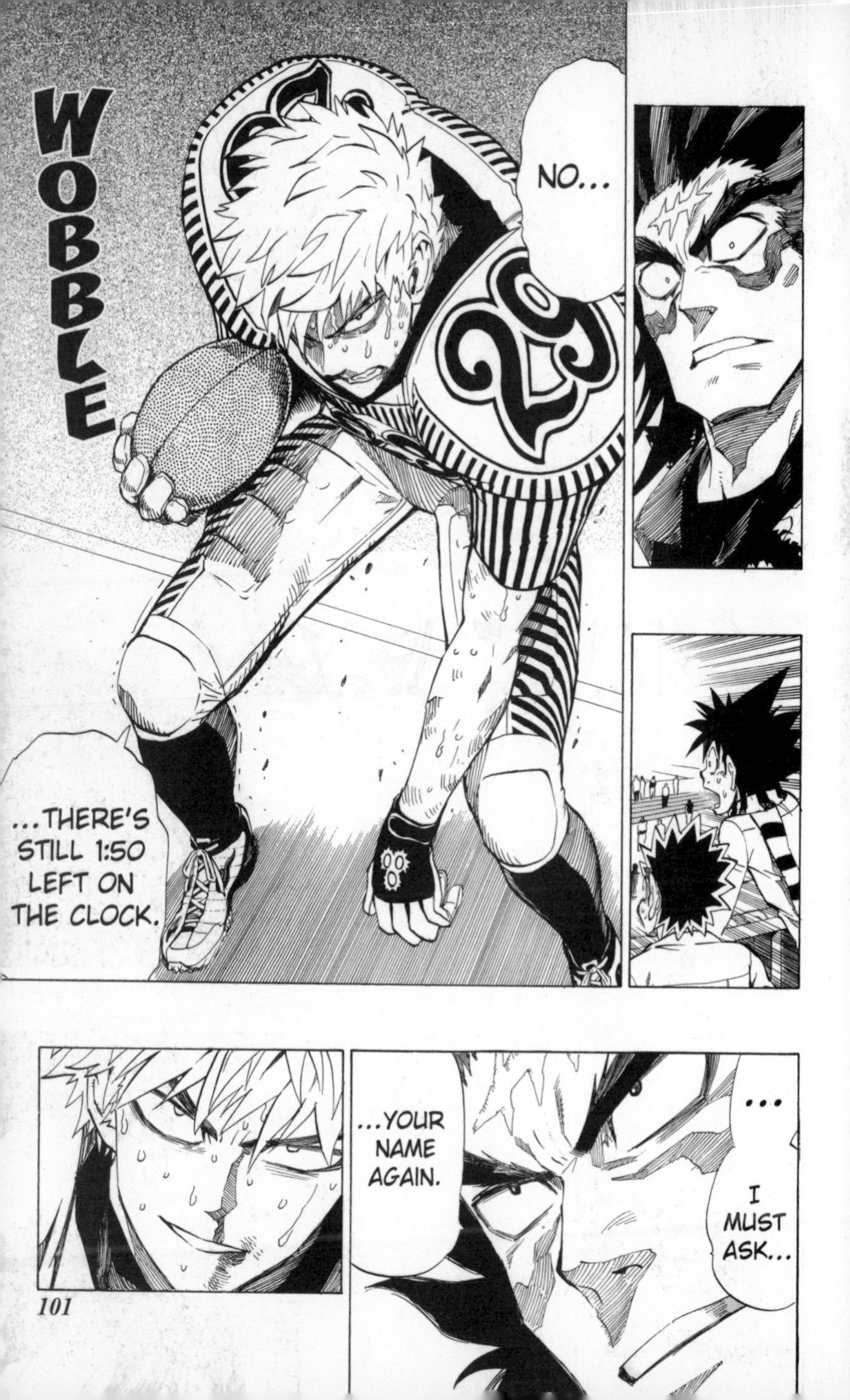
NO...
WOBBLE
...THERE'S STILL 1:50 LEFT ON THE CLOCK.
...
I MUST ASK...
...YOUR NAME AGAIN.

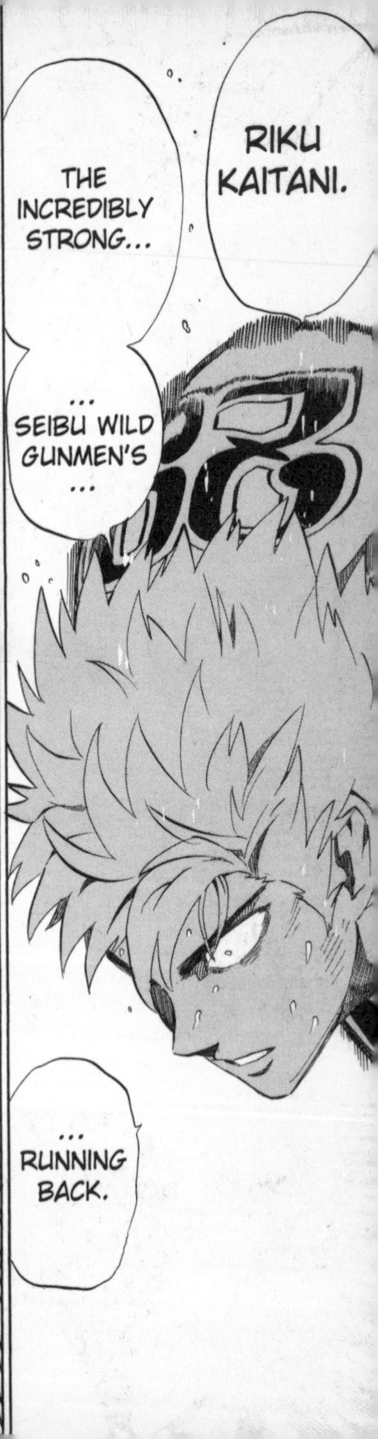
RIKU KAITANI.
THE INCREDIBLY STRONG...
... SEIBU WILD GUNMEN'S ...
... RUNNING BACK.

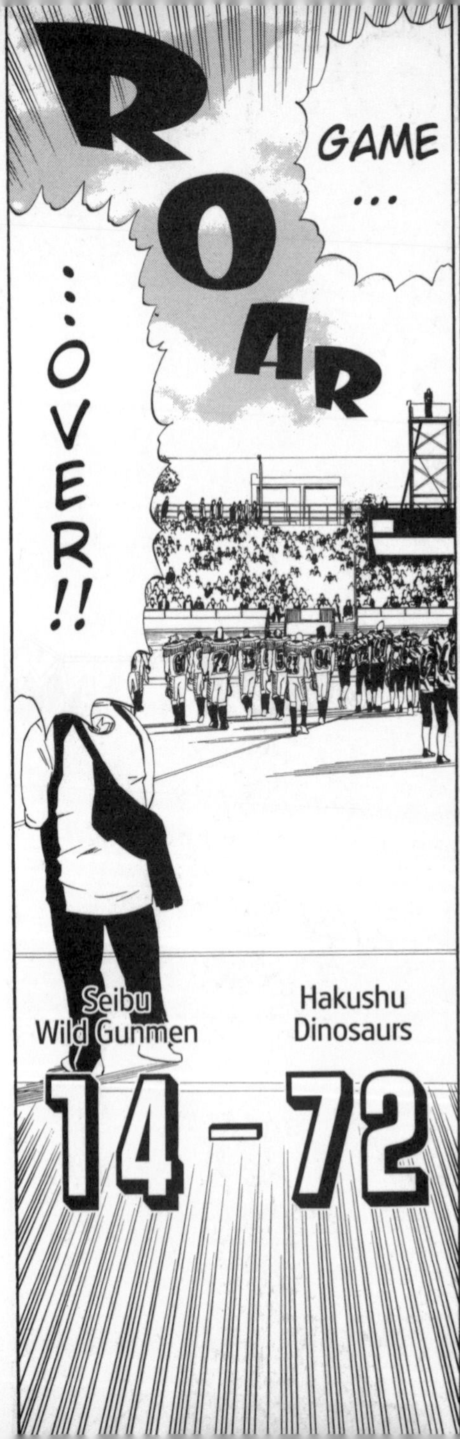
ROAR
GAME ...
...OVER!!
Seibu Wild Gunmen
Hakushu Dinosaurs
14 - 72

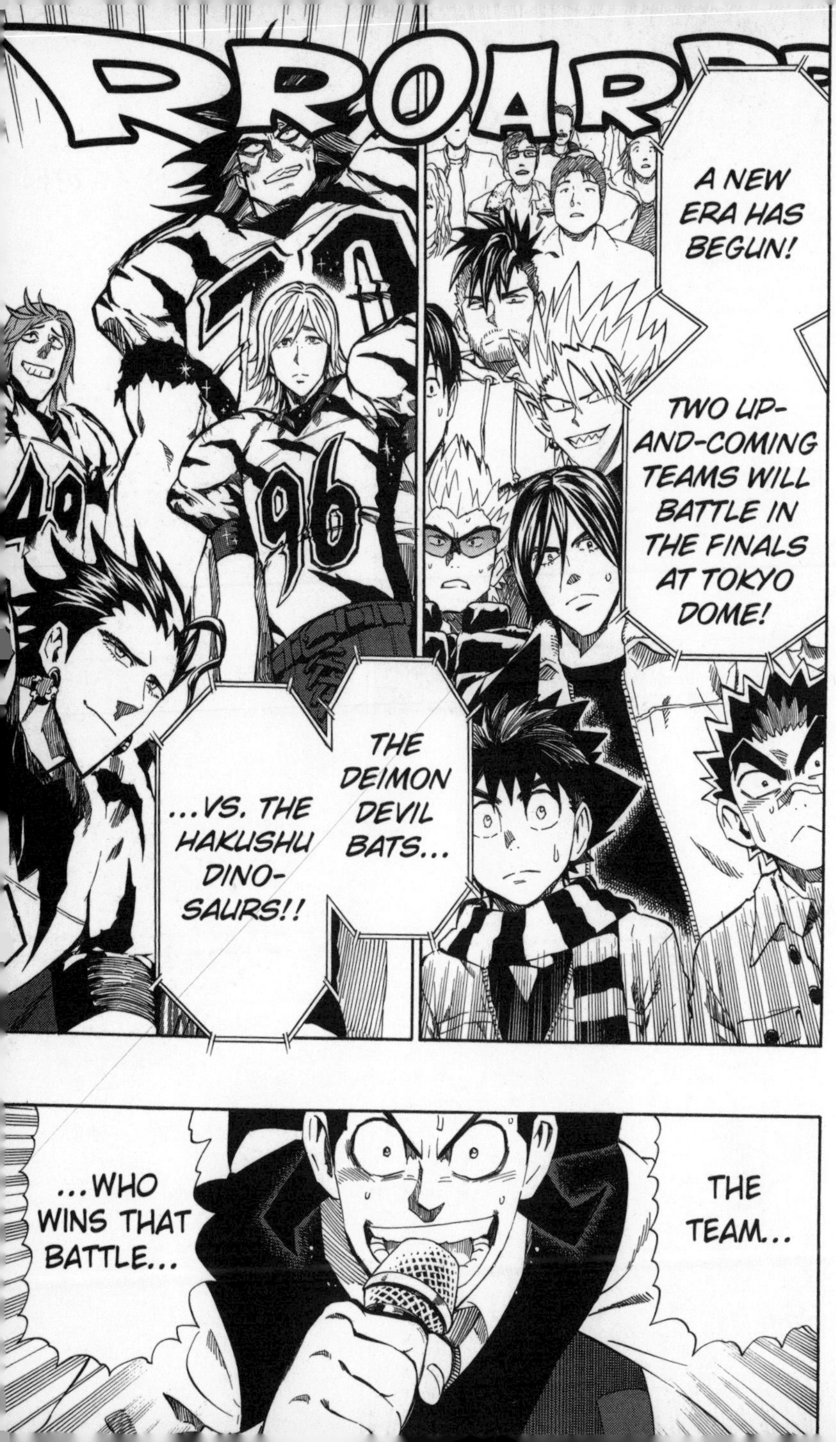
RROAR
A NEW ERA HAS BEGUN!
TWO UP-AND-COMING TEAMS WILL BATTLE IN THE FINALS AT TOKYO DOME!
THE DEIMON DEVIL BATS...
...VS. THE HAKUSHU DINOSAURS!!
THE TEAM...
...WHO WINS THAT BATTLE...

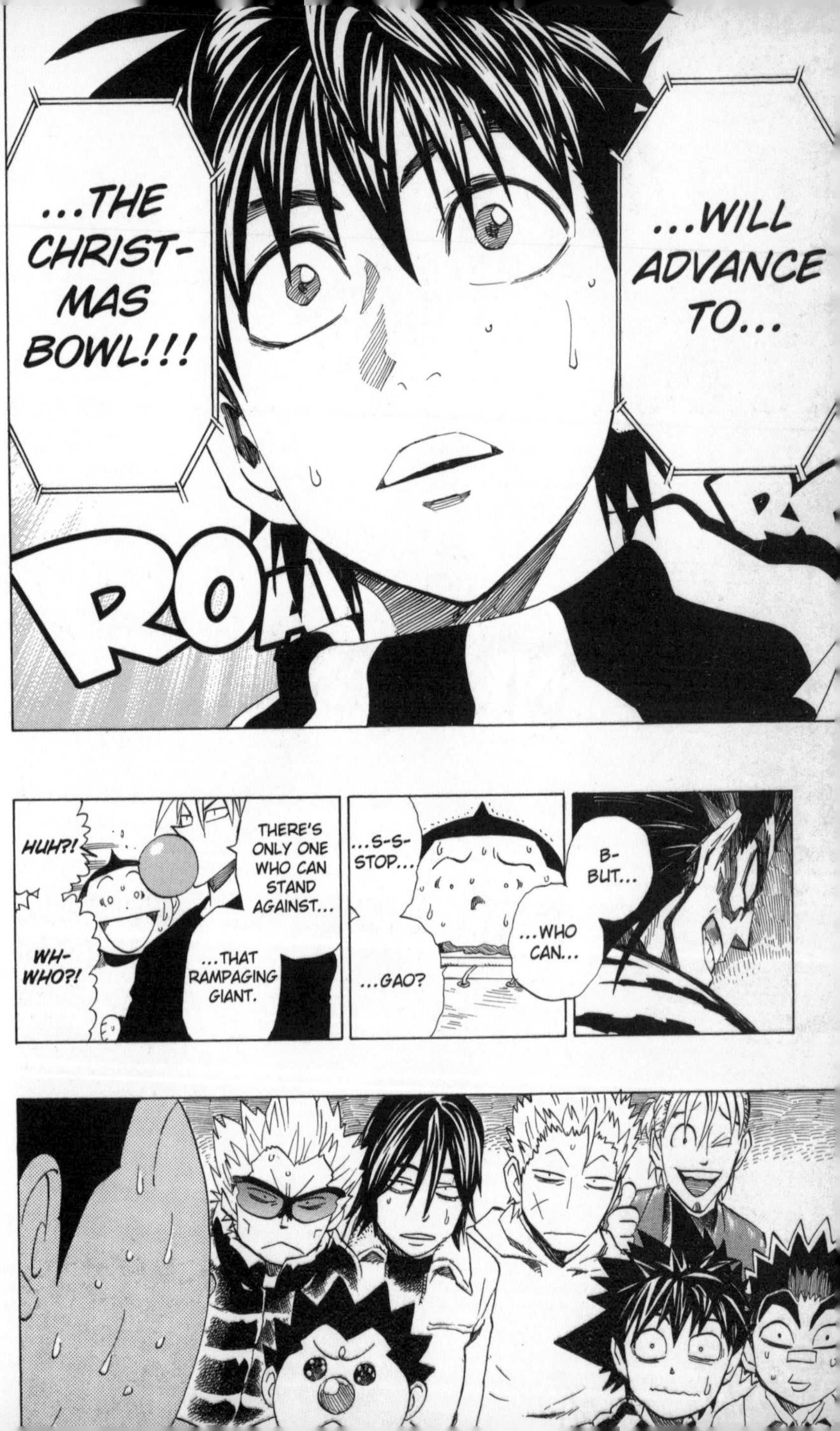
...WILL ADVANCE TO...
...THE CHRIST-MAS BOWL!!!
B- BUT...
...WHO CAN...
...S-S-STOP...
...GAO?
THERE'S ONLY ONE WHO CAN STAND AGAINST...
HUH?!
...THAT RAMPAGING GIANT.
WH- WHO?!

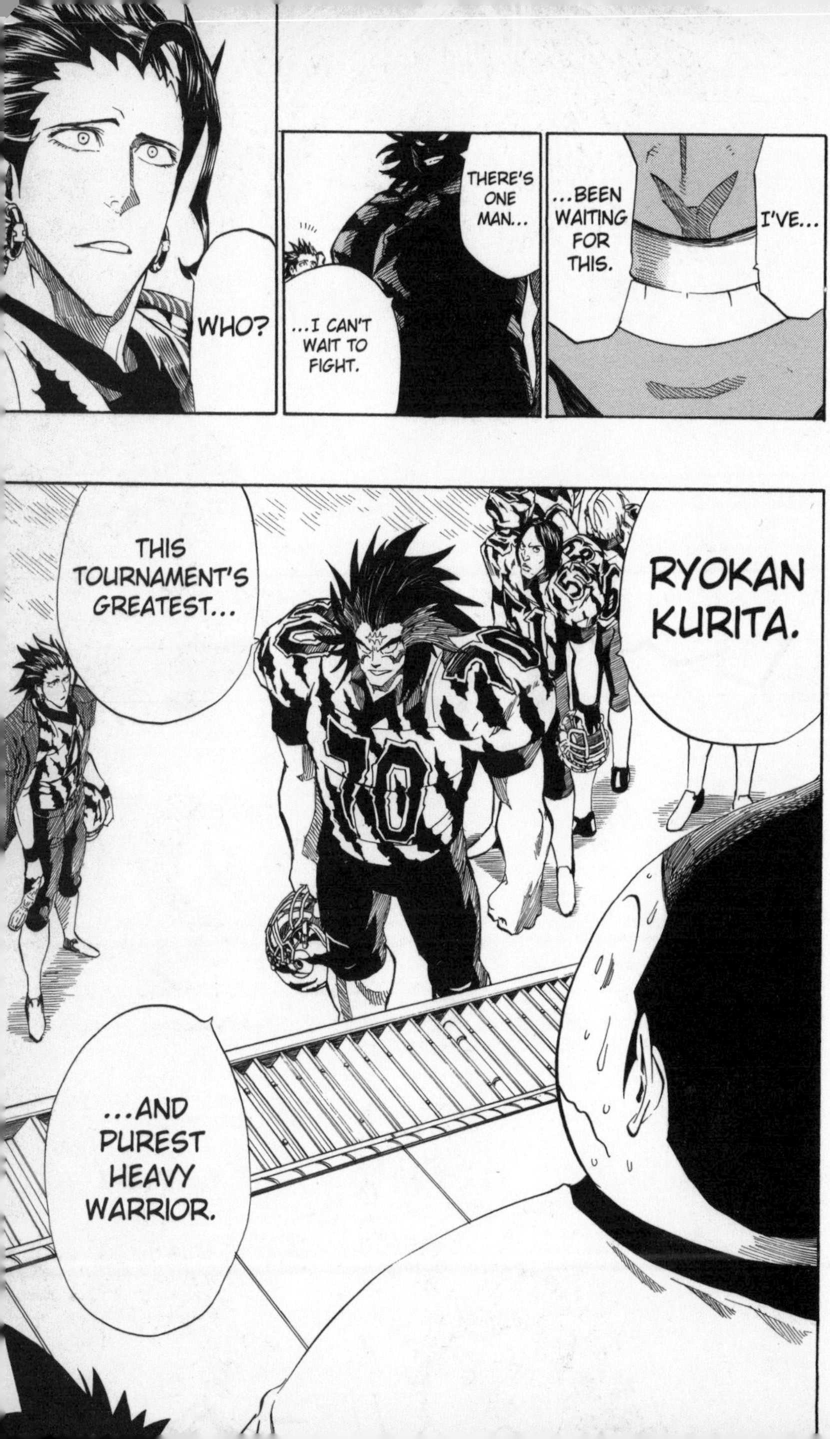
I'VE...
...BEEN WAITING FOR THIS.
THERE'S ONE MAN...
...I CAN'T WAIT TO FIGHT.
WHO?
RYOKAN KURITA.
THIS TOURNAMENT'S GREATEST...
...AND PUREST HEAVY WARRIOR.

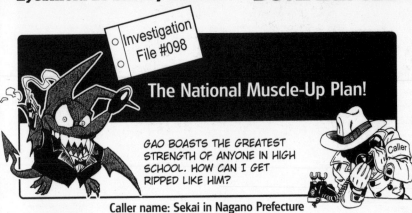

Investigation File #098

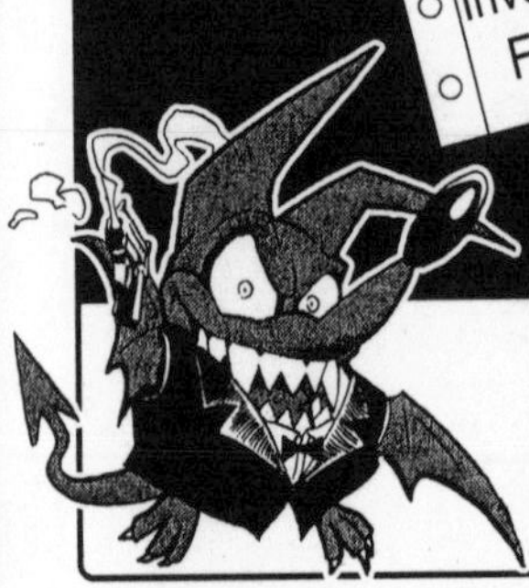

The National Muscle-Up Plan!

GAO BOASTS THE GREATEST STRENGTH OF ANYONE IN HIGH SCHOOL. HOW CAN I GET RIPPED LIKE HIM?

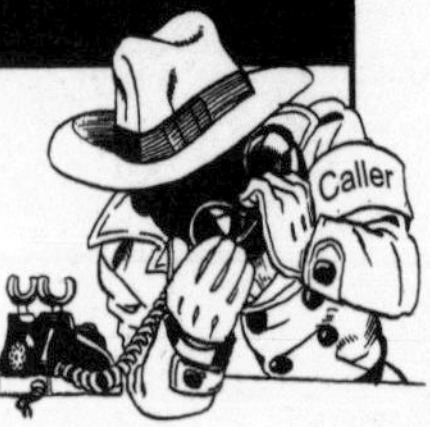
Caller

Caller name: Sekai in Nagano Prefecture

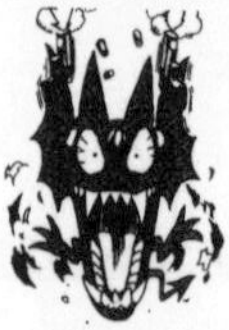

WHEN IT COMES TO BEEFING UP, NOTHING BEATS ***STRENUOUS WEIGHT-LIFTING***.

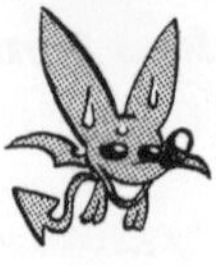

BUT YOU SHOULDN'T OVERDO IT! ENOUGH WEIGHT THAT YOU CAN ***BARELY MANAGE TEN LIFTS*** IS BEST!

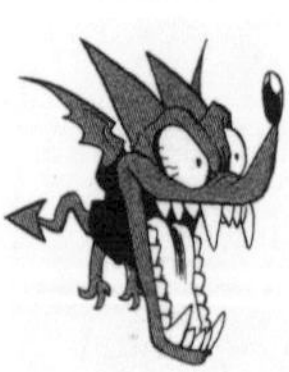

DO ***THREE SETS***, TAKING BREAKS IN BETWEEN!

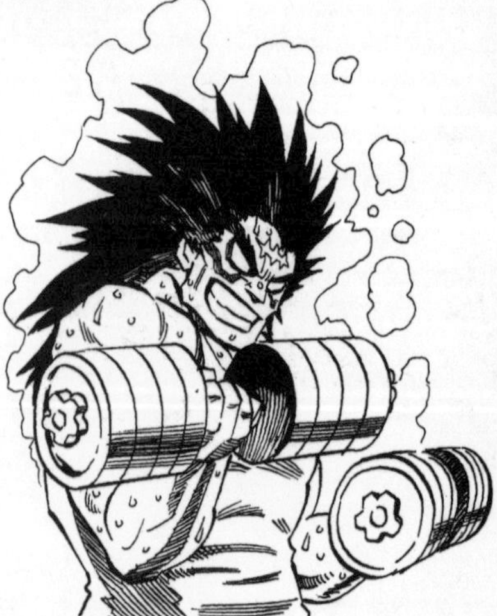

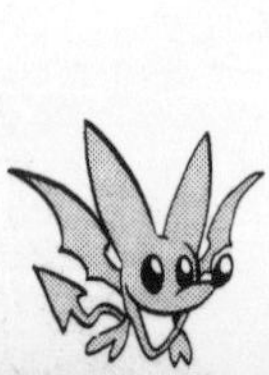

BUT DON'T GET TOO EXCITED! ***DON'T DO IT EVERY DAY!*** DO THREE SETS EVERY TWO OR THREE DAYS! THEN KEEP IT UP OVER TIME! YA-HA!

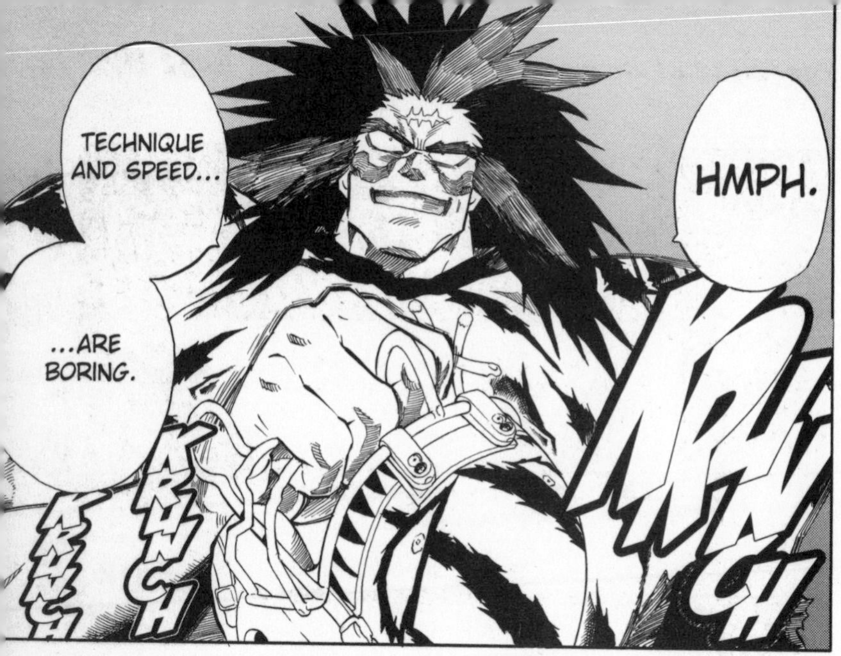
HMPH.
KRUNCH
TECHNIQUE AND SPEED...
...ARE BORING.
KRUNCH
KRUNCH

Chapter 247 Showdown at Tokyo Dome

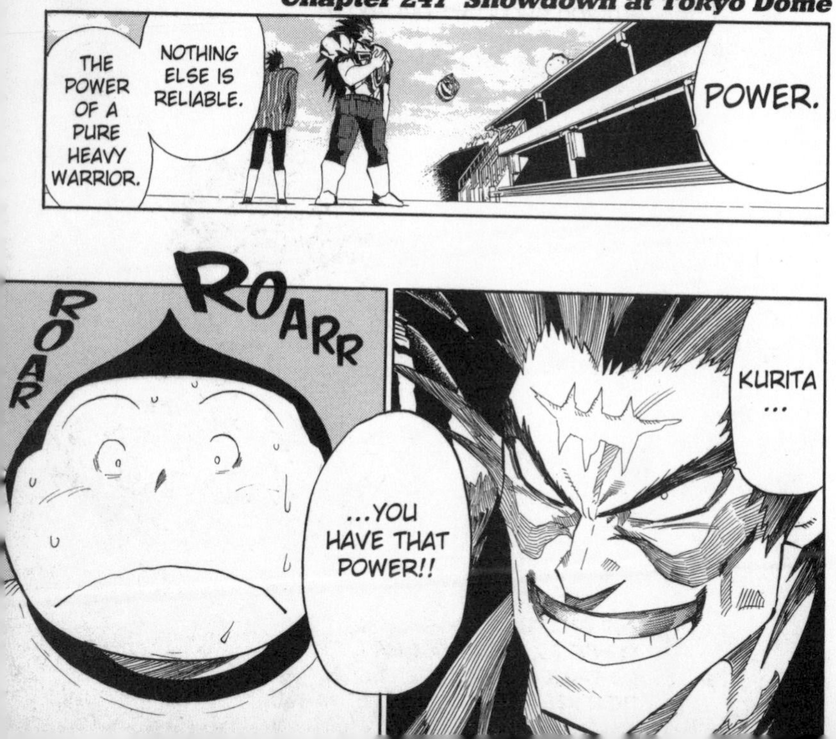
POWER.
NOTHING ELSE IS RELIABLE.
THE POWER OF A PURE HEAVY WARRIOR.
KURITA...
...YOU HAVE THAT POWER!!
ROARR
ROAR

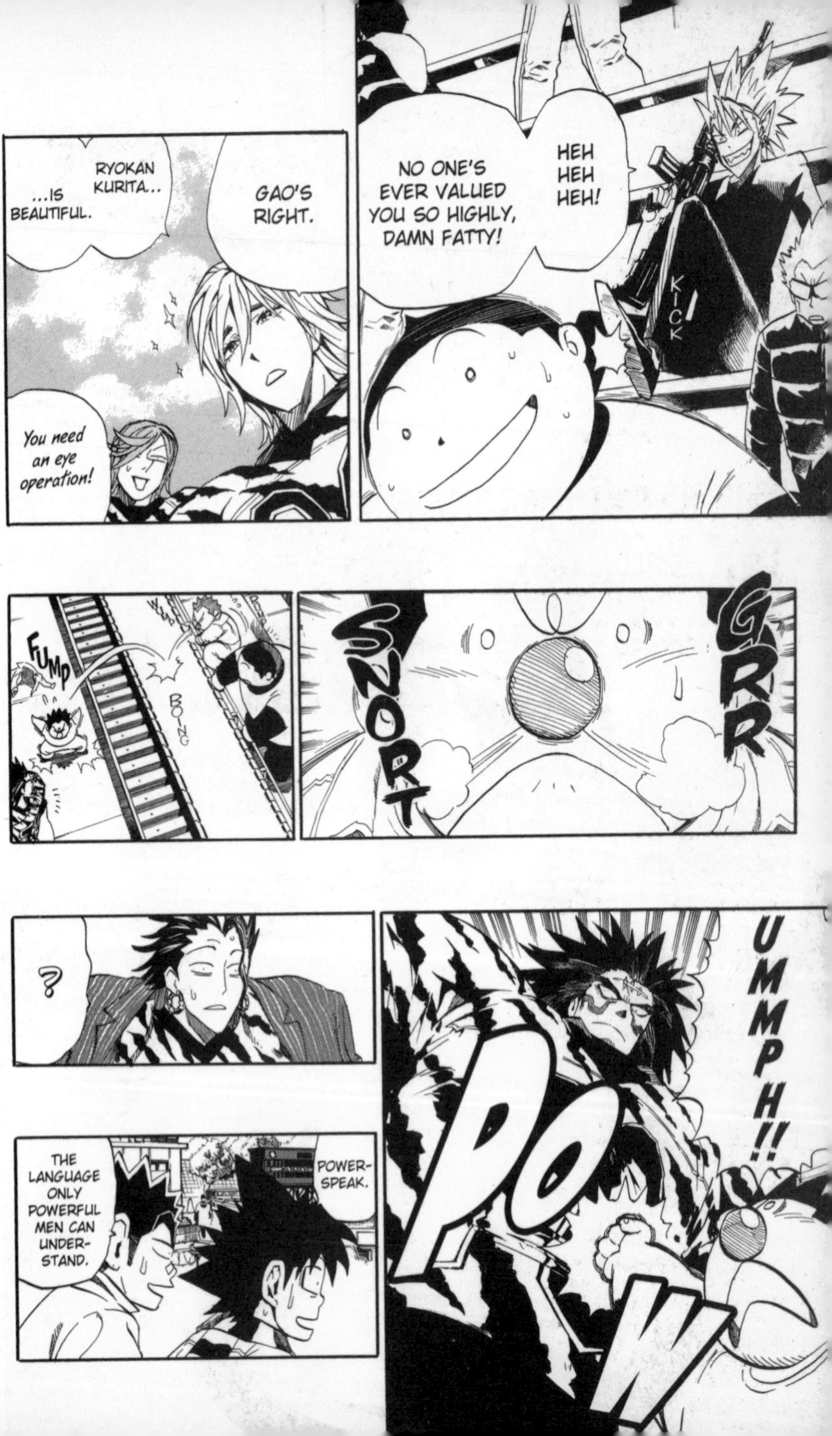
HEH HEH HEH!
NO ONE'S EVER VALUED YOU SO HIGHLY, DAMN FATTY!
KICK
GAO'S RIGHT.
RYOKAN KURITA...
...IS BEAUTIFUL.
You need an eye operation!
GRR
SNORT
BOING
FUMP
UMMPH!!
DOW
?
POWER-SPEAK.
THE LANGUAGE ONLY POWERFUL MEN CAN UNDER-STAND.

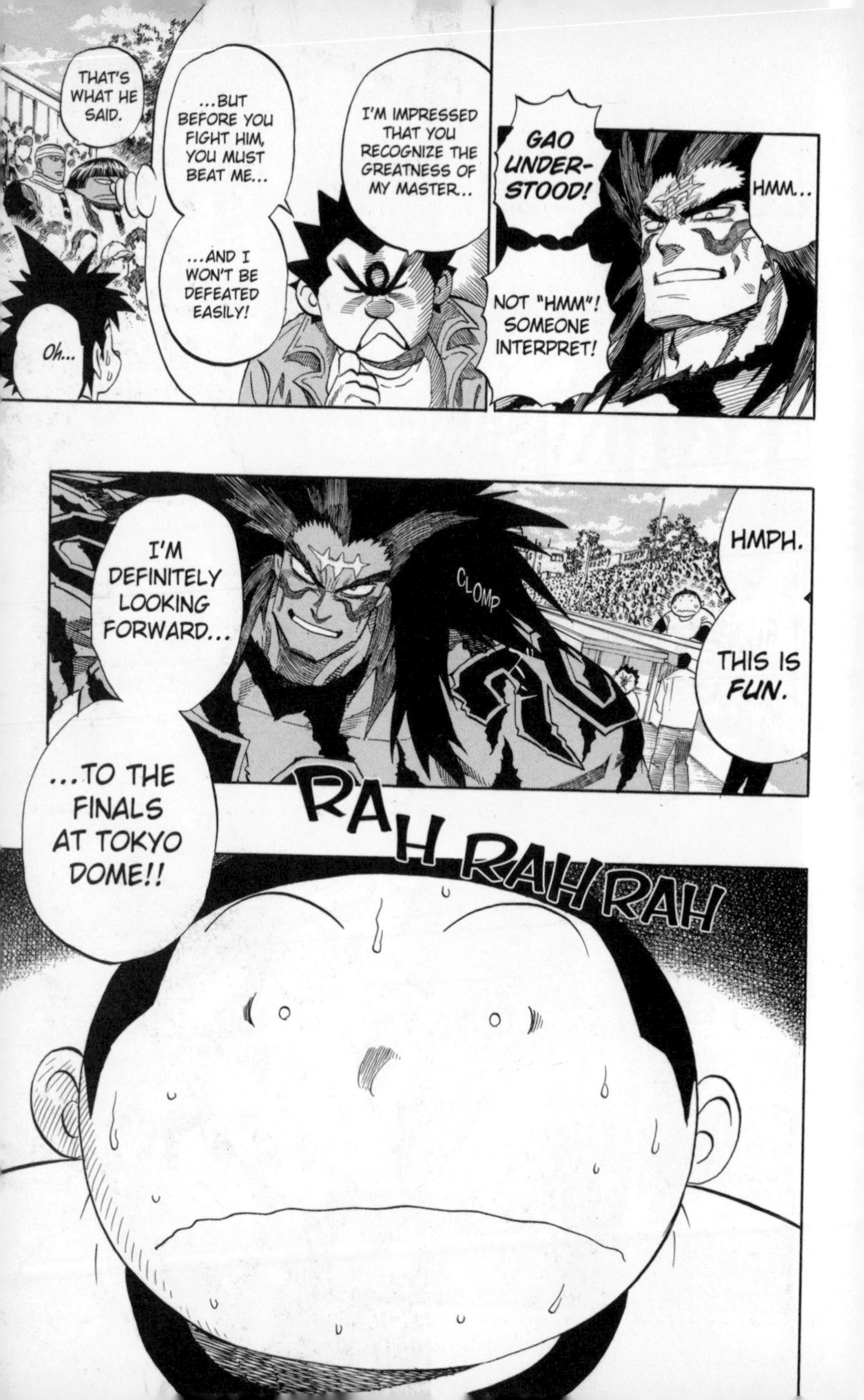
HMM...
GAO UNDERSTOOD!
NOT "HMM"! SOMEONE INTERPRET!
I'M IMPRESSED THAT YOU RECOGNIZE THE GREATNESS OF MY MASTER...
...BUT BEFORE YOU FIGHT HIM, YOU MUST BEAT ME...
...AND I WON'T BE DEFEATED EASILY!
THAT'S WHAT HE SAID.
Oh...
HMPH.
THIS IS FUN.
I'M DEFINITELY LOOKING FORWARD...
CLOMP
...TO THE FINALS AT TOKYO DOME!!
RAH RAH RAH RAH

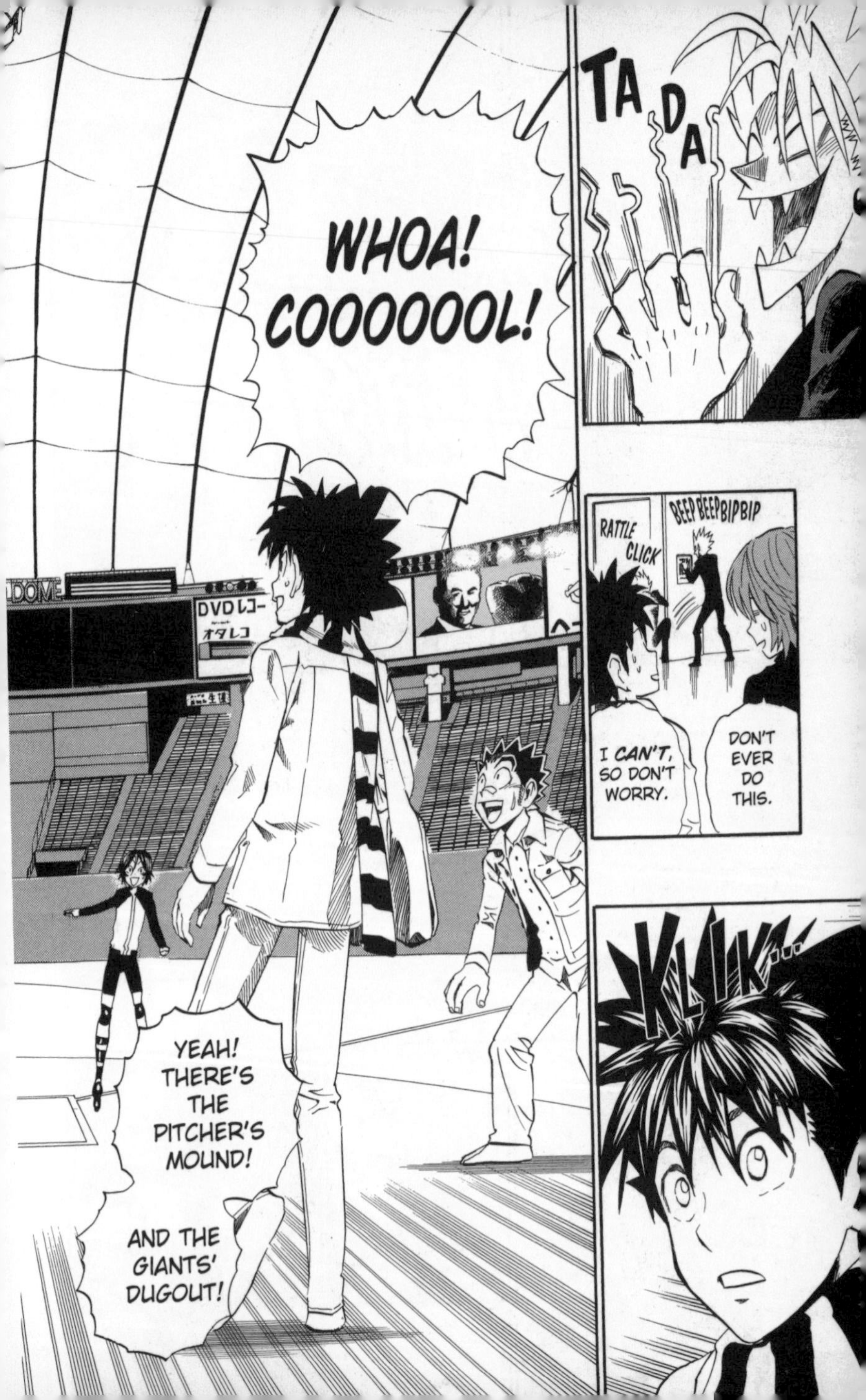
TA DA
BEEP BEEPBIPBIP
RATTLE CLICK
DON'T EVER DO THIS.
I CAN'T, SO DON'T WORRY.
KLIK...
WHOA! COOOOOOL!
DOME
DVDレコー
オタレコ
YEAH! THERE'S THE PITCHER'S MOUND!
AND THE GIANTS' DUGOUT!

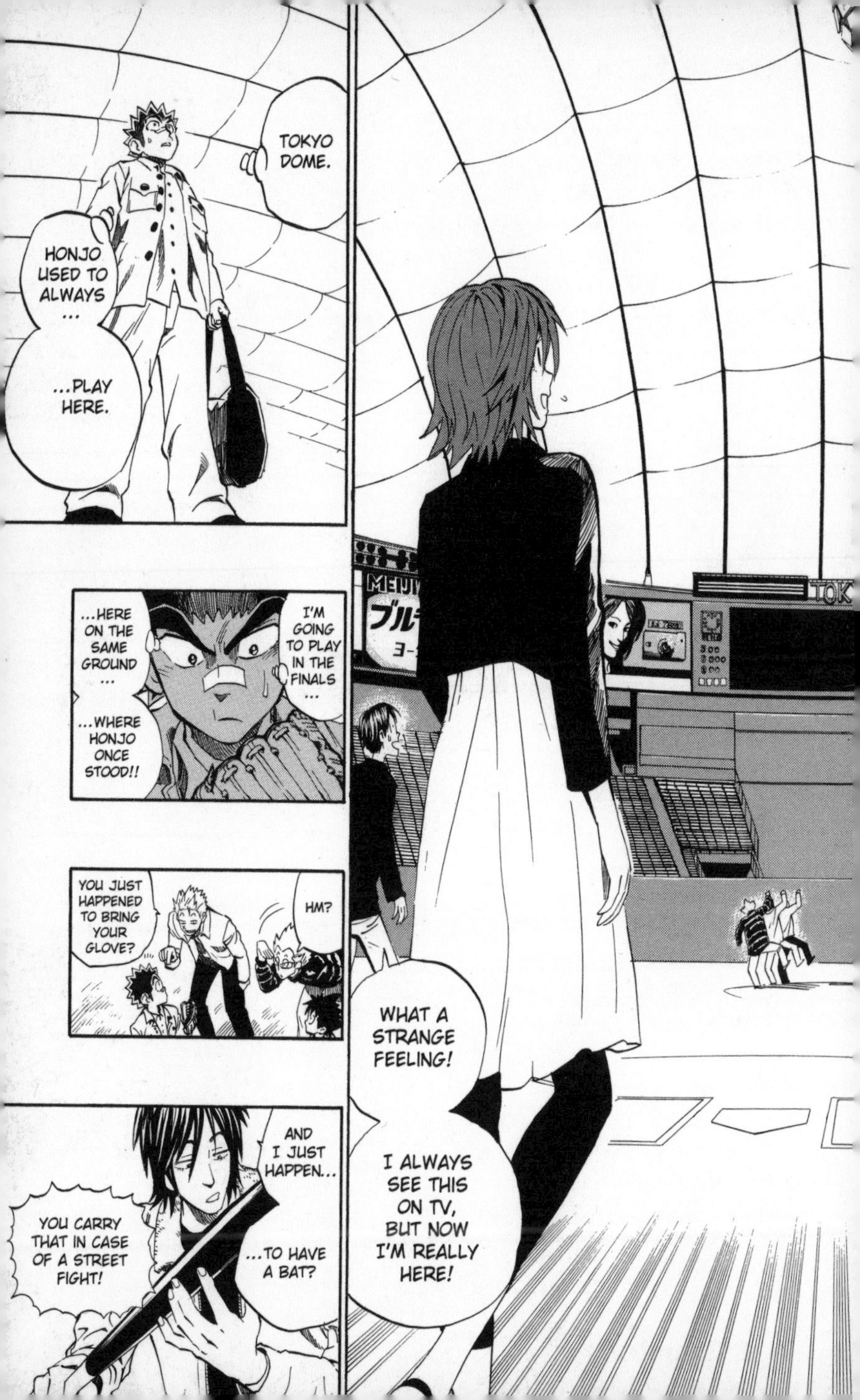
WHAT A STRANGE FEELING!
I ALWAYS SEE THIS ON TV, BUT NOW I'M REALLY HERE!
TOKYO DOME.
HONJO USED TO ALWAYS ...
...PLAY HERE.
I'M GOING TO PLAY IN THE FINALS ...
...HERE ON THE SAME GROUND ...
...WHERE HONJO ONCE STOOD!!
HM?
YOU JUST HAPPENED TO BRING YOUR GLOVE?
AND I JUST HAPPEN...
...TO HAVE A BAT?
YOU CARRY THAT IN CASE OF A STREET FIGHT!

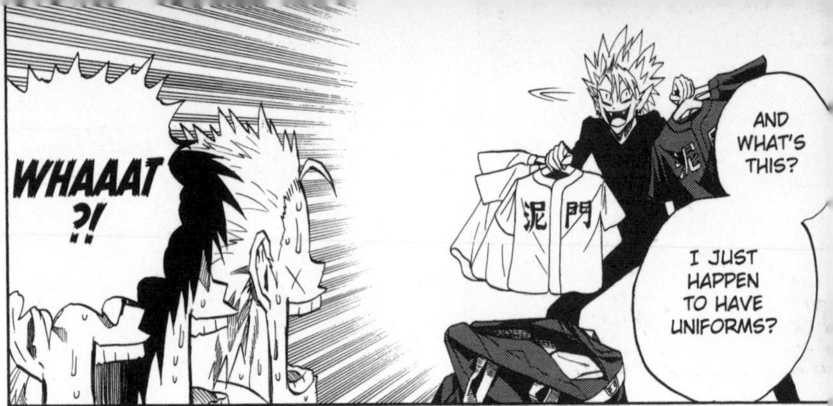
AND WHAT'S THIS?
I JUST HAPPEN TO HAVE UNIFORMS?
泥門
WHAAAT ?!

UNIFORM: DEIMON

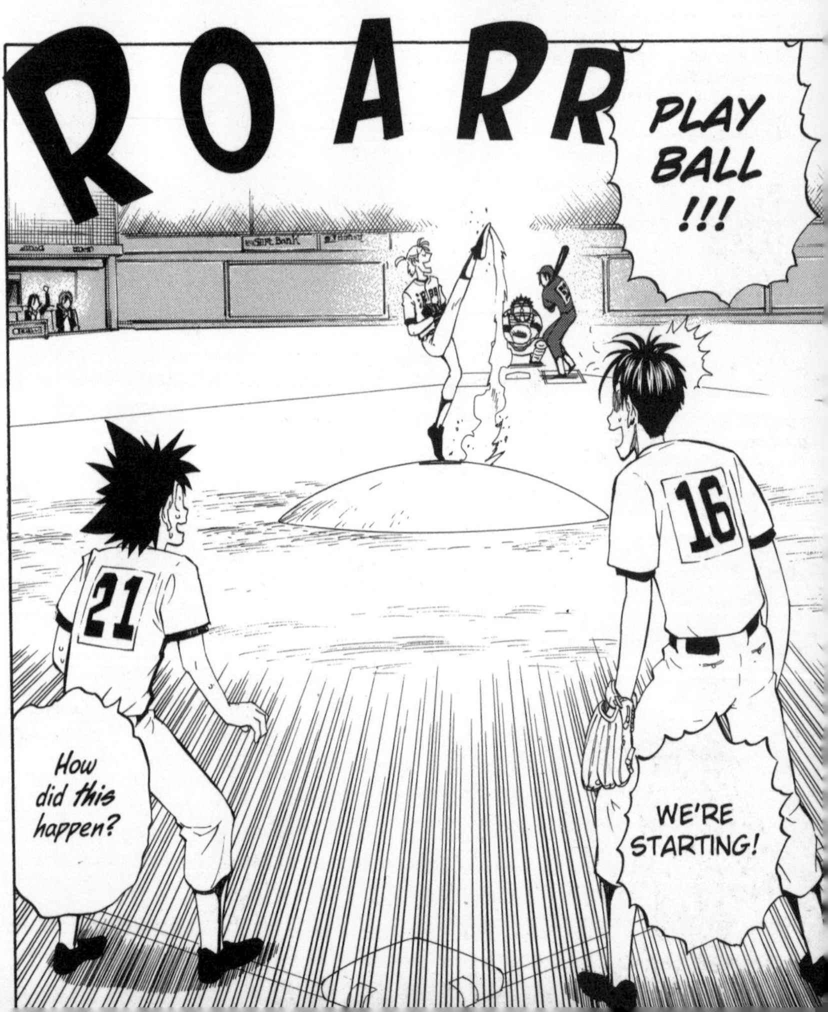
ROARR
PLAY BALL !!!
WE'RE STARTING!
How did this happen?

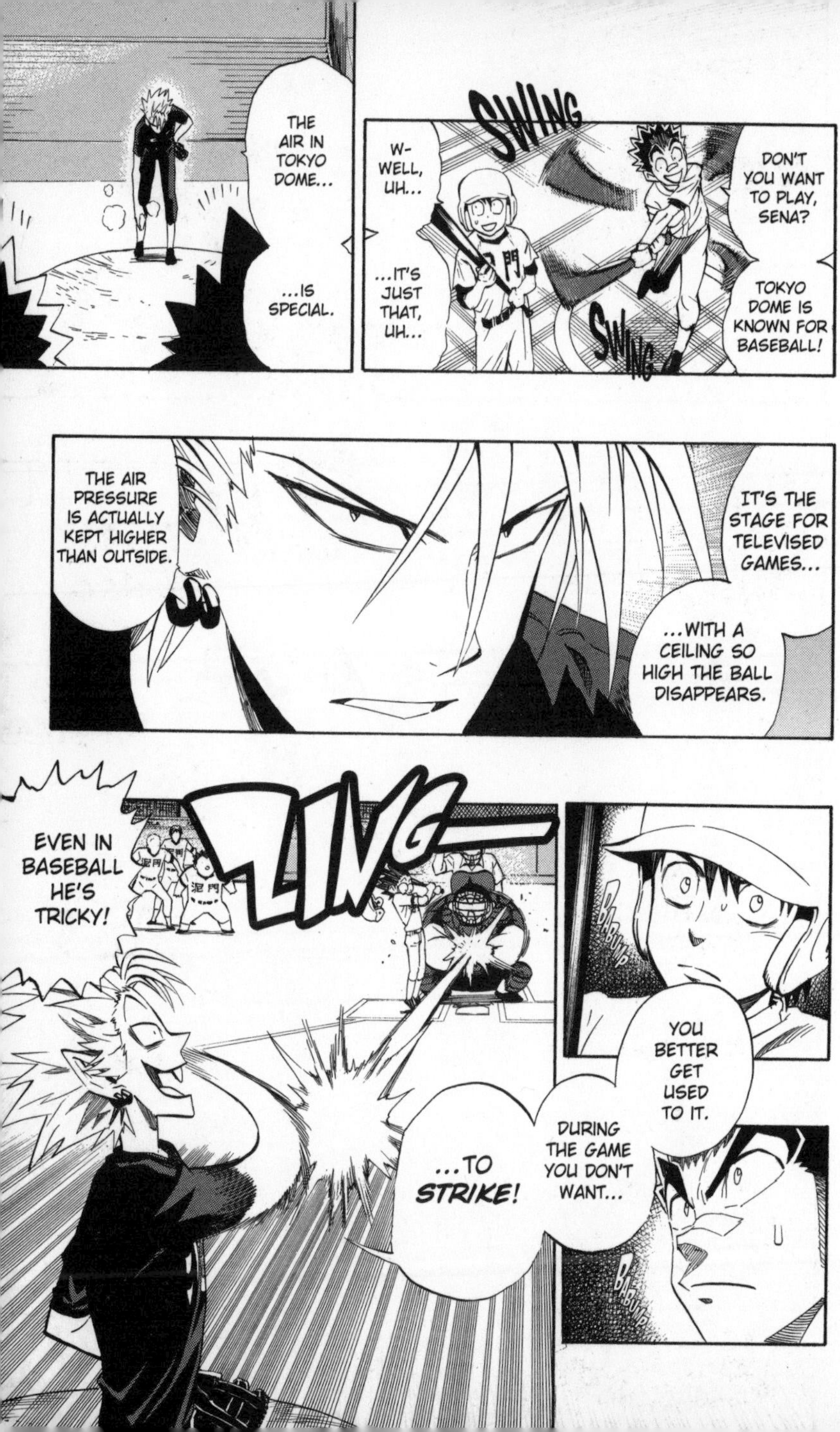
DON'T YOU WANT TO PLAY, SENA?
TOKYO DOME IS KNOWN FOR BASEBALL!
SWING
W-WELL, UH...
...IT'S JUST THAT, UH...
SWING
THE AIR IN TOKYO DOME...
...IS SPECIAL.
IT'S THE STAGE FOR TELEVISED GAMES...
...WITH A CEILING SO HIGH THE BALL DISAPPEARS.
THE AIR PRESSURE IS ACTUALLY KEPT HIGHER THAN OUTSIDE.
FLING
EVEN IN BASEBALL HE'S TRICKY!
BABUMP
YOU BETTER GET USED TO IT.
DURING THE GAME YOU DON'T WANT...
...TO STRIKE!
BABUMP

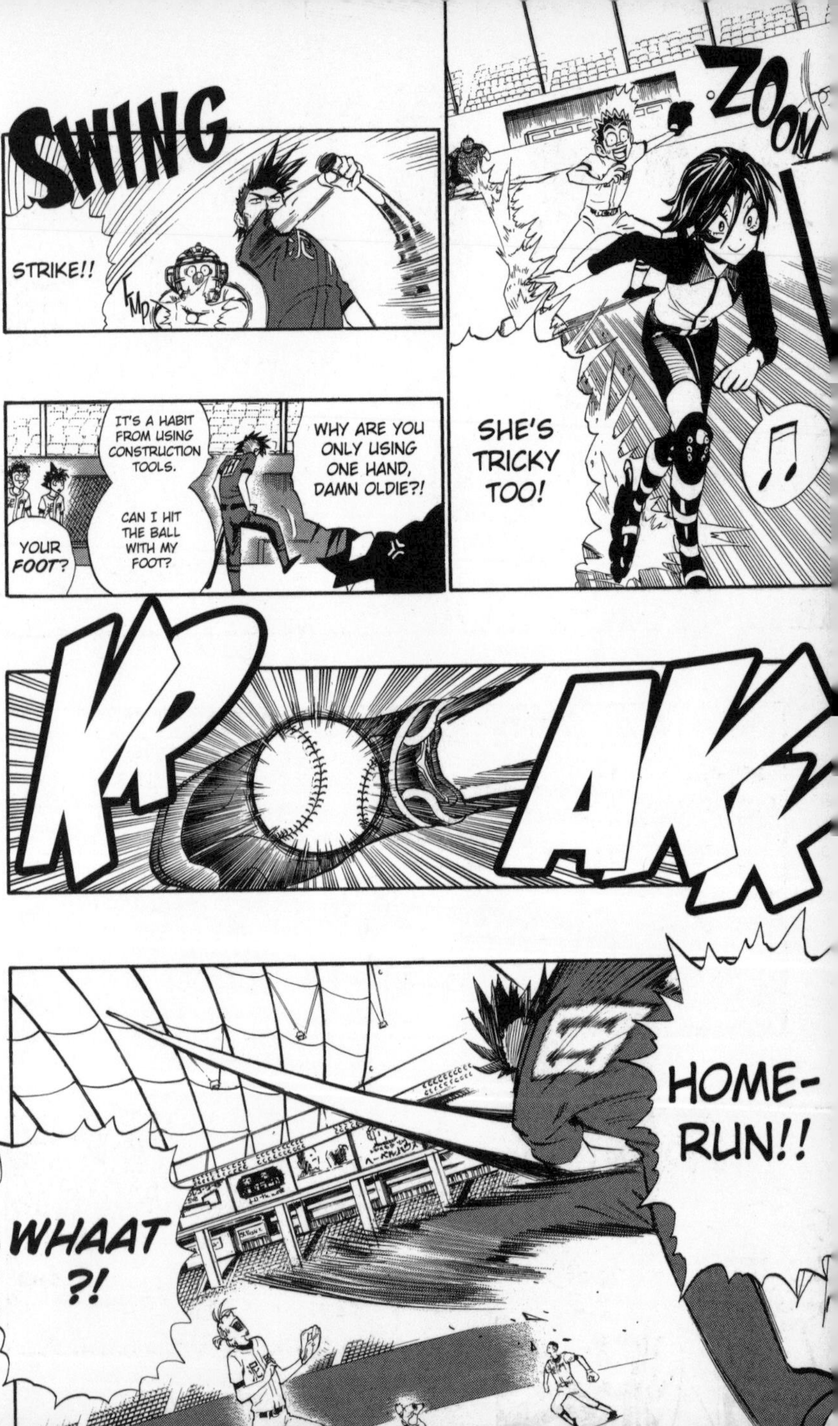
ZOOM
SHE'S TRICKY TOO!
SWING
STRIKE!!
FMP
WHY ARE YOU ONLY USING ONE HAND, DAMN OLDIE?!
IT'S A HABIT FROM USING CONSTRUCTION TOOLS.
CAN I HIT THE BALL WITH MY FOOT?
YOUR FOOT?
KRAK
HOME-RUN!!
WHAAT ?!

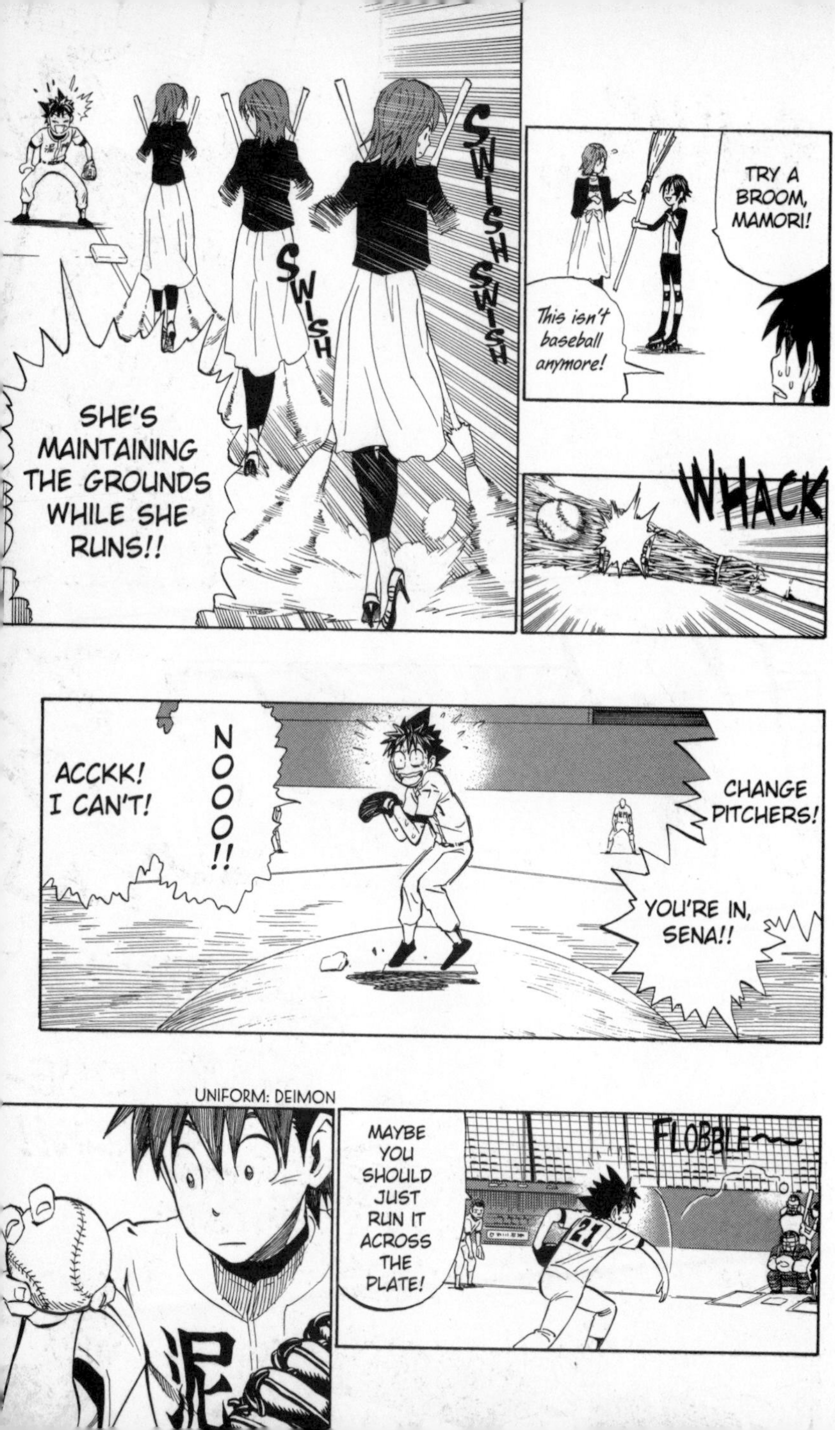
TRY A BROOM, MAMORI!
This isn't baseball anymore!
WHACK
SWISH SWISH
SWISH
SHE'S MAINTAINING THE GROUNDS WHILE SHE RUNS!!
CHANGE PITCHERS!
YOU'RE IN, SENA!!
NOOOO!!
ACCKK! I CAN'T!
MAYBE YOU SHOULD JUST RUN IT ACROSS THE PLATE!
FLOBBLE~~
UNIFORM: DEIMON

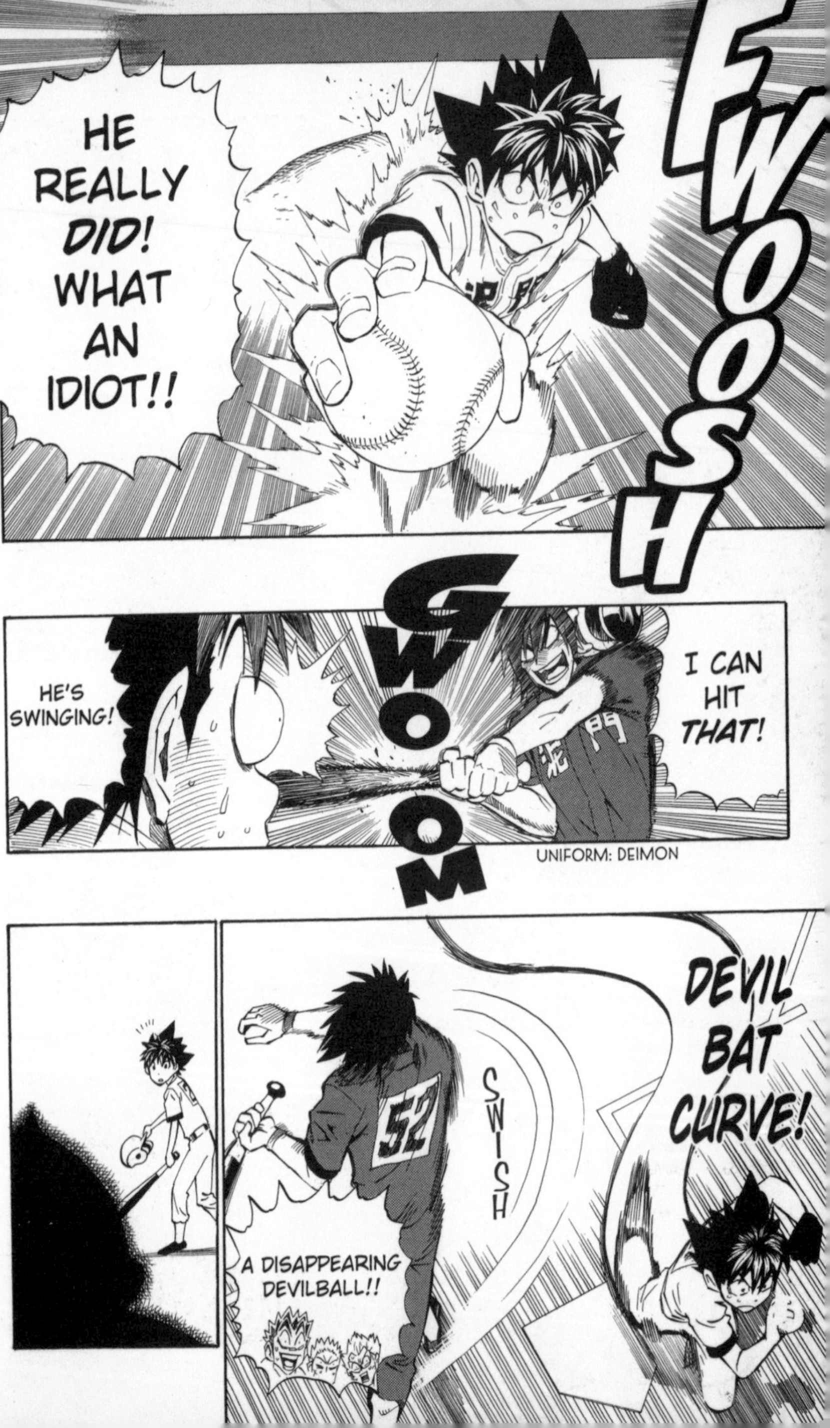
FWOOSH
HE REALLY DID! WHAT AN IDIOT!!
GWOOM
I CAN HIT THAT!
HE'S SWINGING!
UNIFORM: DEIMON
DEVIL BAT CURVE!
SWISH
A DISAPPEARING DEVILBALL!!

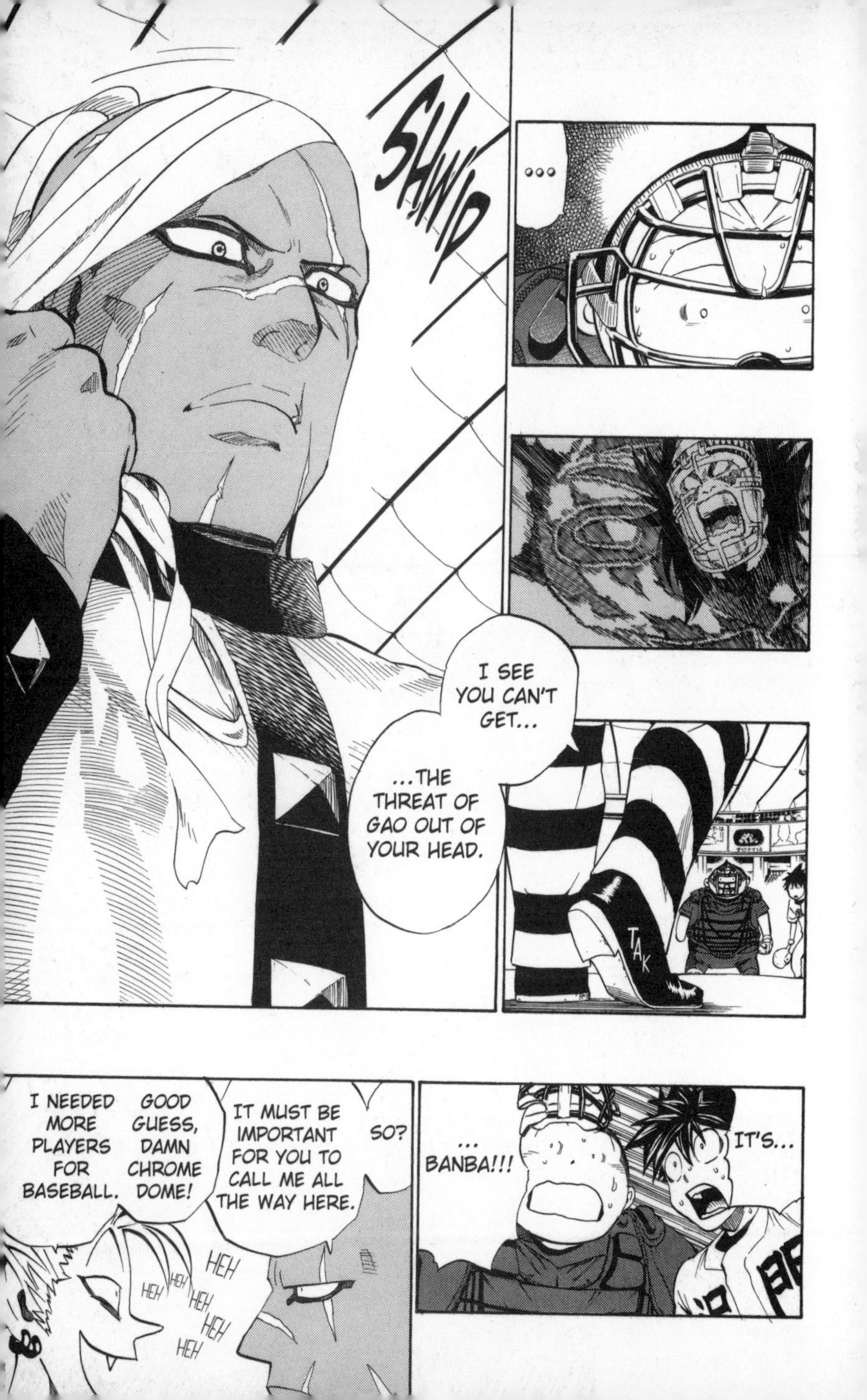
...
TAK
SHWIP
I SEE YOU CAN'T GET...
...THE THREAT OF GAO OUT OF YOUR HEAD.
IT'S...
...BANBA!!!
SO?
IT MUST BE IMPORTANT FOR YOU TO CALL ME ALL THE WAY HERE.
GOOD GUESS, DAMN CHROME DOME!
I NEEDED MORE PLAYERS FOR BASEBALL.
HEH HEH HEH HEH HEH HEH

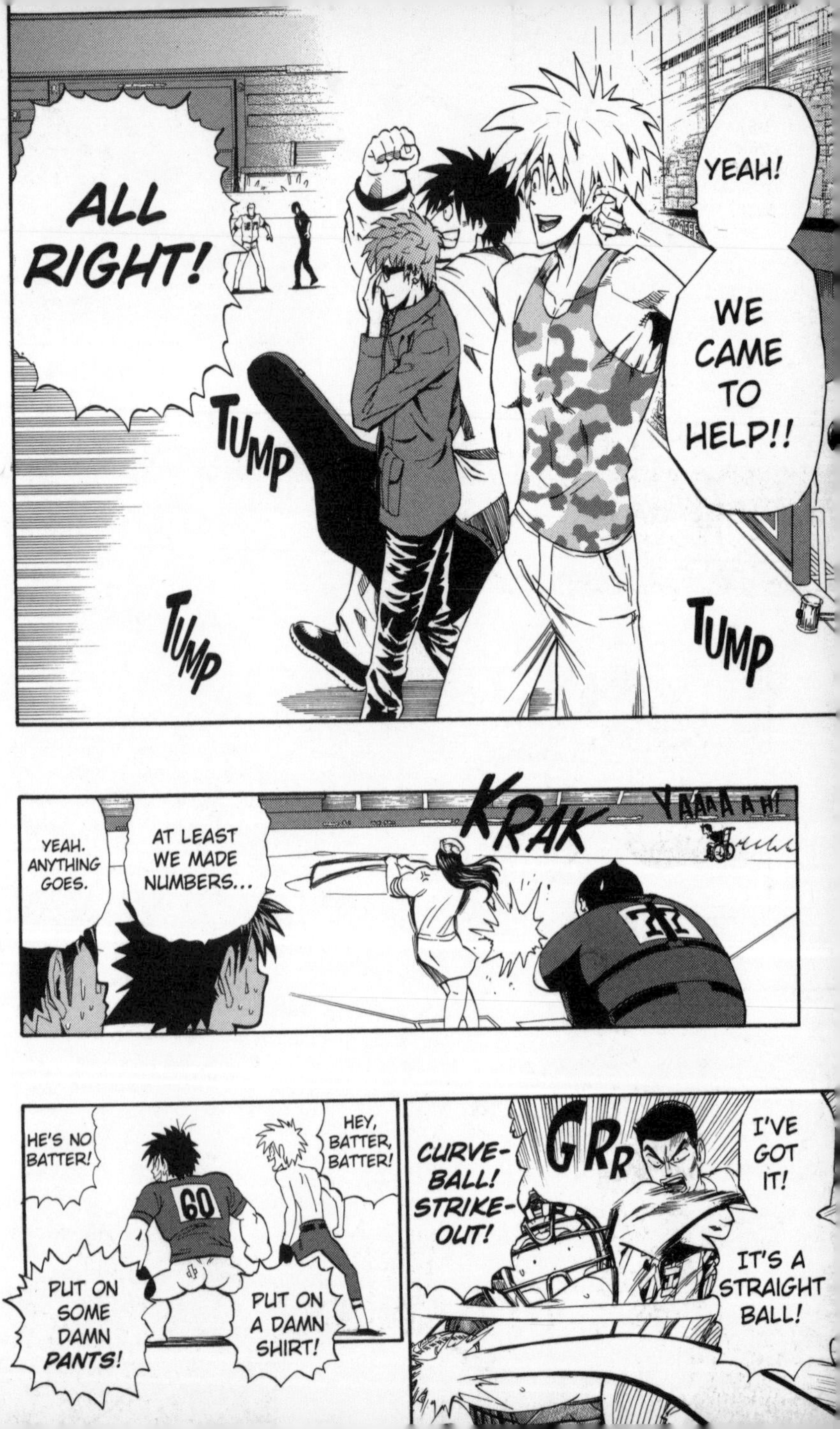
YEAH!
WE CAME TO HELP!!
ALL RIGHT!
TUMP
TUMP
TUMP
YAAAAAH!
KRAK
AT LEAST WE MADE NUMBERS...
YEAH. ANYTHING GOES.
I'VE GOT IT!
GRR
CURVE-BALL! STRIKE-OUT!
IT'S A STRAIGHT BALL!
HEY, BATTER, BATTER!
HE'S NO BATTER!
PUT ON A DAMN SHIRT!
PUT ON SOME DAMN PANTS!

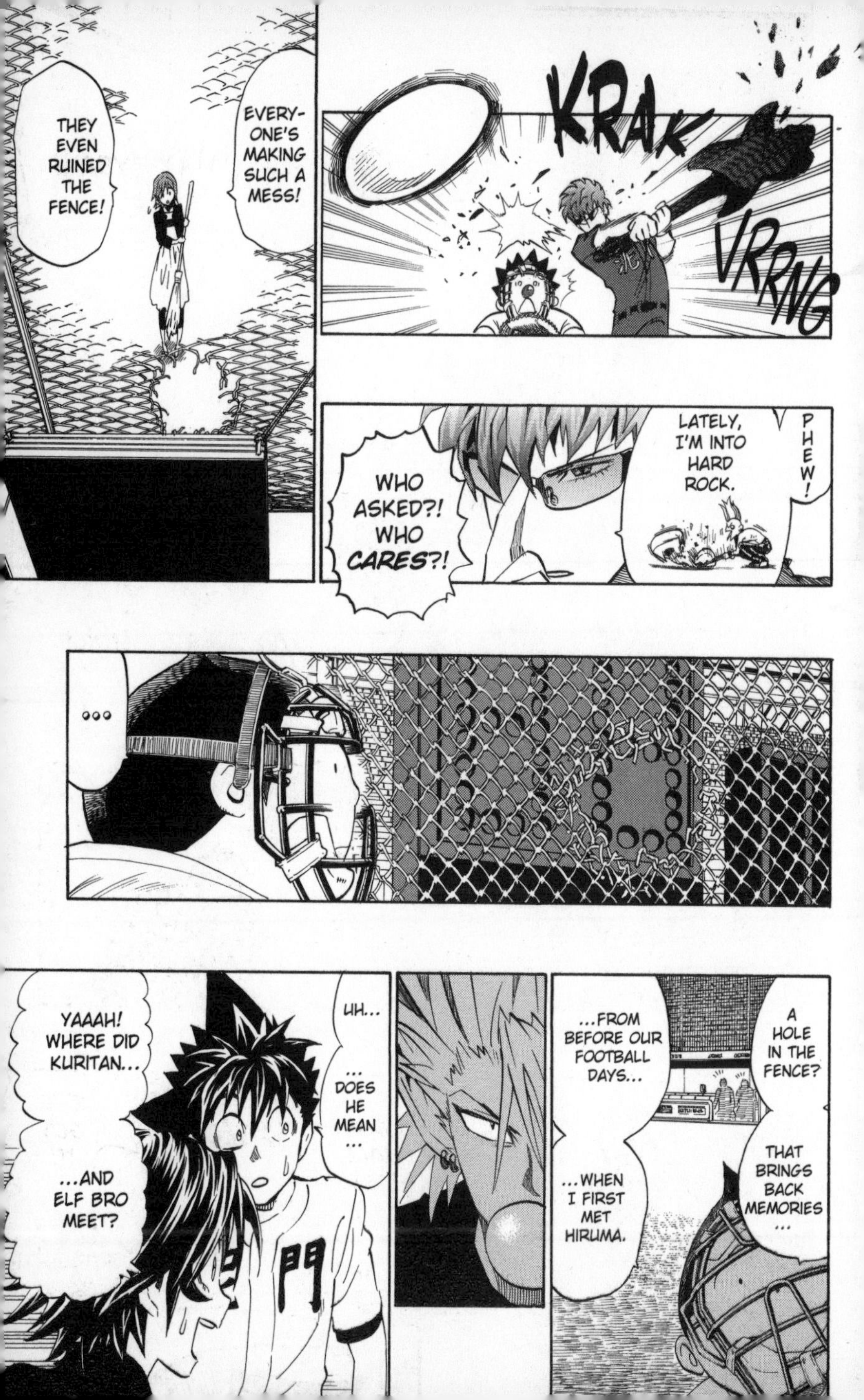
KRAK
VRRNG
LATELY, I'M INTO HARD ROCK.
PHEW!
WHO ASKED?! WHO CARES?!
EVERYONE'S MAKING SUCH A MESS!
THEY EVEN RUINED THE FENCE!
...
A HOLE IN THE FENCE?
THAT BRINGS BACK MEMORIES...
...FROM BEFORE OUR FOOTBALL DAYS...
...WHEN I FIRST MET HIRUMA.
UH...
...DOES HE MEAN...
YAAAH! WHERE DID KURITAN...
...AND ELF BRO MEET?

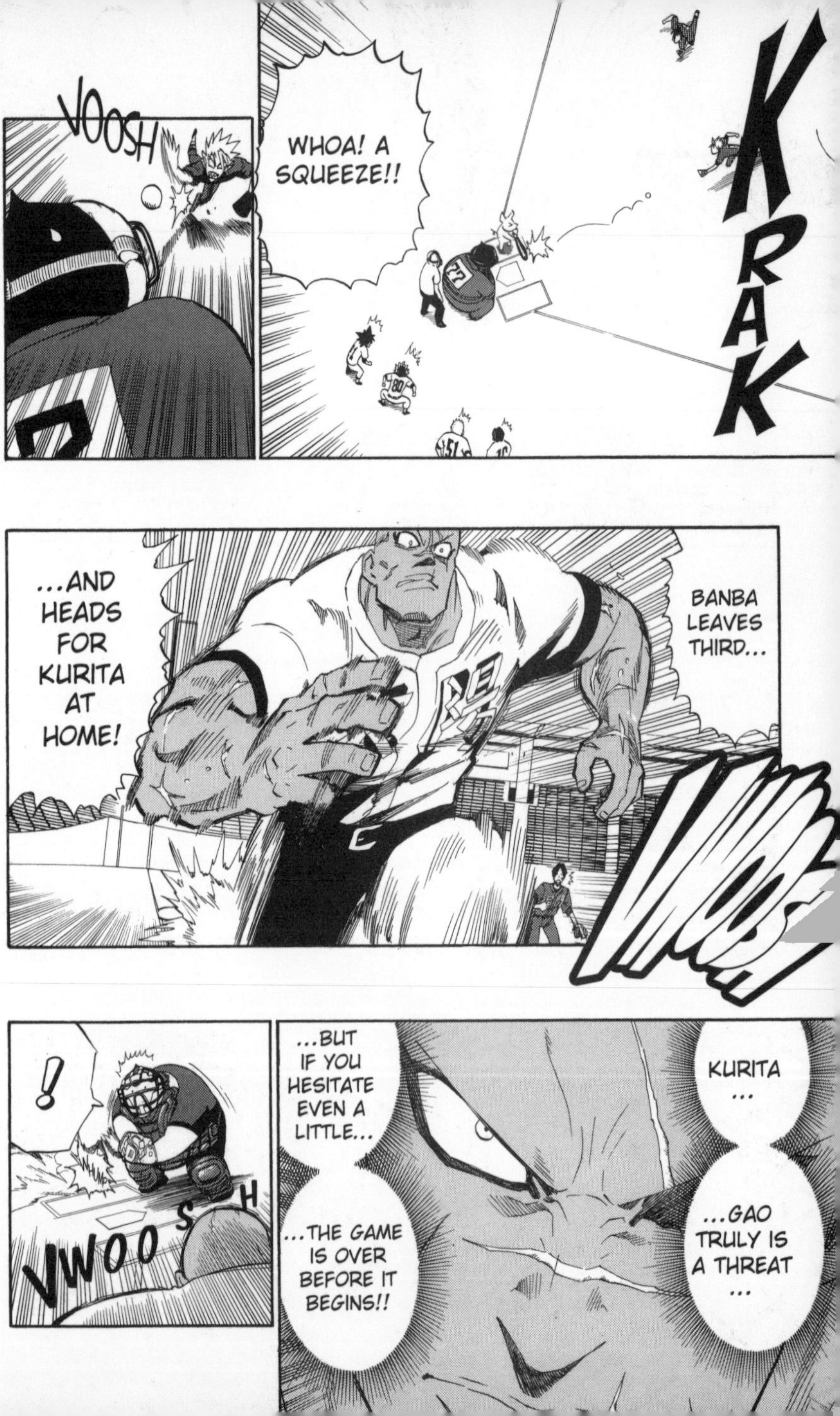
KRAK
WHOA! A SQUEEZE!!
VOOSH
BANBA LEAVES THIRD...
...AND HEADS FOR KURITA AT HOME!
KURITA...
...GAO TRULY IS A THREAT...
...BUT IF YOU HESITATE EVEN A LITTLE...
...THE GAME IS OVER BEFORE IT BEGINS!!
!
WHUMP
VWOOSH

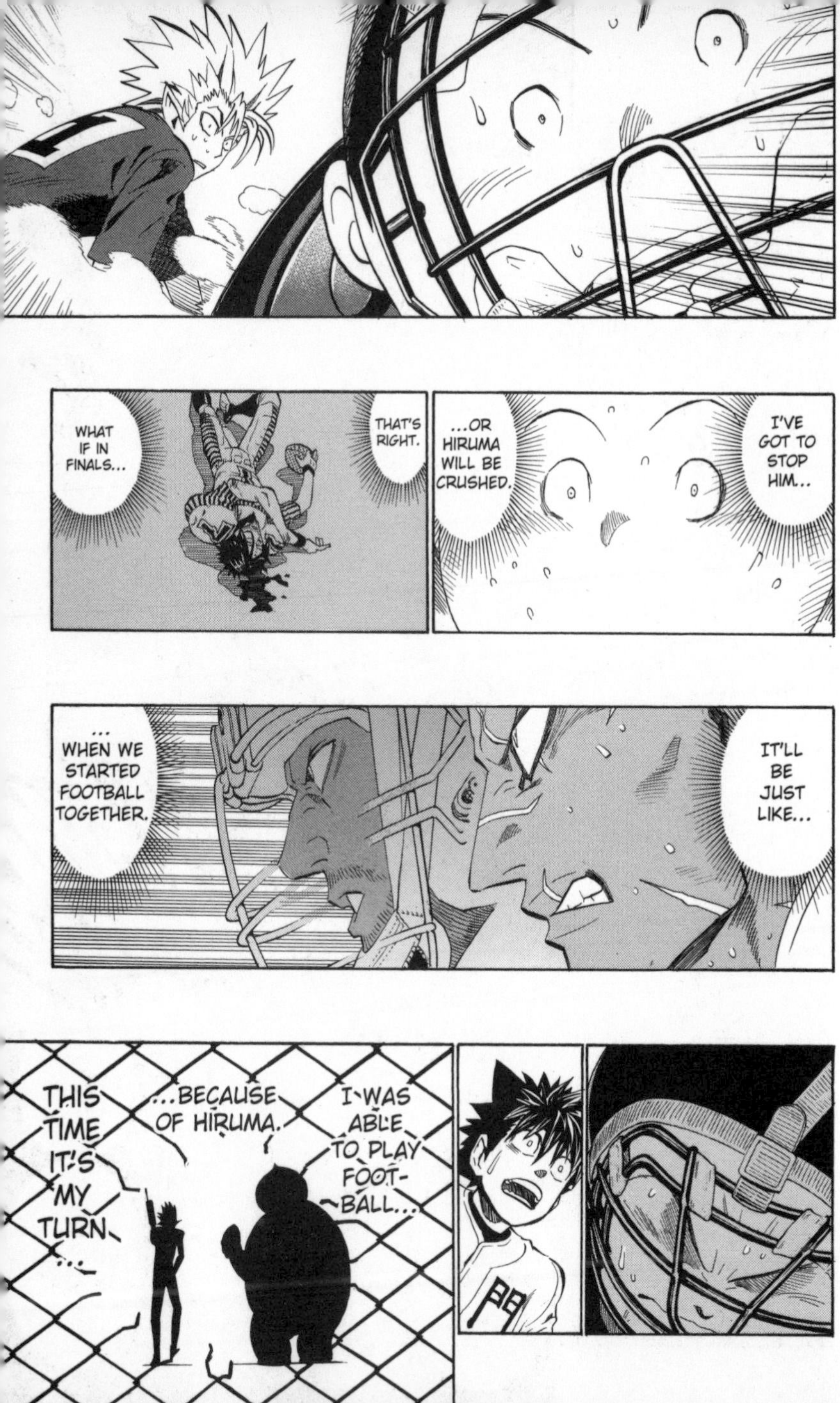
I'VE GOT TO STOP HIM...
...OR HIRUMA WILL BE CRUSHED.
THAT'S RIGHT.
WHAT IF IN FINALS...
IT'LL BE JUST LIKE...
...WHEN WE STARTED FOOTBALL TOGETHER.
I WAS ABLE TO PLAY FOOT-BALL...
...BECAUSE OF HIRUMA.
THIS TIME IT'S MY TURN...

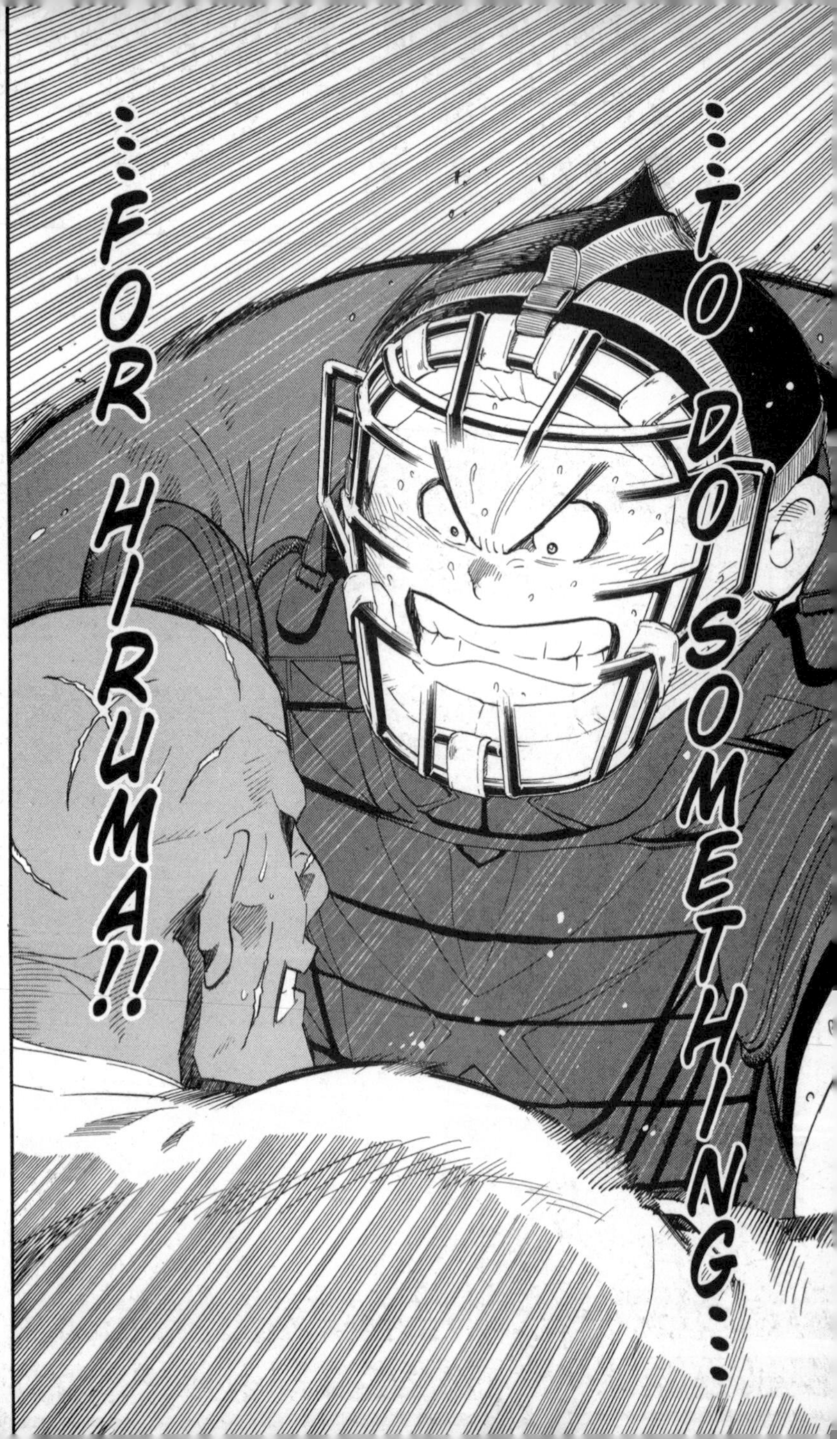
...TO DO SOMETHING...
...FOR HIRUMA!!

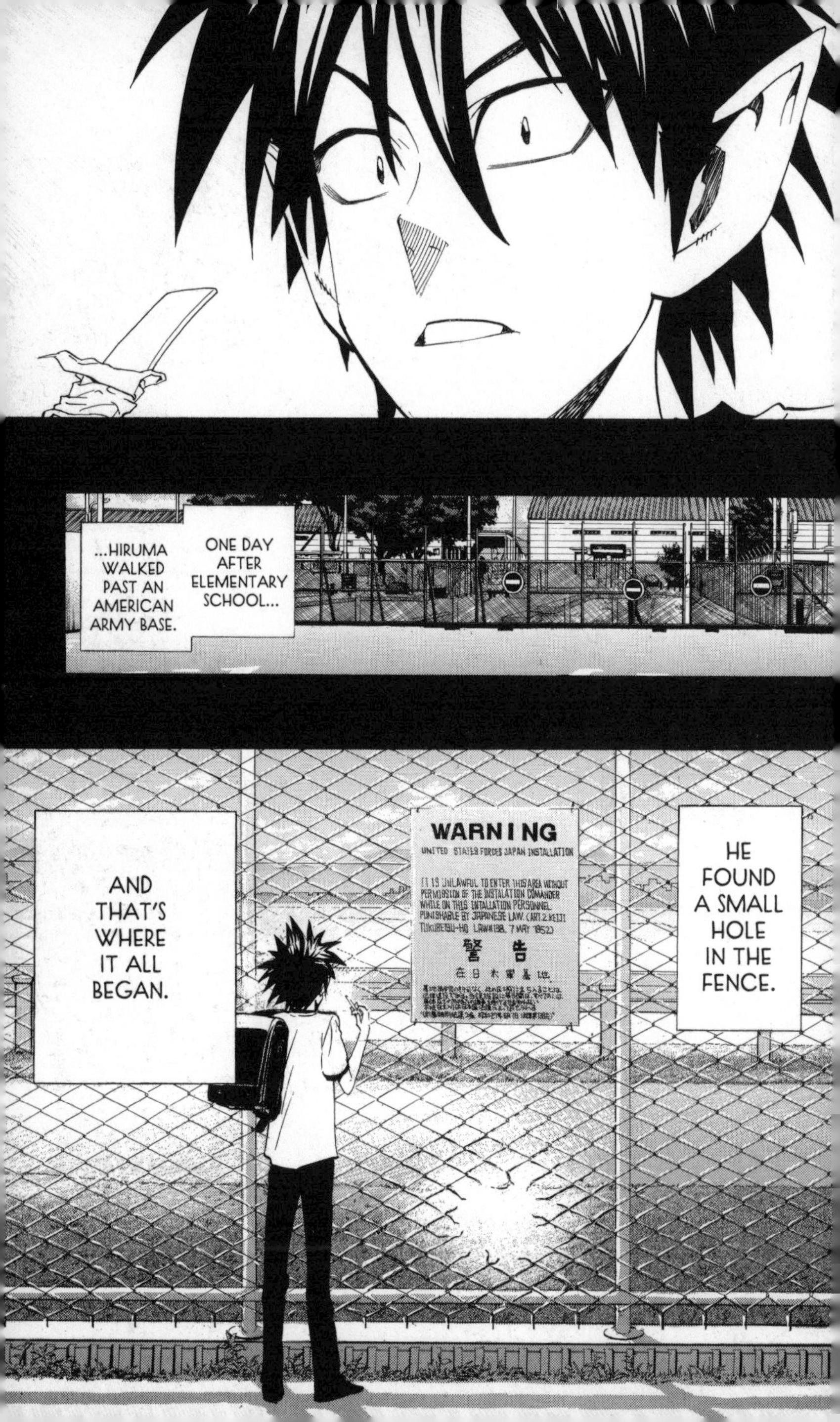
ONE DAY AFTER ELEMENTARY SCHOOL...
...HIRUMA WALKED PAST AN AMERICAN ARMY BASE.
HE FOUND A SMALL HOLE IN THE FENCE.
WARNING
UNITED STATES FORCES JAPAN INSTALLATION
IT IS UNLAWFUL TO ENTER THIS AREA WITHOUT PERMISSION OF THE INSTALATION COMANDER WHILE ON THIS INTALLATION PERSONNEL PUNISHABLE BY JAPANESE LAW. (ART.2 KEIJI TOKUBETSU-HO LAW#138, 7 MAY 1952)
警告
在日米軍基地
AND THAT'S WHERE IT ALL BEGAN.

Devil Bat 021

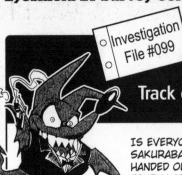

Investigation File #099
Track down the prize spikes!
IS EVERYONE USING THE SAKURABA BRAND SPIKES HANDED OUT TO THE TOKYO TOURNAMENT'S TOP 11 PLAYERS?
Caller

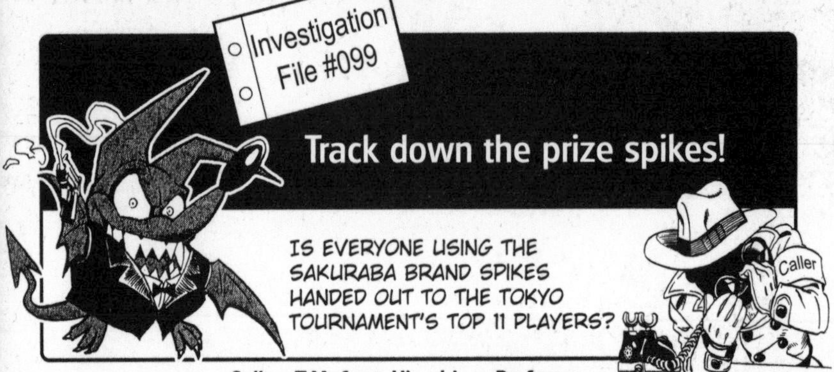

Caller: T.M. from Hiroshima Prefecture

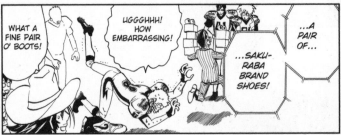

...A PAIR OF...
...SAKURABA BRAND SHOES!
UGGGHHH! HOW EMBARRASSING!
WHAT A FINE PAIR O' BOOTS!

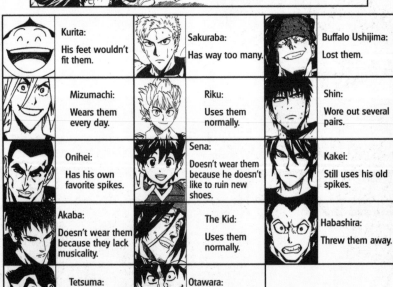

Kurita: His feet wouldn't fit them.	Sakuraba: Has way too many.	Buffalo Ushijima: Lost them.
Mizumachi: Wears them every day.	Riku: Uses them normally.	Shin: Wore out several pairs.
Onihei: Has his own favorite spikes.	Sena: Doesn't wear them because he doesn't like to ruin new shoes.	Kakei: Still uses his old spikes.
Akaba: Doesn't wear them because they lack musicality.	The Kid: Uses them normally.	Habashira: Threw them away.
Tetsuma: Already wore them out.	Otawara: They decayed from his foot odor.	

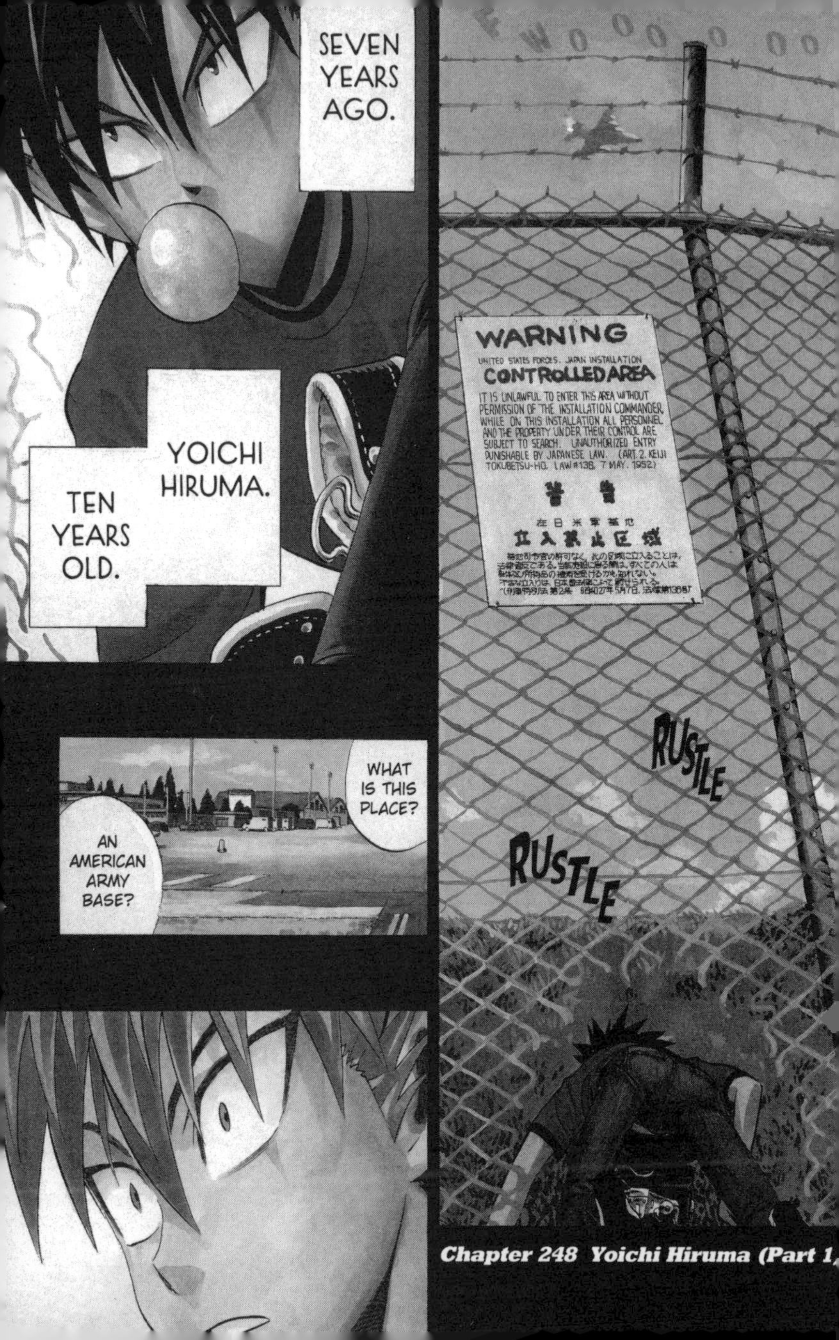
FWOOOO OOO
WARNING
UNITED STATES FORCES, JAPAN INSTALLATION
CONTROLLED AREA
IT IS UNLAWFUL TO ENTER THIS AREA WITHOUT PERMISSION OF THE INSTALLATION COMMANDER. WHILE ON THIS INSTALLATION ALL PERSONNEL AND THE PROPERTY UNDER THEIR CONTROL ARE SUBJECT TO SEARCH. UNAUTHORIZED ENTRY PUNISHABLE BY JAPANESE LAW. (ART. 2, KEIJI TOKUBETSU-HO, LAW #138, 7 MAY, 1952)
警告
在日米軍施設
立入禁止区域
RUSTLE
RUSTLE
Chapter 248 Yoichi Hiruma (Part 1)
SEVEN YEARS AGO.
YOICHI HIRUMA.
TEN YEARS OLD.
WHAT IS THIS PLACE?
AN AMERICAN ARMY BASE?

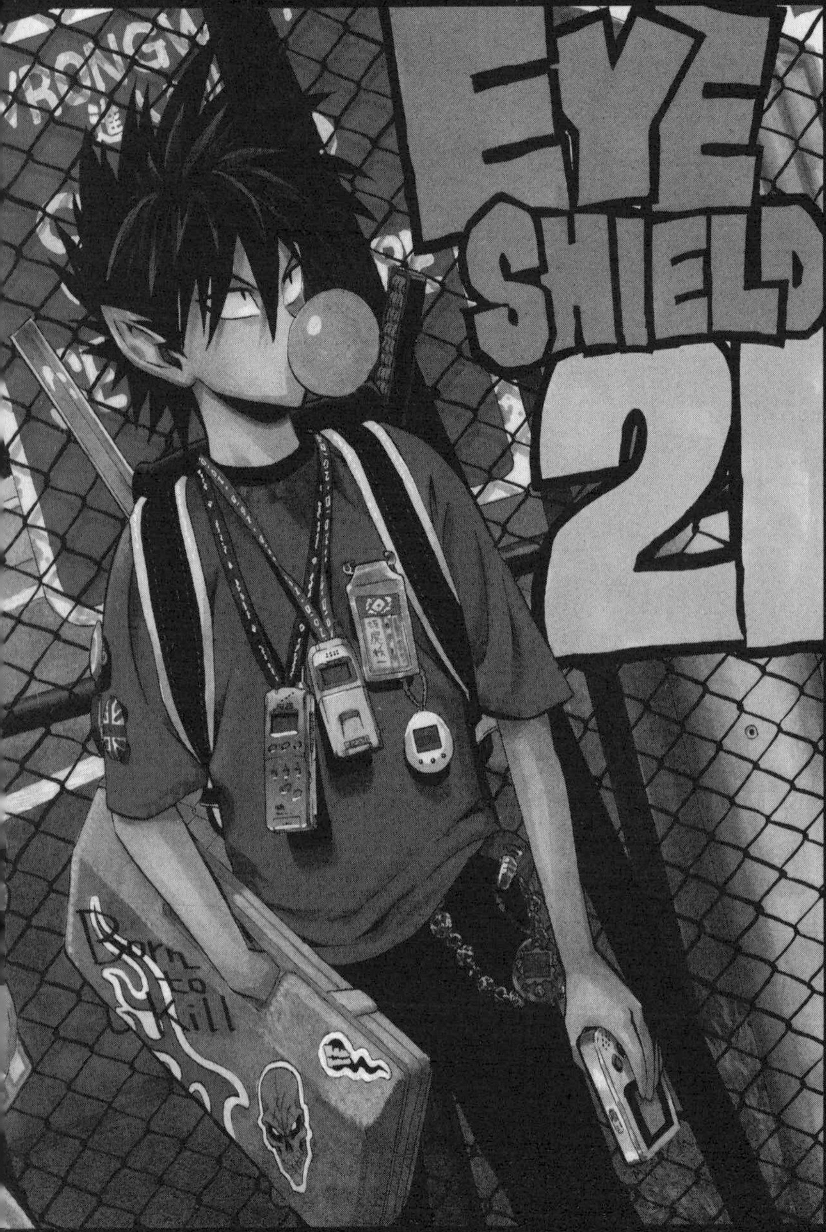
EYE SHIELD 21
Born to Kill

Chapter 248 Yoichi Hiruma (Part 1)

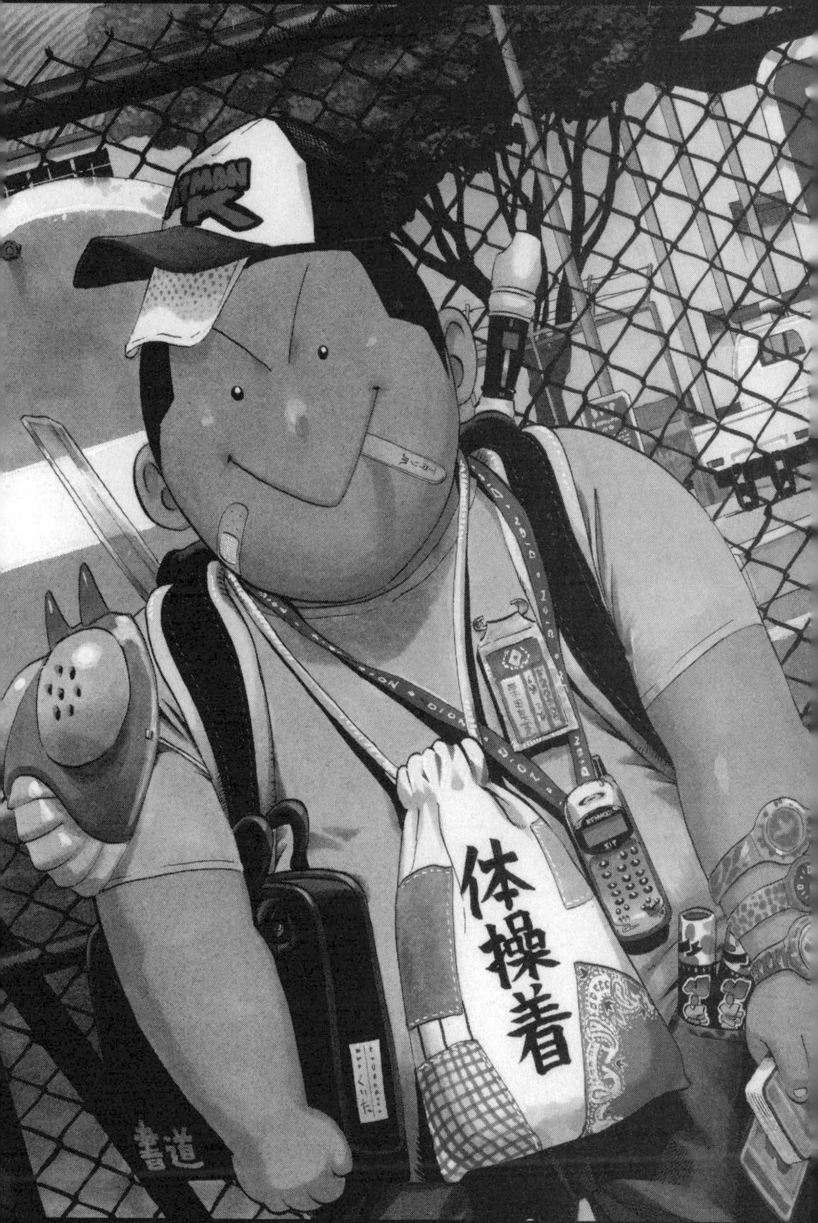
体操着
書道

BAG: P.E. CLOTHES

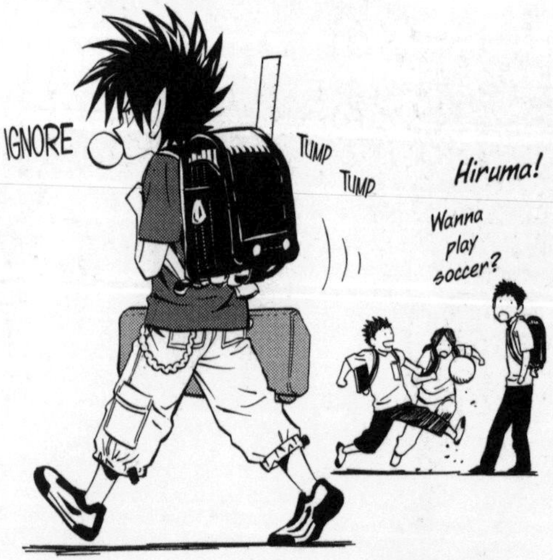
Hiruma!
Wanna play soccer?
TUMP
TUMP
IGNORE

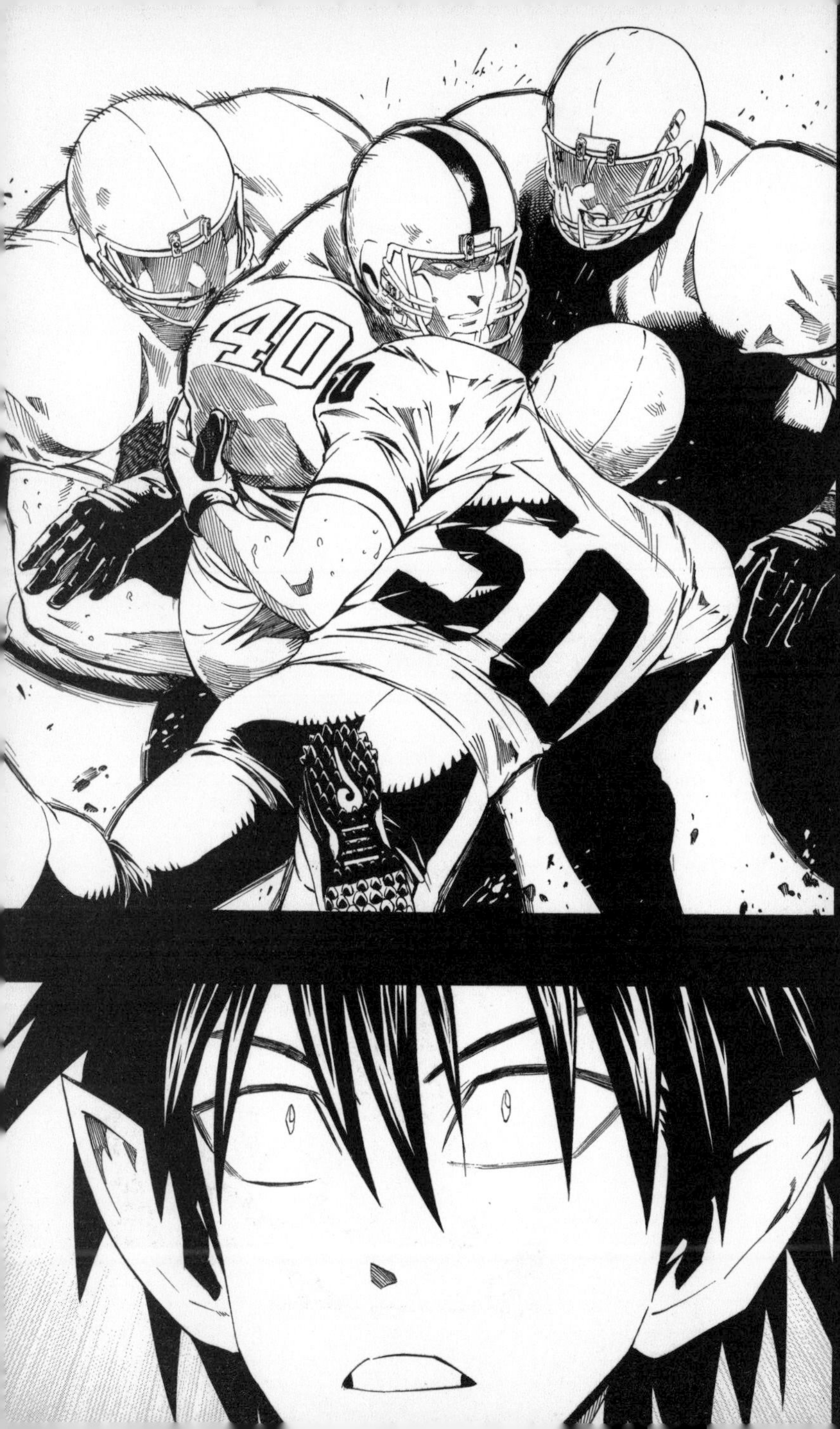

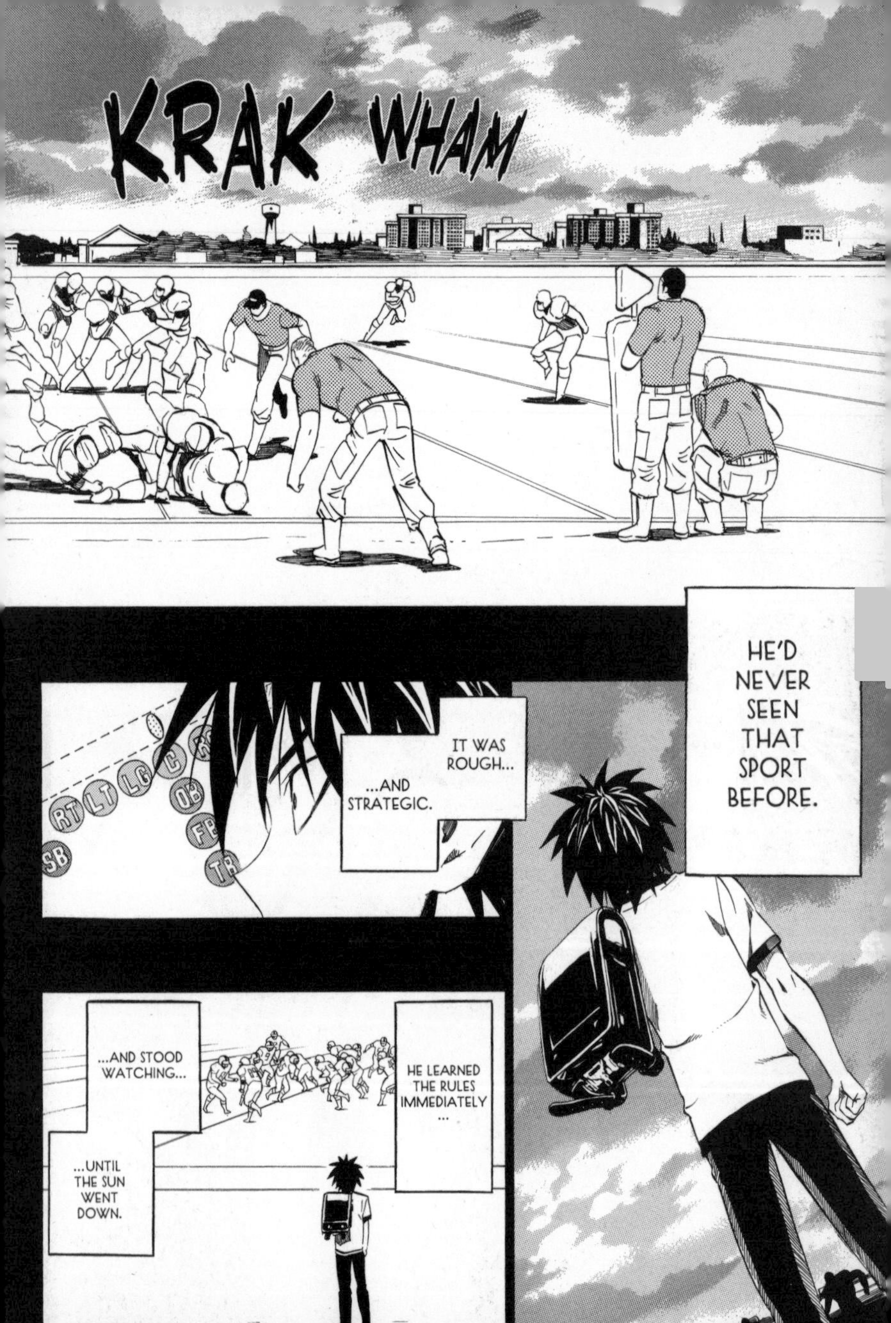
KRAK
WHAM
HE'D NEVER SEEN THAT SPORT BEFORE.
IT WAS ROUGH...
...AND STRATEGIC.
HE LEARNED THE RULES IMMEDIATELY...
...AND STOOD WATCHING...
...UNTIL THE SUN WENT DOWN.

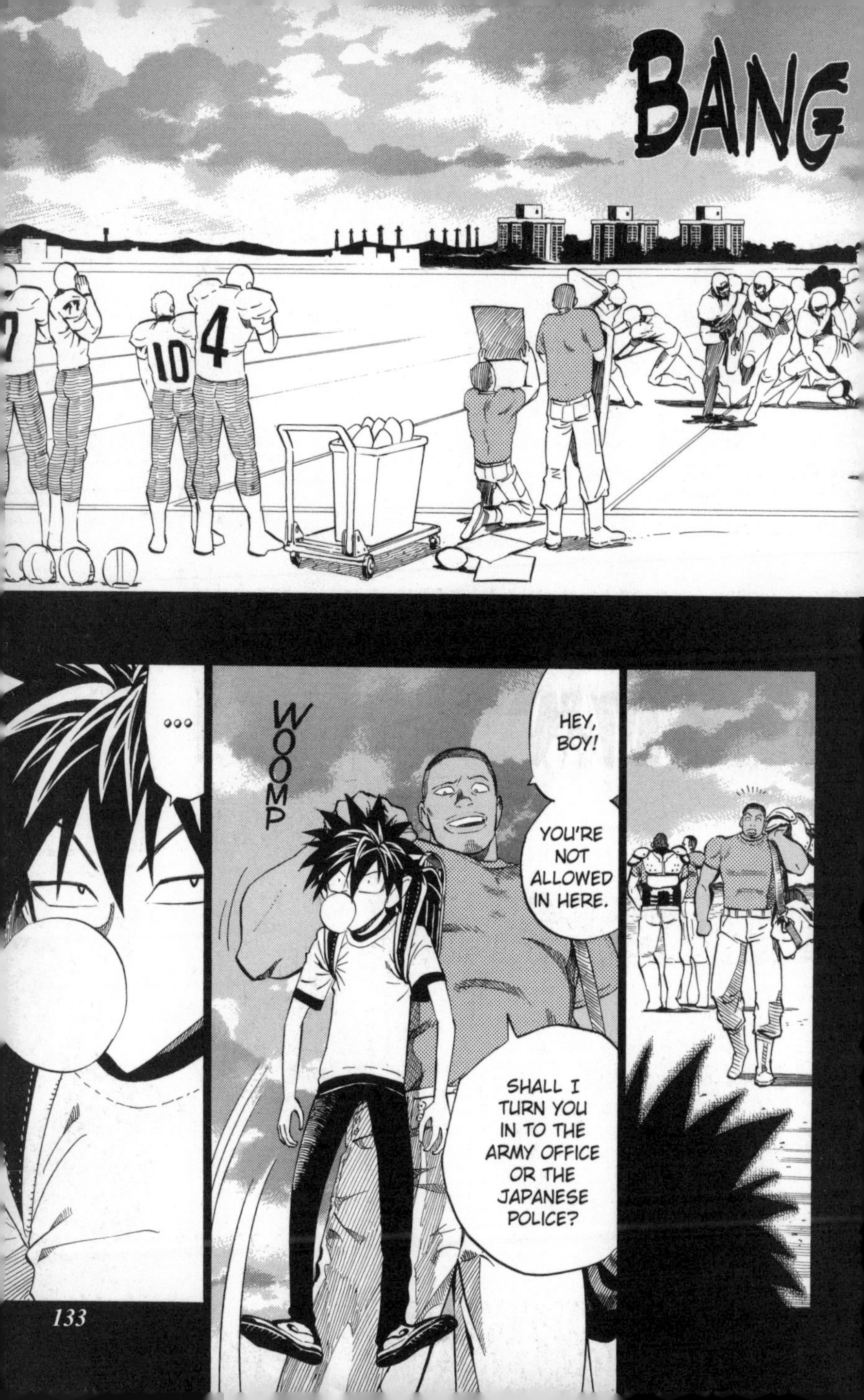
BANG
WOOMP
HEY, BOY!
YOU'RE NOT ALLOWED IN HERE.
SHALL I TURN YOU IN TO THE ARMY OFFICE OR THE JAPANESE POLICE?
...

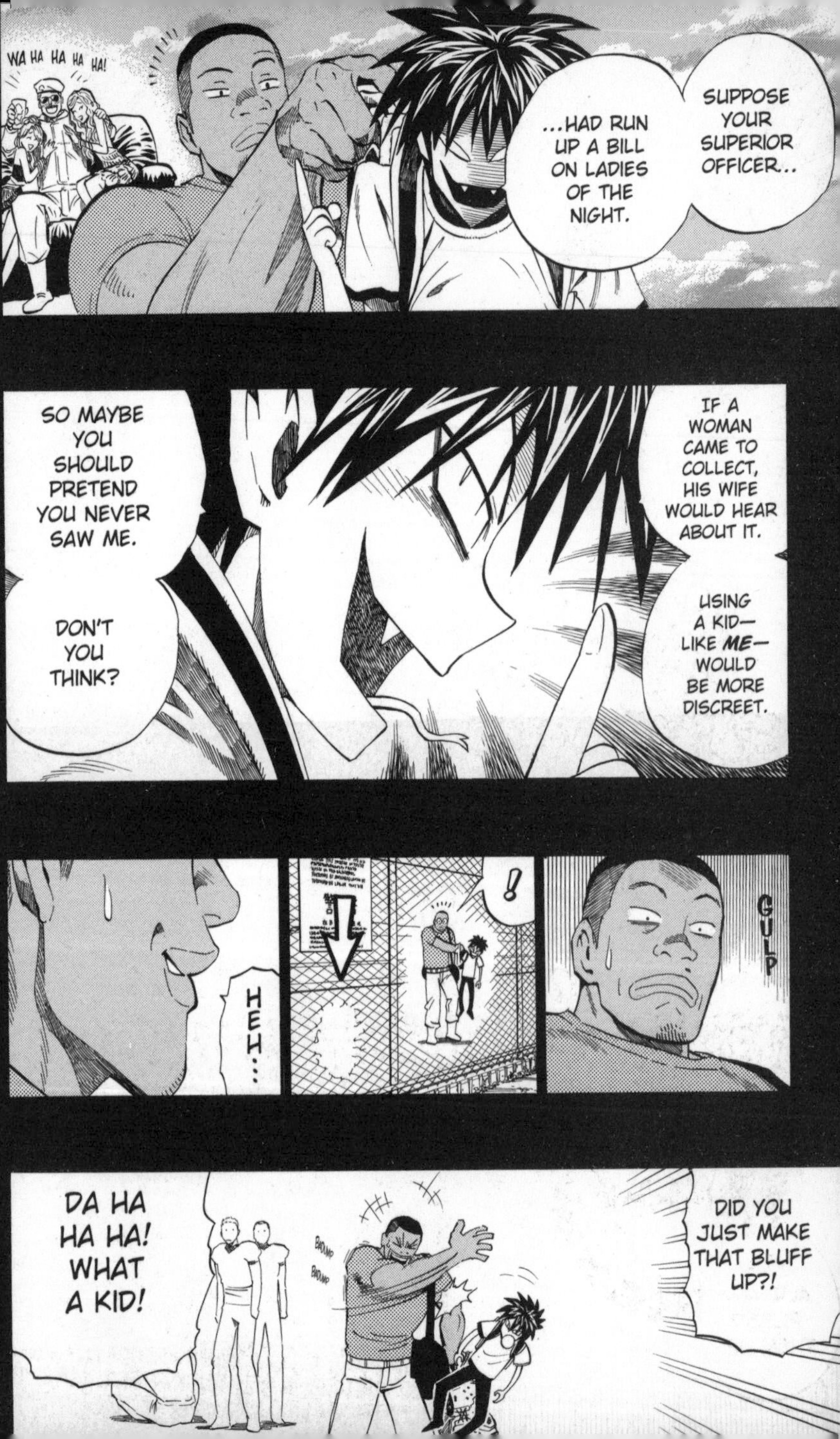
SUPPOSE YOUR SUPERIOR OFFICER...
...HAD RUN UP A BILL ON LADIES OF THE NIGHT.
WA HA HA HA HA!
IF A WOMAN CAME TO COLLECT, HIS WIFE WOULD HEAR ABOUT IT.
USING A KID—LIKE *ME*—WOULD BE MORE DISCREET.
SO MAYBE YOU SHOULD PRETEND YOU NEVER SAW ME.
DON'T YOU THINK?
GULP
!
HEH...
DID YOU JUST MAKE THAT BLUFF UP?!
DA HA HA HA! WHAT A KID!
BADUMP
BADUMP

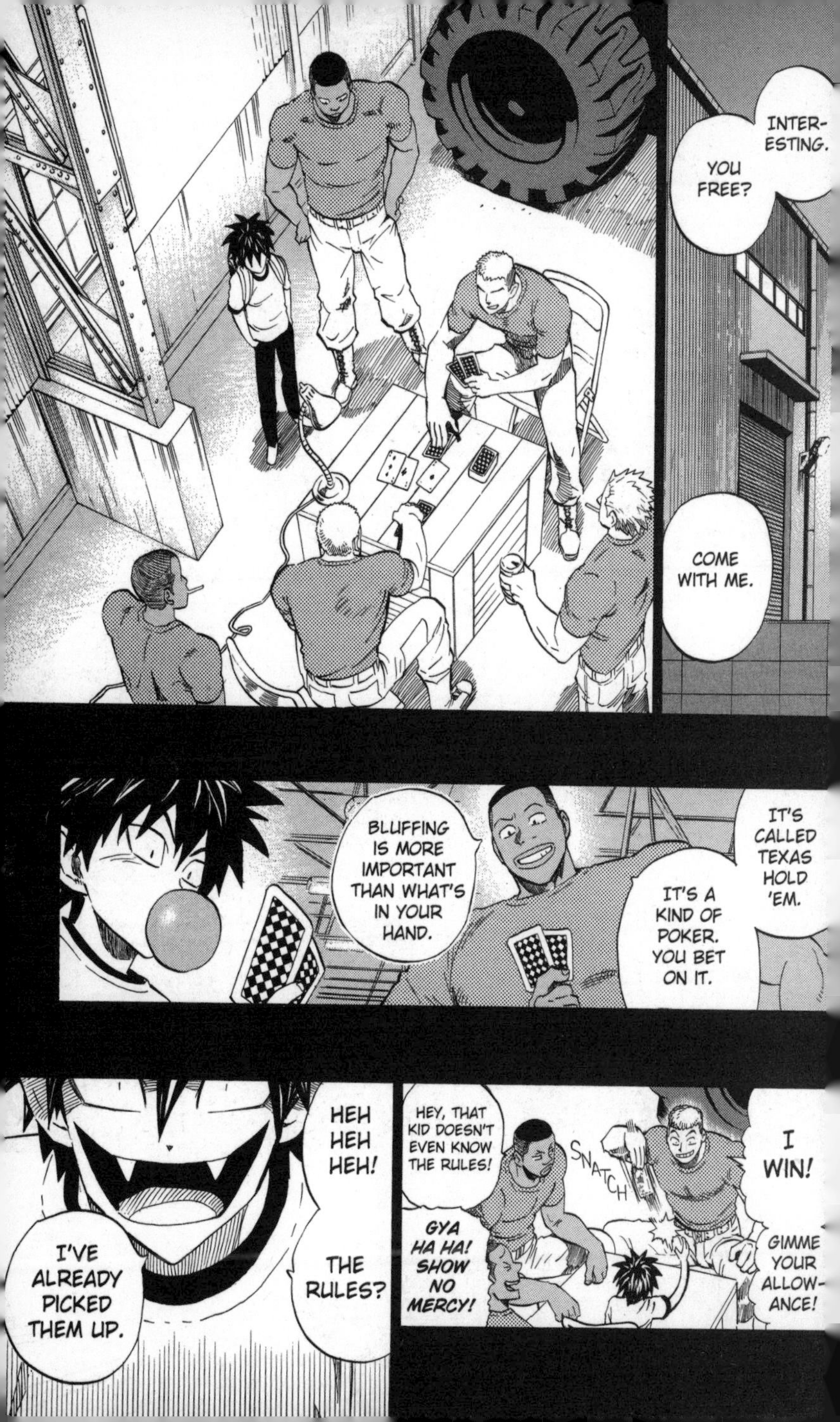
INTER-ESTING.
YOU FREE?
COME WITH ME.
IT'S CALLED TEXAS HOLD 'EM.
IT'S A KIND OF POKER. YOU BET ON IT.
BLUFFING IS MORE IMPORTANT THAN WHAT'S IN YOUR HAND.
I WIN!
GIMME YOUR ALLOWANCE!
SNATCH
HEY, THAT KID DOESN'T EVEN KNOW THE RULES!
GYA HA HA! SHOW NO MERCY!
HEH HEH HEH!
THE RULES?
I'VE ALREADY PICKED THEM UP.

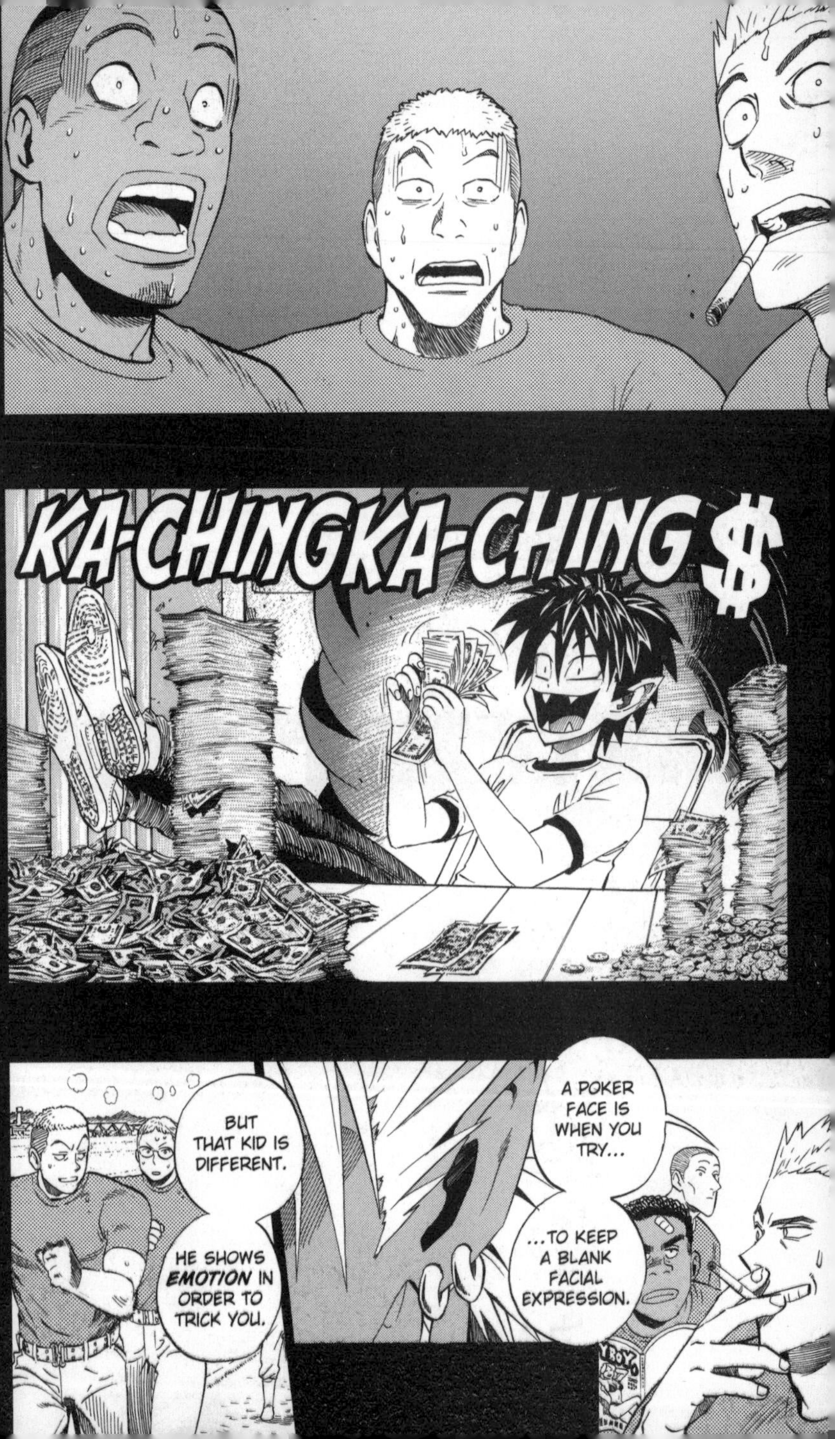
KA-CHING KA-CHING $
A POKER FACE IS WHEN YOU TRY...
...TO KEEP A BLANK FACIAL EXPRESSION.
BUT THAT KID IS DIFFERENT.
HE SHOWS EMOTION IN ORDER TO TRICK YOU.

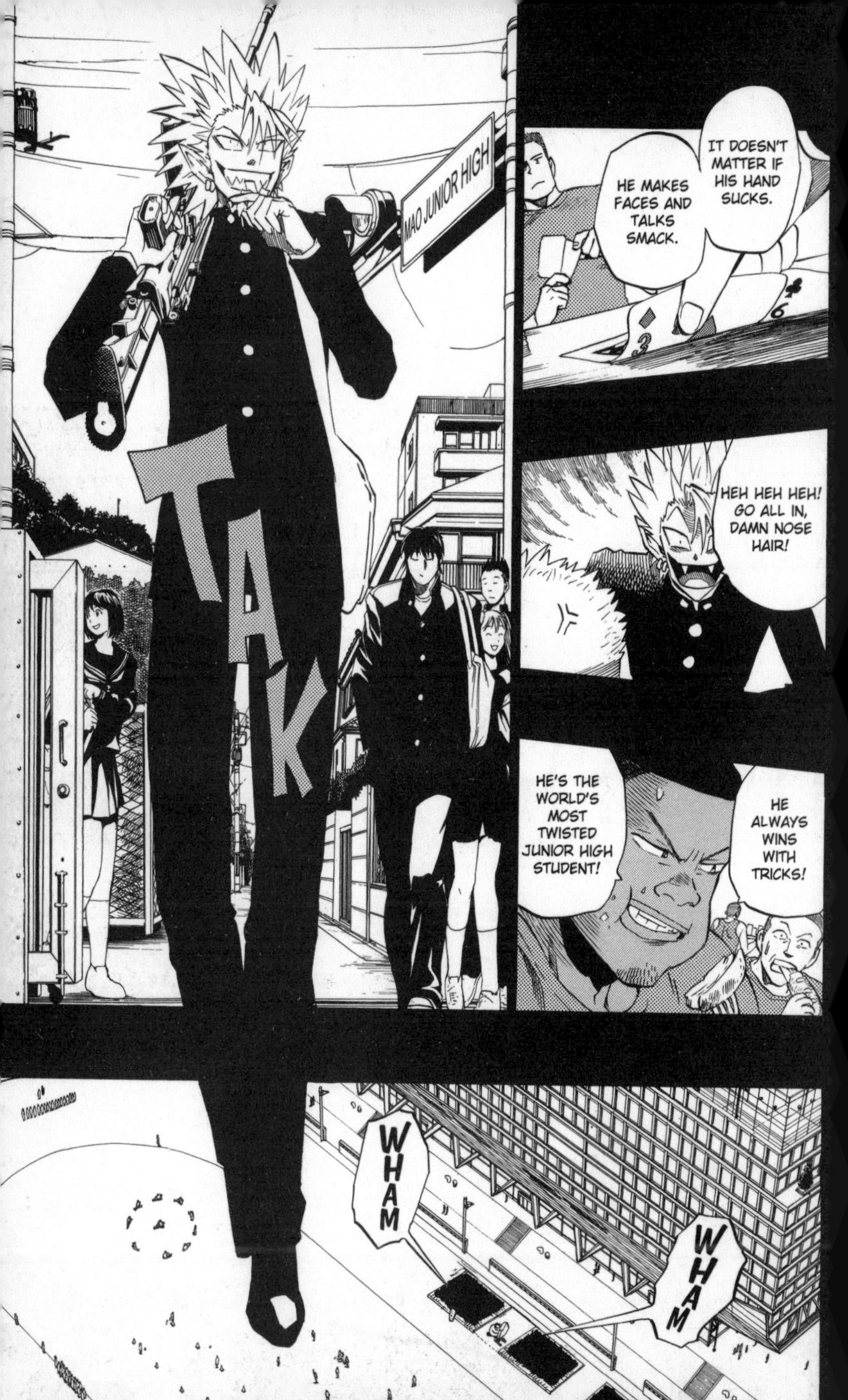
IT DOESN'T MATTER IF HIS HAND SUCKS.
HE MAKES FACES AND TALKS SMACK.
HEH HEH HEH! GO ALL IN, DAMN NOSE HAIR!
HE ALWAYS WINS WITH TRICKS!
HE'S THE WORLD'S MOST TWISTED JUNIOR HIGH STUDENT!
MAO JUNIOR HIGH
TAK
WHAM
WHAM

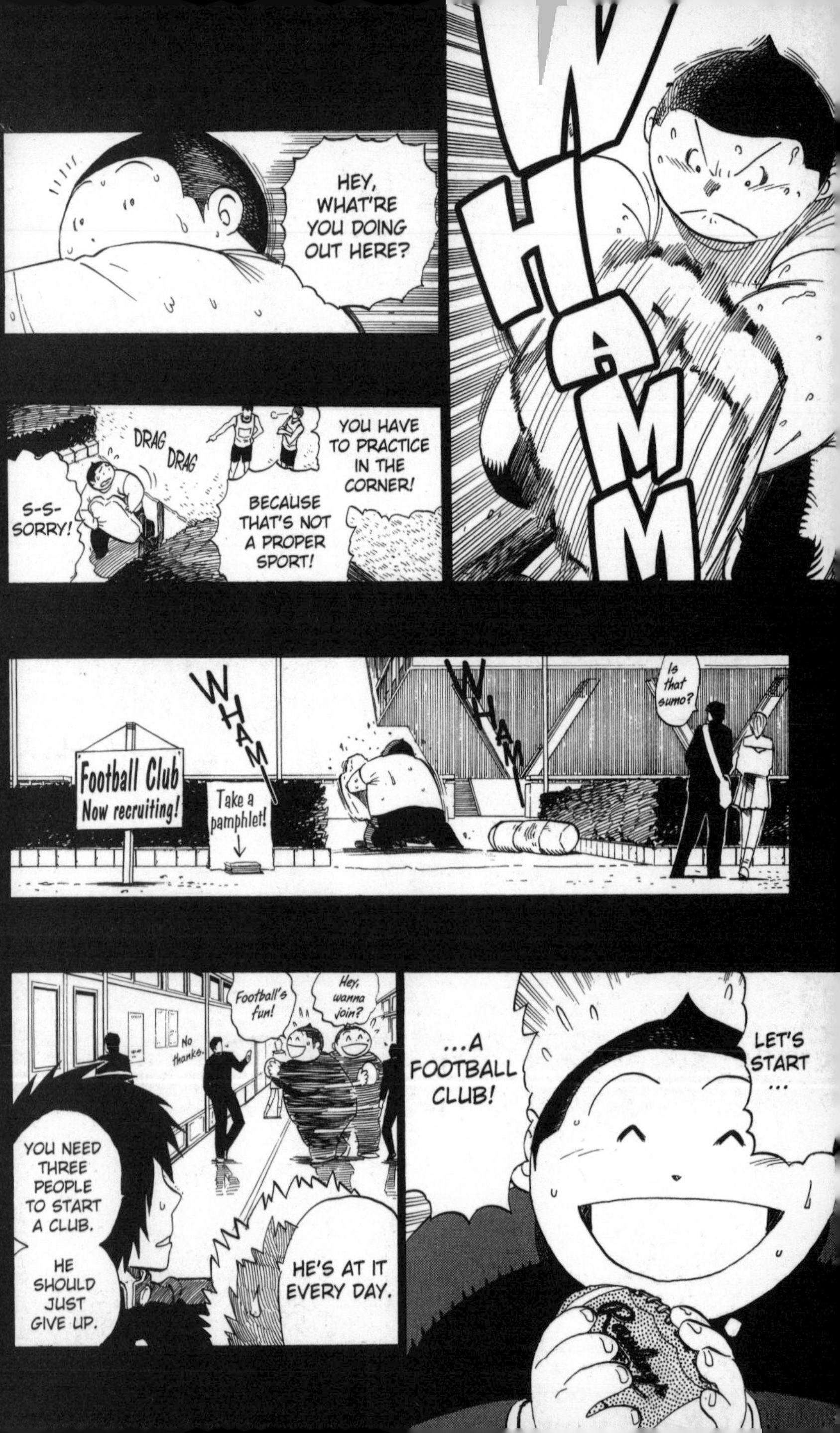
WHAMM
HEY, WHAT'RE YOU DOING OUT HERE?
YOU HAVE TO PRACTICE IN THE CORNER!
BECAUSE THAT'S NOT A PROPER SPORT!
DRAG DRAG
S-S-SORRY!
Is that sumo?
WHAM
WHAM
Take a pamphlet!
Football Club Now recruiting!
LET'S START ...
...A FOOTBALL CLUB!
Hey, wanna join?
Football's fun!
No thanks.
HE'S AT IT EVERY DAY.
YOU NEED THREE PEOPLE TO START A CLUB.
HE SHOULD JUST GIVE UP.

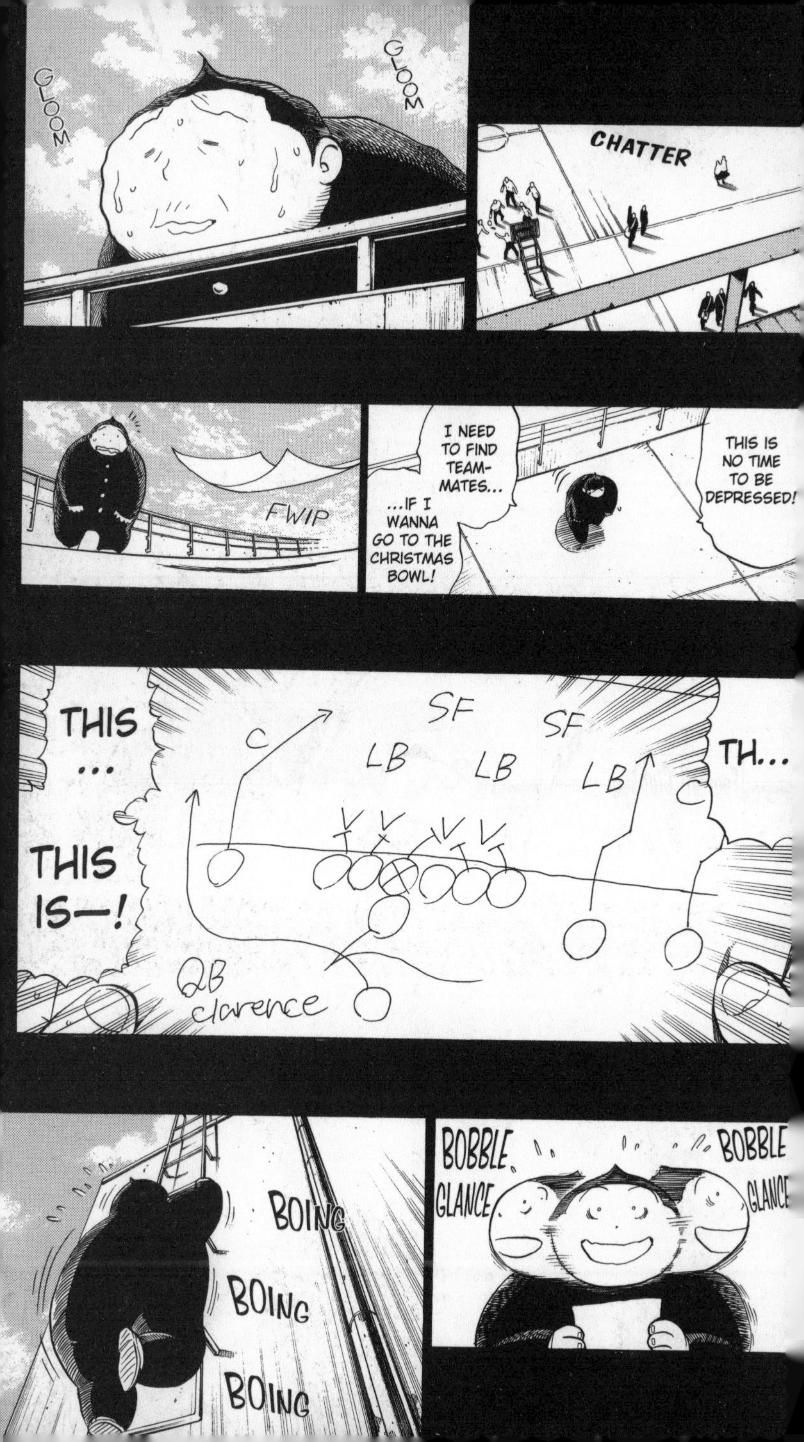
CHATTER
GLOOM
GLOOM
THIS IS NO TIME TO BE DEPRESSED!
I NEED TO FIND TEAM-MATES...
...IF I WANNA GO TO THE CHRISTMAS BOWL!
FWIP
TH...
SF
SF
C
LB
LB
LB
C
QB clarence
THIS...
THIS IS—!
BOBBLE
GLANCE
BOBBLE
GLANCE
BOING
BOING
BOING

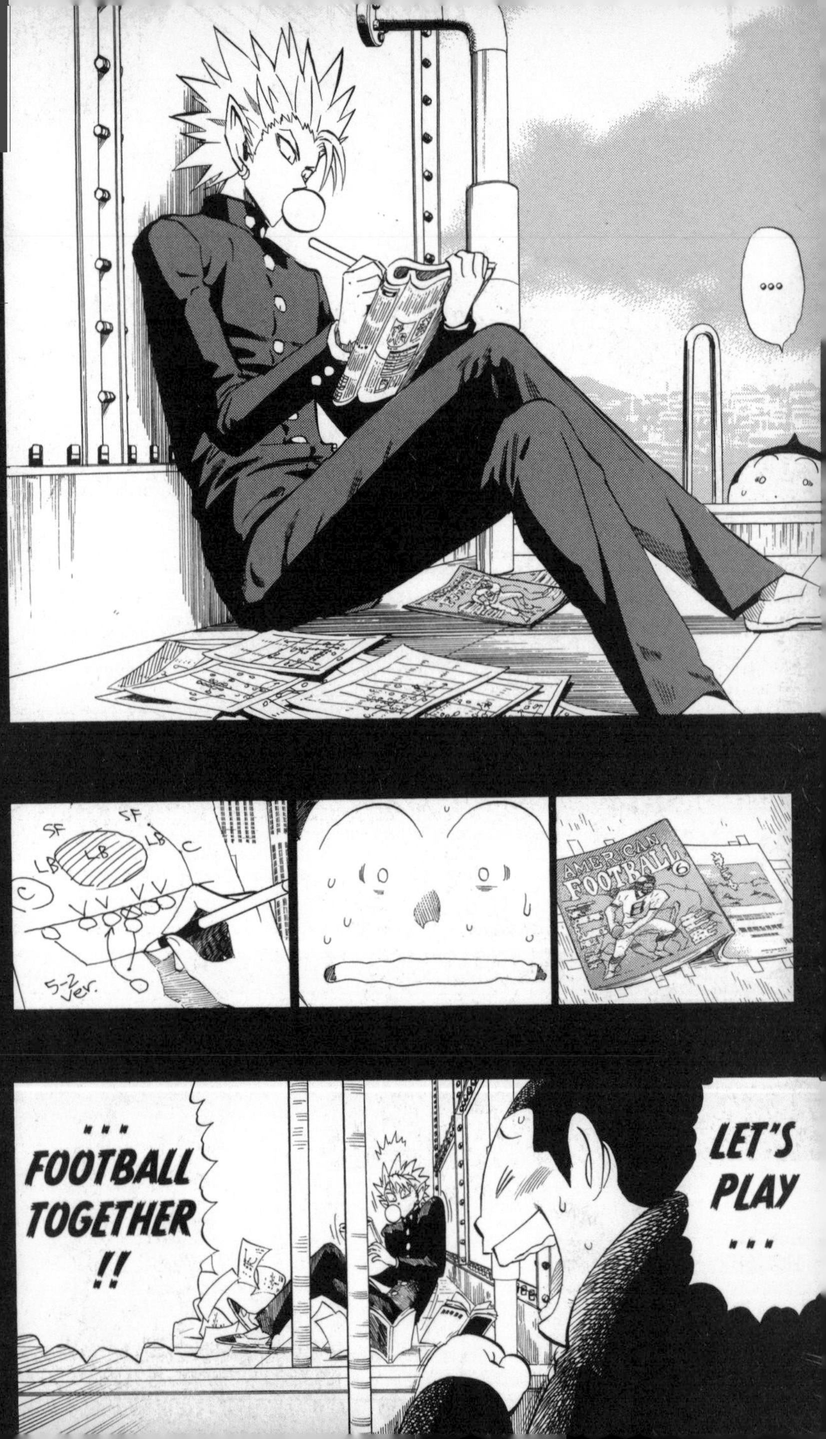
...
AMERICAN FOOTBALL 6
SF
LB
C
5-2 ver.
LET'S PLAY ...
... FOOTBALL TOGETHER !!

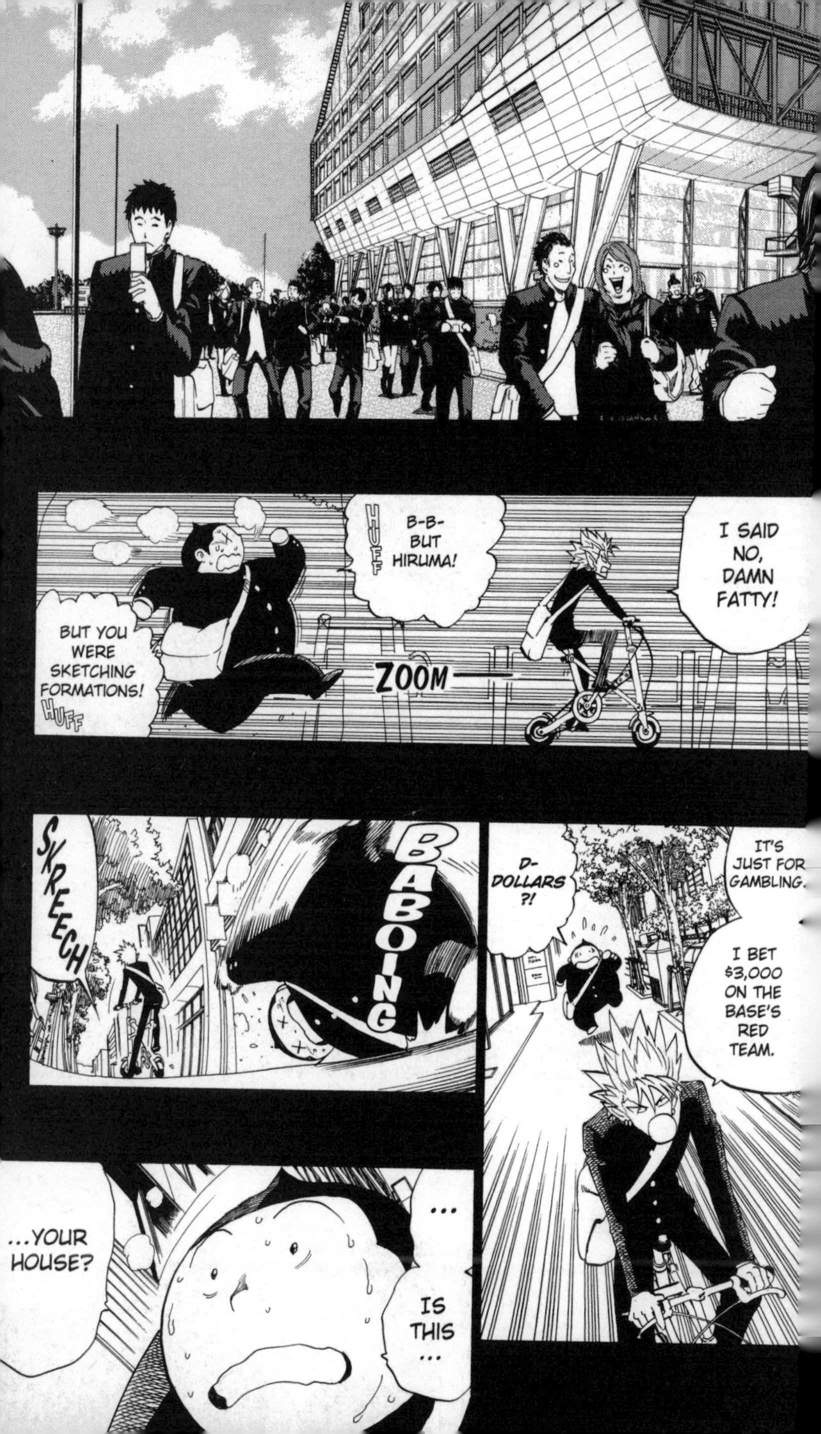
I SAID NO, DAMN FATTY!
HUFF
B-B-BUT HIRUMA!
ZOOM
BUT YOU WERE SKETCHING FORMATIONS!
HUFF
IT'S JUST FOR GAMBLING.
I BET $3,000 ON THE BASE'S RED TEAM.
D-DOLLARS?!
BABOING
SKREECH
...
IS THIS ...
...YOUR HOUSE?

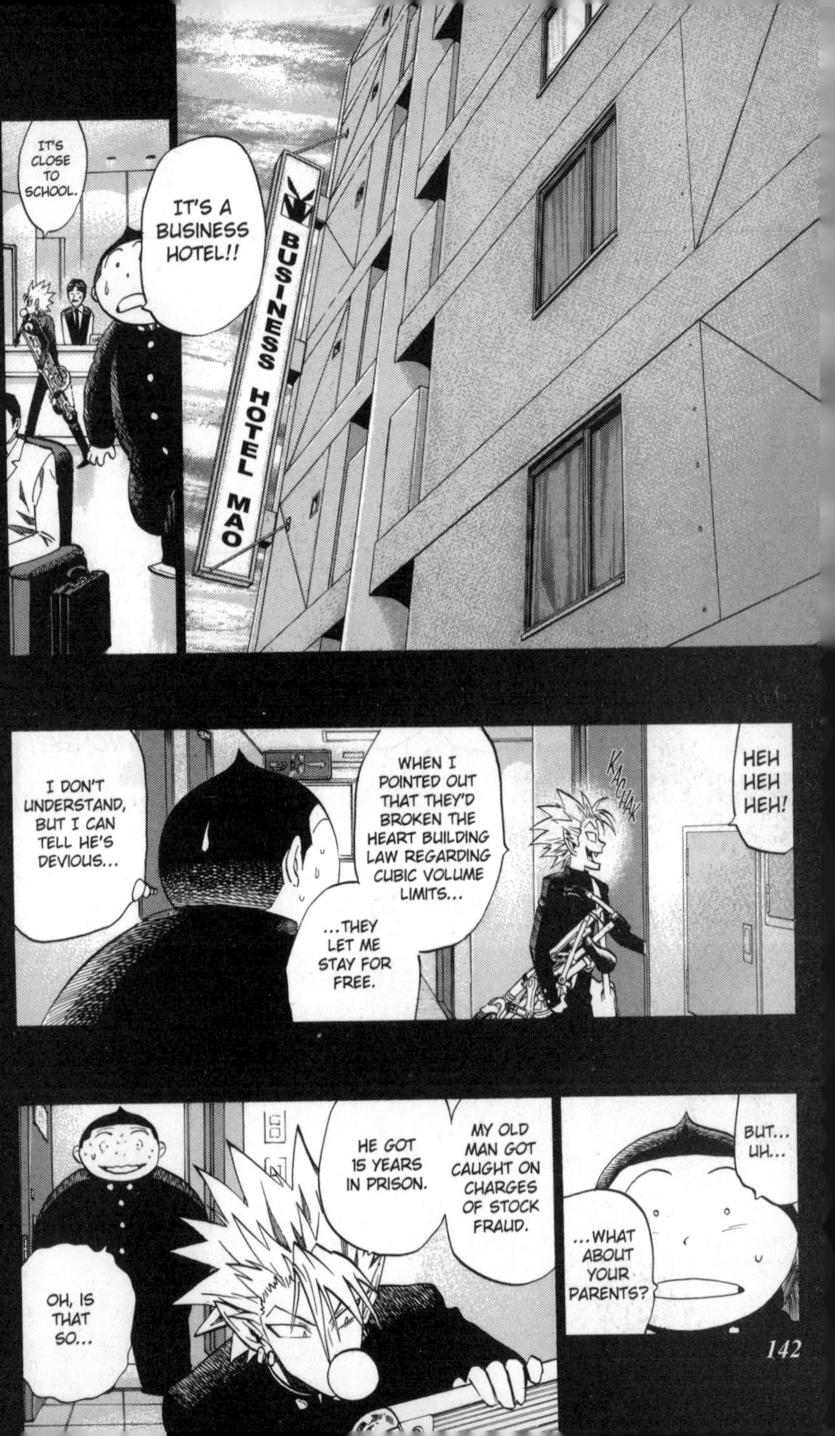
BUSINESS HOTEL MAO
IT'S A BUSINESS HOTEL!!
IT'S CLOSE TO SCHOOL.
HEH HEH HEH!
KACHAK
WHEN I POINTED OUT THAT THEY'D BROKEN THE HEART BUILDING LAW REGARDING CUBIC VOLUME LIMITS...
...THEY LET ME STAY FOR FREE.
I DON'T UNDERSTAND, BUT I CAN TELL HE'S DEVIOUS...
BUT... UH...
...WHAT ABOUT YOUR PARENTS?
MY OLD MAN GOT CAUGHT ON CHARGES OF STOCK FRAUD.
HE GOT 15 YEARS IN PRISON.
OH, IS THAT SO...

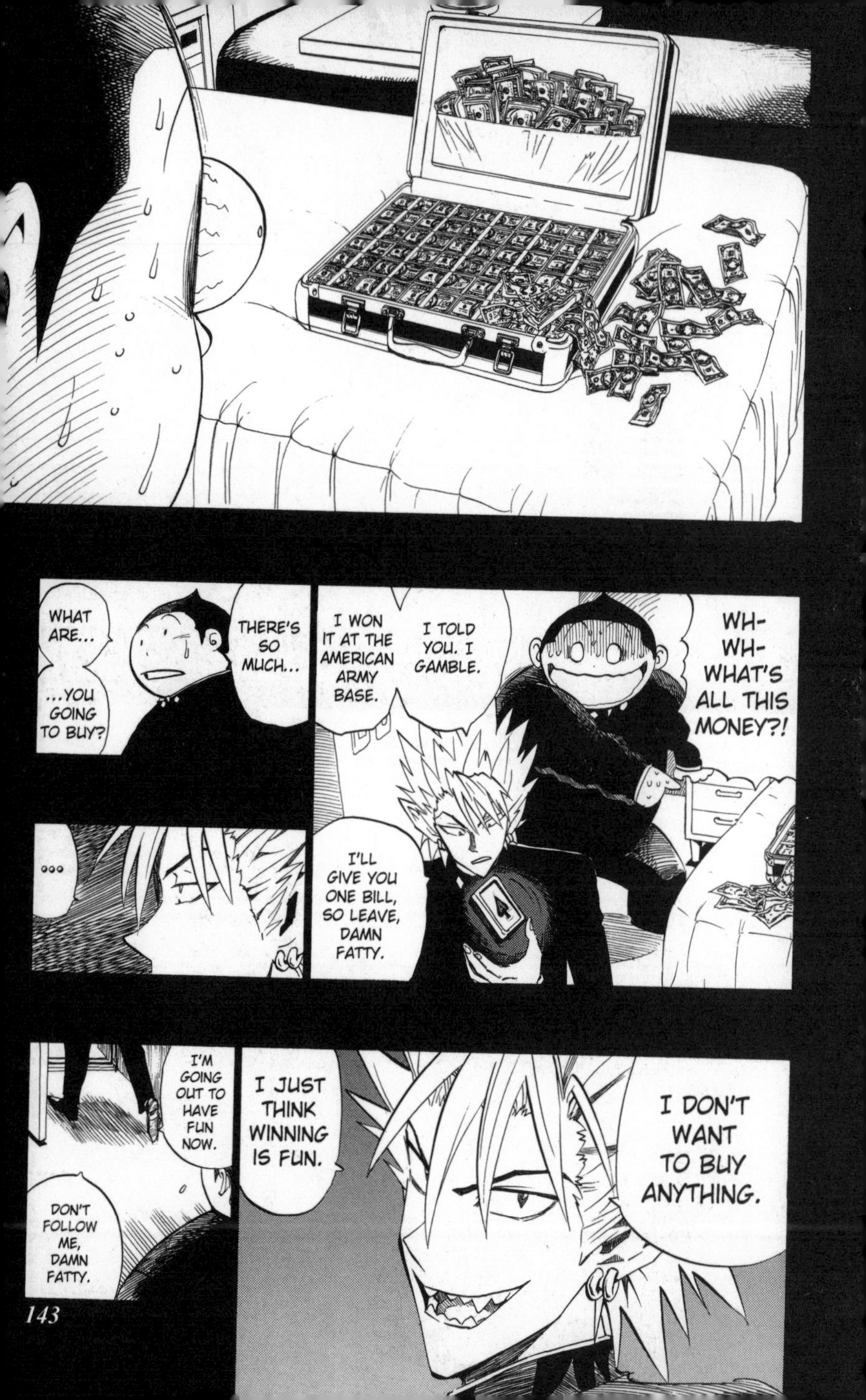
WH-WH-WHAT'S ALL THIS MONEY?!
I TOLD YOU. I GAMBLE.
I WON IT AT THE AMERICAN ARMY BASE.
I'LL GIVE YOU ONE BILL, SO LEAVE, DAMN FATTY.
THERE'S SO MUCH...
WHAT ARE...
...YOU GOING TO BUY?
...
I DON'T WANT TO BUY ANYTHING.
I JUST THINK WINNING IS FUN.
I'M GOING OUT TO HAVE FUN NOW.
DON'T FOLLOW ME, DAMN FATTY.

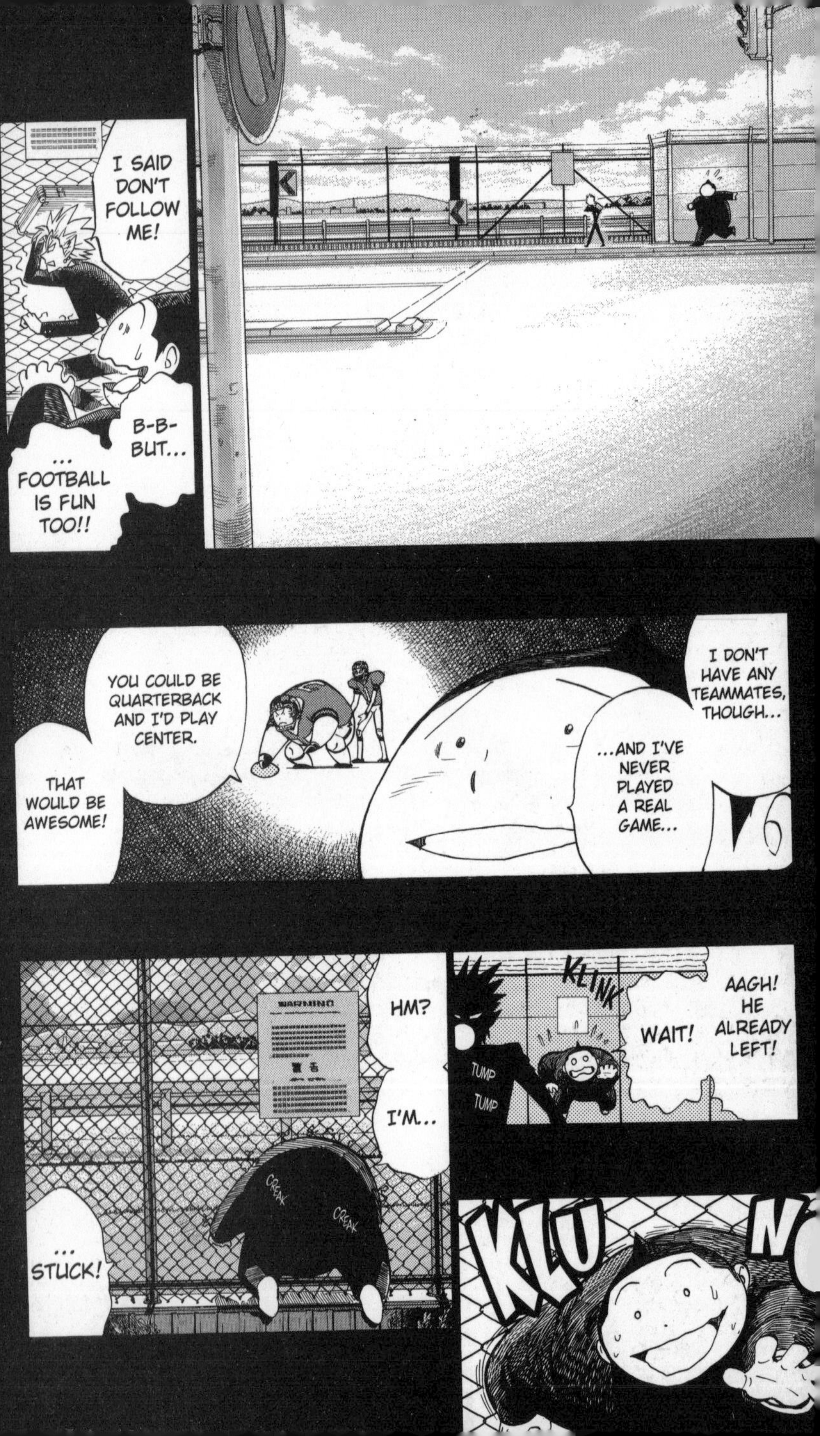
I SAID DON'T FOLLOW ME!
B-B-BUT...
...FOOTBALL IS FUN TOO!!
I DON'T HAVE ANY TEAMMATES, THOUGH...
...AND I'VE NEVER PLAYED A REAL GAME...
YOU COULD BE QUARTERBACK AND I'D PLAY CENTER.
THAT WOULD BE AWESOME!
KLINK
AAGH! HE ALREADY LEFT!
WAIT!
TUMP TUMP
KLU N
HM?
I'M...
CREAK CREAK
...STUCK!

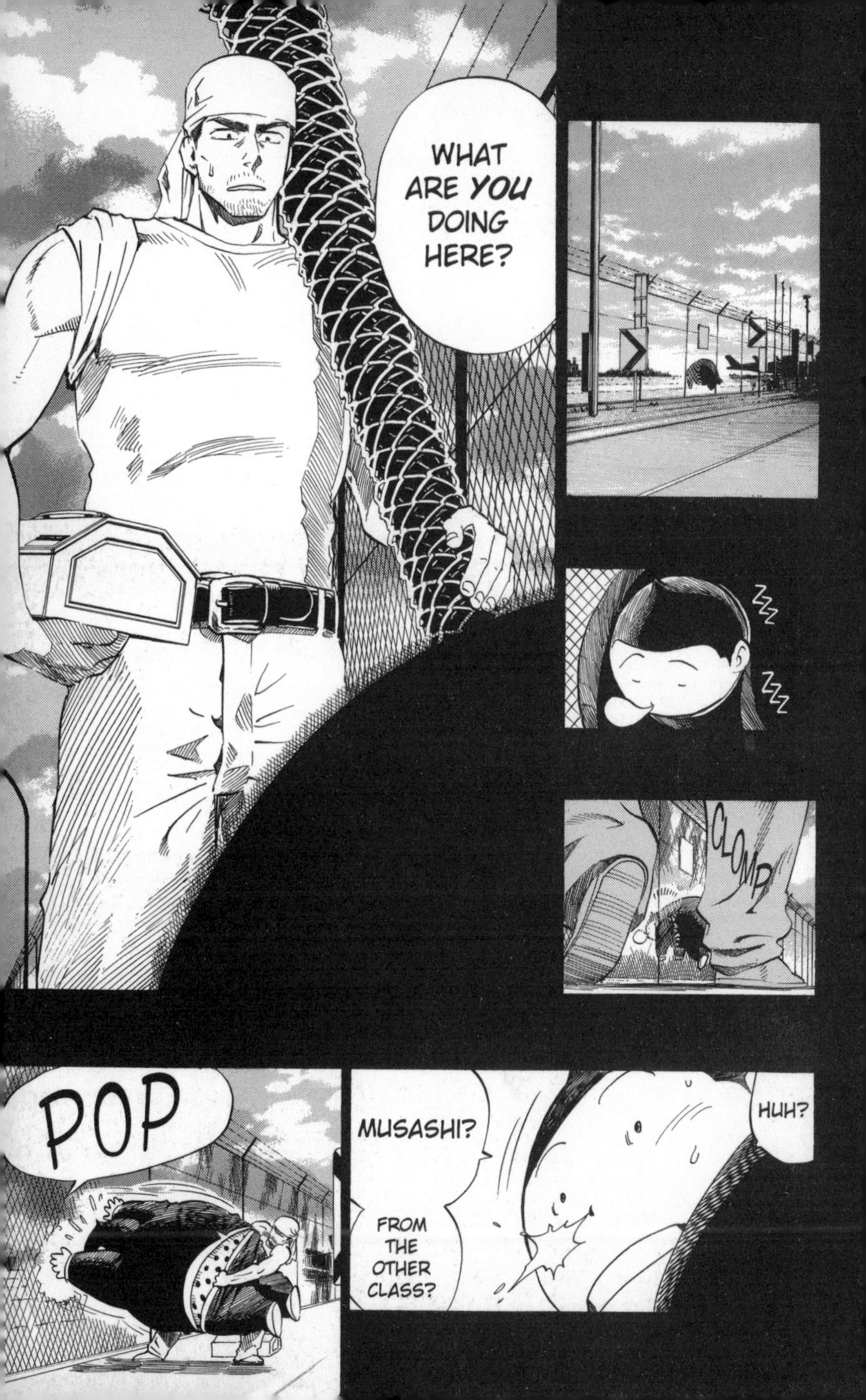
ZZZ
ZZZ
CLOMP
WHAT ARE *YOU* DOING HERE?
HUH?
MUSASHI?
FROM THE OTHER CLASS?
POP

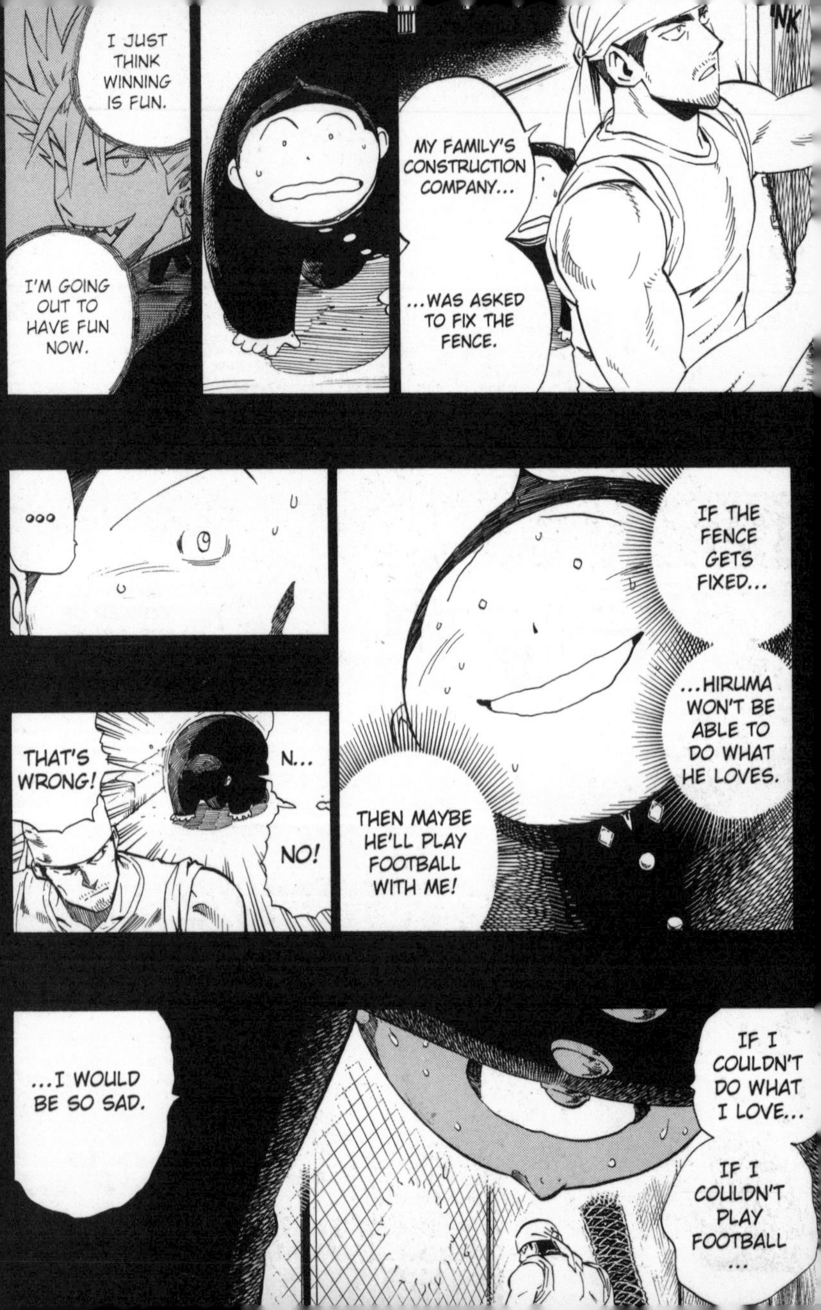
'NK
MY FAMILY'S CONSTRUCTION COMPANY...
...WAS ASKED TO FIX THE FENCE.
I JUST THINK WINNING IS FUN.
I'M GOING OUT TO HAVE FUN NOW.
IF THE FENCE GETS FIXED...
...HIRUMA WON'T BE ABLE TO DO WHAT HE LOVES.
THEN MAYBE HE'LL PLAY FOOTBALL WITH ME!
...
N...
NO!
THAT'S WRONG!
IF I COULDN'T DO WHAT I LOVE...
IF I COULDN'T PLAY FOOTBALL...
...I WOULD BE SO SAD.

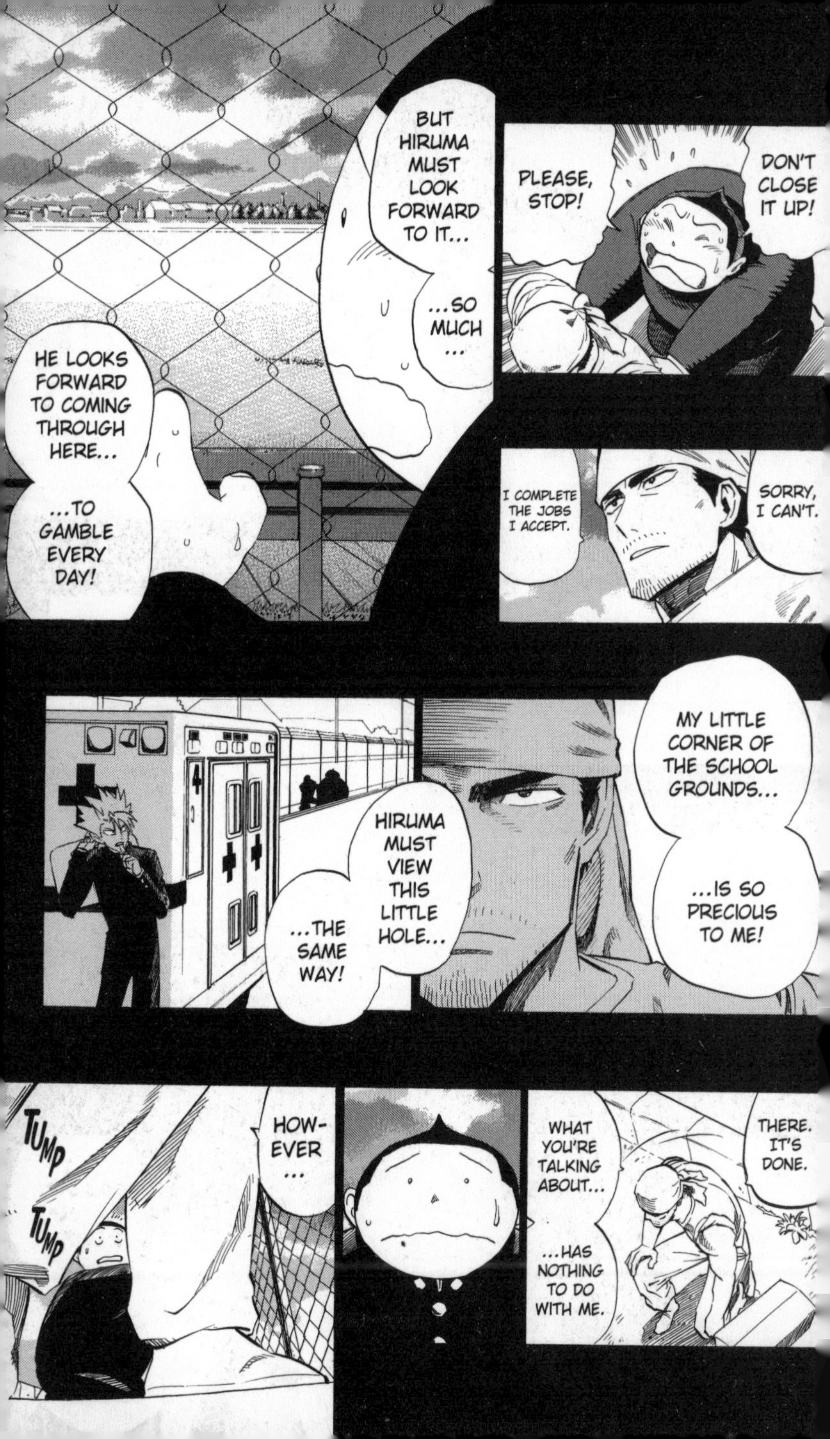
DON'T CLOSE IT UP!
PLEASE, STOP!
SORRY, I CAN'T.
I COMPLETE THE JOBS I ACCEPT.
HE LOOKS FORWARD TO COMING THROUGH HERE...
...TO GAMBLE EVERY DAY!
BUT HIRUMA MUST LOOK FORWARD TO IT...
...SO MUCH...
MY LITTLE CORNER OF THE SCHOOL GROUNDS...
...IS SO PRECIOUS TO ME!
HIRUMA MUST VIEW THIS LITTLE HOLE...
...THE SAME WAY!
THERE. IT'S DONE.
WHAT YOU'RE TALKING ABOUT...
...HAS NOTHING TO DO WITH ME.
HOW-EVER...
TUMP
TUMP

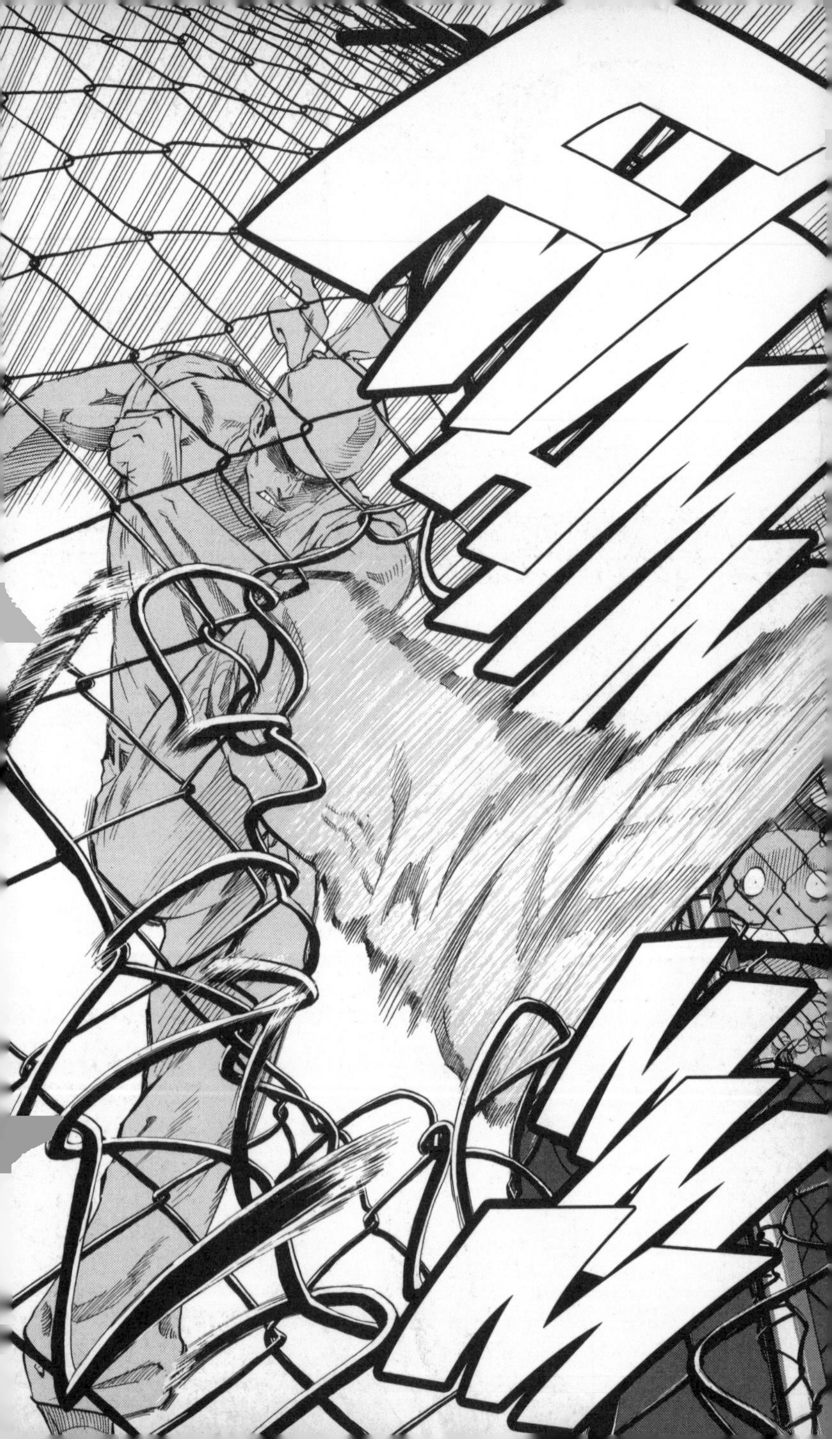

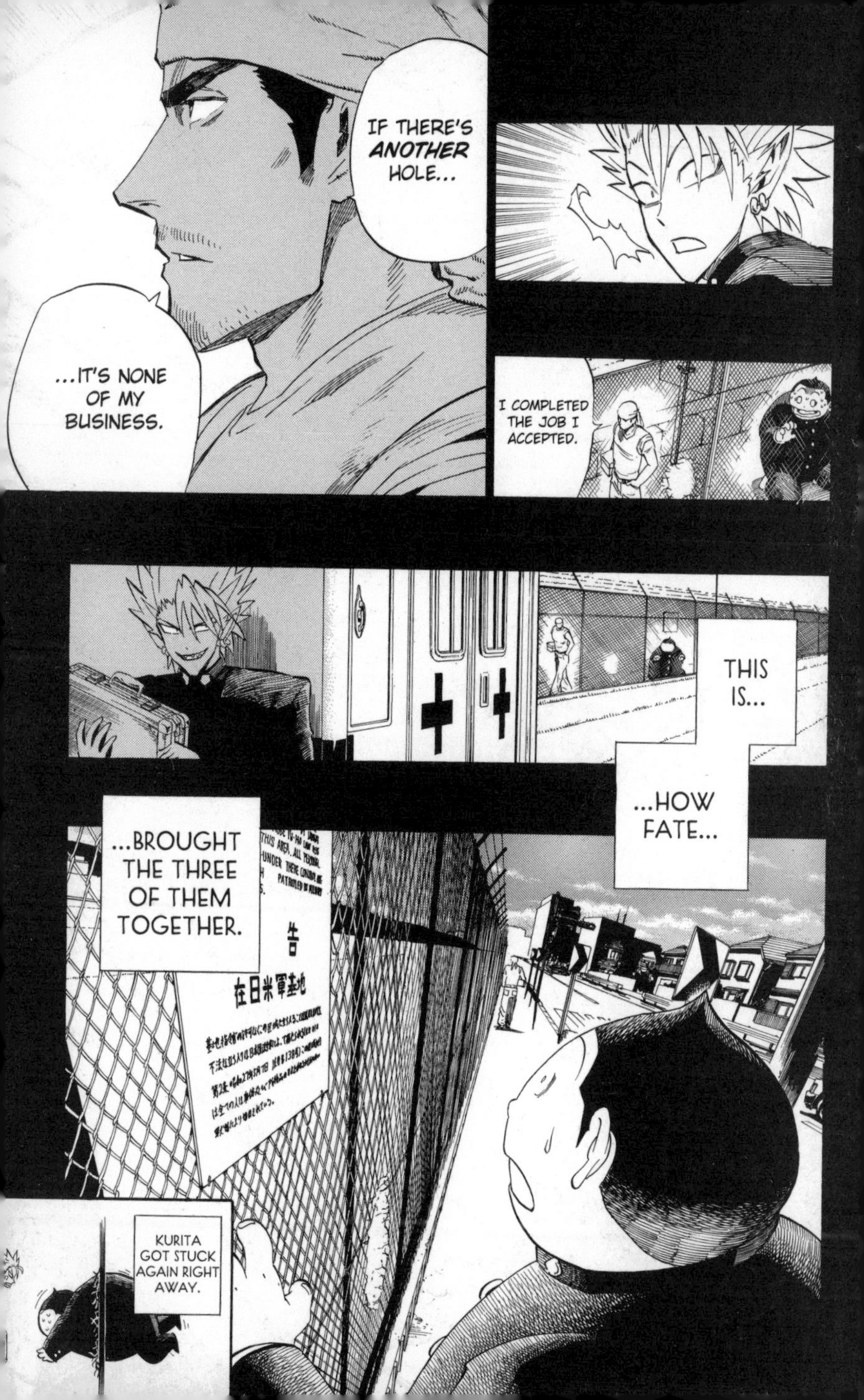
IF THERE'S *ANOTHER* HOLE...
...IT'S NONE OF MY BUSINESS.
I COMPLETED THE JOB I ACCEPTED.
THIS IS...
...HOW FATE...
...BROUGHT THE THREE OF THEM TOGETHER.
告
在日米軍基地
KURITA GOT STUCK AGAIN RIGHT AWAY.

Devil Bat 021

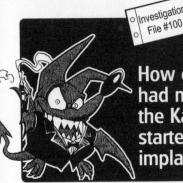

Investigation File #100

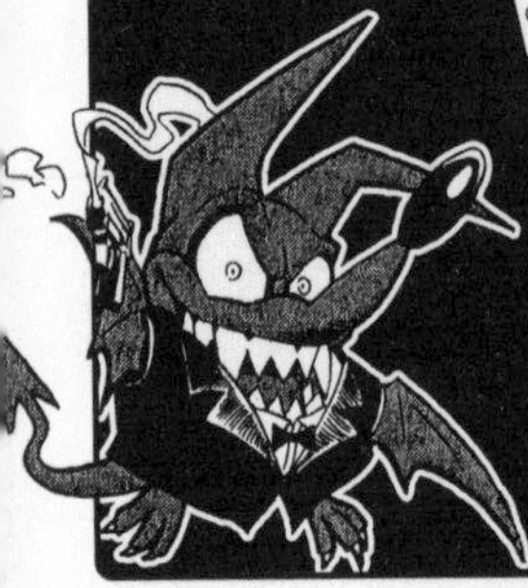

How come Yukimitsu has had more hair ever since the Kanto Tournament started? Did he get hair implants? Or is it a wig?

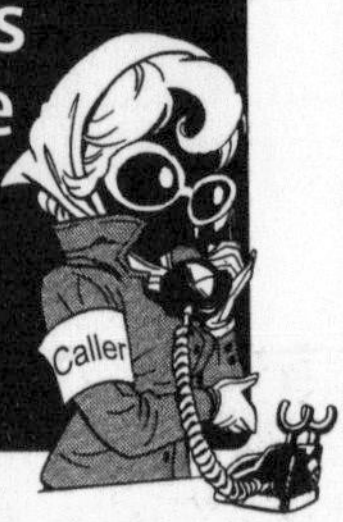
Caller

Caller name: K.M. in Gifu Prefecture.

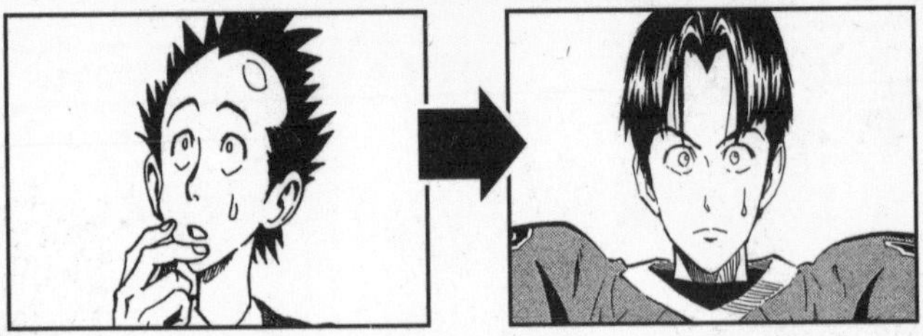

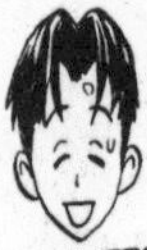

NO, I JUST, UH...GREW MORE HAIR THE NORMAL WAY.

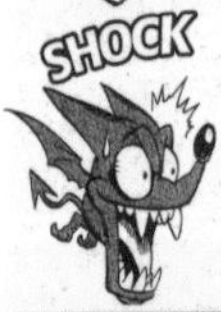
SHOCK

THAT'S ALL WE'VE GOT FOR OUR 100TH INVESTIGATION FILE?! WHAT A LETDOWN!!

Send your queries for Devil Bat 021 here!!

Devil Bat 021
Shonen Jump Advanced/Eyeshield 21
c/o VIZ Media, LLC
P.O. Box 77010
San Francisco, CA 94107

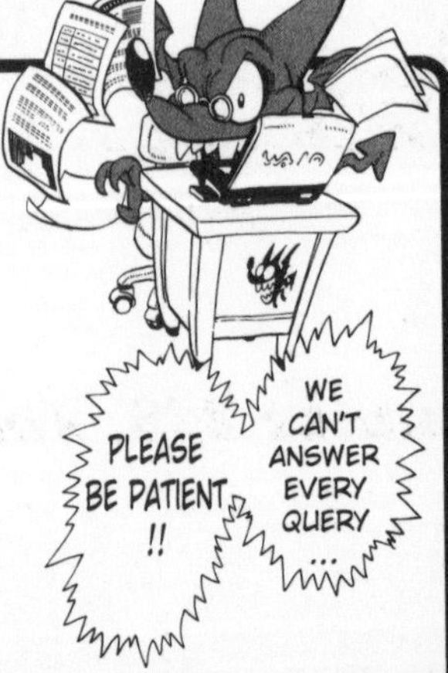
PLEASE BE PATIENT !!
WE CAN'T ANSWER EVERY QUERY ...

Chapter 249 Yoichi Hiruma (Part 2)

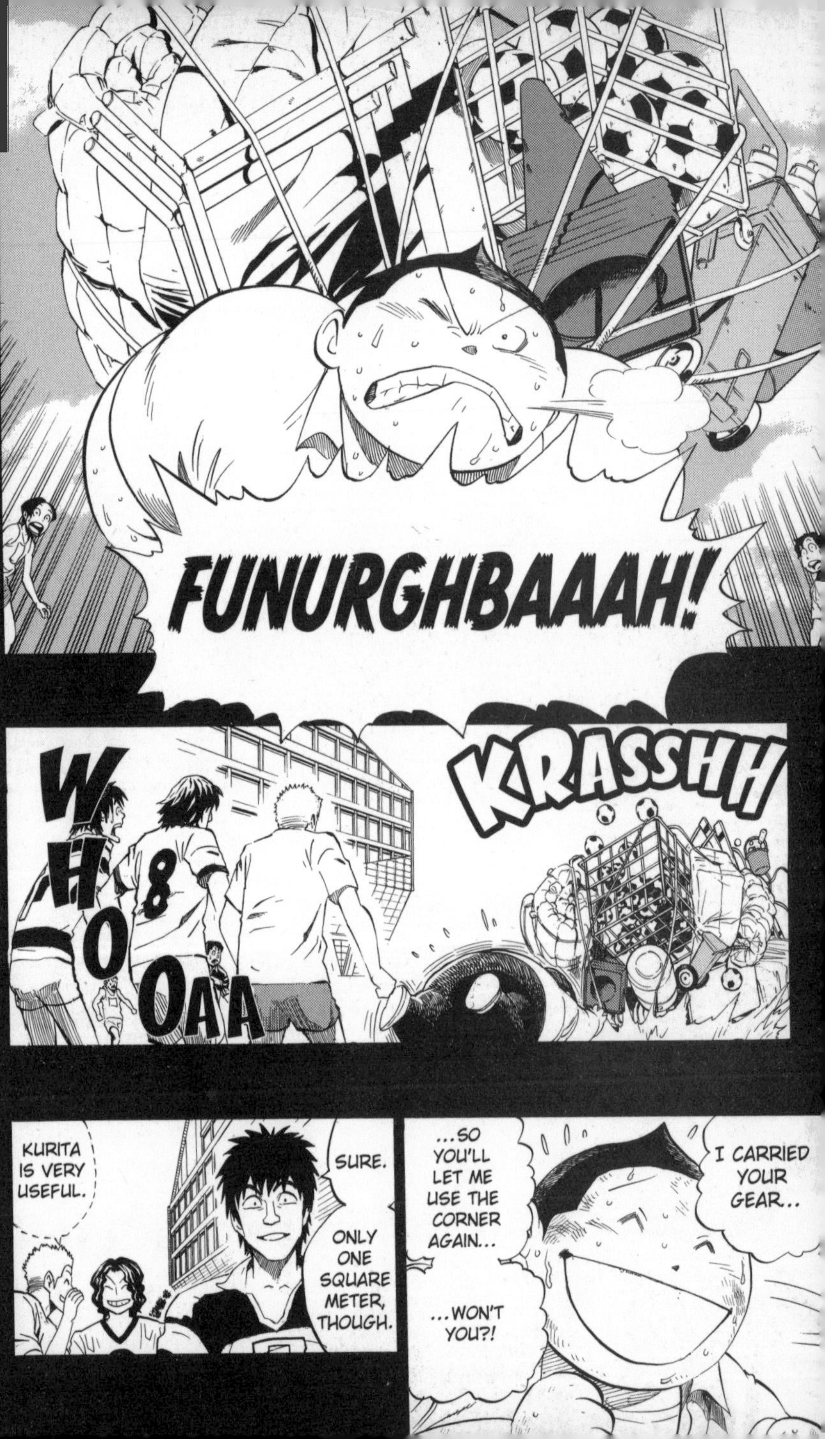
FUNURGHBAAAH!
KRASSHH
WHOOAA
I CARRIED YOUR GEAR...
...SO YOU'LL LET ME USE THE CORNER AGAIN...
...WON'T YOU?!
SURE.
ONLY ONE SQUARE METER, THOUGH.
KURITA IS VERY USEFUL.

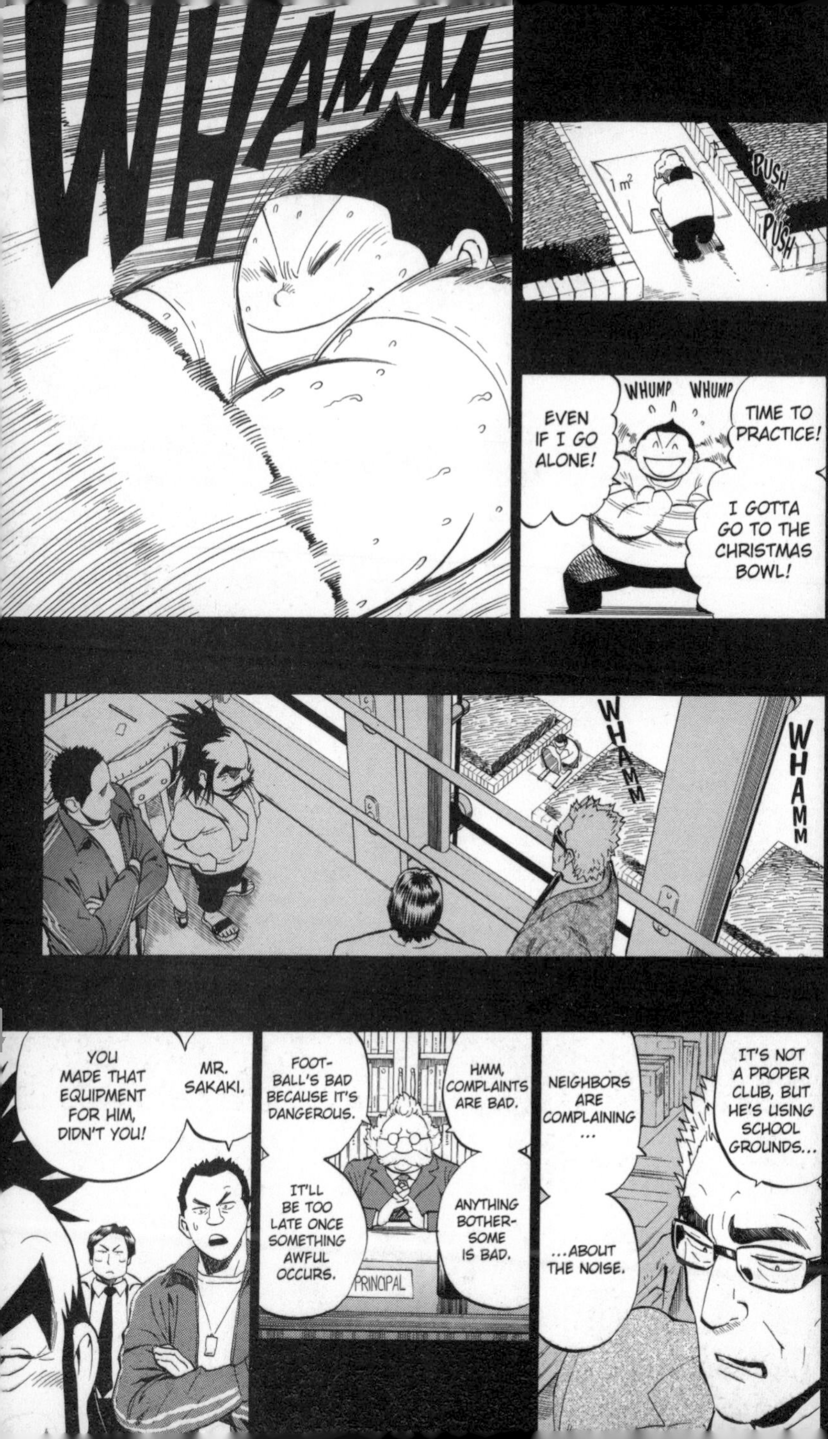
1 m²
PUSH
PUSH
WHUMP WHUMP
TIME TO PRACTICE!
I GOTTA GO TO THE CHRISTMAS BOWL!
EVEN IF I GO ALONE!
WHAMM
WHAMM
WHAMM
IT'S NOT A PROPER CLUB, BUT HE'S USING SCHOOL GROUNDS...
NEIGHBORS ARE COMPLAINING...
...ABOUT THE NOISE.
HMM, COMPLAINTS ARE BAD.
ANYTHING BOTHER-SOME IS BAD.
FOOT-BALL'S BAD BECAUSE IT'S DANGEROUS.
IT'LL BE TOO LATE ONCE SOMETHING AWFUL OCCURS.
PRINCIPAL
MR. SAKAKI.
YOU MADE THAT EQUIPMENT FOR HIM, DIDN'T YOU!

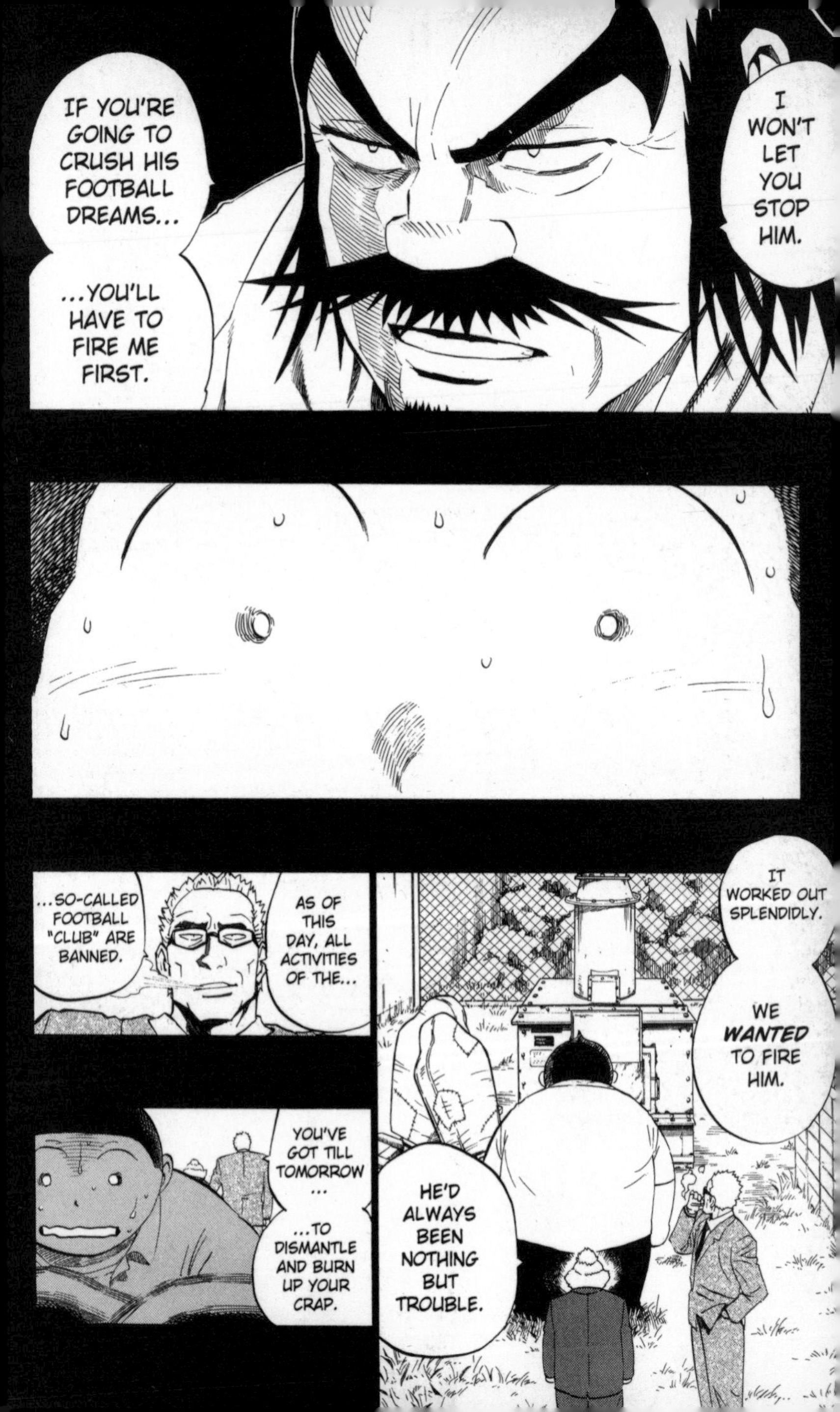
I WON'T LET YOU STOP HIM.
IF YOU'RE GOING TO CRUSH HIS FOOTBALL DREAMS...
...YOU'LL HAVE TO FIRE ME FIRST.
IT WORKED OUT SPLENDIDLY.
WE *WANTED* TO FIRE HIM.
HE'D ALWAYS BEEN NOTHING BUT TROUBLE.
AS OF THIS DAY, ALL ACTIVITIES OF THE...
...SO-CALLED FOOTBALL "CLUB" ARE BANNED.
YOU'VE GOT TILL TOMORROW ...
...TO DISMANTLE AND BURN UP YOUR CRAP.

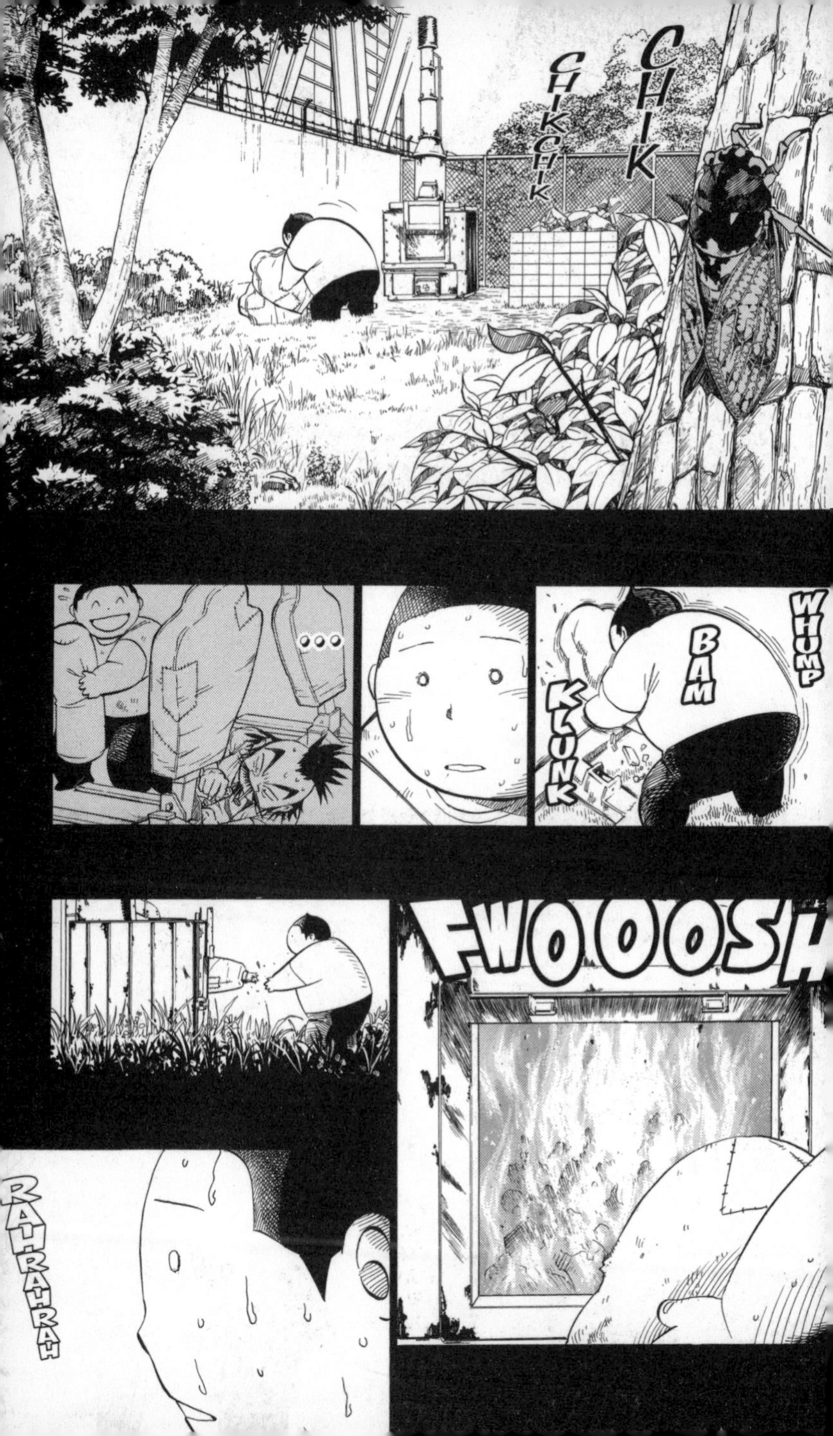
CHIK
CHIKCHIK
WHUMP
BAM
KLUNK
FWOOOSH
RAHRAHRAH

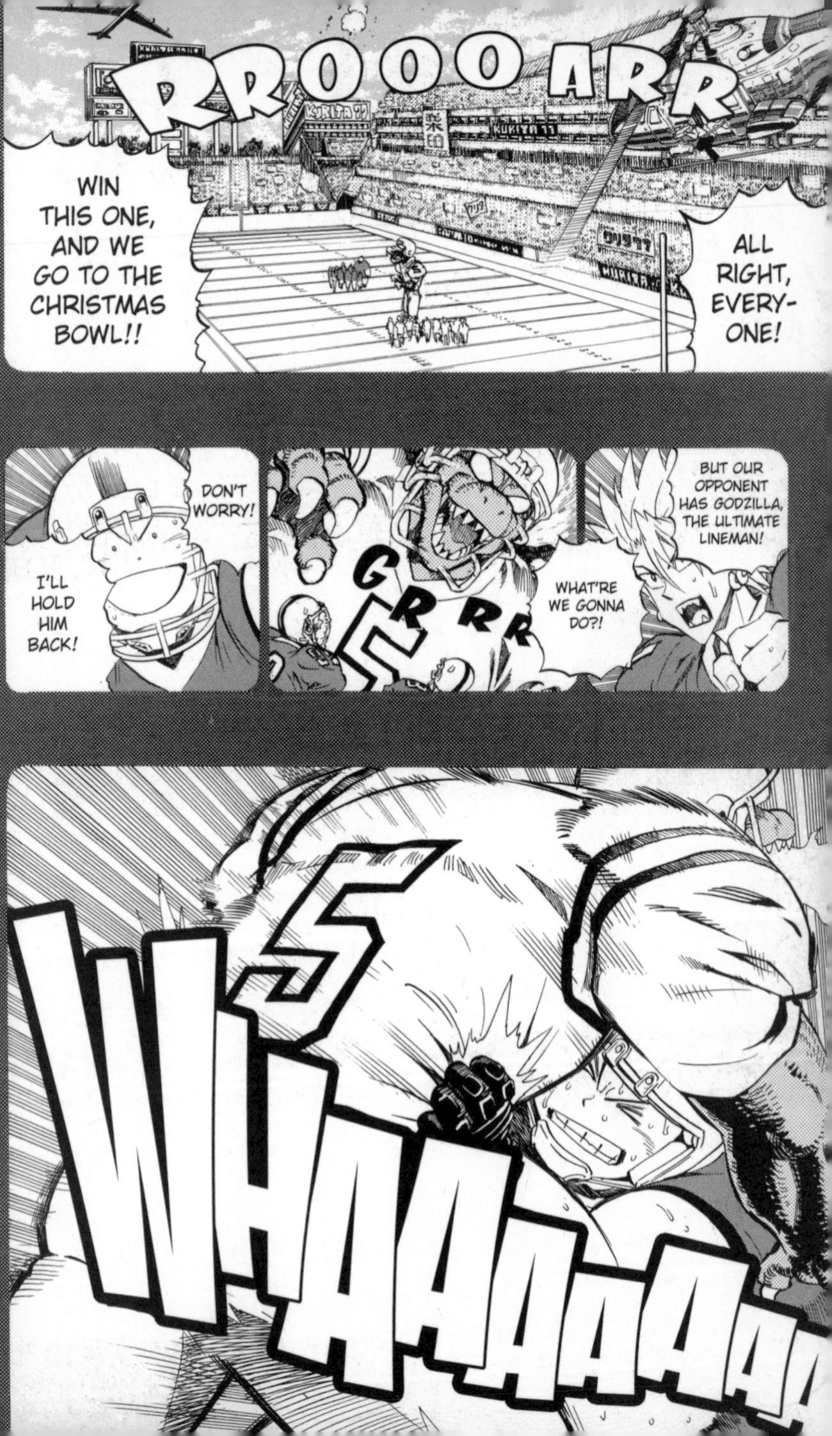
RROOO ARR
ALL RIGHT, EVERY-ONE!
WIN THIS ONE, AND WE GO TO THE CHRISTMAS BOWL!!
BUT OUR OPPONENT HAS GODZILLA, THE ULTIMATE LINEMAN!
WHAT'RE WE GONNA DO?!
GRRRR
DON'T WORRY!
I'LL HOLD HIM BACK!
WHAAAAAAAA!

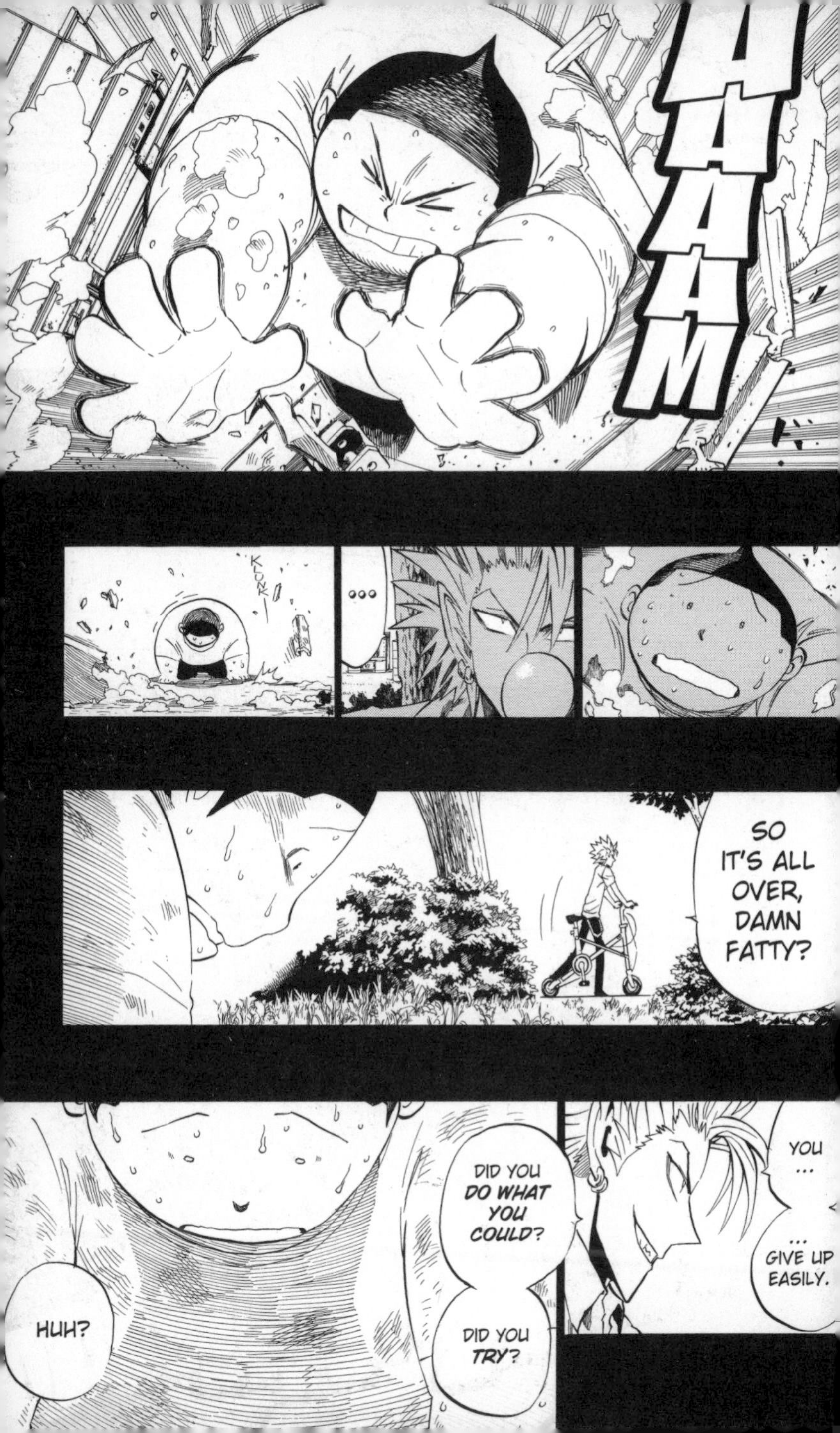
AAAAAM
...
KLUNK
SO IT'S ALL OVER, DAMN FATTY?
YOU ...
... GIVE UP EASILY.
DID YOU DO WHAT YOU COULD?
DID YOU TRY?
HUH?

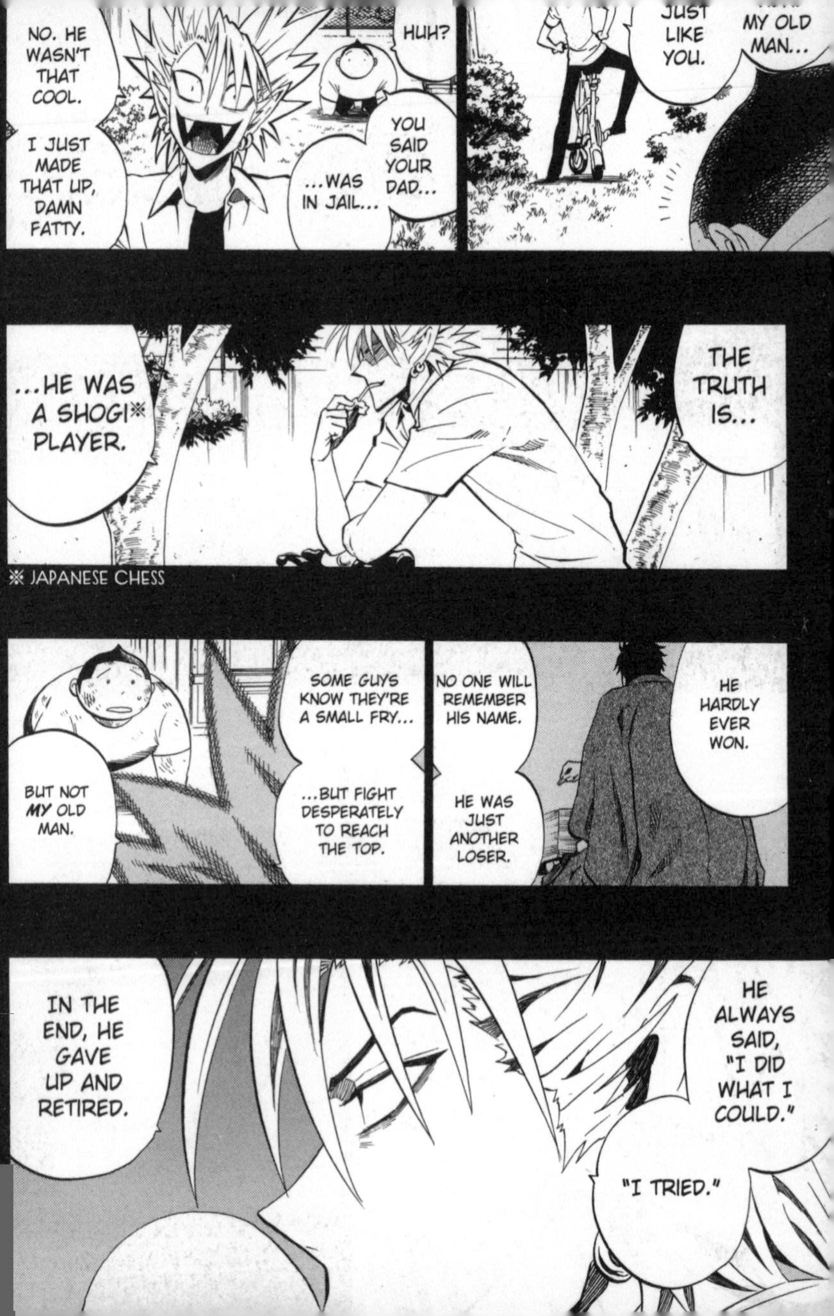
MY OLD MAN...
JUST LIKE YOU.
HUH?
YOU SAID YOUR DAD...
...WAS IN JAIL...
NO. HE WASN'T THAT COOL.
I JUST MADE THAT UP, DAMN FATTY.
THE TRUTH IS...
...HE WAS A SHOGI※ PLAYER.
HE HARDLY EVER WON.
NO ONE WILL REMEMBER HIS NAME.
HE WAS JUST ANOTHER LOSER.
SOME GUYS KNOW THEY'RE A SMALL FRY...
...BUT FIGHT DESPERATELY TO REACH THE TOP.
BUT NOT *MY* OLD MAN.
HE ALWAYS SAID, "I DID WHAT I COULD."
"I TRIED."
IN THE END, HE GAVE UP AND RETIRED.
※ JAPANESE CHESS

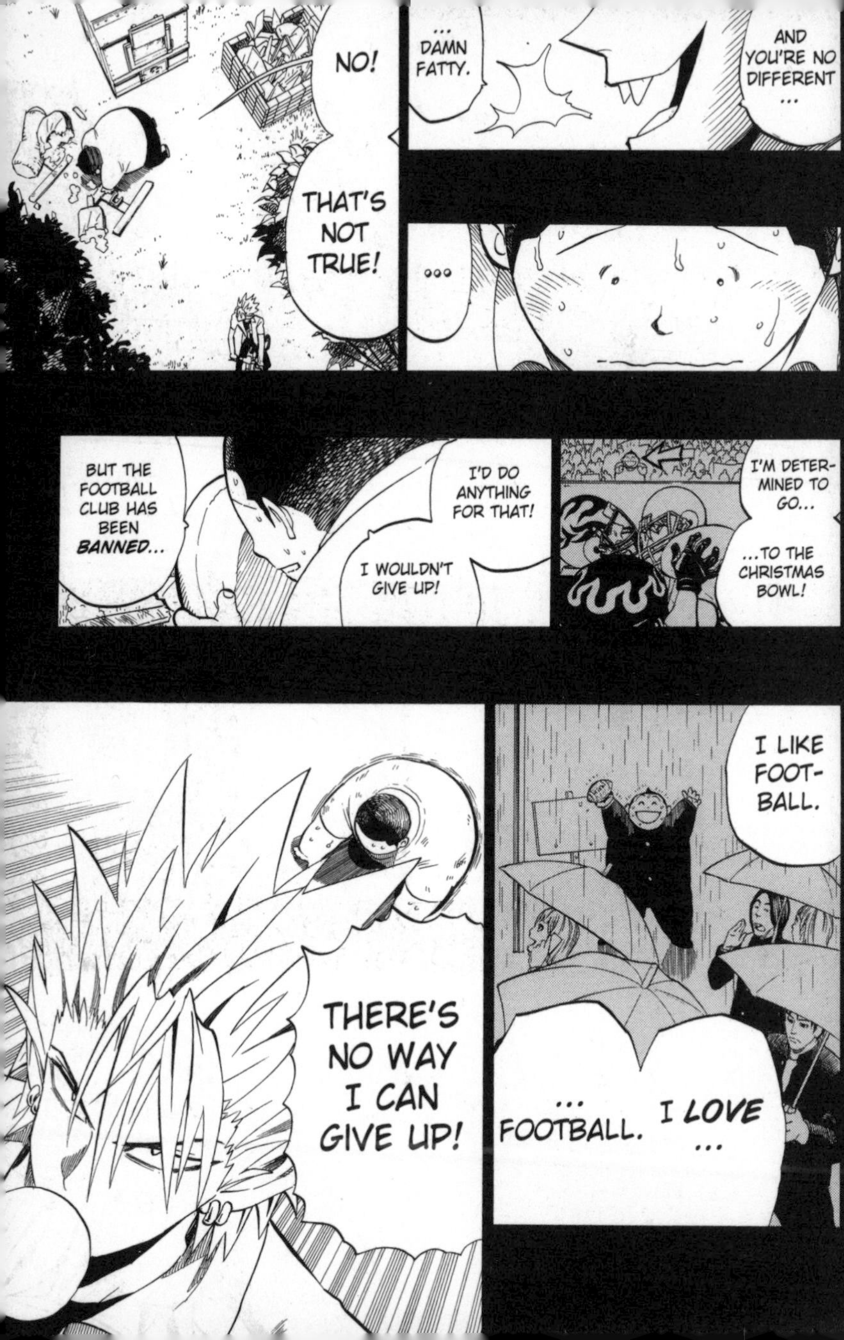
AND YOU'RE NO DIFFERENT ...
... DAMN FATTY.
...
NO!
THAT'S NOT TRUE!
I'M DETER-MINED TO GO...
...TO THE CHRISTMAS BOWL!
I'D DO ANYTHING FOR THAT!
I WOULDN'T GIVE UP!
BUT THE FOOTBALL CLUB HAS BEEN *BANNED*...
I LIKE FOOT-BALL.
I *LOVE* ...
... FOOTBALL.
THERE'S NO WAY I CAN GIVE UP!

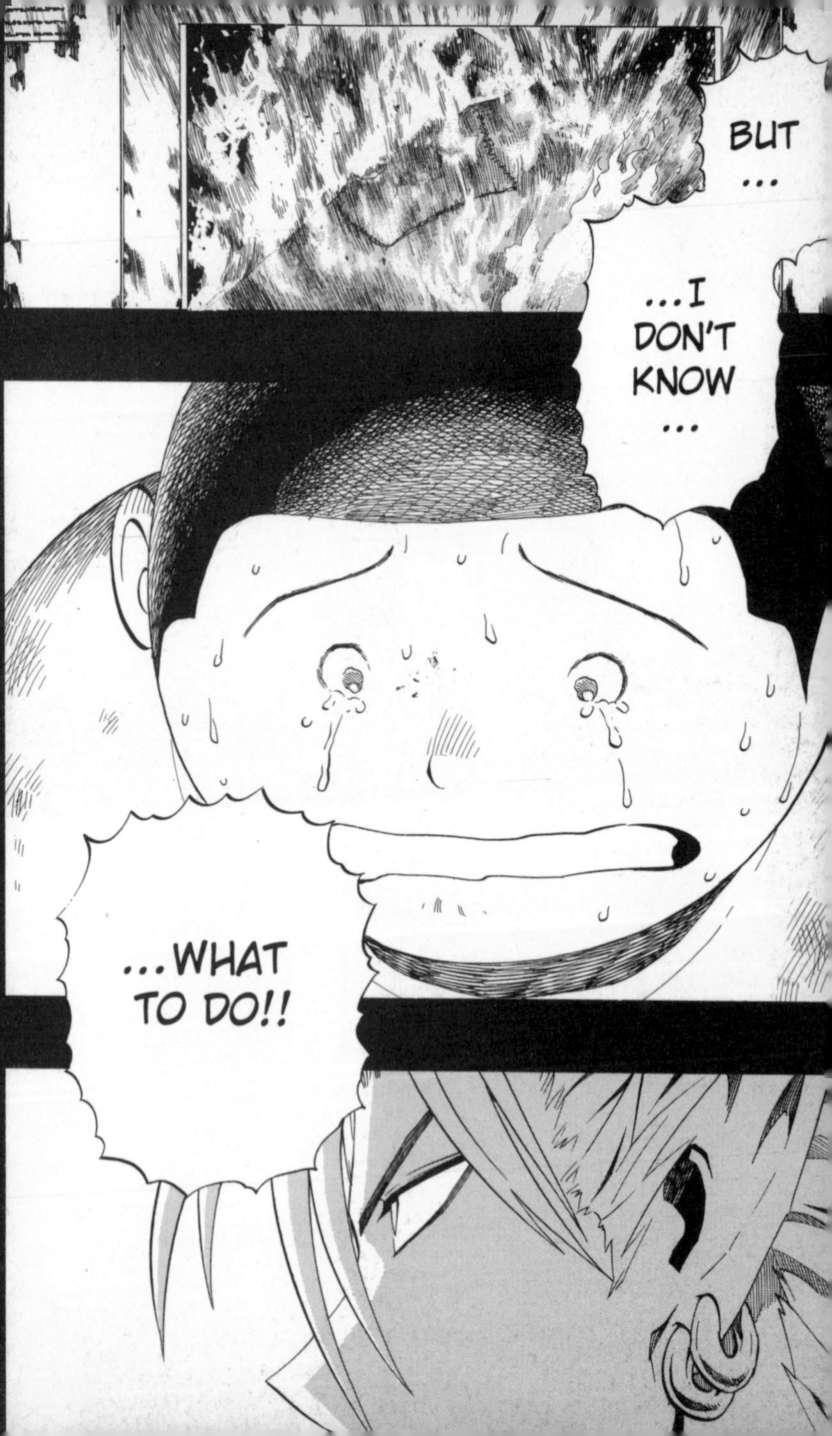
BUT ...
...I DON'T KNOW ...
...WHAT TO DO!!

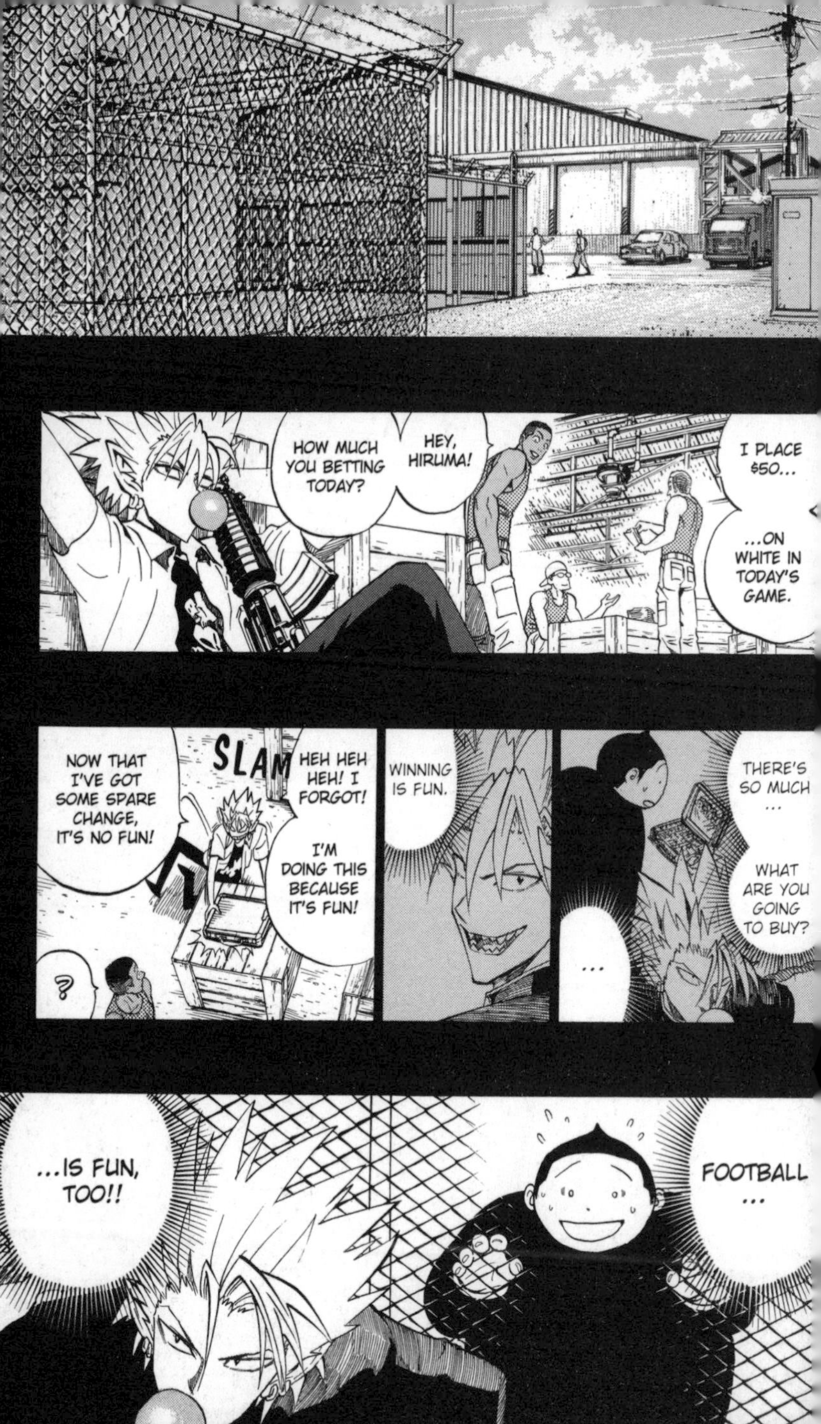
I PLACE $50...
...ON WHITE IN TODAY'S GAME.
HEY, HIRUMA!
HOW MUCH YOU BETTING TODAY?
THERE'S SO MUCH ...
WHAT ARE YOU GOING TO BUY?
...
WINNING IS FUN.
SLAM
HEH HEH HEH! I FORGOT!
I'M DOING THIS BECAUSE IT'S FUN!
NOW THAT I'VE GOT SOME SPARE CHANGE, IT'S NO FUN!
?
FOOTBALL ...
...IS FUN, TOO!!

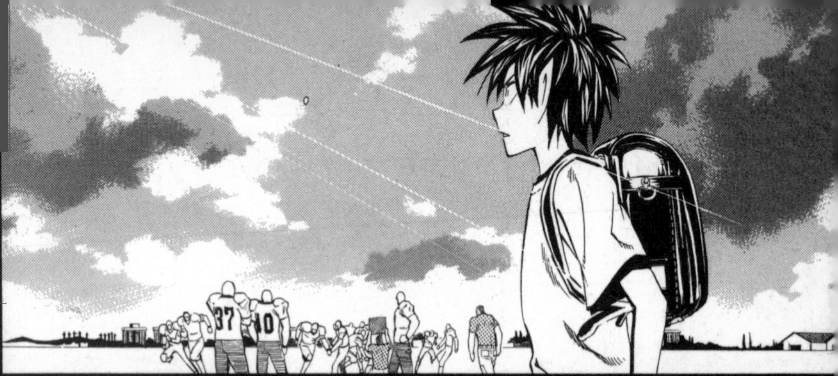

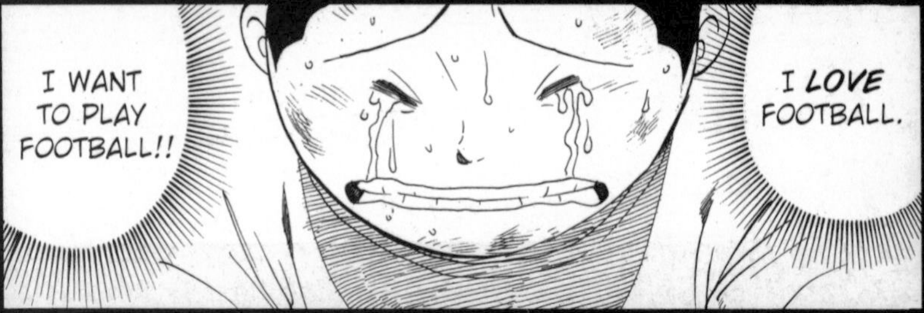
I *LOVE* FOOTBALL.
I WANT TO PLAY FOOTBALL!!

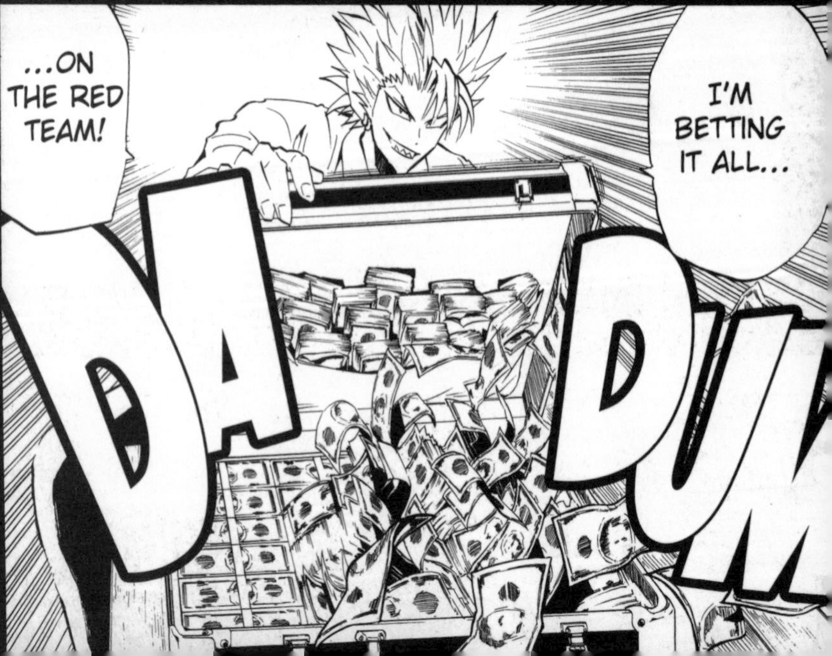
I'M BETTING IT ALL...
...ON THE RED TEAM!
DA
DUM

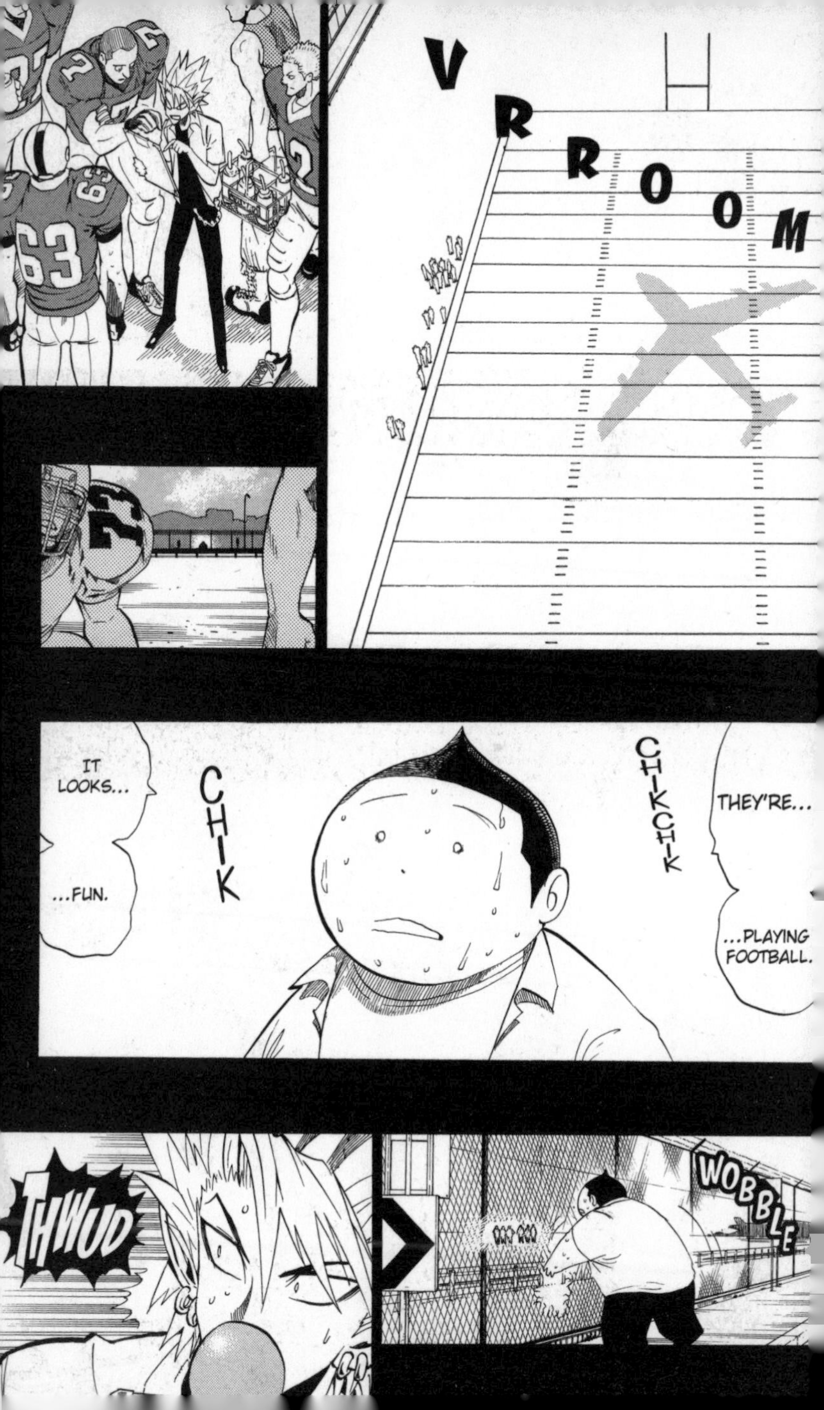
VRROOM
THEY'RE... ...PLAYING FOOTBALL.
CHIKCHIK
CHIK
IT LOOKS... ...FUN.
WOBBLE
THWUD

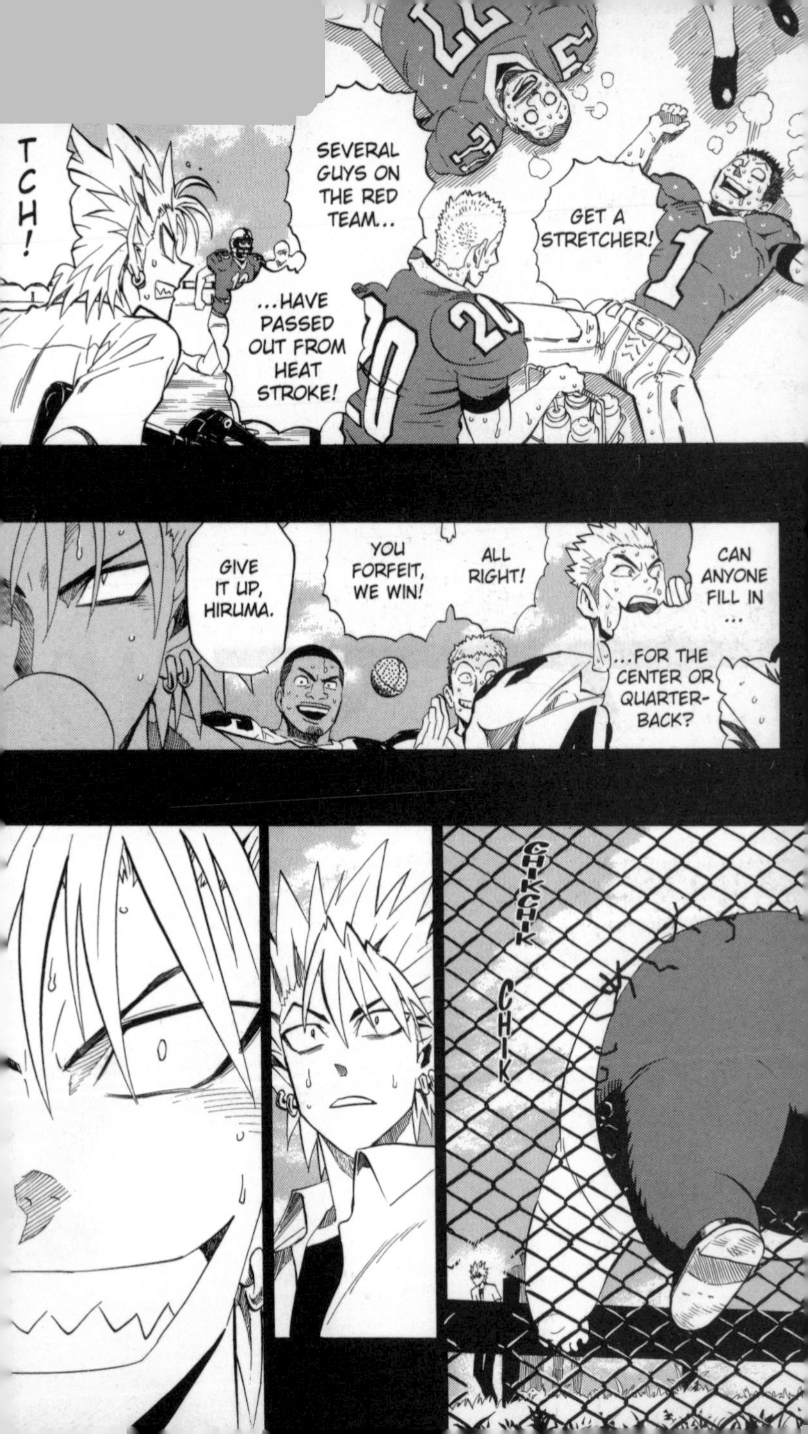
GET A STRETCHER!
SEVERAL GUYS ON THE RED TEAM...
...HAVE PASSED OUT FROM HEAT STROKE!
TCH!
CAN ANYONE FILL IN ...
...FOR THE CENTER OR QUARTER-BACK?
ALL RIGHT!
YOU FORFEIT, WE WIN!
GIVE IT UP, HIRUMA.
CHIKCHIK
CHIK

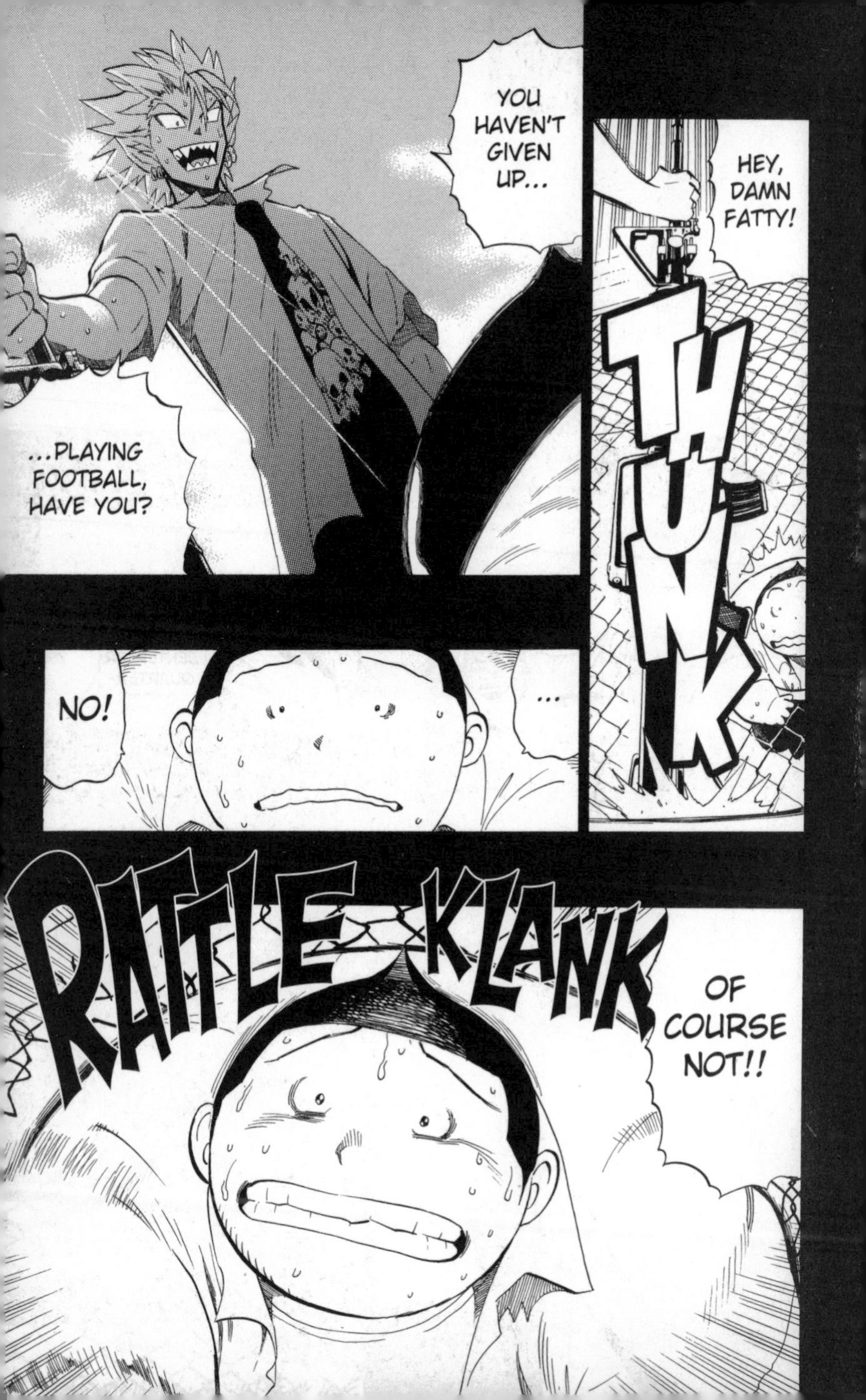
HEY, DAMN FATTY!
THUNK
YOU HAVEN'T GIVEN UP...
...PLAYING FOOTBALL, HAVE YOU?
...
NO!
OF COURSE NOT!!
RATTLE KLANK

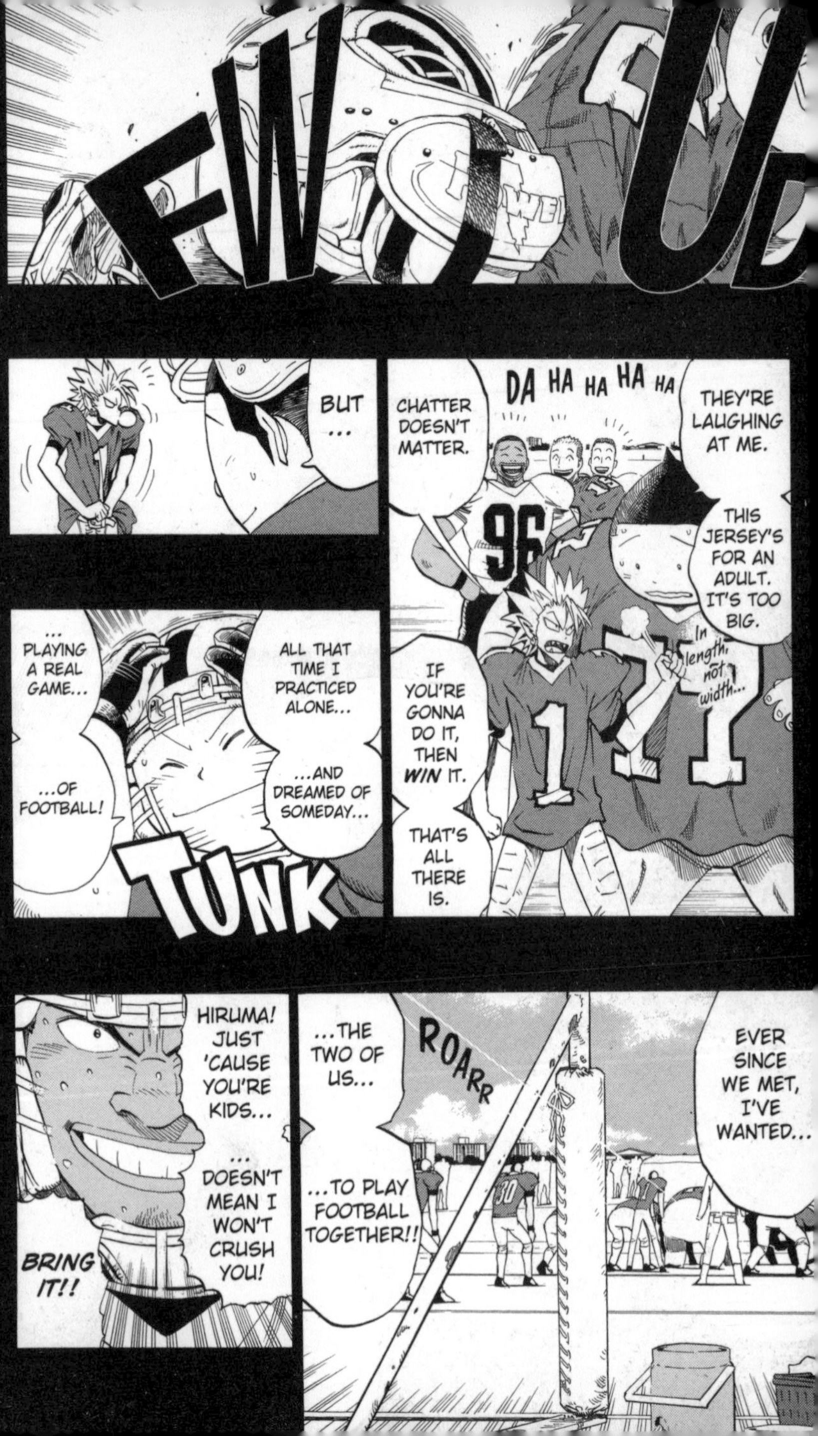
DA HA HA HA HA
THEY'RE LAUGHING AT ME.
THIS JERSEY'S FOR AN ADULT. IT'S TOO BIG.
In length, not width...
CHATTER DOESN'T MATTER.
IF YOU'RE GONNA DO IT, THEN WIN IT.
THAT'S ALL THERE IS.
BUT ...
ALL THAT TIME I PRACTICED ALONE...
...AND DREAMED OF SOMEDAY...
...PLAYING A REAL GAME...
...OF FOOTBALL!
TUNK
EVER SINCE WE MET, I'VE WANTED...
ROARR
...THE TWO OF US...
...TO PLAY FOOTBALL TOGETHER!!
HIRUMA! JUST 'CAUSE YOU'RE KIDS...
...DOESN'T MEAN I WON'T CRUSH YOU!
BRING IT!!

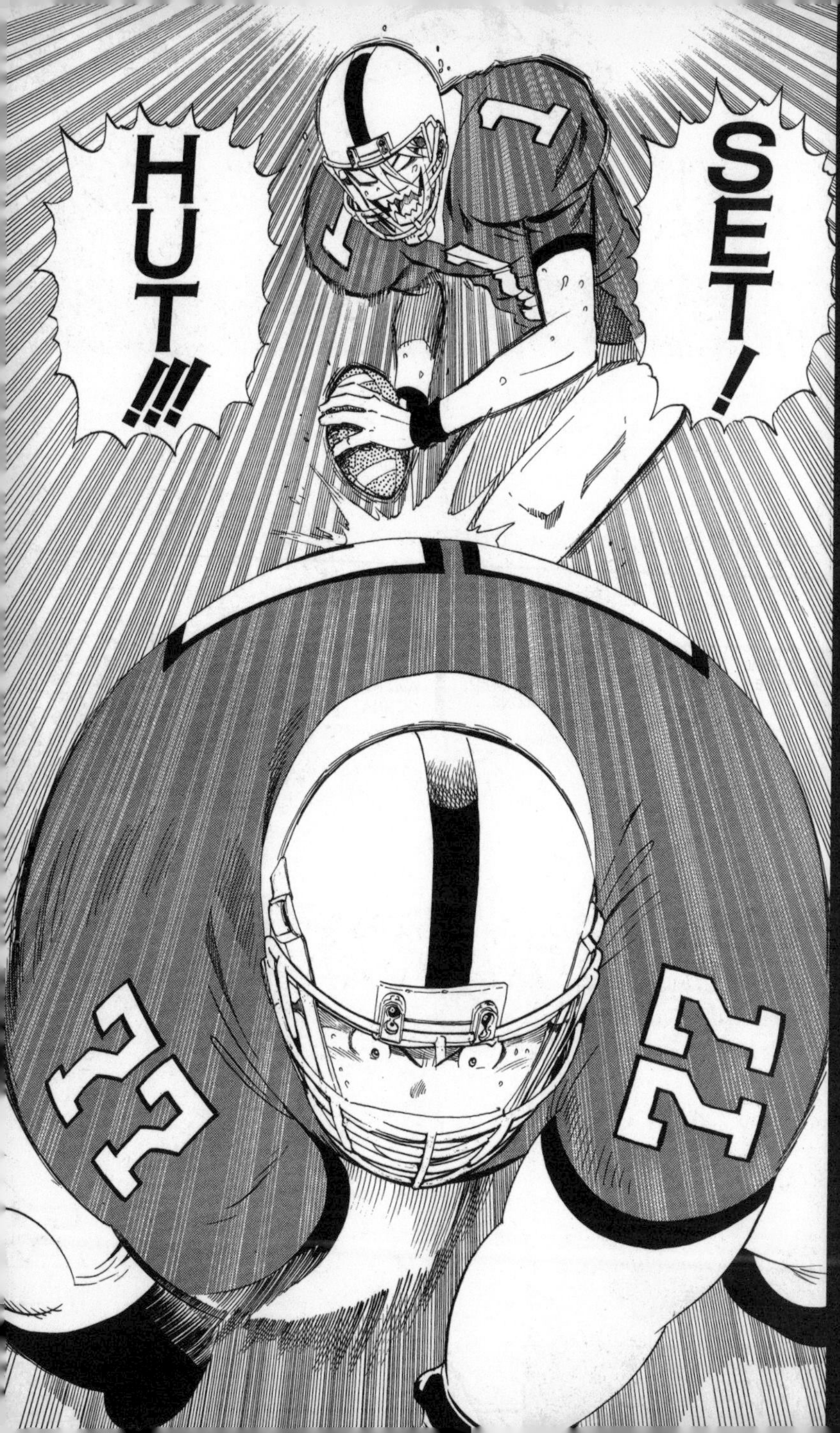
SET!
HUT!!!

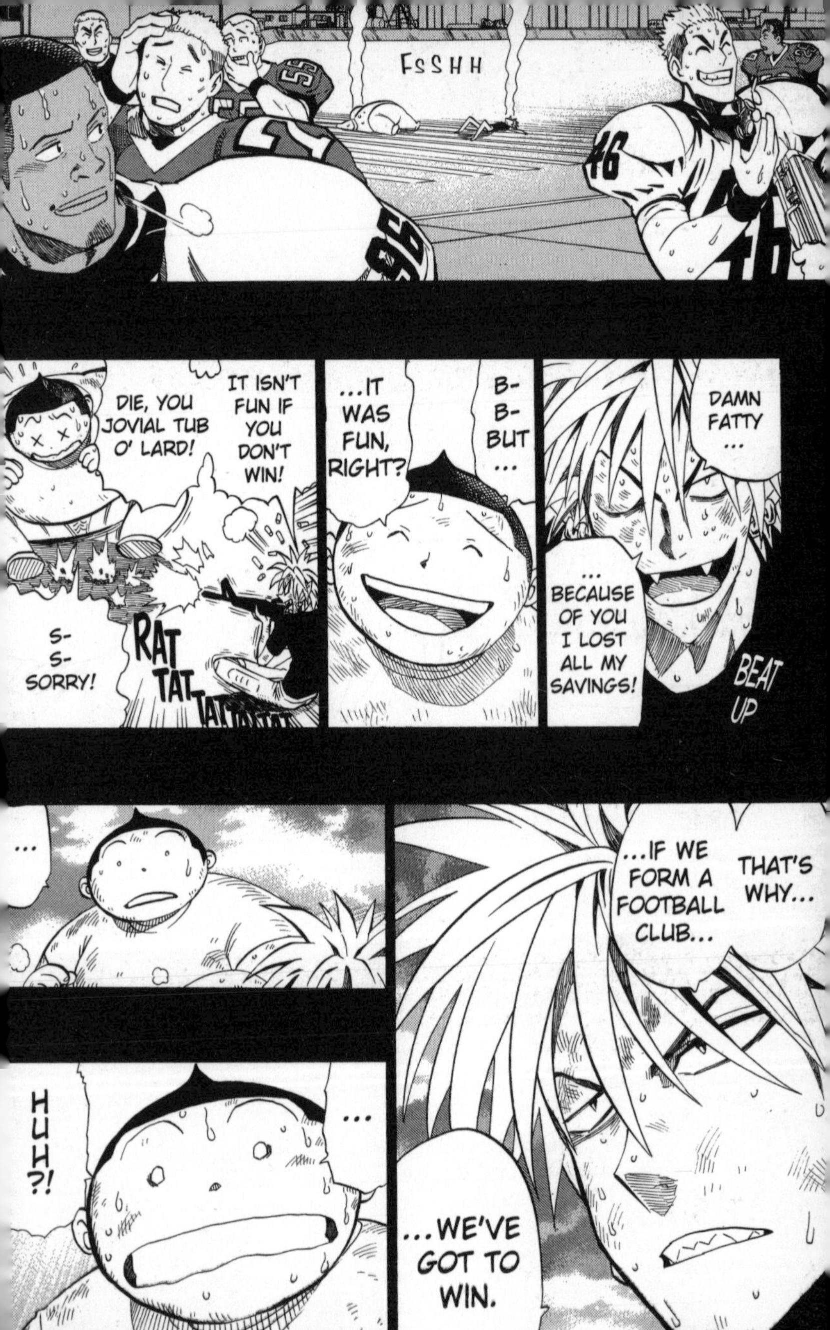
FSSHH
DAMN FATTY...
...BECAUSE OF YOU I LOST ALL MY SAVINGS!
BEAT UP
B-B-BUT...
...IT WAS FUN, RIGHT?
IT ISN'T FUN IF YOU DON'T WIN!
DIE, YOU JOVIAL TUB O' LARD!
RAT TAT TAT
S-S-SORRY!
THAT'S WHY...
...IF WE FORM A FOOTBALL CLUB...
...WE'VE GOT TO WIN.
...
...
HUH?!

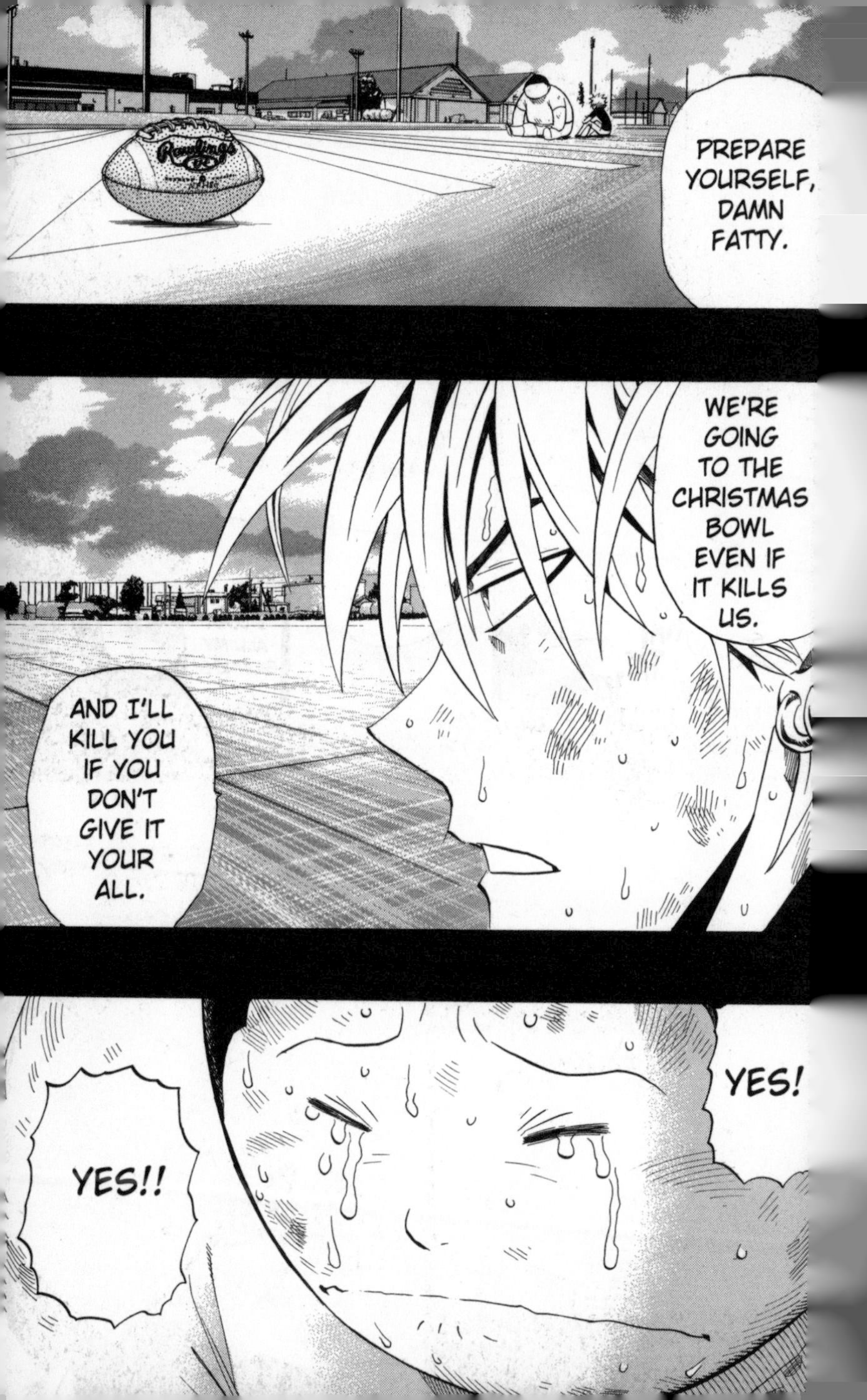
PREPARE YOURSELF, DAMN FATTY.
WE'RE GOING TO THE CHRISTMAS BOWL EVEN IF IT KILLS US.
AND I'LL KILL YOU IF YOU DON'T GIVE IT YOUR ALL.
YES!
YES!!

Deluxe Biographies of the Supporting Cast

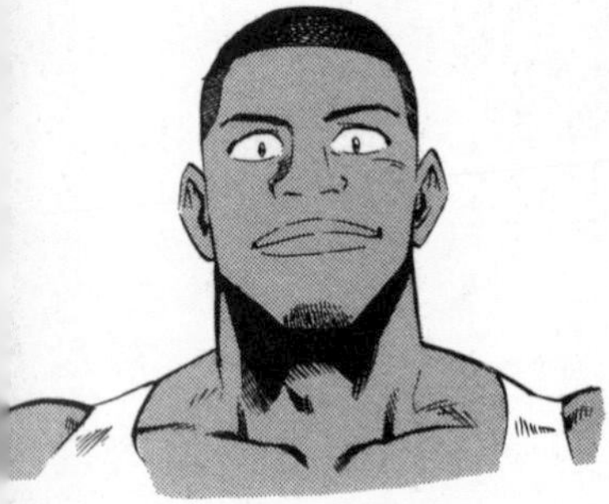

Noriega, American soldier

A ***nice guy*** just going with the flow in ***wasting his life*** by pouring all his pay into betting on football. He was just going with the flow when he got involved with Hiruma, too.

Also going with the flow, he ***"borrows"*** guns for Hiruma from the army base.

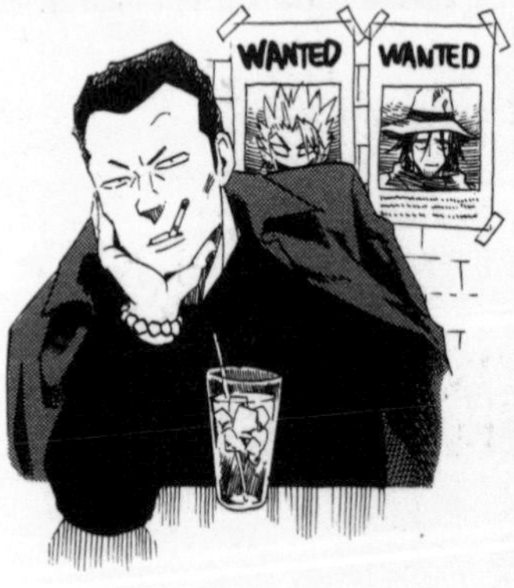
WANTED
WANTED

The Owner of the West darts bar

He was shocked by the two high school kids who piled bull's-eyes on top of one another! He wants to see it again so badly that he put up ***WANTED*** signs for them inside the bar. He will present whoever finds them with ***100 million free tickets for playing darts.***

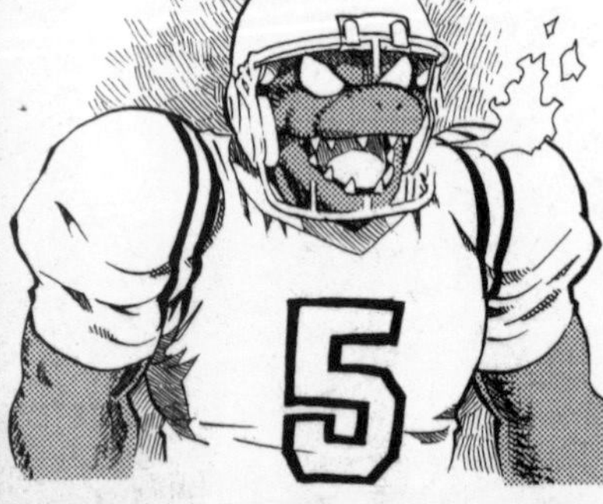
5

Godzilla

The ultimate linebacker Kurita imagined. He can bench press 100 million tons and run 40 yards in 0.1 seconds (in one step). If you face off against him, ***you become as big as he is.*** He's ridiculously huge.

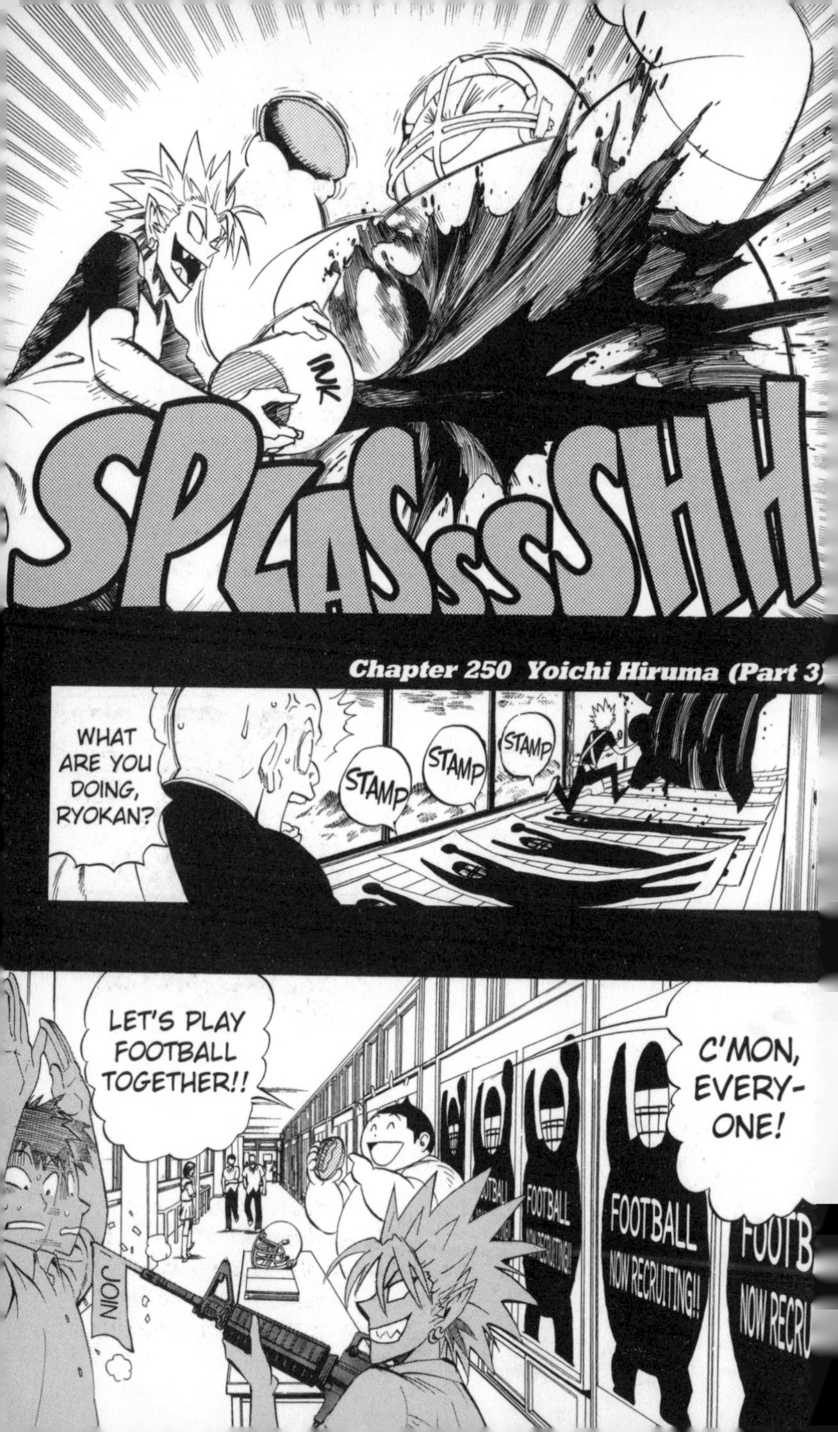
INK
SPLASSSHH
Chapter 250 Yoichi Hiruma (Part 3)
STAMP
STAMP
STAMP
WHAT ARE YOU DOING, RYOKAN?
C'MON, EVERYONE!
LET'S PLAY FOOTBALL TOGETHER!!
FOOTBALL NOW RECRUITING!!
FOOTBALL NOW RECRUITING!!
JOIN

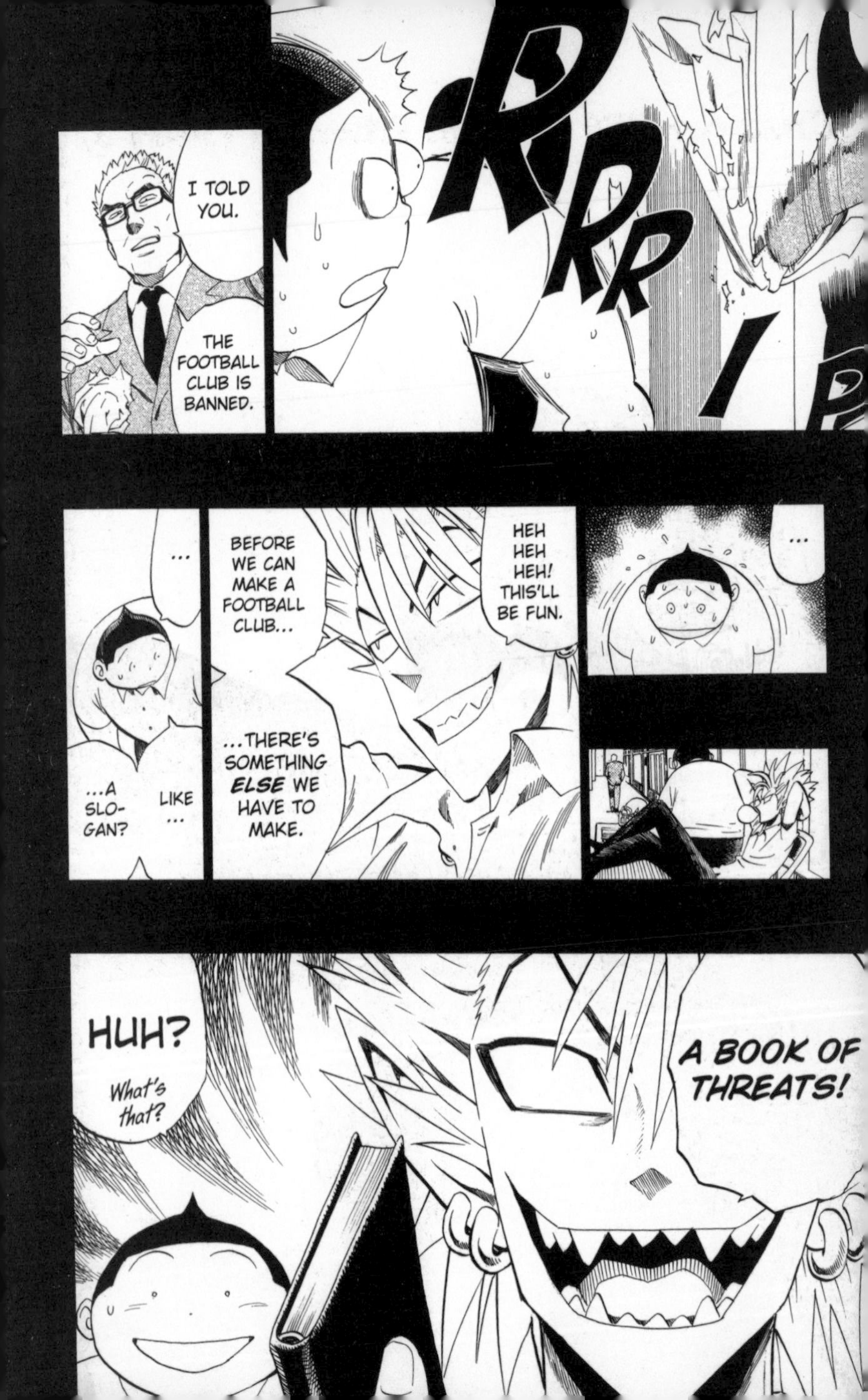
RRRRIP
I TOLD YOU.
THE FOOTBALL CLUB IS BANNED.
...
HEH HEH HEH! THIS'LL BE FUN.
BEFORE WE CAN MAKE A FOOTBALL CLUB...
...THERE'S SOMETHING *ELSE* WE HAVE TO MAKE.
...
LIKE...
...A SLO-GAN?
A BOOK OF THREATS!
HUH?
What's that?

Chapter 250 Yoichi Hiruma (Part 3)

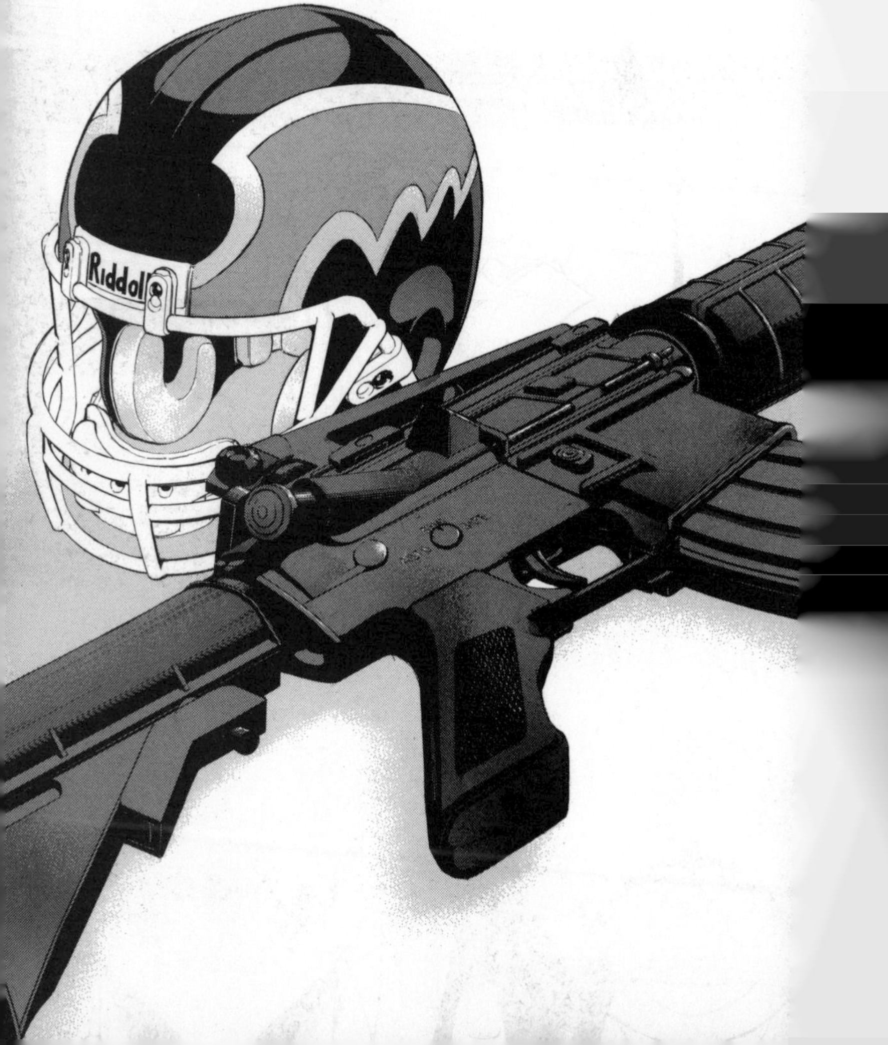
Riddol

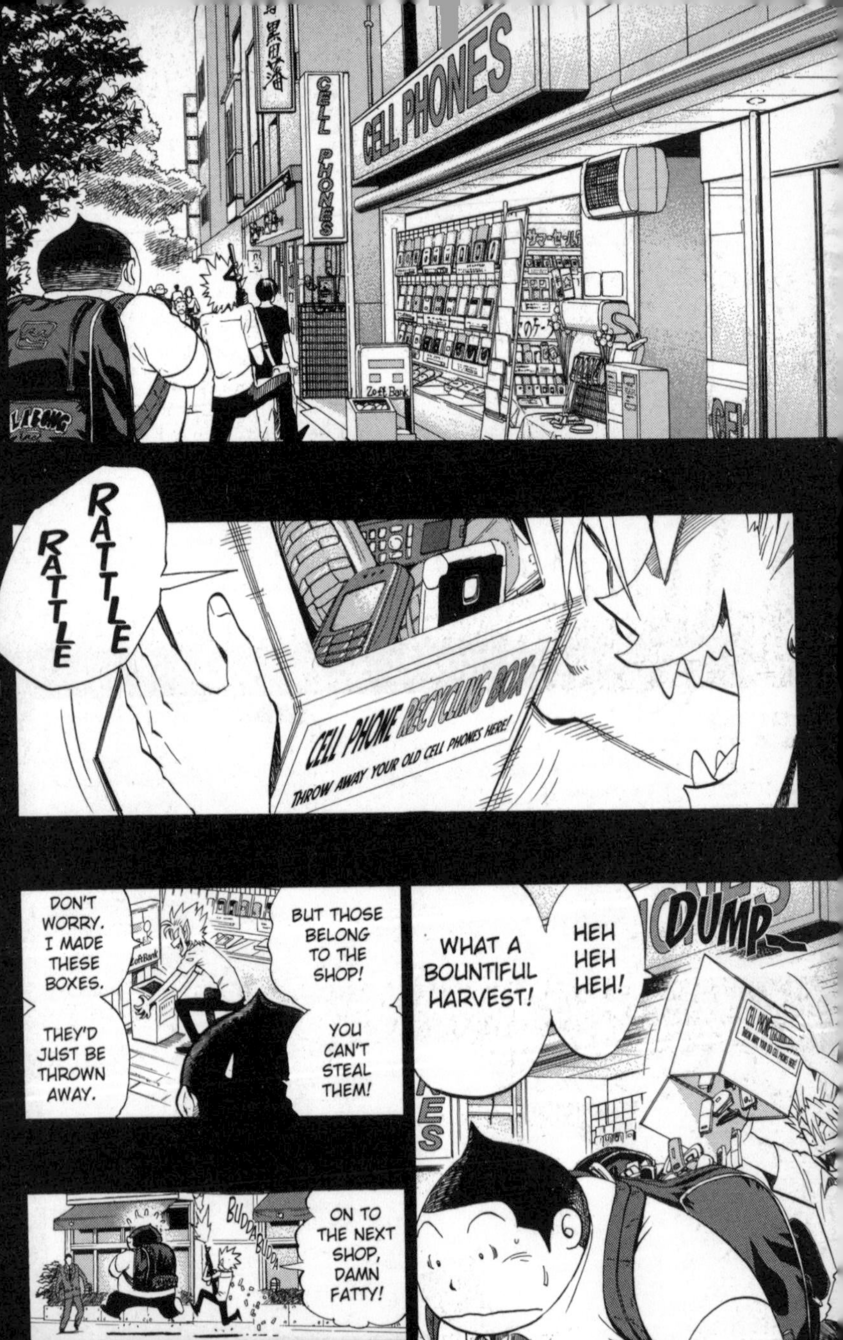
CELL PHONES
CELL PHONES
Zoft Bank
RATTLE RATTLE
CELL PHONE RECYCLING BOX
THROW AWAY YOUR OLD CELL PHONES HERE!
DUMP
HEH HEH HEH!
WHAT A BOUNTIFUL HARVEST!
BUT THOSE BELONG TO THE SHOP!
YOU CAN'T STEAL THEM!
DON'T WORRY. I MADE THESE BOXES.
THEY'D JUST BE THROWN AWAY.
BUDDA BUDDA
ON TO THE NEXT SHOP, DAMN FATTY!

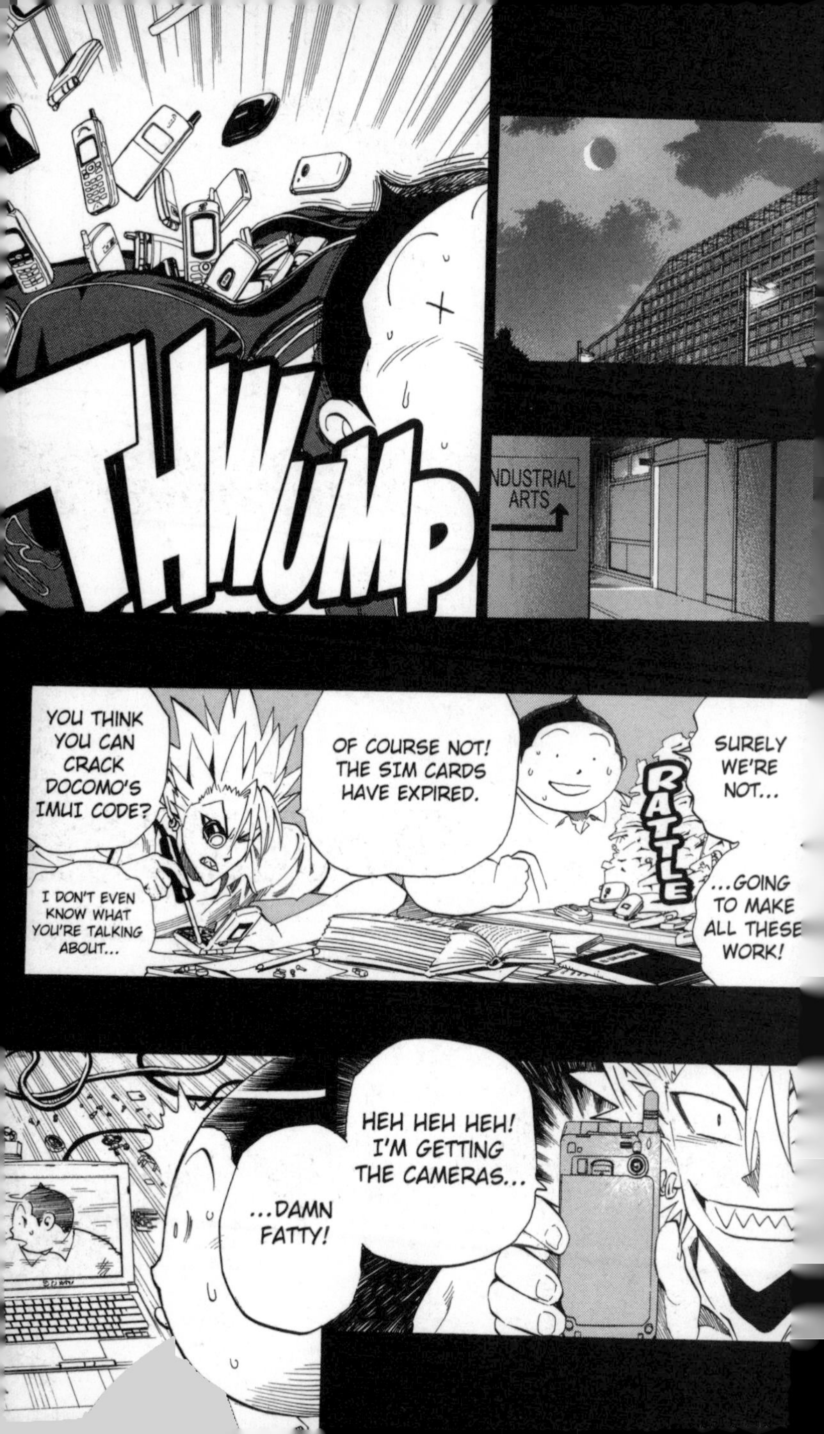
NDUSTRIAL ARTS
THWUMP
SURELY WE'RE NOT...
RATTLE
...GOING TO MAKE ALL THESE WORK!
OF COURSE NOT! THE SIM CARDS HAVE EXPIRED.
YOU THINK YOU CAN CRACK DOCOMO'S IMUI CODE?
I DON'T EVEN KNOW WHAT YOU'RE TALKING ABOUT...
HEH HEH HEH! I'M GETTING THE CAMERAS...
...DAMN FATTY!

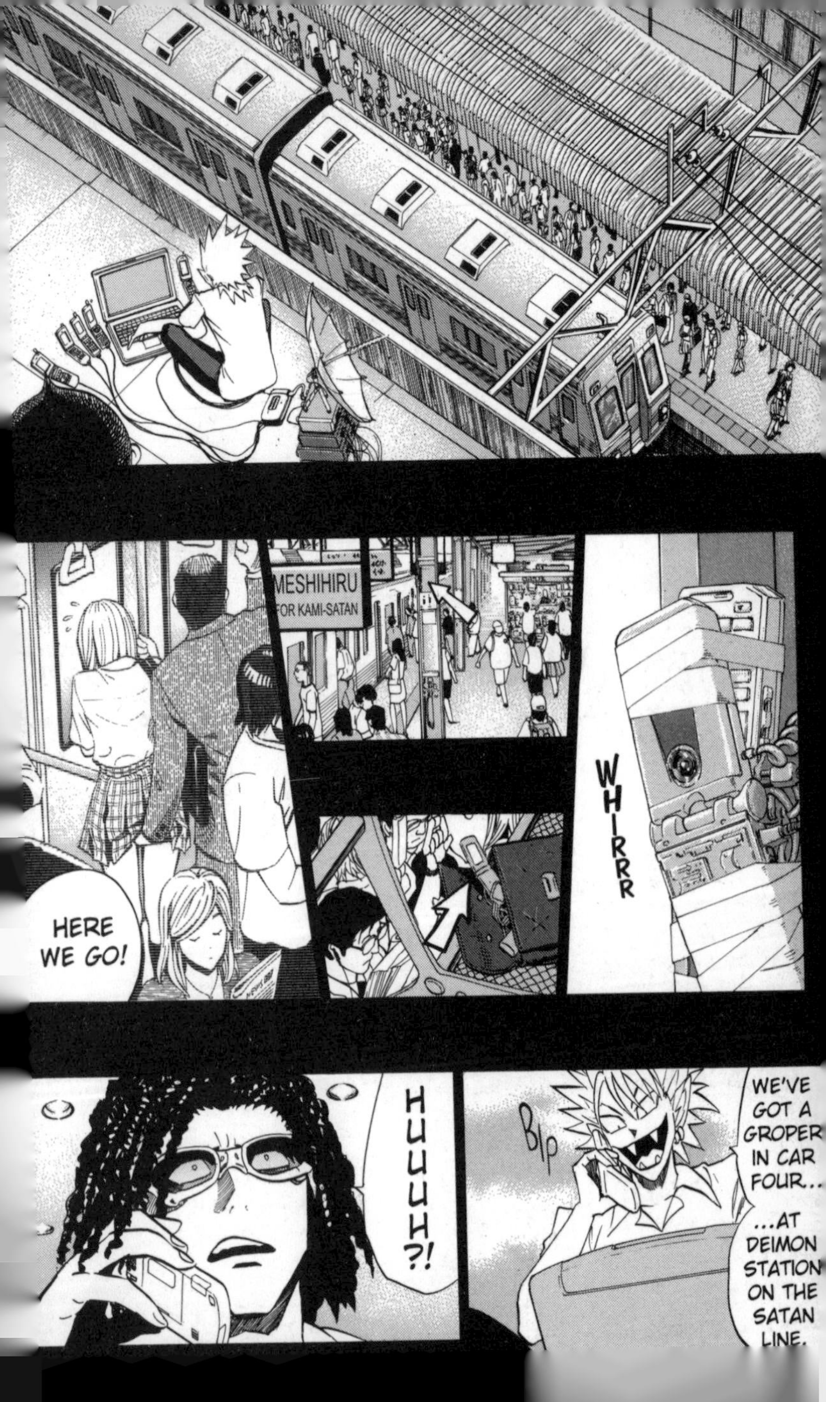
MESHIHIRU
FOR KAMI-SATAN
WHIRRR
HERE WE GO!
WE'VE GOT A GROPER IN CAR FOUR...
...AT DEIMON STATION ON THE SATAN LINE.
BLIP
HUUUH?!

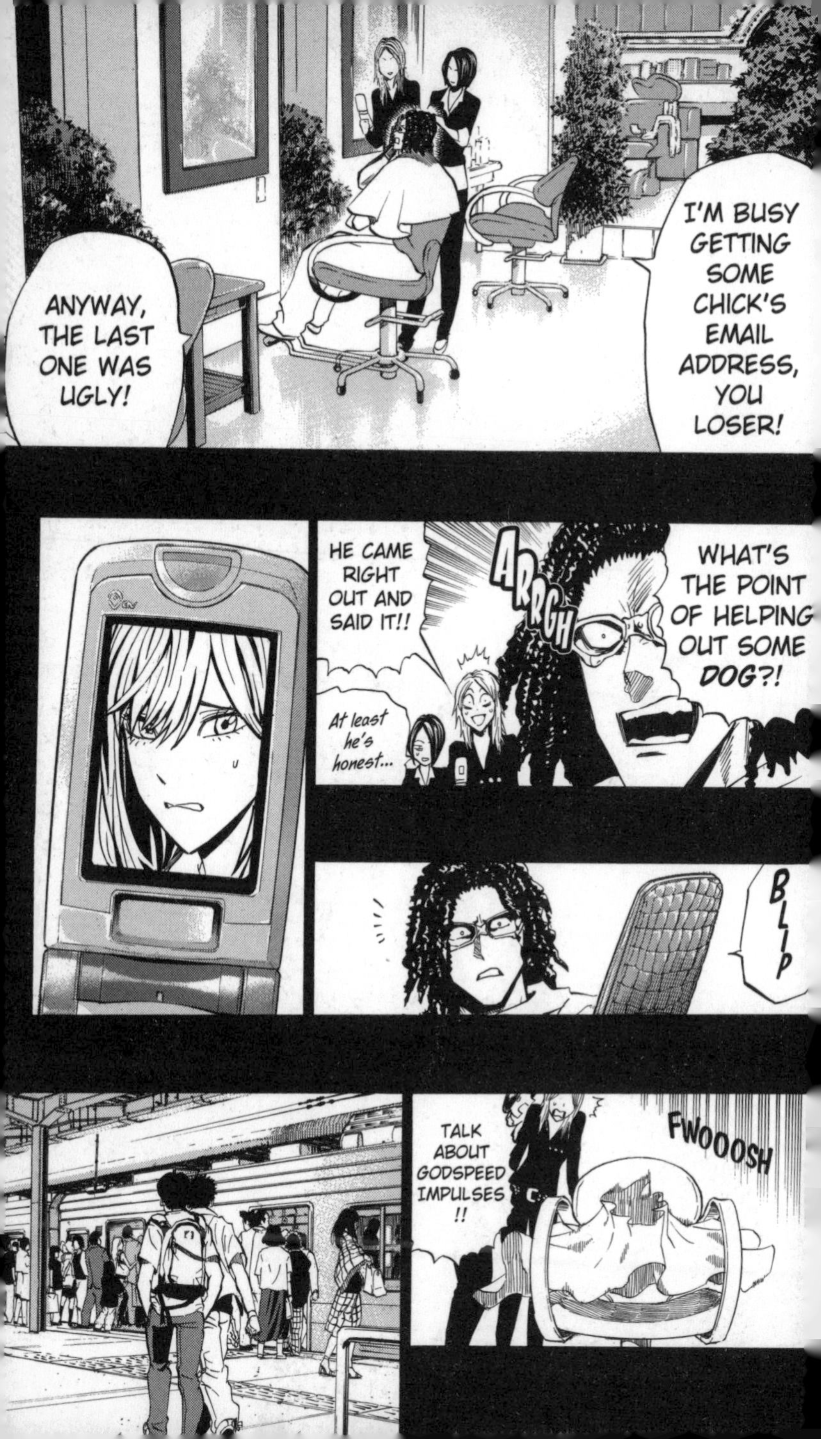
I'M BUSY GETTING SOME CHICK'S EMAIL ADDRESS, YOU LOSER!
ANYWAY, THE LAST ONE WAS UGLY!
WHAT'S THE POINT OF HELPING OUT SOME DOG?!
ARRGH
HE CAME RIGHT OUT AND SAID IT!!
At least he's honest...
BLIP
FWOOOSH
TALK ABOUT GODSPEED IMPULSES!!

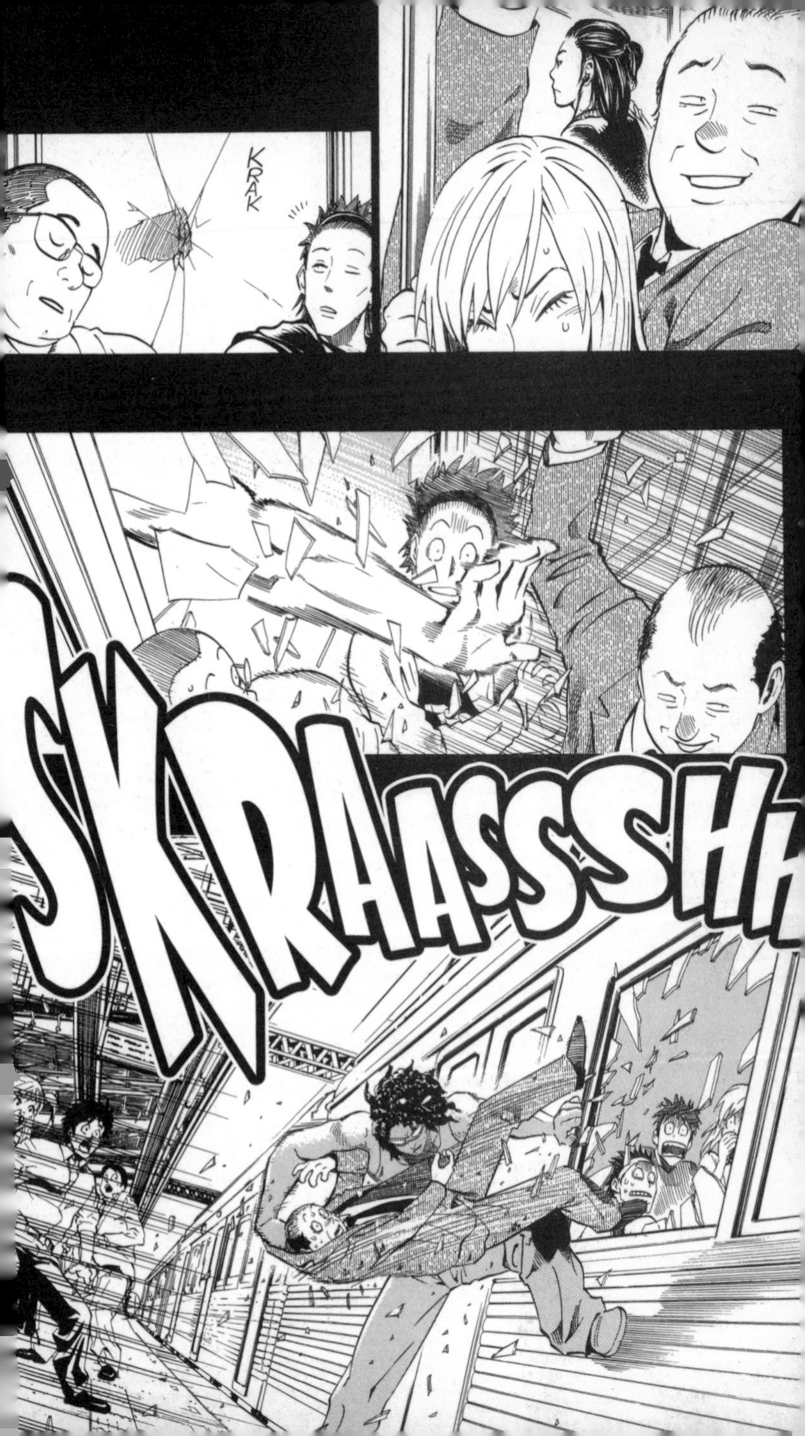
KRAK
SKRAASSH

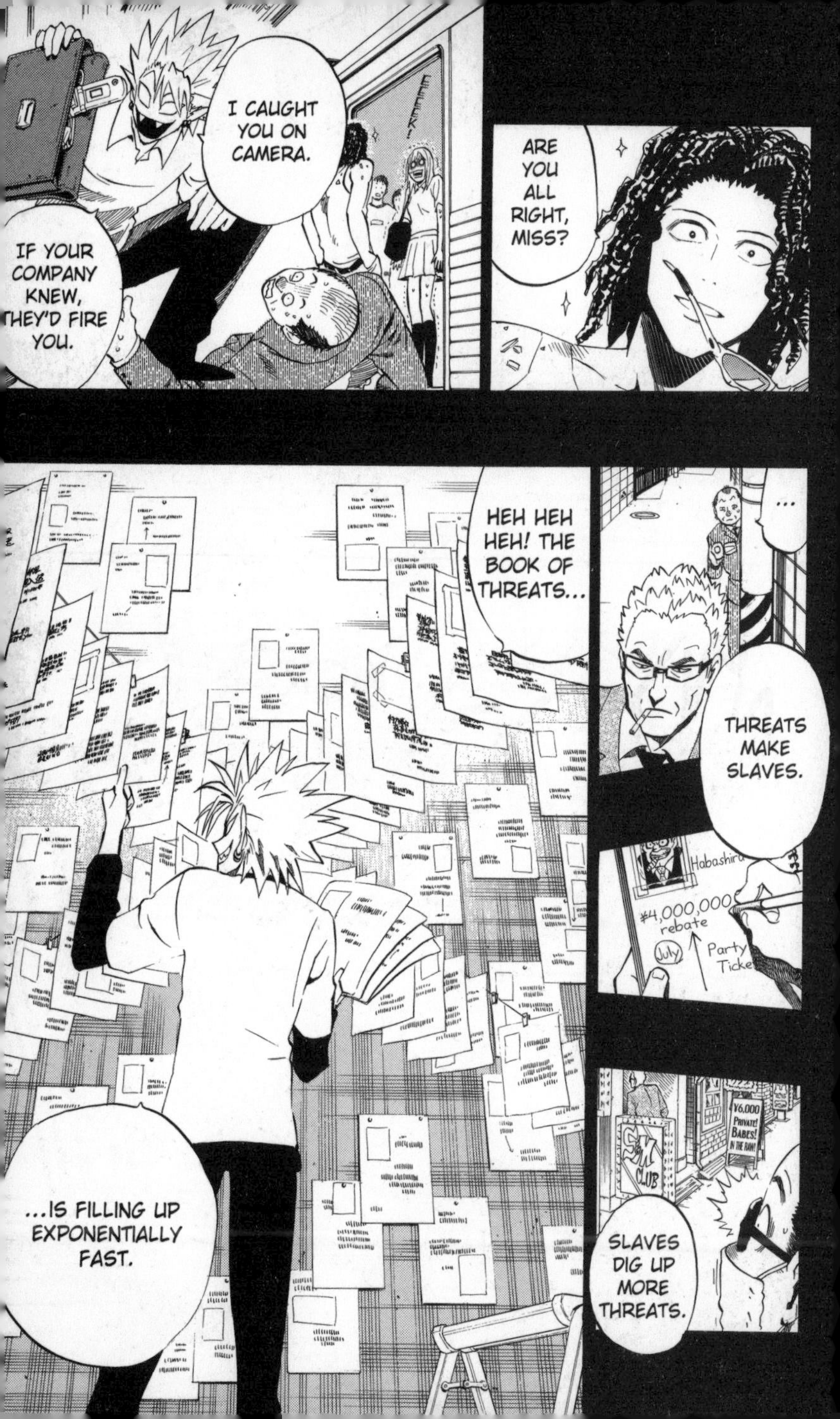
ARE YOU ALL RIGHT, MISS?
I CAUGHT YOU ON CAMERA.
IF YOUR COMPANY KNEW, THEY'D FIRE YOU.
...
THREATS MAKE SLAVES.
Habashira
¥4,000,000 rebate
July
Party Ticke
¥6,000 PRIVATE! BABES! IN THE RAW!
S&M CLUB
SLAVES DIG UP MORE THREATS.
HEH HEH HEH! THE BOOK OF THREATS...
...IS FILLING UP EXPONENTIALLY FAST.

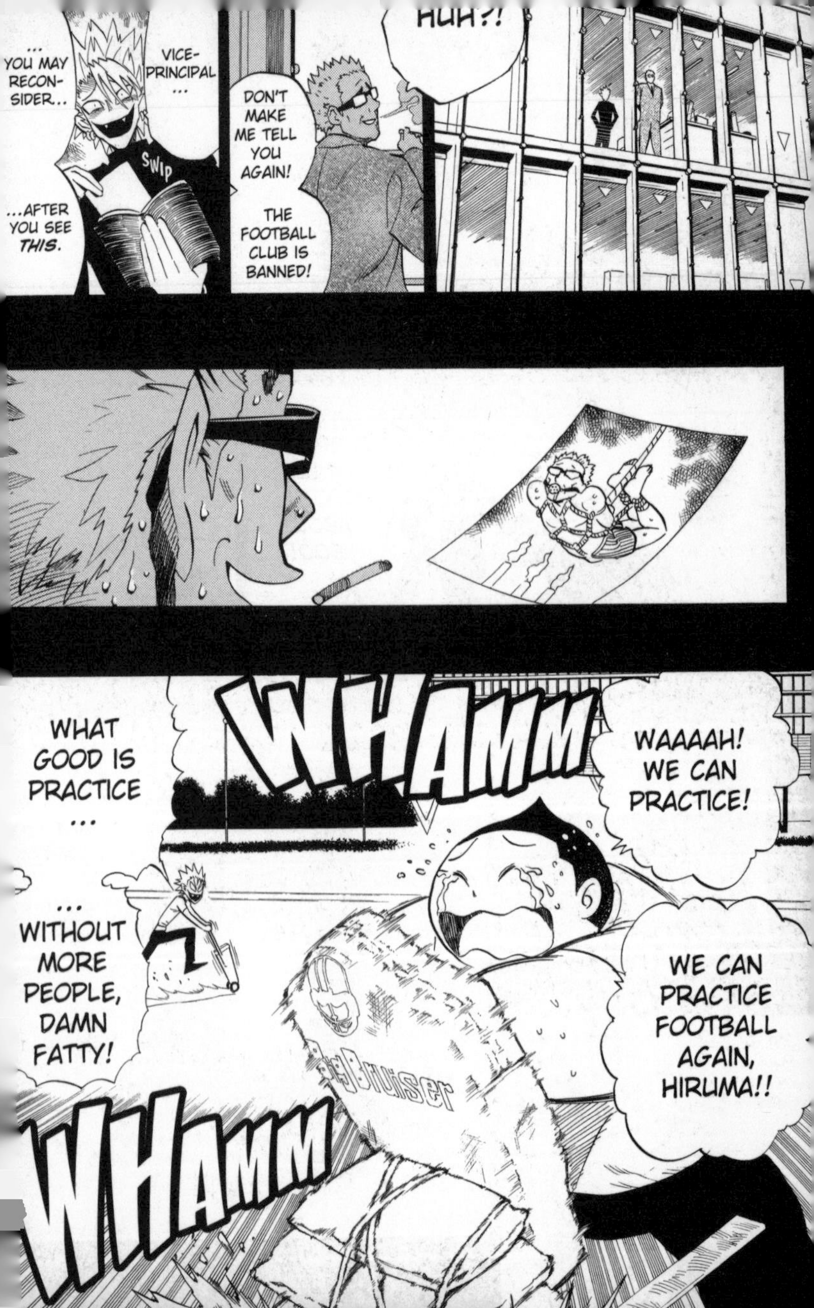
HUH?!
DON'T MAKE ME TELL YOU AGAIN!
THE FOOTBALL CLUB IS BANNED!
VICE-PRINCIPAL...
...YOU MAY RECONSIDER...
SWIP
...AFTER YOU SEE *THIS*.
WHAMM
WAAAAH! WE CAN PRACTICE!
WE CAN PRACTICE FOOTBALL AGAIN, HIRUMA!!
WHAT GOOD IS PRACTICE...
...WITHOUT MORE PEOPLE, DAMN FATTY!
WHAMM

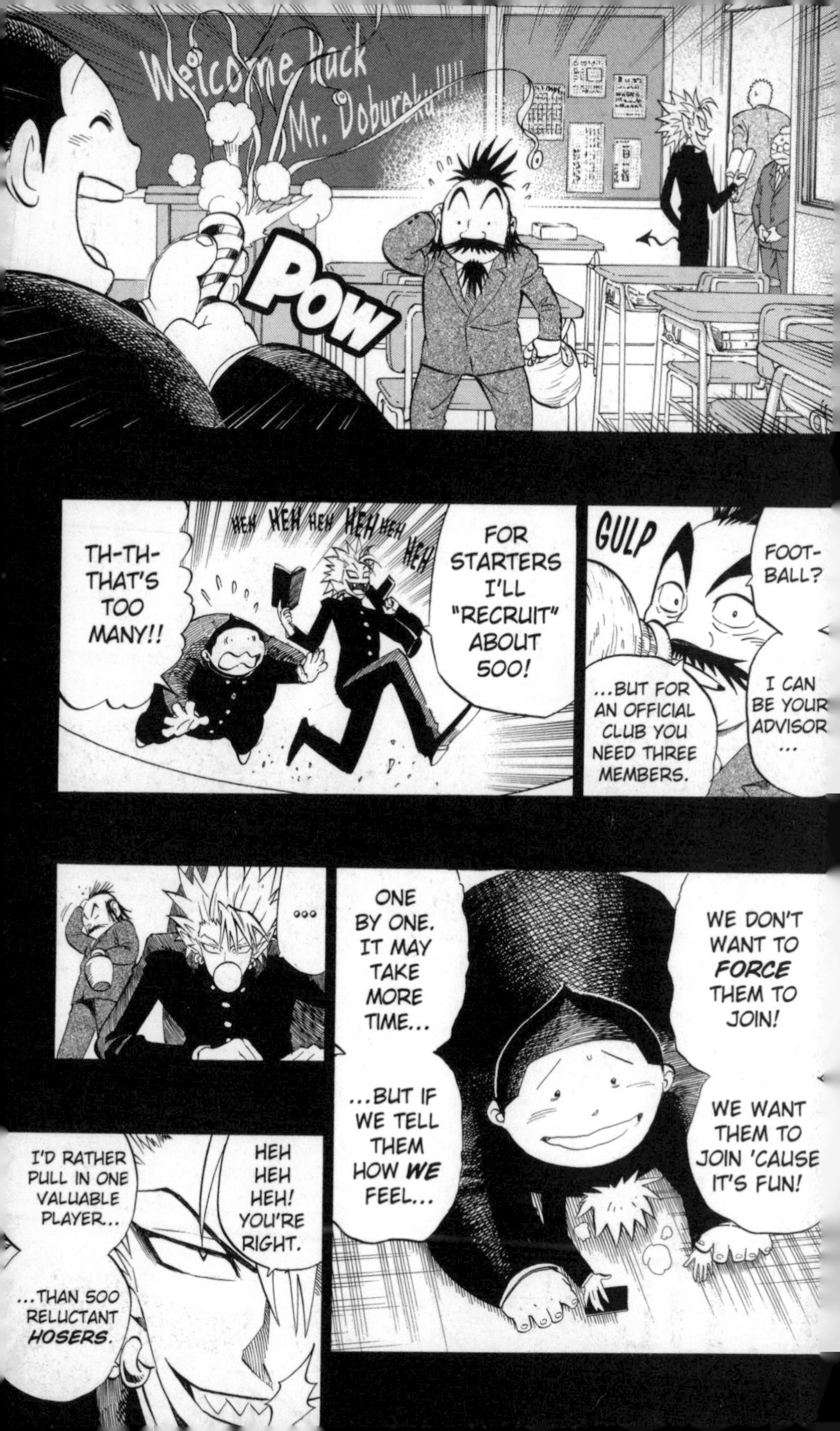
Welcome Back Mr. Doburaku!!!!!
POW
GULP
FOOT-BALL?
I CAN BE YOUR ADVISOR...
...BUT FOR AN OFFICIAL CLUB YOU NEED THREE MEMBERS.
HEH HEH HEH HEH HEH HEH
FOR STARTERS I'LL "RECRUIT" ABOUT 500!
TH-TH-THAT'S TOO MANY!!
WE DON'T WANT TO *FORCE* THEM TO JOIN!
WE WANT THEM TO JOIN 'CAUSE IT'S FUN!
ONE BY ONE. IT MAY TAKE MORE TIME...
...BUT IF WE TELL THEM HOW *WE* FEEL...
...
HEH HEH HEH! YOU'RE RIGHT.
I'D RATHER PULL IN ONE VALUABLE PLAYER...
...THAN 500 RELUCTANT *HOSERS*.

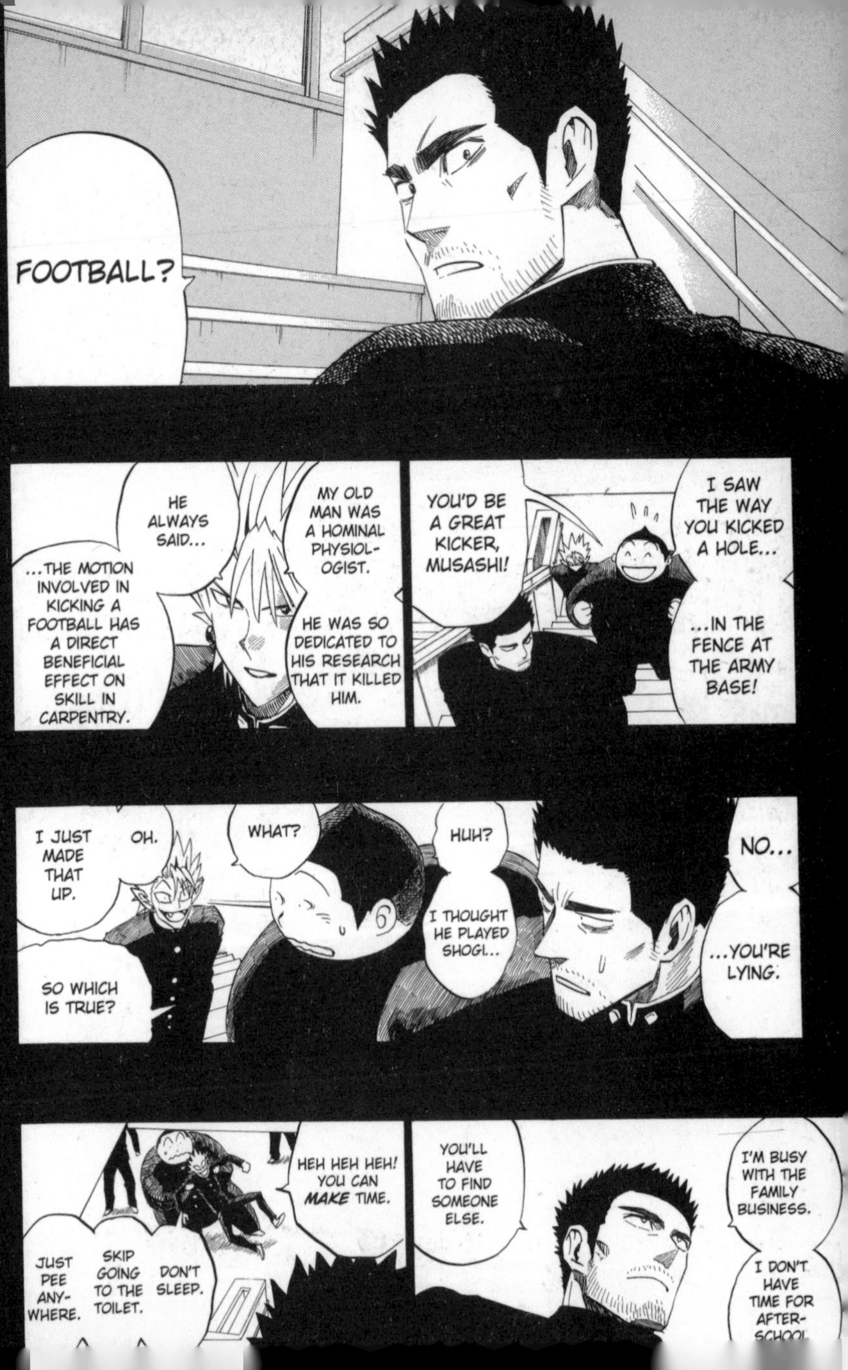
FOOTBALL?
I SAW THE WAY YOU KICKED A HOLE...
...IN THE FENCE AT THE ARMY BASE!
YOU'D BE A GREAT KICKER, MUSASHI!
MY OLD MAN WAS A HOMINAL PHYSIOL-OGIST.
HE ALWAYS SAID...
...THE MOTION INVOLVED IN KICKING A FOOTBALL HAS A DIRECT BENEFICIAL EFFECT ON SKILL IN CARPENTRY.
HE WAS SO DEDICATED TO HIS RESEARCH THAT IT KILLED HIM.
NO...
...YOU'RE LYING.
HUH?
I THOUGHT HE PLAYED SHOGI...
WHAT?
OH.
I JUST MADE THAT UP.
SO WHICH IS TRUE?
I'M BUSY WITH THE FAMILY BUSINESS.
I DON'T HAVE TIME FOR AFTER-SCHOOL
YOU'LL HAVE TO FIND SOMEONE ELSE.
HEH HEH HEH! YOU CAN *MAKE* TIME.
DON'T SLEEP.
SKIP GOING TO THE TOILET.
JUST PEE ANY-WHERE.

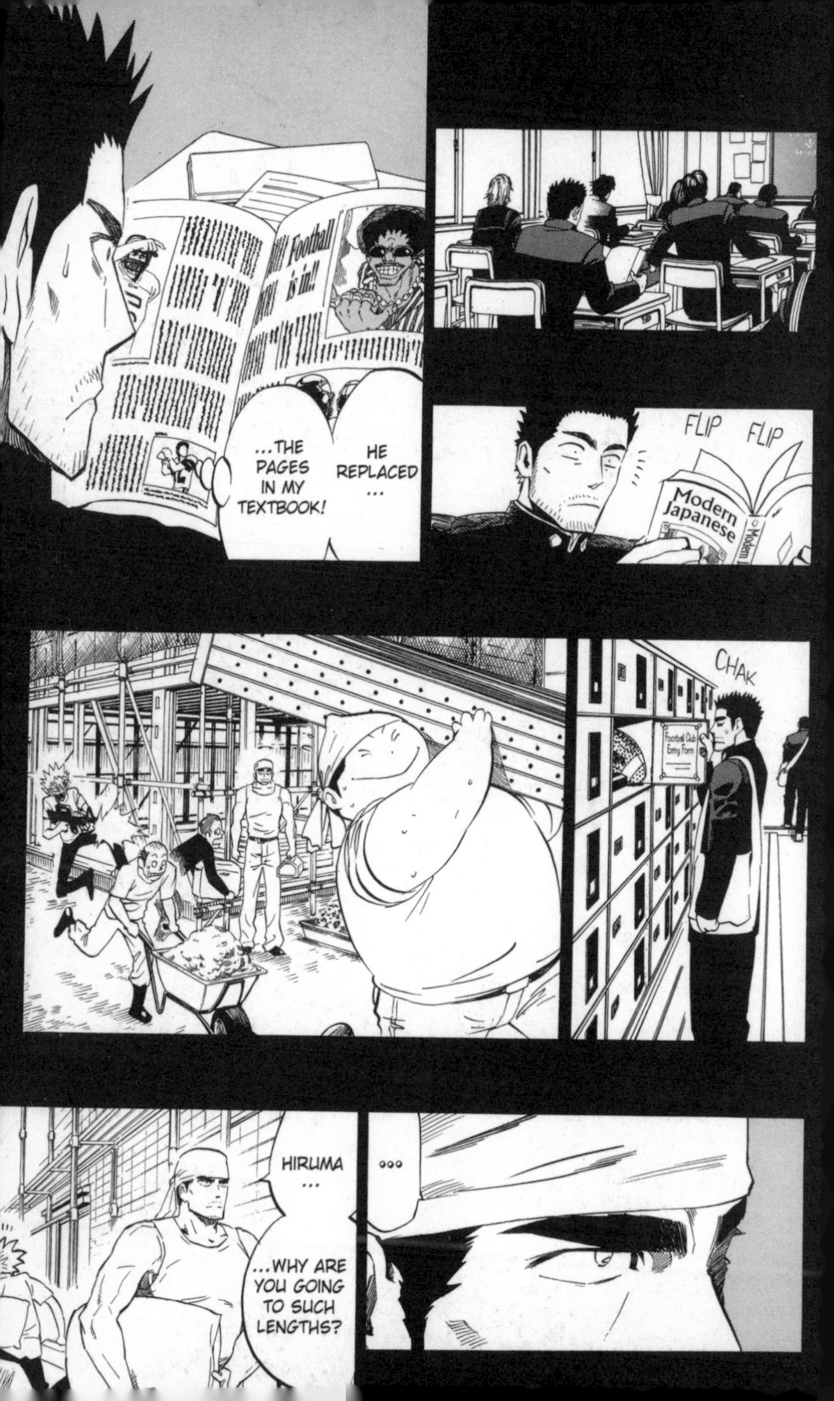
FLIP FLIP
Modern Japanese
Football is in!!
HE REPLACED ...
...THE PAGES IN MY TEXTBOOK!
CHAK
Football Club Entry Form
...
HIRUMA ...
...WHY ARE YOU GOING TO SUCH LENGTHS?

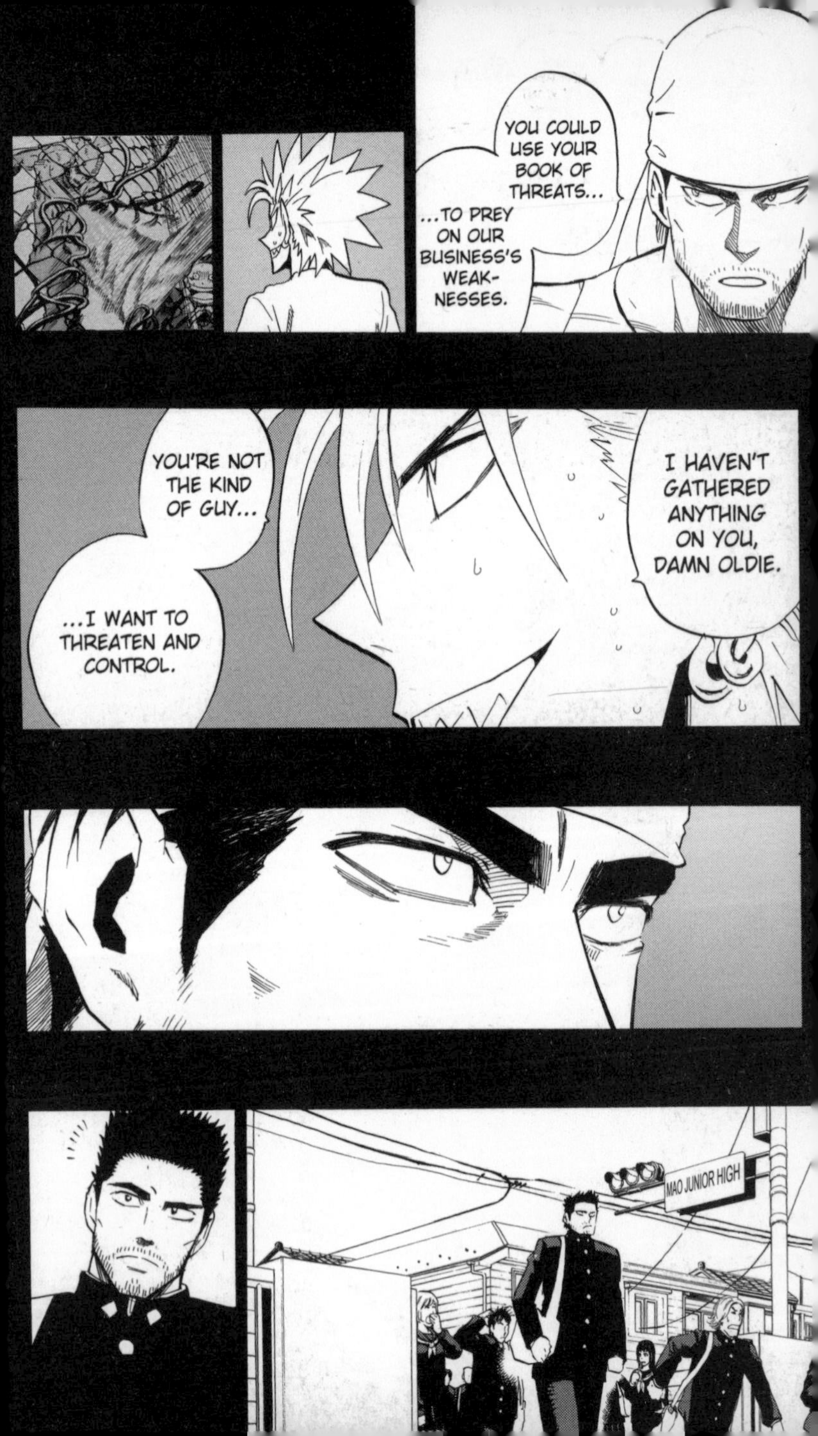
YOU COULD USE YOUR BOOK OF THREATS...
...TO PREY ON OUR BUSINESS'S WEAK-NESSES.
I HAVEN'T GATHERED ANYTHING ON YOU, DAMN OLDIE.
YOU'RE NOT THE KIND OF GUY...
...I WANT TO THREATEN AND CONTROL.
MAO JUNIOR HIGH

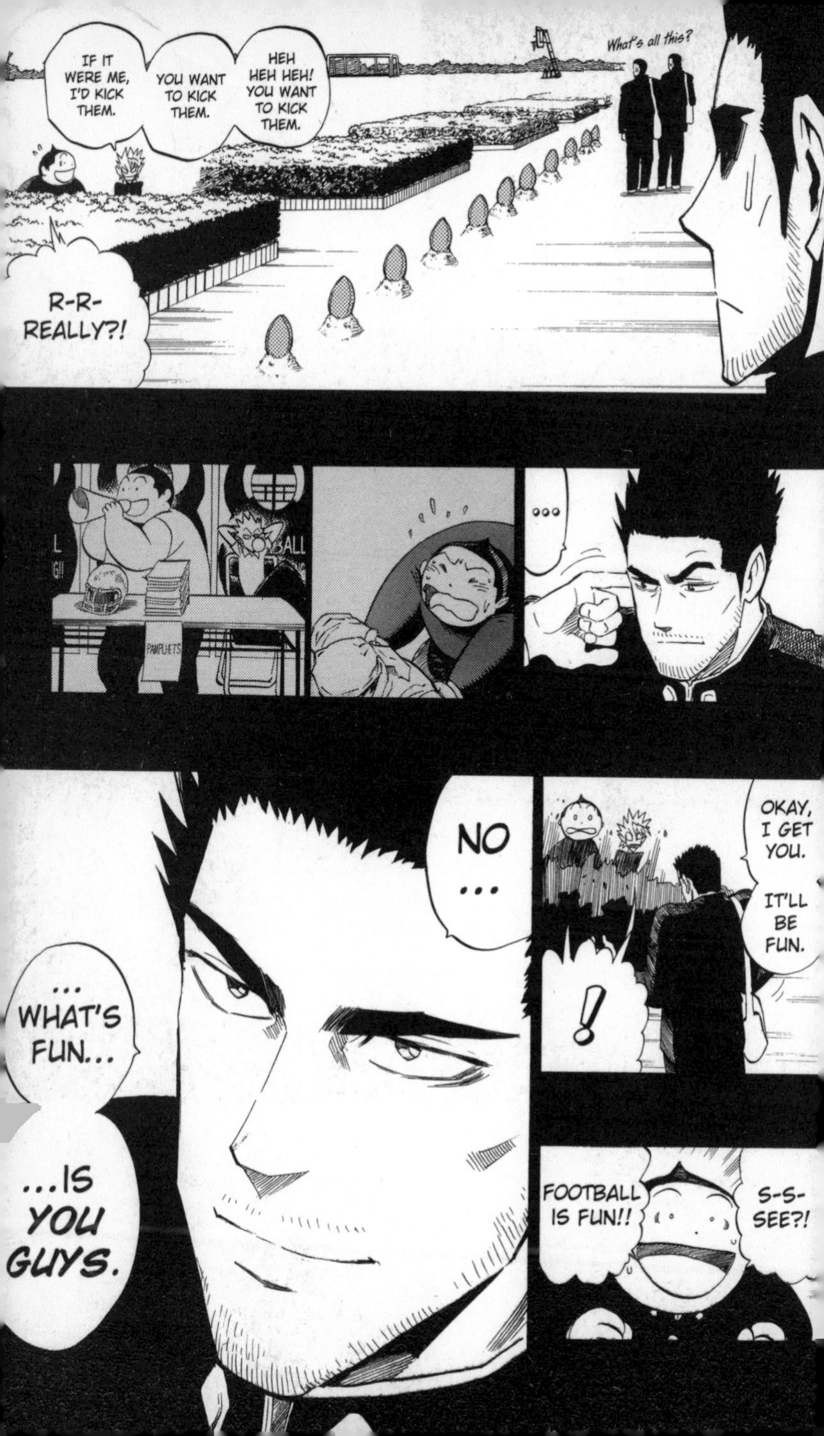
What's all this?
HEH HEH HEH! YOU WANT TO KICK THEM.
YOU WANT TO KICK THEM.
IF IT WERE ME, I'D KICK THEM.
R-R-REALLY?!
...
PAMPHLETS
OKAY, I GET YOU.
IT'LL BE FUN.
!
S-S-SEE?!
FOOTBALL IS FUN!!
NO ...
... WHAT'S FUN...
...IS YOU GUYS.

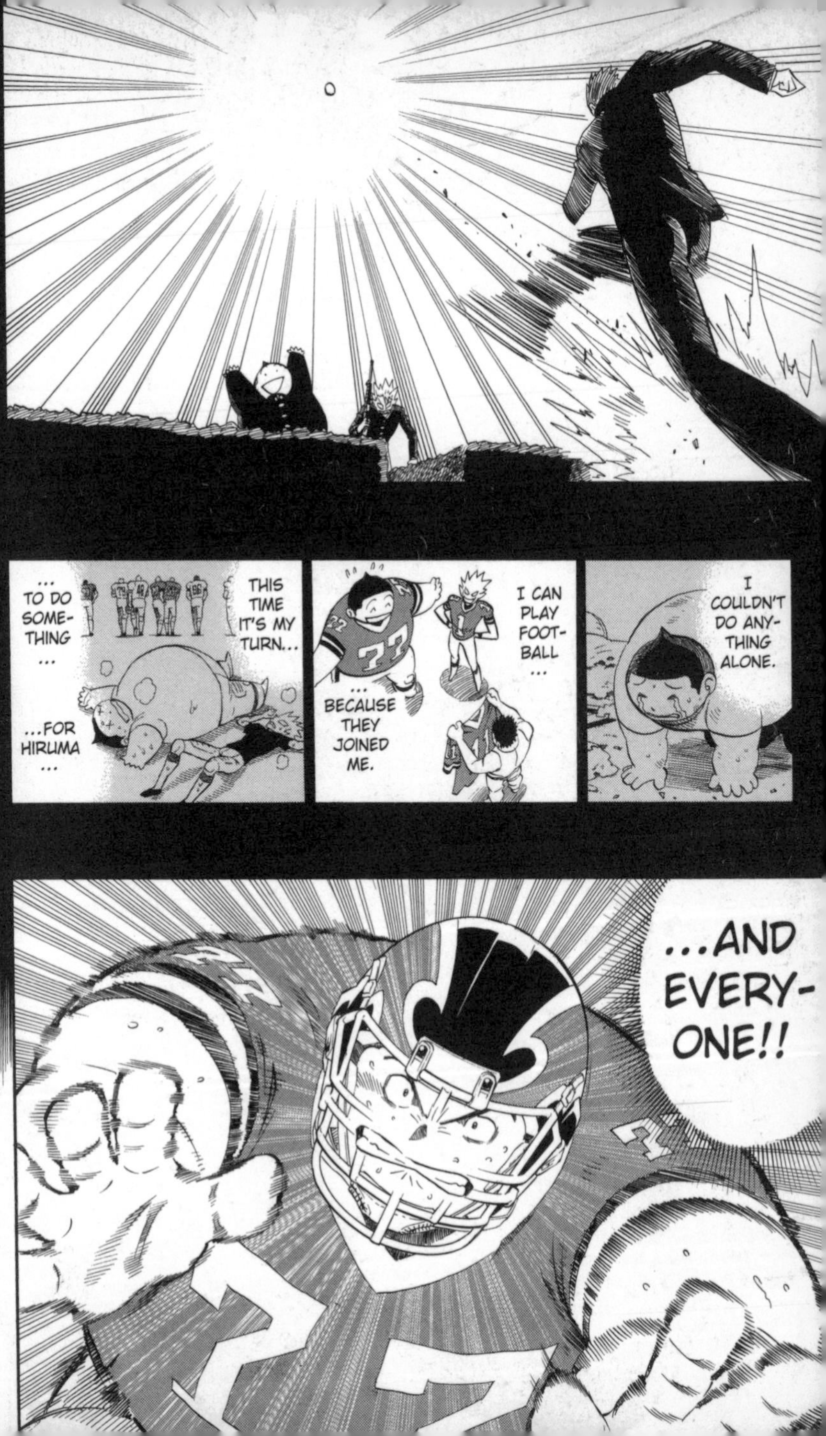
I COULDN'T DO ANYTHING ALONE.
I CAN PLAY FOOTBALL...
...BECAUSE THEY JOINED ME.
THIS TIME IT'S MY TURN...
...TO DO SOMETHING...
...FOR HIRUMA...
...AND EVERYONE!!

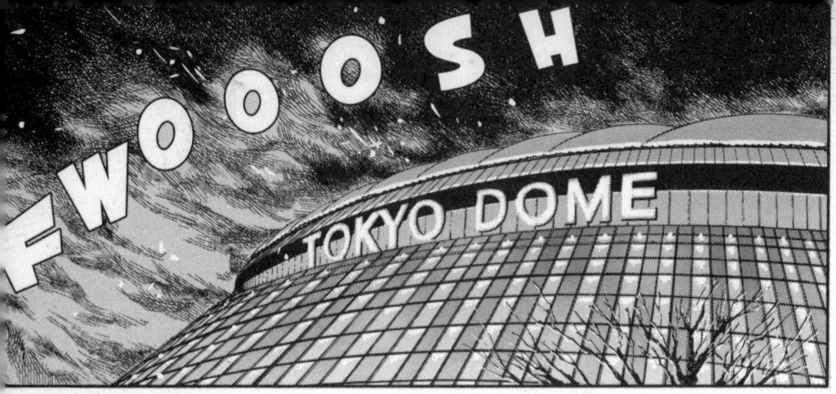
FWOOOSH
TOKYO DOME

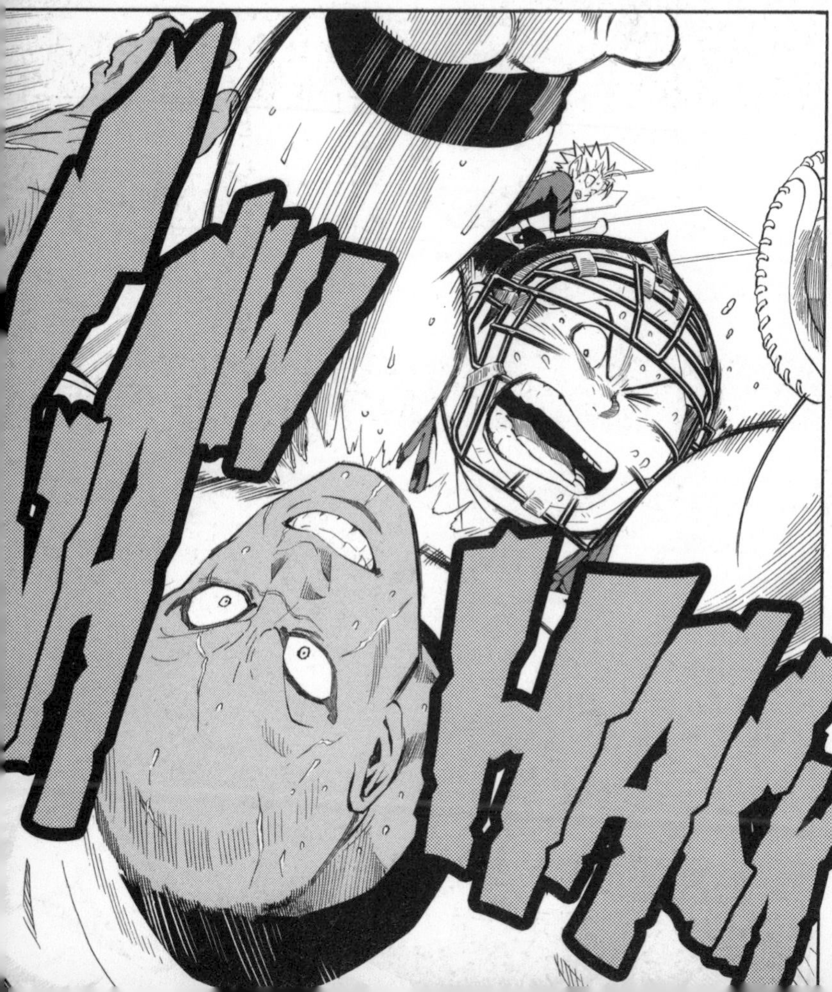

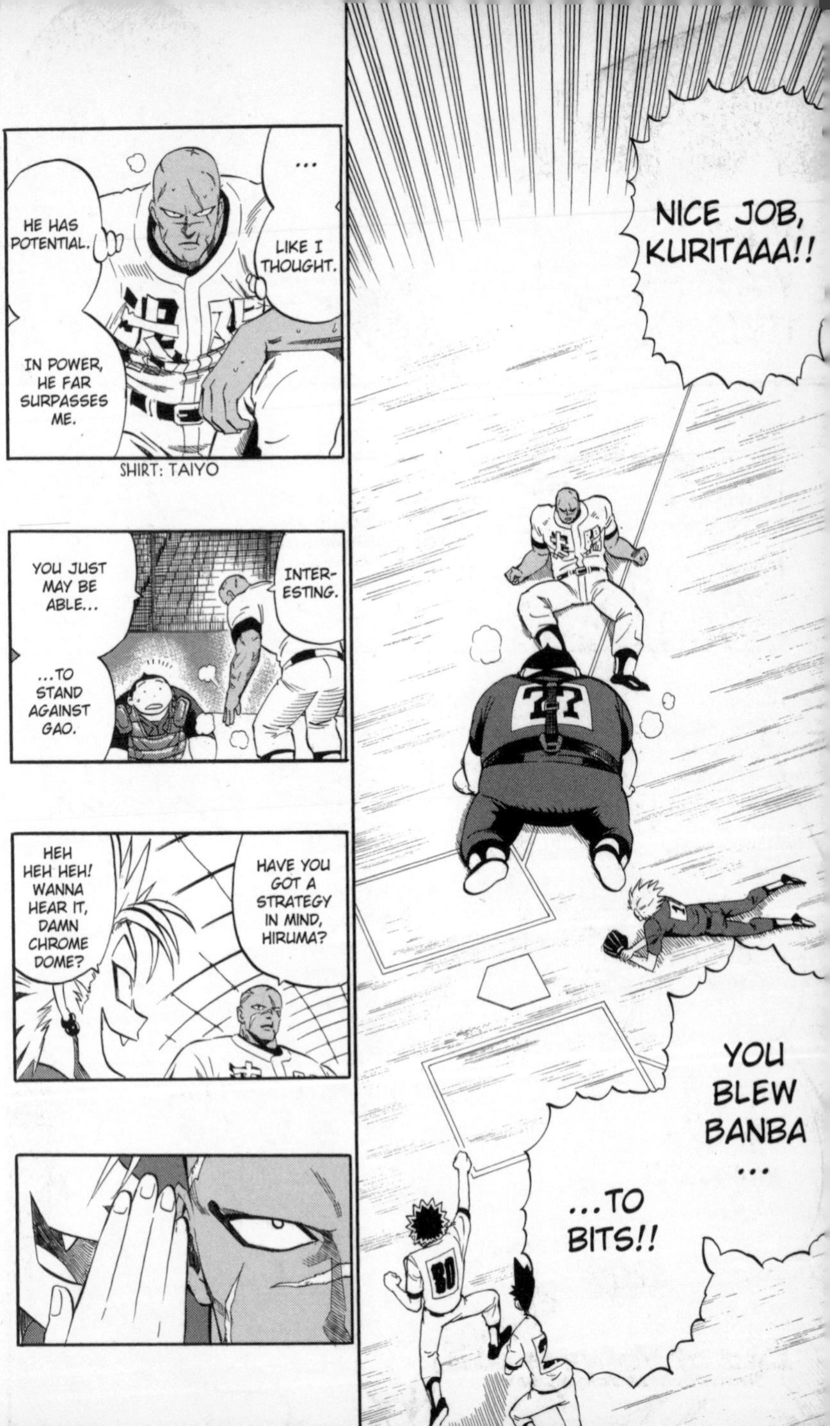
NICE JOB, KURITAAA!!
YOU BLEW BANBA...
...TO BITS!!
...
LIKE I THOUGHT.
HE HAS POTENTIAL.
IN POWER, HE FAR SURPASSES ME.
SHIRT: TAIYO
INTER-ESTING.
YOU JUST MAY BE ABLE...
...TO STAND AGAINST GAO.
HAVE YOU GOT A STRATEGY IN MIND, HIRUMA?
HEH HEH HEH! WANNA HEAR IT, DAMN CHROME DOME?

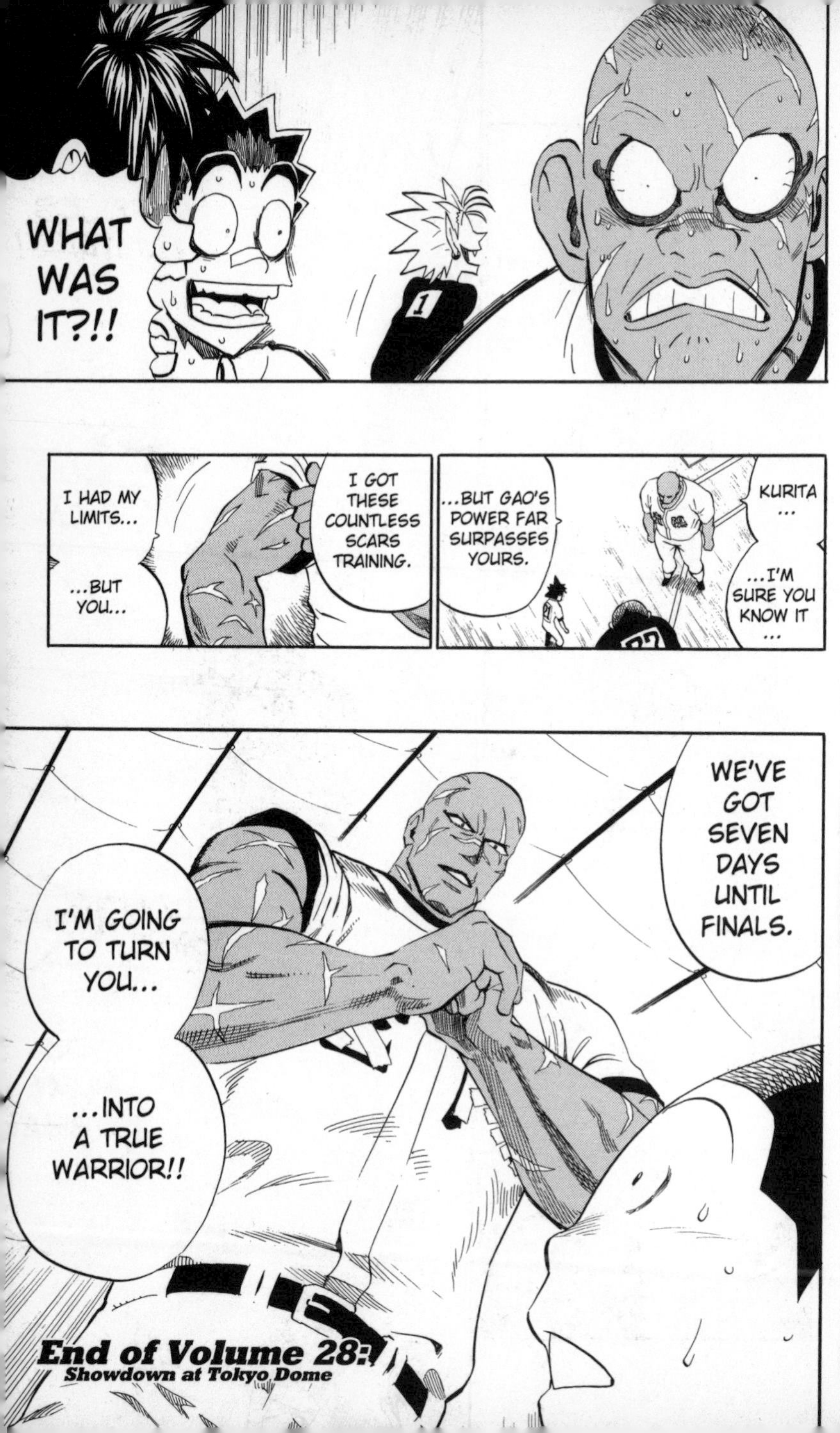
WHAT WAS IT?!!
KURITA ...
...I'M SURE YOU KNOW IT ...
...BUT GAO'S POWER FAR SURPASSES YOURS.
I GOT THESE COUNTLESS SCARS TRAINING.
I HAD MY LIMITS...
...BUT YOU...
WE'VE GOT SEVEN DAYS UNTIL FINALS.
I'M GOING TO TURN YOU...
...INTO A TRUE WARRIOR!!
End of Volume 28:
Showdown at Tokyo Dome

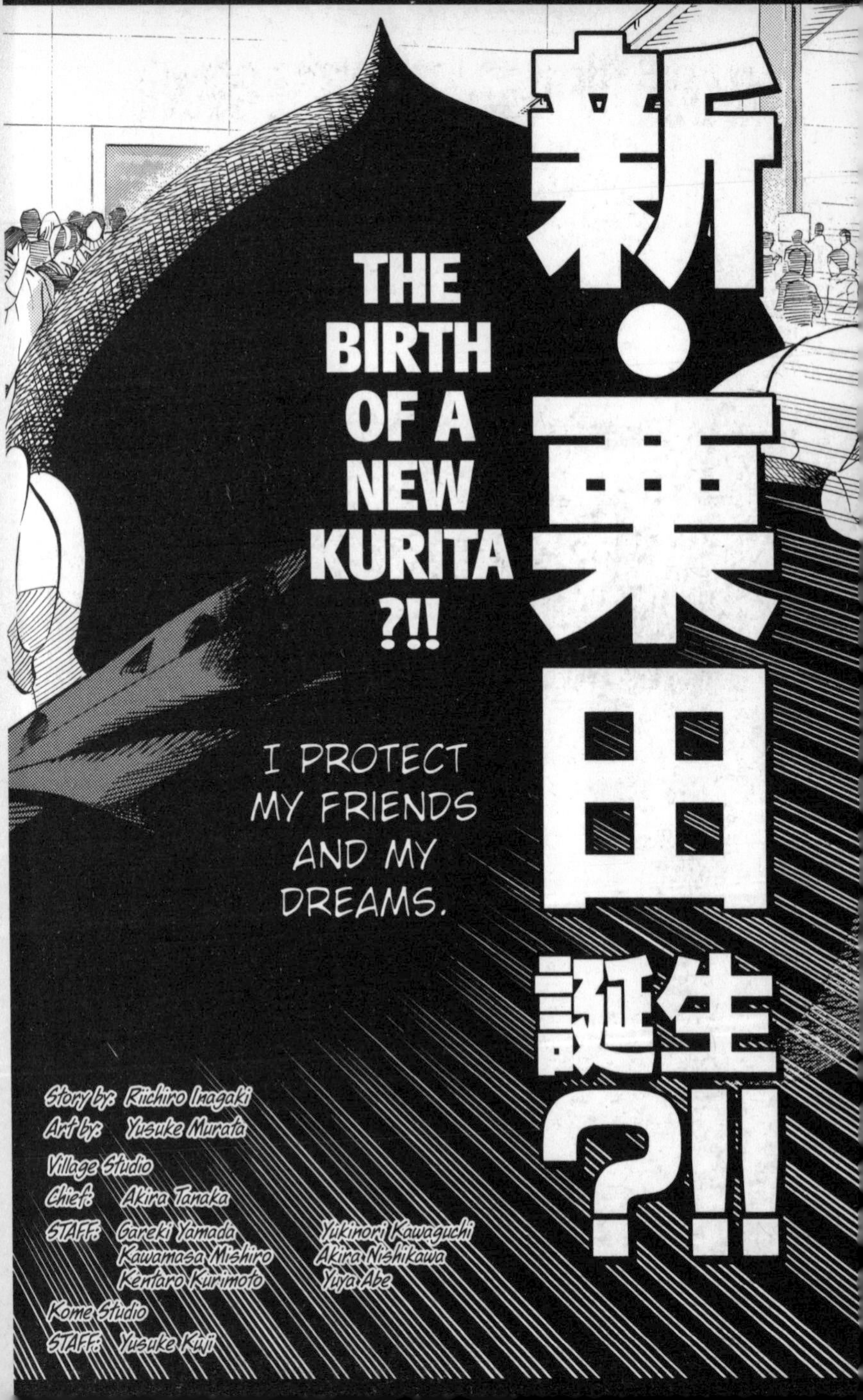
新・栗田誕生?!!
THE BIRTH OF A NEW KURITA ?!!
I PROTECT MY FRIENDS AND MY DREAMS.
Story by: Riichiro Inagaki
Art by: Yusuke Murata
Village Studio
Chief: Akira Tanaka
STAFF: Gareki Yamada
Kawamasa Mishiro
Kentaro Kurimoto
Yukinori Kawaguchi
Akira Nishikawa
Yuya Abe
Kome Studio
STAFF: Yusuke Kuji

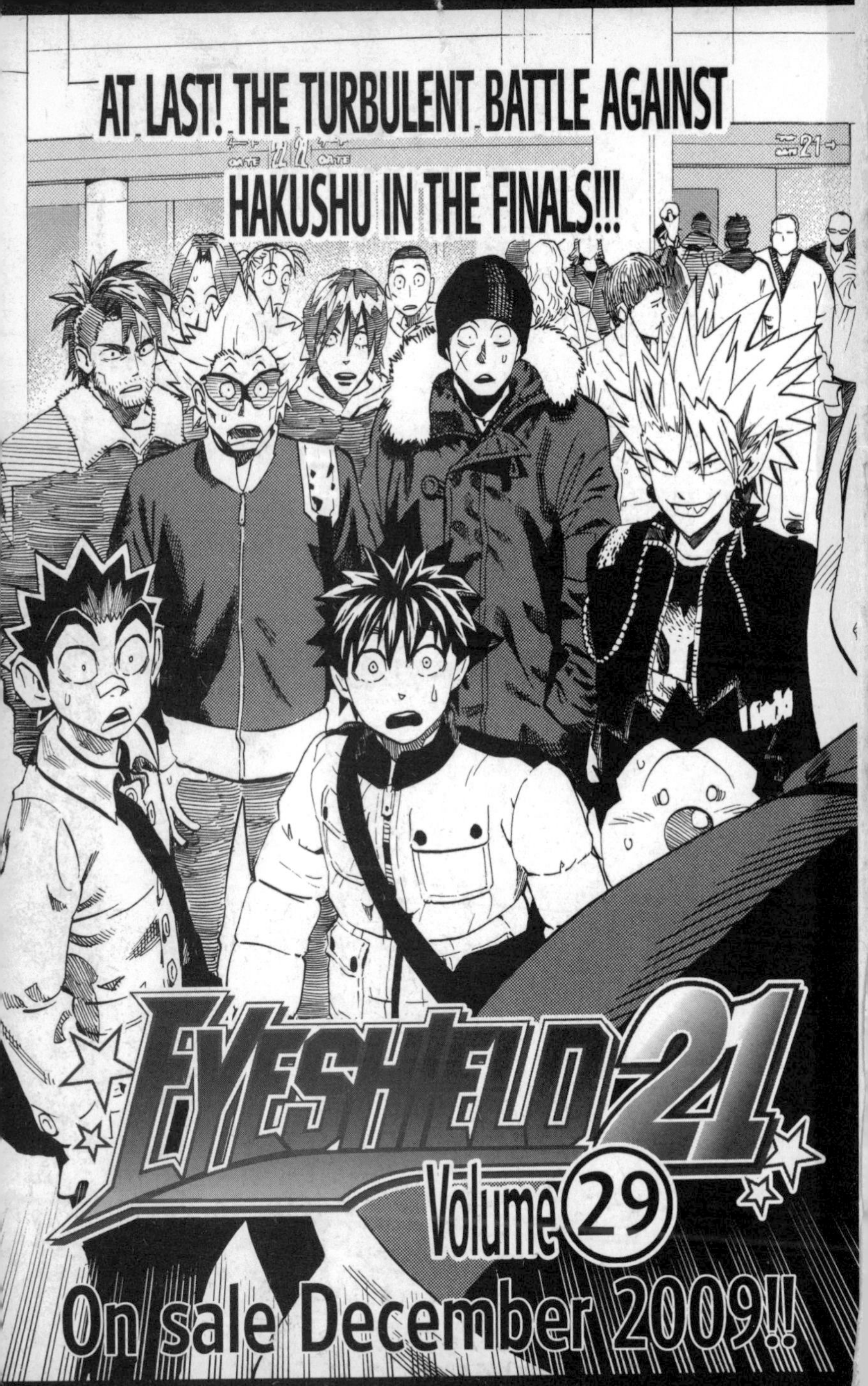
AT LAST! THE TURBULENT BATTLE AGAINST HAKUSHU IN THE FINALS!!!
EYESHIELD 21
Volume 29
On sale December 2009!!

Tell us what you think about SHONEN JUMP manga!

THE REAL ACTION STARTS IN...

SHONEN JUMP
THE WORLD'S MOST POPULAR MANGA
www.shonenjump.com

ViZ media